MERCHANT COLONIES IN
THE EARLY MODERN PERIOD

PERSPECTIVES IN ECONOMIC AND SOCIAL HISTORY

Series Editors: Robert E. Wright
Andrew August

TITLES IN THIS SERIES

MERCHANT COLONIES IN
THE EARLY MODERN PERIOD

EDITED BY

Victor N. Zakharov, Gelina Harlaftis and Olga Katsiardi-Hering

Routledge
Taylor & Francis Group

LONDON AND NEW YORK

First published 2012 by Pickering & Chatto (Publishers) Limited

Published 2016 by Routledge
2 Park Square, Milton Park, Abingdon, Oxfordshire OX14 4RN
711 Third Avenue, New York, NY 10017, USA

First issued in paperback 2015

Routledge is an imprint of the Taylor & Francis Group, an informa business

BRITISH LIBRARY CATALOGUING IN PUBLICATION DATA

Merchant colonies in the early modern period. – (Perspectives in economic
and social history) 1. Mercantile system – Europe – History – 17th century. 2.
Mercantile system – Europe – History – 18th century. 3. Europe – Commerce
– History – 17th century. 4. Europe – Commerce – History – 18th century. 5.
Economic history – 1600–1750. 6. Economic history – 1750–1918.
I. Series II. Zakharov, V. N. (Viktor Nikolaevich) III. Harlaftis, Gelina, 1958–
IV. Katsiarde-Hering, Olga.
382'.094'00903-dc23

ISBN-13: 978-1-138-66467-8 (pbk)
ISBN-13: 978-1-8489-3353-8 (hbk)
Typeset by Pickering & Chatto (Publishers) Limited

CONTENTS

LIST OF FIGURES AND TABLES

LIST OF CONTRIBUTORS

Ina Baghdiantz McCabe is Professor of History at the Department of History at Tufts University, USA. She has degrees from the Sorbonne and Columbia and holds an endowed chair in Armenian History. Her publications include: *The Shah's Silk for Europe's Silver: The Eurasian Silk Trade of the Julfan Armenians in Safavid Iran and India (1590–1750)* (University of Pennsylvania, 1999); *Slaves of the Shah: New Elites of Seventeenth-Century Safavid Isfahan* (London: I. B. Tauris, 2003) as co-author; and *Du bon usage du thé et des épices en Asie Réponses à Monsieur Cabart de Villarmont* by Jean Chardin (Paris: L'Inventaire, Actes Sud, 2002) as editor. Her last book is *Orientalism in Early Modern France: Eurasian Trade, Exotism, and the Ancien Régime* (Oxford and New York: Berg, 2008).

Iannis Carras studied Ancient History and Philosophy (Lit. Hum.) at Oxford University (Lincoln College) in the United Kingdom, and Politics and Economics with a specialization in Russia at the School of Advanced International Studies of Johns Hopkins University in Bologna, Italy and Washington, DC in the United States. He completed a doctorate supervised by Paschalis Kitromilides entitled 'Trade, Politics and Brotherhood: Greeks in Russia 1700–1774' (in Greek) at the Faculty of Political Sciences and Public Administration of Athens University. He has spent two years researching in Russia at the invitation of the Institute of Slavic Studies of the Russian Academy of Sciences and has also spent time researching in and writing about Ukraine. Outside academia, he has worked as a policy analyst in issues related to energy and the environment. He is currently working on the 'Thalis' research programme on economic and social development of twenty Black Sea port cities during the eighteenth to twentieth centuries led by the Department of History of Ionian University.

Beverly A. Dougherty earned her Ph.D. at Fordham University, N.Y. (1992), MA at Niagara University, N.Y. with credits from the University of Kent, Canterbury, England. She received a Teaching Fellowship from Fordham University, a Graduate Study Fellowship from the Richard III Society and taught at George Mason University and Northern Virginia Community College. Beverly, an Independent Scholar, continues research at the Library of

Congress and the Folger Shakespeare Library in Washington, D.C. expanding on aspects of medieval statutes (dissertation) such as the *Piepowder* Courts, prejudice, foreign colonies and treason. Annual papers have been presented at Arizona State University, The U. S. Military Academy, West Point, Cambridge University, England, and the National University of Ireland, Dublin. Most recently, she presented papers at the United Arab Emirates University, Al-Ain, U.A.E. (2009), World Economic History Congress, Utrecht (2009), Venice, Italy for the Renaissance Society (2010) and Lisbon for the Portuguese Association of Economic and Social History (2010). She also writes and presents on travels to the Middle East and Asia and continues interests in music studied at the Eastman School of Music, N.Y.

Gelina Harlaftis is Professor of Maritime History in the Department of History of the Ionian University. She graduated from the University of Athens and completed her graduate studies at Cambridge University (MPhil) and Oxford University (DPhil). She was President of the International Maritime Economic History Association (2004–8) and visiting Fellow at universities of Canada, the United States and the United Kingdom. Among her recent publications are *Diaspora Entrepreneurial Networks. Five Centuries of History* (Oxford: Berg, 2005) with I. Baghdiantz McCabe and I. Minoglou; *Leadership in World Shipping: Greek Family Firms in International Business* (Palgrave Macmillan, 2009) with Ioannis Theotokas; and *The New Ways of History* (London: I. B. Tauris, 2010) with Nikos Karapidakis, Kostas Sbonias and Vaios Vaiopoulos. Since 2012 she has been the project leader of the 'Thalis' research programme on the economic and social development of twenty Black Sea port cities during the eighteenth to twentieth centuries.

Pierrick Pourchasse graduated from the University of Rennes and Lorient (PhD in 2003) and received the 'Agrégation d'histoire' in 1994. He is a senior lecturer and Research Fellow in the Department of History at the University of Bretagne Occidentale in Brest. His research deals with economic relations between France and northern Europe in the eighteenth century. He is the author of *Le commerce du Nord. Les échanges commerciaux entre la France et l'Europe septentrionale au XVIIIe siècle* (Rennes: PUR, 2006). He is one of two coordinators of 'Navigocorpus', a project which aims to compile important data on merchant shipping between 1650 and 1850 and put it at public disposal.

Olga Katsiardi-Hering is Professor of History in the Faculty of History and Archaeology at the University of Athens. She has published over thirty-five articles in Greek, German, Italian and English and her books include: *The Greek Community of Trieste, 1750–1830* (Athens, 1986) (in Greek); *Forgotten Horizons of Greek Merchants: The Fair of Senigallia (18th to the Beginning of* *the 19th Century* (Athens, 1989) (in Greek); *Artisans and Cotton-Yarn Dyeing Methods. From Thessaly to Central Europe (Eighteenth to the Beginning of the Nineteenth Century). Addendum: The 'Company' of Ambelakia (1805)* (Athens: Herodotos, 2003) (in Greek). She was twice visiting professor at the University of Vienna. She is a member of the International Scientific Committee of the Institute for Economic History 'F. Datini'. She has published three books and many articles on the above subjects. *The Venetian Chartography of the Morea, (end of the 17th to the Beginning of the 18th Century)* will be published under her care by the Cultural Foundation of National Bank of Greece: http://users.uoa.gr/~olkats/katsiardi_en.pdf.

Jarmo Kotilaine studied Economics and Economic History at the universities of Oxford (BA, MA), Cambridge (MPhil) and Harvard (AM, PhD). He subsequently joined the faculty at Harvard where his primary focus was the long-term economic and institutional development of Eurasia and international trade and finance. Jarmo Kotilaine joined NCB Capital as Chief Economist in May 2008. He previously oversaw financial services consultancy at Control Risks Group (CRG), a London-based international business risk consultancy firm. His publications include: *Modernizing Muscovy*, ed. with M. Poe (London, 2003); *Foreign Trade and Russia's Early Modern Economic Expansion* (Leiden, 2004); *Stuarts and Romanovs*, with P. Dukes and G. Herd (Dundee, 2009); and *Enemies at the Market Place: Russian Trade with Eastern Europe* (Cambridge, MA, forthcoming).

Evrydiki Sifneos is a historian and Senior Research Associate at the Institute for Neohellenic Research of the National Hellenic Research Foundation in the programme of History of Enterprises and Industrial Archaeology. She received her doctorate from the École des Hautes Études en Sciences Sociales in Paris. Her interests include the economic and social history of the Aegean region, the history of the olive oil trade and the history of the Greek diaspora in New Russia. She manages a database on 'The Greeks in Odessa, according to the 1897 All-Russian Census'. She is a leading manager of the project 'The Contribution of the Greeks to the Development of the Azov Sea Ports, 19th Century' together with Gelina Harlaftis from the Ionian University and The Russian Academy of Sciences, south Russian branch (2007–9) sponsored by the F. I. Kostopoulos Foundation. She is fluent in English, French, Spanish and Italian and is currently studying Russian. She is author of the recent publication: *Greek Merchants in the Azov Sea. The Power and the Limits of Family Business* (Athens, 2009) (in Greek).

Jan Willem Veluwenkamp studied History at Leiden University and graduated in 1976, taking his doctorate there in 1981. From 1981 to 1991 he worked as a management staff member at the Dutch Postal Giro and Post Office Savings

Bank and, subsequently, at the Dutch Savings Bank Association. From 1991 to early 2009 he was a lecturer at the Arctic Centre and the Department of History, University of Groningen. Since early 2009 he has been a full-time lecturer in the Department of History, University of Groningen. Among his publications are (with F. de Goey, ed.), *Entrepreneurs and Institutions in Europe and Asia, 1500–2000* (Amsterdam: Aksant, 2002); 'International Business Communication Patterns in the Dutch Commercial System, 1500–1800' in H. Cools, M. Keblusek and B. Noldus (eds), *Your Humble Servant. Agents in Early Modern Europe* (Hilversum, 2006) pp. 121–134; 'Kaufmännisches Verhalten und Familiennetzwerke im niederländischen Russlandhandel (1590–1750)' in M. Häberlein and C. Jeggle (eds), *Praktiken des Handels. Geschäfte und soziale Beziehungen europäischer Kaufleute in Mittelalter und früher Neuzeit* (Konstanz, 2010) pp. 379–405. Since 2009 he has been the scholarly project manager of *Sound Toll Registers online*, the electronic database for the complete Sound Toll Registers which is gradually becoming available on www.soundtoll.nl.

Joost Veenstra studied History at Leiden University (propaedeutic) and the University of Groningen (BA and MA). In 2009 Veenstra concluded the two-year research master 'Modern History and International Relations' in which he specialized in economic and social history. In his master thesis Veenstra studied the rise of shipmasters from the north of the Netherlands in international shipping at the start of the nineteenth century. Since his graduation in 2009 he has taken up a PhD position at the Faculty of Economics and Business at the University of Groningen and studies Europe's inability to keep up with the pace of economic growth set by America during the early twentieth century.

Victor N. Zakharov graduated from the Moscow State Lomonosov University (History Sciences, 1983) and from the Moscow State Regional University (Doctor of History Sciences, 2001); he was awarded a Professorship in 2008. He is a senior lecturer on Russian history at Moscow State Regional University, chair of Russian Medieval and Early Modern History (since 2002) and the dean of the Faculty of History, Political Sciences and Law (since 2009). His main academic interest lies in the economic history of Russia during the seventeenth to early nineteenth centuries, and with the activity of the foreign entrepreneurs in Russia. He is the author of *West-European Merchants in Russian Trade of the 18th Century* (Moscow, 2005). He has co-edited *The History of Taxes in Russia* with Yu. A. Petrov and M. K. Shatsillo (Moscow, 2006), and has written many papers on this topic. He participated in the international project 'Wirtschaftliche Wechsellagen im hansischen Wirtschaftsraum, 1300–1800' (Lübeck, 1995–9) and 'CLIOHRES: A New History Research Agenda for Citizens of a Growing Europe' (2005–10).

INTRODUCTION

Victor N. Zakharov, Gelina Harlaftis and Olga Katsiardi-Hering

The purpose of this book is to examine the history of 'merchant colonies' and their importance in the European international trade in the early modern period (late fifteenth–eighteenth centuries). Traditionally the term 'merchant colony' has been used in connection with the formation of European economic empires as territories under the immediate political control of an empire. This book, however, is not about European colonization in overseas territories but about foreign merchant colonies or 'merchant communities' in Europe established to carry international and national trade between empires and states.

Frederic Mauro defines a merchant community as an association or unit of merchants who shared a similar background and provided each other with any cooperative assistance needed in their foreign environment.[1] He then proceeds into a chronological and systematic distinction of the merchant colonies in two periods: the first one covers the period of the fourteenth–sixteenth centuries and the second one from the seventeenth to the eighteenth century. It is commonly accepted that European land and seaborne trade has traditionally been connected with the establishment of foreign merchants in major European cities where the terms 'merchant community' and 'community of foreign merchants' were often synonymous. The foreign merchant communities were characterized by solidarity, mutual aid, kinship and a desire to preserve their culture. They 'had a similar international commercial outlook' as well as 'sufficient capital, credit or connections, and adequate commercial experience'. Moreover, they shared a sectarian outlook that interlocked families in chains of partnerships and marriages.[2] This kind of attitude and practices are generally attributed to the 'ethnic minorities of eastern origin'. 'International business has always implied cultural minorities and the European "miracle" would never have taken place without entrepreneurial minorities', Antony Reid has also written.[3]

The significance of the issue of the merchant colonies is highlighted by their influence on inter-local and world economic development throughout history. Long-distance transnational trade has traditionally been carried out by foreign merchants in the main Eurasian fairs and cities. The foreign merchants were either western European traders, such as the Italians, French, Spanish, Portuguese, English, Dutch, Germans or Scandinavians, or eastern European traders such as the Russians, or eastern European/'Levantine' traders like the Greeks, the Armenians or the Jews who formed their own merchant colonies in foreign lands. In current bibliography, these foreign merchants residing in different countries often tend to be studied by scholars of their own ethnicity, and, consequently, not only is the comparative perspective lost, but 'nationalistic' interpretations along the lines of superiority and uniqueness are also quite common. The present collection has made a conscious effort to overcome narrow national or nationalistic lenses in their articles and examines these foreign merchants within and beyond the national boundaries.

The term 'merchant colonies', which can also be termed 'communities of foreign merchants', 'nations', 'ethnic minority merchants', 'diaspora merchants' 'confraternities' or '*compagnies*' characterizes the establishment of groups of merchants of a shared ethnicity in foreign lands and the creation of international commercial networks in the early modern period. The function of the merchant colonies became particularly significant when foreign trade expansion became the most influential factor in economic growth initially in a number of European countries and subsequently the world over. The merchant colonies increased turnover, boosted profits and developed various forms of economic activities (trade companies, banks, insurance companies, etc.) nursing the essential prerequisites for the Industrial Revolution of the eighteenth–nineteenth centuries and consequently the modern world economy.

In the last decade, the upsurge of globalization has stimulated interest in global economic history and this trend has drawn greater attention to the history of the fifteenth–eighteenth-century world trade. Academic interest focuses largely on the structure and dynamics of trade and shipping. Additionally entrepreneurship has attracted a good deal of attention over the last couple of decades, particularly the organization of individual firms and family companies including their national and international contacts and networks. Scholars of several countries have also touched upon the activities of merchant colonies and a considerable body of material has already been accumulated. There are, however, no comprehensive studies focusing on the history and function of merchant colonies. What is more, most of the studies of merchant colonies in the early modern period focus either on a specific nation, like the Dutch or British, or an ethnic minority, like the Jews or Huguenots, or a specific city-port like Livorno or London, or a specific geographical region, like western Europe and its overseas territories of the big merchant maritime empires such as the Venetian, the Portuguese, the English and Dutch.

Essentially this book, rather than focusing on a specific merchant community of an ethnic minority in a part of Europe, proposes to bring together the study of the most important merchant colonies of both western and eastern Europeans in the whole of Europe, western and eastern. This is considered one of the main strengths of this volume as the merchant colonies in the Russian, Habsburg and Ottoman Empires, are currently so underrepresented in English-speaking publications.

The distinction of westerners and easterners has long been made by Frederic Mauro who has indicated 'large ethnic formations of eastern origin, which stood out against the purely European western background'. Equally, Philip Curtin, a pioneer on the subject of trade diasporas, addressed both western Europeans and 'the ethnic formations of eastern origin' trading beyond their territories as 'trade diasporas'.[4] This book reveals that merchant colonies shared similar organizations, structures and development in the English, Dutch, French, German, Russian, Greek and Armenian cases in European cities in the early modern period. Merchant colonies have also been described as 'trade diasporas'. The term coined by Abner Cohen refers to 'a nation of socially interdependent, but spatially dispersed communities'.[5] Philip Curtin in his seminal book examines various groups of trade diasporas that carried international trade transcending national boundaries by forming world-wide networks.[6] Historical diasporas, particularly the three classical ones, those of the Armenians, Greeks and Jews, epitomize the resilience of traditional forms of association in certain groups who for centuries transcended the boundaries of states and empires. In the present study we do not adopt the concept of 'diaspora' for two reasons. Firstly, we deal with both western and eastern Europeans and this term does not apply to English, Dutch, German, etc. merchant colonies. Secondly, the term 'diaspora' has taken another connotation as it has been used by cultural and postcolonial studies to form the discipline of diaspora studies with an immense literature; over thirty new groups have found shelter now under this term.[7] Concerning diaspora people this book focuses on the trade diasporas of Greeks and Armenians, keeping a comparative perspective with the Jews. The reason for not including Jewish merchant colonies in this volume is that Jews were dispersed in all major western and eastern European countries for centuries so they, usually, formed part of the local societies. Furthermore, Jewish diaspora has been extensively studied in the Anglo-Saxon bibliography and also in a comparative perspective and in many of the chapters of this volume comparisons with the Jewish merchants are drawn (see for example, Chapter 3 by Pierrick Pourchasse, Chapter 4 by Ina Baghdiantz McCabe and Chapter 8 by Iannis Carras).[8]

The comparative dimension is also another one of the strengths of the present volume. Most chapters deal with more than one ethnic merchant colony in one or more countries. For example, English merchant colonies are examined in comparison with the Scottish and the Dutch in the Baltic and Mediterranean ports; German and Italian merchant colonies are examined in English ports; German, Dutch and Swedish merchant colonies in Atlantic French ports; Russian merchant colonies in Scandinavian Baltic ports; Ottoman and Iranian Armenian merchant colonies in Mediterranean ports; Ottoman and Venetian Greek merchant colonies in ports and landlocked cities in the land and sea trade of Ottoman, Habsburg and Russian Empires; Hanseatic, Dutch, German, English, Italian, Armenian and Greek merchant colonies in the Russian Empire.

The chapters also deal with merchant colonies in port cities and 'land' cities. Both land and maritime trade activities of the foreign merchant colonies are examined in the early modern period in the city-ports of the European waters, the Baltic Sea, the North Sea, the Atlantic Ocean, the Mediterranean and the Black Sea. Therefore, the book tends to address extraordinary structures and processes as generally prevailing, and on the other hand, generally prevailing structures and processes as extraordinary. In this way, *Merchant Colonies in the Early Modern Period* provides a much wider view of the international trade of the era under examination both chronologically and geographically. It enables researchers to place their work in a broader context and avoid unnecessary misinterpretations. It unveils patterns which serve as points of reference for future research. It contributes to the understanding of the early stages of commercial globalization.

Some chapters of this book were presented at the XV International Economic History Association Congress in the session 'Merchant Colonies in the Context of the International Commerce in the Early Modern Period' in Utrecht 2009, organized by Victor Zakharov and Jan Willen Veluwenkamp. More authors have been invited to participate and all papers have been rewritten according to the guidelines set by the editors. Main issues that all papers discuss are as follows:

What is a colony? The concept of 'merchant colony' or merchant community
Why and when were merchant colonies formed? The politico-economic dimension
How were they formed? a) The institutional dimension: legal status and privileges, b) The economic dimension: types of organization and their evolution
How they functioned? a) Cooperation, interaction and competition with local and foreign merchants, b) Interconnections between partners in the mother country and abroad, the emergence of the networks connecting merchants from different countries in the system
What was the effect of the formation of merchant colonies in Europe?
What happened to them? a) evolution or change of this role and perspectives, b) The process of integration, adaptation and assimilation or the formation of a multiple identity of the members of a merchant colony in host countries. Crucial was the role of the naturalization on the part of the host countries and therefore the bourgeoisification of the colonists.

Although most authors tackle the first issue of what a merchant colony is according to the needs of their study, a preliminary discussion on what is a merchant colony is needed along with an analytical approach of the terminology used. Many of the authors (like Pierrick Pourchasse, Victor Zakharov, Olga Katsiardi-Hering and Iannis Carras) emphasize the ambiguity and multiplicity of the term. It is rather ironic that the editors, a Russian and two Greeks, agree in their chapters that the term 'merchant colony' is not just right for their cases; the term is more appropriate for the merchant colonies of the Dutch or English empires. In order to make things clearer we will use the paradigm from Greek antiquity. Ancient Greek historiography makes a clear distinction between the ancient *apoikies*, i.e. colonies of the Greek city states - in the framework of the first and second colonization[9] - and the modern *paroikies*[10], in German *Niederlassungen*, i.e. communities or ethnic minority groups settled in a host country. This not only reflects a nominal difference but a functional one too. Both the ancient *apoikies* and the early modern colonies were groups of people who settled in distant lands, formed powerful economies but remained under the political jurisdiction of their native land. The ancient *apoikies* and the early modern colonies were related to a particular city state, the metropolis, and though politically sovereign, were characterized by the exploitation of the colonized region. By contrast, the *paroikies* balanced a dual role as they had to accept the rules and laws of the host countries and to retain the linkages with the homeland that allowed them to survive economically by a continuous back and forth movement of its members and to maintain their ethnic identity (see also Chapter 2 by Beverly A. Dougherty). Saying that, for the English and the Dutch the term 'colony'/'*apoikia*' as is evident by Chapter 1 of Jan Willem Veluwenkamp and Joost Veenstra applies better.

The reason to use the Greek word *paroikia* in order to describe the merchant communities of the early modern times lies on the difference among a politically autonomous ancient colony and a settlement of a legally recognized ethnic minority group that enjoyed privileged status in a country that had its own rules and political administration to which the members of a *paroikia* were subordinate and tended to integrate. The usage of the term *paroikia* in Greek is probably preferable to the word *koinotita* (community) which indicates both the total population of a diaspora group in a new settlement and a specific form of social organization of its people that could be identified with the General Assembly of its adult members.

It might be worth noting that the studies in this volume do not examine the 'community' from a socio-anthropological point of view but from a socio-economic one. They do, however, often use the term 'community' alternatively, on the one hand to describe the established group of foreigners as individuals in a host city being examined, and on the other as business institutions analyzing their administrative and organizational structure and mechanisms.

Apart from terminology issues, another theme that must be explored in the study of the *paroikies* is the point of view, the methodological angle from which we observe and study the communities of foreign merchants. Historical trends usually conform to established policies or desired concepts. Therefore, when national-ism and colonialism were dominant doctrines, the *paroikies* were studied within a nationalistic framework, pointing out their role towards the national question, which related them mainly to their natal land, and the activities of their members were viewed from the angle of benefit or ignorance of their homeland. Another approach that followed was to view merchant communities as an influential fac-tor that contributed to the evolution of the host country. A third view, similar to the second one but even more enriching, is the comparative approach, that is the study of ethnic minority groups in relation to others as well as to the indigenous population that operates in the same territory. Contemporary studies take into consideration the previous trends but emphasize the comparative approach.

Although some Greek *paroikies* took advantage of European state policies, they were often founded on or near classic or Byzantine settlements. Marseille and Taganrog are good examples of this statement. Moreover, the merchant colonies form part of a continuity in the Mediterranean, that of the classic diasporas involved in international business.[11] The formation of Greek merchant communities beyond the Ottoman or Venetian state were the result of a mobil-ity organized within family and commercial networks, with profit as the sole purpose for their movements, and much less due to an organized, massive immi-gration instigated by 'push and pull' factors.

Ina Baghdiantz McCabe in Chapter 4 raises, however, an important issue. Looking through an ethnic lens historians tend to look at Armenians and Greeks as 'stateless' people and as a group. Armenians, however, in the seven-teenth century, for example, were Ottoman and Iranian subjects, and the Greeks were Ottoman and Venetian subjects. They were used and treated according to the Empire or state they came from by the Russian or Habsburg Empires.

The second issue that the studies of this volume tackle is why and when were merchant colonies formed? In the early modern period merchant colonies served as a tool for the expansion of merchant empires. They have been associated to long-distance inter-local and international trade, by land or sea routes organized in companies or leagues in the north like the English Company of Merchant Adventurers, the Hanseatic League or in the south like the Venetian group of merchants or the Levant Company in the Ottoman Empire. At a time of difficult spatial communications and trade barriers merchant colonies operated as a cata-lyst in the expansion and integration of European markets. Mercantilist policy, state protection, commercial privileges, capitulations, free ports, tax-free regimes were some of the many politico-economic instruments used by the European authorities for the support and promotion of foreign merchant colonies.

The third issue concerns how these merchant colonies were formed, and in which institutional framework they prospered and in what types of entrepreneurial institutions they operated. Merchant colonies were firstly organized with the establishment of a few commercial agents followed by the establishment and organization of a 'nation'. In that sense 'the term "nation" was used for the merchant association of a certain nationality'[12] and/or of the same geographical origin, see Chapters 3, 4 and 7 in the present volume. Foreign merchants established a formally organized 'community' according to special privileges given by the host states. These communities were organized as confraternities/communities/*compagnies* (see Chapters 7 and 8). The merchant colonies functioned in the administrative framework of the host countries and covered a gap in the economic development of these countries.

There were certain states that formed a regulated commercial system, like that of the English and the Navigation Act of 1651 that introduced protectionism and enforcement of national monopoly in international trade. The English also introduced a system of privileges to regulated chartered companies that monopolized trade in specific geographical areas. In all host countries there were regulations on settlements of foreign communities. In Russia, for example, for a merchant to become part of the merchants' system, the 'merchant guilds', one had to become a Russian subject and was classified in the first, second or third 'guild' according to his capital (see Chapter 9); in France, in Nantes one could become citizen by naturalization or by a sojourn of twelve consecutive years (see Chapter 3).

As Chapter 2 by Beverly A. Dougherty and Chapter 1 by Jan Willem Veluwenkamp and Joost Veenstra indicate there are two types of merchant colonies: one type evolved during the period from the mid-sixteenth to the mid-seventeenth century, that of the chartered companies, for example of the English chartered company of Merchant Adventurers, the Muscovy Company, the Eastland Company, the Levant Company that instigated the formation of merchant communities in the European cities like that of Moscow, Constantinople, Livorno, Naples or Messina. The second type was that of the 'deregulation', of the trading companies and the emergence of many independent companies. Merchant colonies were formed to overcome trade barriers, asymmetry of market information and communication problems. When these were dissolved Veluwenkamp and Veenstra support the view that merchant colonies disappear. The latter happened in north-western Europe but it continued in northern, northeastern and south-eastern Europe where the trade barriers and the markets were difficult and distant. They point out how the system of chartered companies continued in the regions with trade barriers.

The fourth issue examines how the merchant colonies carried out their business. Merchant colonies or communities consisted of groups of foreign merchants involved in international business. They developed into networks of ethnic-religious groups that formed their own 'unofficial' international market, enabling them to operate independently of the countries or states in which they were established. The merchant colonists, whether as independent merchants or companies, were international operators that adapted the conduct of their businesses to the economic needs of nations which were engaged in imperial expansion. They sought out factors that would make them more competitive, exploiting the resources and advantages of the institutional environment that were available to them. They facilitated international trade flows 'because they reduced search, negotiation and transaction costs in unfamiliar and risky environments' (see for example Chapter 9 and Sifneos and Harlaftis).[13]

To overcome the main problems of communication and trust they created informal institutions, international business networks. Business theory of networks and principal-agents are combined with historical evidence to explain the dynamism and integration of merchant colonies in the host country's business environment as Pierrick Pourchasse indicates in Chapter 3. The structure of merchant companies was heavily based on family ties, on trust, which did not exclude resources in case of disputes to an informal system of arbitration and to systems of local justice as Chapter 6 by Victor Zakharov and Chapter 8 by Iannis Carras indicate. These kinds of trading companies have been described as network firms.[14] A network is defined as a particular type of relationship that links a particular group of people, and the study of this form of relationship is performed through network analysis.[15] Networks are based on the formation of an institutional framework that minimizes entrepreneurial risk and provides information flow. They allowed the establishment of transnational connections based on personal relations, bypassing official market mechanisms. Furthermore in all cities where foreign merchants were established in order to overcome difficulties in their host countries they tried to make alliances with the local government officials as well as with the local merchants.

The fifth question that is tackled by the authors of this book is what was the effect of the formation of merchant colonies in Europe? The merchant colonies in Europe were needed as they covered an organizational gap in the economic and commercial development of the host countries. They became an instrument to develop new markets; Veluwenkamp and Veenstra in Chapter 1 test this hypothesis by looking more closely at the English trade system which was, along with the Dutch system, one of the great commercial systems to bloom in the second half of the seventeenth century. As all chapters indicate, these colonies were formed and evolved as long as the host states needed them: German and Italian merchant colonies in England in the beginning of the early modern period (Beverly A. Dougherty in Chapter 2); the English merchant colonies in Scandinavia, the Netherlands, Italian states and the Ottoman Empire (Jan Willem Veluwenkamp and Joost Veenstra in Chapter 1); the 'nations' of the Germans and the

Dutch in France in the eighteenth century (Pierrick Pourchasse in Chapter 3); those of the Russians in Sweden (Jarmo Kotilaine in Chapter 5); the merchant communities of the Italian, the English, the Dutch, the German and the French in Russia (Victor Zakharov in Chapter 6); the ones of the 'Greeks' and Armenians in central Europe and Russia in the seventeenth and eighteenth centuries (Ina Baghdiantz McCabe in Chapter 4, Olga Katsiardi-Hering in Chapter 7, Iannis Carras in Chapter 8, Evrydiki Sifneos and Gelina Harlaftis in Chapter 9); or the establishment of the 'privileged' Venetians in the Ottoman Empire.

In the meantime, apart from maintaining the flow of trade and its smooth operation, they contributed to the evolution and diffusion of information and commercial know-how in the places and societies of the east and west. In this way, on one hand the French 'nations' and partially the English ones played an important role through the *beratlis* (protected) system[16] in the formation of local groups of merchants in the Ottoman Empire and their transformation in independent merchant groups fully engaged in the international European trade. On the other hand the merchants from the east established in central Europe and western European city-ports diffused their institutions, business and artisan techniques in the host societies.

As long as they were useful, the foreign merchants were supported; when the local merchants learned the business and foreigners hindered their interests they were either kicked out or forced to integrate and eventually assimilate. An evident example is given in Chapter 2 by Dougherty when the German merchant colony in the Steelyard of London was ended by Elizabeth I and merchants were asked to leave. It is also evident in the Russian colonies in Sweden as Jarmo Kotilaine indicates in Chapter 5. Similarly the Greeks in Hungary had to become naturalized by the end of the eighteenth century in order to maintain a trade business as is evident in Chapter 7 by Olga Katsiardi-Hering. The cycle of a merchant colony, its rise and decline in the trading cities of Europe, is discussed by Veluwenkamp and Veenstra in Chapter 1 relating to theories that try to understand the economic development of Europe.

The sixth issue deals with what happened to merchant colonists. According to the time of establishment of the colonies in host countries, some had a lifespan of one or two generations, others a longer one, that, according to the migration rhythms of the moving groups of foreign merchants, reached sometimes more than a century as all chapters in the present volume indicate. In the latter case, different timing of integration and assimilation of the colonists is observed, depending on the rate of development of the local society.

In the urban web of the host cities merchant colonists usually formed neighborhoods or places where they resided. For example, in London there was the Steelyard for Germans; in Moscow there was, until the beginning of the eighteenth century, the so-called *Nemetskaia sloboda* (German quarter or settlement), where not only Germans lived, but also foreigners from other western European countries; in Nantes the 'Little Holland' for the Dutch; in Venice the *Campo dei Greci* or the *Sottoportego dei Armeni*; in Vienna the *Griechengasse*; and in Smyrna the *francomahalla* (Frankish neighborhood).[17] They also contributed to the urban and residential expansion as well as to the differentiation and renewal not only of city regions, but also of cities themselves (see for example Jarmo Kotilaine in Chapter 5 and Evrydiki Sifneos and Gelina Harlaftis in Chapter 9). It is worth noting that the tendency of integration and assimilation was stronger among the eastern groups of merchants established in central and eastern Europe. The fact that they resided in distinct neighborhoods did not prevent many of them from fully integrating in the local society either as members of the local authorities or local aristocracy or the local business circles; see the case of the merchant colonies of Italian city states in England and central Europe (Chapter 2 by Beverly A. Dougherty and Chapter 7 by Olga Katsiardi-Hering). The process of naturalization did not hinder the preservation of the ethno-religious identity of merchant colonists in almost all the cases examined in this volume. The case of the commercial interaction between Sweden and Russia as presented by Jarmo Kotilaine in Chapter 5 about the permanent – and sometimes semi-permanent – presence of large numbers of ethnic Russians in Swedish-controlled areas, the so-called Ingrian and Karelian Russians, is indicative.

In many cases the host-cities were characterized by cosmopolitanism and as Pierrick Pourchasse mentions 'cosmopolitanism seems to be a characteristic feature of all international emporium'. However, were many city-ports really cosmopolitan or was there a parallel symbiosis with the locals? In new city-ports like Trieste, Odessa or Taganrog, formed by immigrants, the society was mixed. In other north-western European port cities with more rigid structures of societies the foreign merchants seldom became integral members.

This collection of essays consists of two kinds of articles geared to bringing out historiographical results and methodological discussions. The first one is composed of surveys, some of them more or less historiographical, and the second one of research articles based on archival research, incorporating discussion of the historiography. All merchant colonies studied by the scholars of this volume indicate the importance of groups of foreign merchants in seaports, river ports or 'land ports' in promoting international trade. Merchant colonies or communities have played a major role in the process of globalization trading beyond boundaries.

1 EARLY MODERN ENGLISH MERCHANT COLONIES: CONTEXTS AND FUNCTIONS

Jan Willem Veluwenkamp and Joost Veenstra

Introduction

In the early modern period, many European commercial towns, including the main Turkish, Italian, Spanish, French, English and Russian ports, harboured communities of foreign merchants. The present article aims to contribute to the explanation of this phenomenon – the settlement of merchants abroad. Up till now, the literature has not addressed this question in a structural way. The historiography on merchant colonies is mainly limited to the study of commercial settlements in particular cities, for example the foreign merchants in Hamburg or in Bergen.[1] The topic is less frequently studied from the opposite direction, i.e. by focusing on a country's merchant communities in foreign cities. The latter approach places merchant settlements within the broader context of a country's commercial network. Quite extensive work has already been done on the dispersion of Greek and Jewish communities in south-east Europe.[2] Research focusing specifically on the pattern and function of north-west European trade settlements is rare, however. Fifteen years ago, a first attempt in this direction was made by the second author of the present paper, who studied the case of Dutch merchant colonies.[3] In this paper we pursue a similar strategy by studying British merchant colonies during England's commercial expansion from the late sixteenth century onwards.

Veluwenkamp's earlier article discusses the function of merchant colonies in the Dutch commercial system from 1550 to 1750.[4] He argued that through these colonies the Dutch developed new markets in the late sixteenth and seventeenth centuries. The colonies were instrumental in the expansion of Dutch trade and were founded in countries where indigenous traders did not possess the level of sophistication required to meet Dutch commercial standards.[5] Veluwenkamp's implicit suggestions are, first, that the Dutch merchant colonies were unique and, second, that the colonies were a condition for the development of 'Dutch primacy in world trade'.[6] There is reason to question the accuracy of these suggestions. With regard to the first suggestion, it should be noted that merchants of other nations, such as Italians, English and Scots, founded colonies too.[7] Furthermore, the Dutch merchant colonies might have been a necessary condition for the development of Dutch primacy, but they cannot have been a sufficient condition. The Scottish merchant colonies, indeed, did not lead to Scottish dominance of world trade. One could suspect that the Dutch commercial communities abroad were of a special nature which distinguished them from the other nations so that, yes, they did produce primacy after all. But there are, so far, no indications that this was the case. The Dutch presence abroad did not differ fundamentally from that of other nations.

Katsiardi-Hering discusses the relatively rich historiography on Greek merchant colonies in the present volume.[8] The Greek communities abroad seem to have been the result of flight from repressive policies of the state of departure and immigration policies of the states of destination. Accordingly, their development is usually characterized as a diaspora. They doubtlessly facilitated and even boosted international trade – at least in central and south-eastern Europe. But the historiography hardly analyses their development as a product of deliberate commercial action of individual merchants or trading organizations. In this respect the Greek diaspora differed fundamentally from the Dutch 'colonization'.

Clearly, more research is needed to understand the rise and decline of European merchant colonies in the early modern period. Fortunately, much has been written about the role of business networks in modern international trade. This strand of literature in development economics stresses that transnational networks, such as merchant colonies, serve to overcome barriers to trade.[9] Even nowadays, trade barriers limit the movement of goods between countries. These barriers can appear in many forms. For instance, trade can be hindered by fixed effects, such as geography. Furthermore, formal institutional barriers, for example protectionist policies, can limit the scope of trade. It has been argued, however, that the most important constraints on trade are of informal institutional nature. Inadequate information about international trading opportunities and weak enforcement of international contracts restrain entrepreneurs from expanding their international trade.[10] Respectively, the key notions here are communication and trust. Transnational networks can, first of all, match supply and demand by providing a means of communication between domestic and foreign markets.[11] Secondly, by controlling foreign markets, merchant colonies eliminate indigenous elements from the chain of trade.[12] This decreases opportunistic behaviour as both the agents of merchant colonies and the companies they represent belong to the same 'moral community'.[13]

Can these theories help one understand the developments of European merchant colonies in the early modern period? As argued by Veluwenkamp, in the case of the Dutch, the size of the settlements shrank when trade became routine.[14] This is in line with the literature on international business networks, which predicts that merchant colonies disappear when barriers to trade dissolve. At some point, after a period of regular trade, the Dutch developed an understanding of foreign markets, stimulating trust and improving communication. Foreign markets were included in the Dutch network, which, other things being equal, reduced the need for merchant colonies.[15] However, it remains unclear whether the same applies to merchant colonies of other countries. In this paper we zoom in on the commercial settlements of England, which succeeded the Netherlands as the predominant centre of commerce in Europe during the early modern period. Did English merchant colonies disappear when barriers to trade broke down? Can we identify a similar pattern of development as with the Dutch? In this paper, the years between 1550 and 1650, which saw the emergence of the English trading network under supervision of chartered trading companies, are discussed first. In a second step, the period characterized by the 'deregulation' of the trading companies between 1650 and 1750 is analysed. Furthermore, a third section will briefly discuss Italian and Scottish merchant colonies in order to broaden the scope of the analysis and see whether the same dynamics can be identified in settlements of other origins.

The Initial Expansion of the English Commercial System, 1550–1650

The Dutch merchant colonies, then, were not unique. The commercial systems of other countries, too, included trader communities abroad. England, which came to dominate international trade in the eighteenth century, is probably the most pronounced example showing this.

The proliferation of the English merchant colonies traces back to the second half of the sixteenth century, when England emerged as a still modest, but developing, player in the international marketplace. Its foreign trade by that time was of very limited size and scope and consisted mainly of the export of woollen cloth and the import of luxuries. Some of this commerce was conducted directly with the Baltic and the Mediterranean. These two trades were firmly in the hands of Hansards and Italian merchants, respectively, and English merchants played only a marginal role in them. The greater part of England's foreign trade was carried on with Antwerp and handled by the royally chartered Company of the Merchant Adventurers. The Merchant Adventurers did not need to go farther than Antwerp as traders from all over Europe met there to do business. In Antwerp the English sold their cloth and bought the products England needed in return. From Antwerp continental merchants distributed the English cloth over a large area. The town on the river Scheldt had an English merchant colony within its walls as the Adventurers had their apprentices resident there to facilitate their trade.[16]

After 1550 big changes occurred in England's foreign trade. The demand for English woollen cloth stagnated in its traditional European markets. Cloth exports were, in addition, hampered by the difficulties which resulted from religious troubles and war in Antwerp, which lost its position as England's outlet when, in 1585, during the Dutch Revolt, the port fell into Spanish hands and the Dutch henceforth blockaded its access to the sea. All these problems led to a 'commercial push' of English merchants into new areas in Europe and beyond.[17]

Finding new markets was vital. From the early 1550s the quest led the English to Russia via the White Sea, to the Baltic and to the Mediterranean. Direct access to these markets was developed and maintained by companies that were founded expressly for that purpose. The Russia Company originated in 1555, the Eastland Company in 1579 and the Levant Company in 1581. Accordingly, the majority of the English merchants continued to trade as members of a chartered company provided by the Crown with a monopoly of a particular branch of trade.[18] The new companies brought no growth of England's total export volume but they did bring about a geographical expansion and redistribution of its foreign trade.[19] In addition, after 1585, the English found new access to the old markets in the Low Countries and the German Empire via Hamburg and a succession of Dutch towns.

Direct access to the Russian market was realized as a side effect of a great endeavour. In 1553 a large group of London entrepreneurs organized an expedition to find a north-east passage, acquire their own access to the riches of the East Indies and find new markets there for their cloth.[20] The expedition did not reach the East Indies but one of its three ships, under Richard Chancellor, ended up in the White Sea. Chancellor travelled on to Moscow and was received by Tsar Ivan IV. The results of this meeting induced Chancellor's principals to found, in 1555, the Muscovy Company, the English Crown to charter it with the exclusive right to trade with Russia and the tsar to grant it permission to do business in Russia.[21]

The English found the Russia trade risky, foresaw high costs and low returns and did not expect it to reach a large volume. They considered it therefore not worthwhile for individual merchants to employ their own factors in Russia. Instead, the Muscovy Company was organized as a joint-stock company, doing business as one body, working with the capital of its stockholders. England's trade with Russia basically involved the export of English products, mainly cheap woollen cloth and non-ferrous metals such as copper, lead and tin, and the import of Russian commodities for its own interior market, mainly cordage, flax, tallow, skins, furs and wax.[22]

The Company established several factories in Russia to take care of its business on the spot. By 1589 it had 'households' in Moscow, Yaroslavl, Vologda, Kholmogory and St Nicholas. And from the 1560s to 1581 it had one in Narva, too. Each of these factories probably consisted of not more than one or two dozen merchants, apprentices and craftsmen. They were managed by English agents who supervised the Company's other servants in Russia.[23] It is clear that

England traded with Russia through merchant colonies on the spot, consisting of men working for the Muscovy Company.

English merchants gained direct access to the Baltic markets exploiting the opportunities offered by the wane of the Hanse. They moved into the Baltic from the beginning of the sixteenth century, but their traffic gained momentum only in the 1560s, '70s and '80s, after which they made little progress until the middle of the seventeenth century. They made their way into the Baltic as free traders, but in 1579 Queen Elizabeth I abolished the Hanseatic privileges in London and chartered the Eastland Company, reserving trade with Norway, Sweden and the Baltic to Company members. Unlike the Muscovy Company the Eastland Company was not a joint-stock company but, like the Company of Merchant Adventurers, a regulated company whose members traded individually with their own capital and on their own account within the rules set by the Company.[24]

The Eastland trade consisted in bilateral barter up to the mid-seventeenth century. The vital factors of the Eastland merchants' initial success were the increase of the demand for English finished cloth in the Baltic and the increase of the English demand for such Baltic products as naval stores and grain. In the first half of the seventeenth century 90 per cent of England's export to the Baltic consisted of cloth, shipped in English vessels by English merchants almost exclusively to Eastland proper, i.e. the Prussian ports of Danzig, Elbing and Königsberg, the gateways to the basins of the rivers Vistula and Niemen. The English imports from the Baltic mainly consisted of grain, hemp, cordage, flax, linseed, linen, canvas, timber, potash, pitch, tar and iron, the bulk of which came from, again, Danzig, Elbing and Königsberg. Nevertheless, in the same period, the scope of the English Baltic trade expanded. By 1646, about half the hemp came from Riga and some iron began to come from Stockholm. Nearly all this trade was handled by English merchants. Merchants of the Baltic did not as a rule export to England even the products of their own countries in any considerable quantity.[25]

Like the English Russia merchants, the Eastland merchants, too, traded through merchant colonies on the spot. Initially, the English established factories in Danzig and also in Bergen. After the foundation of the Eastland Company they moved, in 1583, from Danzig to the little town of Elbing, where they could play a leading role. Company members employed factors and brokers here and had sons, servants and apprentices on the spot. Together they formed an English merchant colony. The English had their own house in Elbing, which they used for commercial, administrative and religious purposes. The Company's deputy governor represented the London-based directors on the spot. Local merchants must have been employed, too, as the Eastland Company's by-laws of 1618 forbade Company members to employ foreigners as factors and brokers.[26]

The Eastland Company's by-laws of 1618 restricted trade with Eastland proper (Danzig, Elbing and Königsberg) to Elbing. This suggests that, in practice, trade was conducted elsewhere, too. There were, indeed, in 1618, English merchant houses in both Elbing and Danzig. The water connections of Elbing with the Polish hinterland were inferior to those of Danzig so that, soon, Elbing proved to be less attractive than hoped for. In the 1630s the Eastland merchants transferred their foreign residence from Elbing to Danzig. The English mercantile agents left Elbing, and the colony of some one or two dozen English factors in Danzig came to full development as Danzig again became the main Baltic staple of the English.[27]

The 1618 Eastland Company's by-laws declared it lawful to trade with Denmark, Norway, Sweden and the towns of Riga and Reval in Livland and in all these places Eastland merchants did do business. In our brief survey of the historiography we have found no references to English merchant colonies there, but the Elbing and Danzig examples make it likely that these colonies did exist. This assumption is backed by a suggestion Hinton provides. Hinton does not explicitly discuss the reason why the Eastland Company established representatives abroad. But he does refer to the disadvantages of 'selling off the ship's keel', as the phrase went. If a trader could not store unsold merchandise on the spot, he would be forced to sell at any price or send his merchandise back to England. Apparently, selling off the ship's keel did happen, but storage was preferable and only feasible with permanent representatives on the spot.[28]

When, in the course of the sixteenth century, the first signs of decline in the trade of Italian city states became apparent, the English and other newcomers appeared in the Mediterranean business, especially in the trade with the Ottoman Empire. English commerce with the Ottomans was initiated in the 1570s as a result of the growth of their demand for tin, which they needed for the production of bronze cannon and which the English could offer in abundance. As in the case of the Russian trade, the length of the journey to the markets of the Levant and the small volume of business induced the English to organize trade via a dedicated joint-stock company, in this case the Levant Company, formed in 1581.[29] The Levant Company's charter granted its members the English monopoly of the trade with the Ottoman Empire.[30] An additional benefit was the fact that the Company could conduct the diplomatic functions necessary in this business.[31] The sultan had granted trading rights, known as capitulations, to the French as early as 1535.[32] In 1580 he had agreed with private English merchants on similar rights for English subjects – but under French pressure had withdrawn them almost immediately.[33] The Levant Company regained them in 1583.[34]

The Mediterranean tin market turned out to be rather small but soon, in the decades following the collapse of the Antwerp entrepôt, the English 'new draperies' began to find ready sale in the Ottoman market while the return cargo consisted of currants, wine, cotton and silk.[35] From Aleppo, one of the main markets of the Levant, the Levant Company mainly exported silk, a large portion of which originated in Persia.[36]

The success of the new draperies induced the English merchants to ignore the Levant Company and embark upon private business.[37] The force of this tendency led, in 1605, to the reorganization of the Company into a regulated company following the set-up of the Eastland Company.[38] Now, the Levant merchants legally conducted business on their own account while the commerce conducted by the Levant Company itself petered out. Company membership was still required for the Levant merchants, but even this rule was increasingly ignored. Nevertheless, the Company continued to play an important role dealing collectively with Ottoman officialdom.[39]

The Levant Company set up factories at Constantinople and Aleppo in an early stage and small resident communities of some ten or twenty English merchants and commercial agents developed in these cities. Individual London Levant merchants conducted their business exclusively through these factors, some of whom stayed for many years.[40] The factors had to abide by the rules of the Company and lived protected by the capitulations while the local English consul represented their collective interests and individual affairs before the authorities. In business matters, nevertheless, they were individually only responsible to the Company members in London who provided their operating capital.[41]

In the second decade of the seventeenth century the Levant Company established a trading factory in Smyrna, present-day Izmir. Agents of English merchants began arriving in town and by mid-century a significant English merchant community prospered in the Aegean port.[42] Smyrna was attractive to European merchants as it had a large hinterland and extensive maritime and terrestrial commercial networks.[43]

In the western Mediterranean, especially in Spain and Italy, the 'new draperies' found a ready market, too. But this region had few exports to balance the import of English fabrics. One option for the English merchants was to have their ships sail on to the Levant and take in cargo there. Another was to buy Levantine goods in Livorno, which developed into an emporium where such commodities were collected for resale in the last quarter of the sixteenth century. Soon, English merchants settled in the Tuscan port and conducted entrepôt business on behalf of themselves or principals elsewhere.[44] In this way, an English merchant colony had developed in Livorno by 1600.

After the peace with Spain of 1604 English merchants settled for the first time in Naples and Sicily, the Spanish dominions in Italy. Gradually, small permanent English merchant communities developed in Naples, Messina and Palermo and in the course of the seventeenth century Englishmen firmly established themselves and their trade in these southern ports.[45]

The English commercial initiatives in the White Sea, the Baltic and the Mediterranean areas do not alter the fact that well beyond 1640 by far most of England's export continued to be routed through the Low Countries and Germany. For a long time, this trade continued to be dominated by the Merchant

Adventurers, who received a new royal charter granting them a monopoly of the cloth trade to Germany and the Low Countries in 1564. At the same time, the problems the Adventurers met in Antwerp induced them to look for alternative commercial channels. They settled in Hamburg as early as 1567 and after the fall of Antwerp in 1585 they traded through various other towns, looking for places to re-establish their traditional staple. They finally chose Hamburg and a succession of Dutch towns. On the basis of a treaty they concluded with Hamburg in 1611 English merchants resided there to at least the early nineteenth century. Also, Middelburg served as the Adventurers' Dutch staple from 1611 to 1621, Delft from 1621 to 1635 and Rotterdam from about 1635 to the mid-1650s.[46]

Even though the empirical data is limited, the examples presented above show that there is ample evidence that the opening of the new markets coincided with the development of English merchant colonies in the relevant regions – in Russia, in the Baltic and in the Mediterranean – in the century after 1550. Especially in the case of the Baltic trade, there are indications that English merchants initially made the return trip on the ships to do business, but soon established themselves in key market towns to gain the competitive edge. It is evident that the men abroad were needed to surmount all kinds of barriers to trade, varying from lack of knowledge of local markets and poor postal connections to adverse local institutions and cultural idiosyncrasies. The men abroad built up trust. They acquired market knowledge and established commercial relations. They dealt with the authorities, who sometimes resisted the English initiative in order to protect the local merchants, but eventually, realizing that they could reap large benefits, yielded.

Structural Changes of the English Commercial System, 1650–1750

One would suspect that by 1650 most trade barriers between England and its foreign markets would have been overcome and that the English merchant colonies would have lost their reason for existence. But the caution the historiography shows is appropriate. The general picture as drawn by Ashton, Åström and Clarkson shows that many bigger merchants still had branch houses overseas, manned by junior partners or employees, often related to them by family ties, to look after their affairs and sometimes to serve several other merchants, too. Also, smaller English merchants would still appoint a supercargo – often the shipmaster – who travelled with the goods and did business abroad. And a few even continued to accompany their goods on board ship themselves, although this became less usual since this required long absences abroad.[47]

The persistence of the merchant colonies originated in big commercial innovations which were closely connected to institutional reforms. The institutional reforms originated in the frustration about the Dutch commercial dominance of England's trade, since well into the second half of the seventeenth century most of England's foreign trade passed through the Dutch Republic. Cromwell's Navigation Act of 1651 marked the beginning of a policy to emancipate England's commerce from the Dutch and to rescue trade from their hands. Henceforth goods were to be imported into England exclusively from where they were grown or produced and only in vessels from the same area or in English vessels. These conditions excluded both the Dutch entrepôt and Dutch ships. The Navigation Act of 1651 was followed by the Navigation Act of 1660 which tightened up the earlier regulations.[48]

The counterpart of the Navigation Acts was the gradual, no less mercantilist disintegration of the chartered companies in the European trade.[49] The commerce of the trading companies was continually infringed upon by interlopers, individual merchants who did not share their privileges. In the second half of the seventeenth century these illicit practices gained such dimensions that, indeed, the companies lost their commercial prominence and individual merchants took over.[50] Both the constant activity of these interlopers and the opposition from within London's merchant community eventually lead to 'deregulation'.[51] In 1673, the Eastland Company lost its monopoly of England's trade with Sweden, Norway and Denmark; its privileges were reduced to the inner Baltic area and it was compelled to admit new members. Deregulation of the massive trade with the Low Countries and Germany, traditionally reserved for the Merchant Adventurers, followed in 1689, when Parliament opened it up to all. And the same thing happened to the commerce with Russia in 1699 as, from then on, anyone could become a member of the Russia Company.[52] The Levant Company retained its monopoly until 1825 and continued to protect the English merchants trading in the Ottoman Empire by diplomatic means even if many did business without paying the Company dues.[53]

In this way the English mercantilist state dismantled the individual monopolies of the privileged companies and introduced protectionism and the enforcement of the national, 'joint' monopoly of the navigation code instead. This policy was successful. From the 1670s, for example, Amsterdam's role as a Baltic entrepôt for England was largely eliminated. An additional major change in the English commercial system and a symptom of England's emancipation from the Dutch was the introduction of triangular trade in the North Sea area, developing into an integrated system during the first half of the eighteenth century. Indeed the English copied the old and proven methods of the Dutch and began to carry out intermediate commerce of their own.[54]

Perhaps as another result of the English government's new, aggressive mercantile policy, English foreign trade quite suddenly expanded in the last quarter of the seventeenth century. The exports of English produce – as always mainly woollen textiles – more than doubled in the decades up to 1740. At the same time, re-exports increased sensationally. By 1660 their value was still negligible but by 1740 it amounted to about 40 per cent of that of internally produced exports. The first growth spurt was between about 1665 and 1690 and involved mainly tobacco and sugar from the English possessions in America and calico from India. From about 1720 growth resumed when coffee, from the Near East, and, to a lesser degree, tea, from China, were added to the range of re-exports. Reversely, articles of continental origin, mainly wine and German linen, were re-exported to the English settlements across the Atlantic.[55]

While intermediate commerce, exports and colonial re-exports increased, there were major shifts in the pattern of commercial destinations in Europe. Great changes occurred in the Baltic trade at an early stage.[56] In the mid-seventeenth century the backbone of the Eastland trade, the export of cloth to the Prussian ports, went through a crisis from which it never recovered. Simultaneously, the destinations for the purchase of flax and hemp for the English market shifted eastwards from Danzig: first to Königsberg, then to Riga and Narva. And, finally, there was a sudden and large increase of export of Swedish iron from Stockholm and Gothenburg directly to England. These changes in destinations and cargoes – 'from cloth to iron' – took a long time, but the turn of the tide occurred between 1660 and 1675.[57]

The dominance of Dutch and German ports as commercial destinations gradually crumbled off. By 1740 only about a third of all English export, increasingly consisting of re-exports, went to Amsterdam and Hamburg and other ports of the Low Countries and Germany. English produce increasingly went to southern Europe: mainly Portugal and Spain, and wine and Spanish wool were shipped from there to England. And, in addition, the English gradually took over the Mediterranean carrying trade between foreign countries at the expense of the Italians. The Levant commerce expanded rapidly during the 1650s, '60s and early '70s but, in the first half of the eighteenth century, was hit hard by competition from silks from China and Bengal, cotton from the Caribbean and coffee being shipped by the East Indian companies, and from fashion and technical shifts in the case of mohair yarn and galls. Consequently, English trade with Turkey was in sharp decline throughout the middle decades of the eighteenth century.[58]

The great structural changes in English foreign trade in the period between 1650 and 1750 – deregulation, emancipation from the Dutch, the introduction of intermediate commerce, growth of re-export of colonial commodities and shifts in destination patterns – mainly happened between 1650 and 1700. It is true that English export grew vigorously into the early 1750s and that coffee and tea entered the market only after 1720, but the tendency is that after about 1700 English commerce rather stabilized than structurally changed. This stabilization reached the edge of ossification after about 1760. It might be tempting to look for signs of a fundamental economic reorientation leading to the Industrial Revolution in these years. Nevertheless, as Murphy has argued slightly ironically, the basic tendency in the English economy of the later 1760s, the 1770s and the early 1780s, 'far from being a cumulative building up to revolutionary force, was a wasting decline into stagnancy'.[59]

Just as in the case of the period after the great commercial changes in the century between 1550 and 1650, now, again, after the commercial changes of the half century between 1650 and 1700, one would suspect that most of England's foreign commerce had become routine and that, with trade barriers down, the English merchant colonies would have lost their reason for existence and disappeared. This time, this seems to be true in at least some cases. Ormrod argues that, in the first half of the eighteenth century, trade via English agents on the Continent gave way to direct trade with local businessmen abroad 'in all branches of overseas trade with regions which contained strong indigenous merchant groups', extending, specifically, from Holland and Germany to Scandinavia and the Baltic, excluding Russia.[60] But Ormrod also mentions that the use of English factors abroad persisted in 'more distant and less predictable markets', such as Portugal, the Levant and Russia, where colonies of merchants and factors continued to exist.[61] According to Ormrod the disappearance of the English merchant colonies in northern and north-western Europe may be explained by the inclination of the English to invest their capital in the lucrative Atlantic economy and by the fact that this was facilitated by the influx of continental capital into England's European trade.[62] By implication, Ormrod seems to suspect that 'more distant and less predictable markets' lacked sufficient local capital and entrepreneurship to allow this shift.

Three examples may illustrate the various ways the English merchant colonies developed between 1650 and 1750 and to what extent their development can be explained by the development of trade barriers, specifically the structural changes and subsequent stabilization of England's foreign trade, or – in Ormrod's terms – by the extent the markets they served were nearby and predictable and had strong indigenous merchant groups or were more distant and less predictable and lacked such groups. These three examples include Sweden, the Ottoman Empire and the Dutch Republic.

The great changes of the second half of the seventeenth century included the expansion of England's trade with Sweden. This expansion coincided, indeed, with the rise, from the 1650s, of colonies of English factors in Stockholm, Gothenburg, Riga and Narva. In Stockholm and Gothenburg, the factors arrived to buy iron from Swedish merchants. The heyday of the English factors colony in Stockholm was during the Swedish-Danish war of 1675–9 when about thirty English factors were active in the Swedish capital. After the war, the Swedish authorities, instigated by the big Stockholm burghers, took up a policy of either shutting out the English factors from trade or pressing them to citizenship, usually in vain as the English were little anxious in this respect. The authorities now stripped the English of their customs concessions and began to strictly enforce the trade regulations and to limit the length of their yearly stay.[63] According to Åström, Sweden, nevertheless, for the time being, was unable to do without the English factors, which, by this time, provided the Swedish iron production and export with credit.[64] In the 1680s, indeed, the English were still responsible for two thirds of the iron export from Stockholm to England. At the same time, however, several large local, Stockholm merchants sent the bulk of the rest directly to English merchant houses in London and clearly could do without the services of the English factors. In 1698 there were only three English factors left among Stockholm's iron exporters. Two years later this number had risen to six or seven again and after the outbreak of the Great Northern War the regulations concerning foreign residents immediately ceased to have effect.[65] Only after the war did the policy to shut out the factors gradually take effect. According to Åström, all English factors had left Stockholm by the 1730s.[66] Müller seems to confirm Åström's conclusion, with a slight lag, showing that, in the first half of the eighteenth century, English merchants still had a prominent role in the Stockholm iron export, about 50 per cent of which went to Britain. Two of the seven leading iron export houses of Stockholm between 1730 and 1745 may be categorized as English. The other five firms originated in Ireland, Scotland, the Dutch Republic, France and Sweden. The two English companies had left the scene by 1750 – ten or twenty years later than one might gather from Åström's argument. In 1750 and 1760 the five firms originating in Ireland, Scotland, the Dutch Republic, France and Sweden were still dominant. Their combined share in Stockholm's iron export in those two years was 59 and 51 per cent, respectively.[67]

The Stockholm example seems to show the full cycle of a merchant colony in a nutshell. The English arrived to start Swedish iron export to England but they lost their indispensability when the remnants of soon crumbling trade barriers proved, at least in peacetime, not so high as to prevent direct business between Englishmen in England and Swedes in Sweden. Only war frustrated direct trade. In the first half of the eighteenth century, many English were finally driven out by the mercantilist policy of the Swedish government and trade via English agents gave way to direct trade. On the other hand, it seems odd that the Stockholm iron export in 1750 and 1760 was still dominated by foreign – but not English – houses. One explanation for this may be that these houses could no longer be considered as foreign, as the members of most of them had come to Sweden already in the seventeenth century.

Just as in Stockholm, in Swedish Riga and Narva, too, English trade was supported by a colony of English residents. Åström provides a fuller picture for Narva than for Riga. He shows that Narva's governor had already tried to attract Englishmen to the town in the early seventeenth century. The Swedish government wanted to make the port on the Gulf of Finland a staple for the Russian trade and in this way to attract traffic from Arkhangelsk to the Baltic. It seems, nevertheless, that a colony of English factors did not really take shape until the 1670s. By 1679 it consisted, perhaps, of about seven merchant houses, apparently agents of English firms. In 1696, again, seven English companies were established in Narva, including, in all, twelve people, mostly working in partnerships of two.[68]

The English factors and naturalized English dominated Narva's business with England. The town's local merchants did not have a chance to take over from the English colony after trade had become routine. Before that could happen, war ended Narva's commercial prominence. The Russian conquest of the town in 1704, the founding of St Petersburg and the rerouting of Russia's foreign trade there hit Narva's trade hard and led to the disintegration of its English colony. Instead, after peace had come in 1721, St Petersburg became the centre of Russian trade. English commercial houses found the new town on the river Neva an attractive new gateway to the Russian market and soon attained a leading position in St Petersburg's trade with western Europe.[69] Foreign merchant communities here continued to be indispensable throughout the eighteenth century as Russian merchants lacked the knowledge, experience, credit and government support to do direct international business.[70]

The second example illustrating the various ways the English merchant colonies developed between 1650 and 1750, and to what extent their development can be explained by the development of trade barriers, involves the Dutch Republic. The Dutch Republic was, just like Sweden, one of Ormrod's near and predictable markets with strong indigenous merchant groups. Quite obviously, the need for the use of English factors would be expected to have disappeared here, as it disappeared in Sweden, in the course of the first half of the eighteenth century when English foreign trade stabilized after the great changes of the previous half century. The opposite, however, is true. However predictable the Dutch market was and however strong its indigenous merchant groups were, the English navigation codes raised a great trade barrier which could only be overcome by the use of an extensive English merchant colony in Rotterdam, which consequently continued to flourish.

The bulk of the Anglo-Dutch trade had been concentrated in Rotterdam since 1635 but the First Anglo-Dutch War (1652–4) brought commercial relations to a standstill, resulting in the abandonment of Rotterdam by the Merchant Adventurers. After the war, the Adventurers resettled in Dordrecht and struggled on in Holland in the face of heavy competition from interloping merchants, many of whom were based in Rotterdam. In the 1660s, company members began to transfer their business to Hamburg and in 1672 the last few remaining company factors in Holland left Dordrecht and moved to Hamburg. In the meantime,

Rotterdam's community of English interlopers had taken over Dutch re-export to England. The restrictive English import policies, laid down in the Navigation Codes since 1651, formally excluded Dutchmen from this business and the interlopers were happy to stand in, handling the lion's share of Anglo–Dutch trade. English businessmen based in Rotterdam – 'Little London' – continued to dominate Dutch trade and shipping with the British Isles throughout the eighteenth century.[71] By 1743 Rotterdam's English colony numbered between 3,000 and 4,000 individuals – about 8 per cent of the total population.[72]

The third example illustrating the development of the English merchant colonies involves the Ottoman Empire. As mentioned above, English merchant communities had developed in Aleppo, Constantinople and Smyrna, in the early seventeenth century. These colonies persisted throughout the seventeenth century and far into the eighteenth century. It was via the English factoring houses in these great trading cities and staying in touch with them by frequent correspondence that the English Levant merchants, usually based in London, conducted their business abroad. These business relationships, however, were not exclusive. The factors competed for orders, each of them acting for several principals at the same time, for the most part merchants in London, with occasional commissions from foreign merchants in Marseilles, Leghorn and Amsterdam. The factoring houses often included a young partner for whom his father had bought a partnership to be introduced to the trade and they would accommodate a son of a Levant merchant as an apprentice.[73]

The development of the English merchant colonies in the Levant followed quite neatly that of the trade and coincided with the general shift of the western European commercial activities from Aleppo to Smyrna.[74] Thus, by the end of the seventeenth century, when trade flourished, the English factors in Aleppo numbered thirty or forty, comprising perhaps fifty traders and partners, but in the first half of the eighteenth century, when commerce waned, their number began to decrease. By 1760 the Aleppo trade was in full decline and from the middle decades of the eighteenth century the English lost interest and largely abandoned the Aleppo trade. To the same effect, in the second quarter of the eighteenth century, the English had to leave the great market of Constantinople to the French. The English merchant community in Smyrna fared better. It is true that the English saw their trade with Smyrna decrease, too, after the turn of the seventeenth century, but they continued to buy some Persian silk there and they experienced a revival of the cotton trade in the Aegean port in the second half of the eighteenth century. By the end of the century Smyrna had replaced Aleppo as England's main market in the Levant.[75]

As noted above, Ormrod mentions that English merchant colonies persisted in 'more distant and less predictable markets', such as the Levant. And, although the colonies in the Ottoman Empire waned with the trade, it seems to be true that trade via English agents here did not give way to direct trade with local businessmen – as did happen in Sweden. Apparently, commercial barriers were not overcome. The question is justified if this was because of the remoteness or the unpredictability of the Ottoman market. Throughout the eighteenth century the English principals at home were not willing to have Ottoman merchants act as their agents or correspondents in Smyrna. They would not allow Ottoman merchants to participate in their commercial networks and kept the trade to and from England in their own hands. All the same, the local merchants seem to have been quite capable of doing the job. Unlike the English, Dutch businessmen based in the Dutch Republic did include local Ottoman merchants in their commercial network and accepted them, at times, as their correspondents in Smyrna in the eighteenth century. It seems that the English and the Dutch applied different commercial strategies and raising commercial barriers was part of the English strategy.[76]

The three examples presented above show that English merchant colonies changed along different lines in the period between 1650 and 1750, creating an ambiguous pattern of development. While several colonies, such as the merchant settlement in Stockholm, deteriorated over time, others were more persistent. Due to different causes, merchant colonies remained intact in both the Dutch Republic and the Levant. In the former case, the Navigation Codes involved a formal institutional barrier to trade and made a permanent English settlement necessary. In the case of the Levant, it is less clear why the English chose to hold on to their merchant colonies. But, as the Russian case suggests, too, it seems likely that markets, which were less predictable as a consequence of cultural differences, permanently needed a representation of domestic merchants.

Italian and Scottish Merchant Colonies

After the decline of the Dutch trade system, the English dominated commerce. Of course, the transition was gradual. The Dutch merchant colonies did not suddenly disappear, but gradually shrank in size and lost importance. Likewise, many English merchants could already be found abroad during the Golden Age of Dutch trade. Although in terms of trade supremacy the English system succeeded the Dutch merchant network, for most of the time colonies of both countries coexisted. Furthermore, in addition to the Dutch and the English, merchants from other countries founded their own colonies abroad as well. In this section we study the literature on Italian and Scottish merchant colonies. These two nations differed considerably in terms of size, economic interests and geographical position. Italy was not yet unified during the early modern period. Several city states, which eventually would join the Italian state, benefited hugely from the Asian trade, entering Europe through the Levant. Scotland was much smaller than the combined Italian city states, yet it is peculiar to see that in some merchant cities, such as Bergen, Rotterdam and Hamburg, large Scottish communities existed. Because of the highly diverse nature of these countries, the demands on the business networks of Scotland and Italian city states were different as well.

The rise of north-west European commercial empires, such as those of England and the Low Countries, coincided with a decline of the trade of the Italians.[77] During the fifteenth and first part of the sixteenth centuries, the economies of city states such as Venice, Florence and Genoa had expanded rapidly as a consequence of increased export trade.[78] From the late sixteenth century onwards, however, the trade of Italian city states encountered several setbacks. First, they had lost their key position in the trade with Asia after the sea route via the Cape of Good Hope was established and subsequently exploited by the seafaring nations of northern Europe.[79] Secondly, and more decisively, the export products of Italian commercial cities, i.e. high quality manufactured goods (textiles mainly), came to compete with products made in the Low Countries or England. Due to lower production costs and a lower level of quality, the latter were cheaper and undercut prices set by Italian states.[80]

Often, the low-quality produce of north-west European origin provided a substitute for the more expensive manufactures of Italian city states. As a result, Italian export industries received some blows, a process reinforced by the increased competition in shipping. The French, English and Dutch increasingly shipped goods previously handled by Italian merchants. Nevertheless, low and high quality products were not perfect substitutes and the price elasticity of demand was therefore limited: luxury goods produced in or re-exported through Italian states remained in demand in north-west Europe. Consequently, Italian companies maintained their overseas branches in order to cling on to their European markets.

An elaborate account of merchant colonies of the Italian city states (henceforth, Italian merchant colonies) is provided by M. E. Bratchel, specifically focusing on Italian merchants in London. Overall, his description of Italian merchants in London nicely fits with the business-network theory mentioned above. Especially in the early stages of settlement, during the late Middle Ages, Italian merchant colonies were founded on a family basis. Family members were easily trusted and reliable links between London and Italian city states were established. However, in the fifteenth and sixteenth centuries this pattern changed. The decreasing share of family members among overseas companies coincided with the emancipation of the commission agent. Small firms, unable to maintain an elaborate network of agents themselves, traditionally used representatives of larger firms to look after their overseas interests. However, at the end of the sixteenth century these branches of large firms also cut back on their employee roster. Instead, more and more business was conducted through professional agents, leading to a declining population size of Italian merchant settlements.[81] Nevertheless, in places where the legal institutions offered little support to the substitution of agents for family members, such as Antwerp, this trend was less profound.[82]

In contrast to the Italian city states, the Kingdom of Scotland was a minor commercial nation in Europe. During the late Middle Ages, Scottish merchants settled on the coasts of Normandy and Flanders.[83] Subsequently, during the sixteenth and seventeenth centuries, the focus of Scottish merchants expanded further northward. As a consequence, merchant settlements were also erected in the Baltic countries as well as the Netherlands and Norway.[84] In some merchant cities, like Hamburg, the identity of Scots was less distinct and the Scottish community seemed to have been part of a larger British network.[85] During the first phase of the expansion of the Scottish trade network, the Scots were concerned with the export of salmon, raw wool, hides, plaiding and coal. This encouraged them to settle in cities such as Bruges and Rotterdam. There, the Scots established staples so that goods could be sold at a common price by specified factors, who returned the proceeds to the originating merchant minus a commission. Contracts that established a staple were drawn up between a local community and the Scots. One of the major benefits of having staples is that Scottish merchants enjoyed certain rights, freedoms and privileges, among which was the exemption from duties.[86] However, the factors who found buyers for the Scottish goods did not necessarily have to be Scottish themselves. For instance, in Rotterdam all wholesale transactions were managed by municipal brokers organized in guilds. In the case of the Scottish coal trade, both Scottish and Dutch brokers were employed. Catterall argues that it was wise to use Scots as brokers, since they knew and understood the Scots coal trade.[87]

While the Scots were, at the turn of the sixteenth century, still in an early phase of commercial development, Italian trade communities appeared to have entered the closing stages of their existence. In this period, the set-up of many Italian businesses in London changed significantly. The previously described development of Italian businesses in the merchant colonies from being traditional, based on family relations, to a more open structure took place during the sixteenth century in particular. An important encouragement to involving outsiders in the family business was the increasing size of trade. When merchant colonies expanded, non-relatives started to enter the Italian enterprises. Perhaps even more relevant was the increased need for capital in the sixteenth century as a consequence of increased competition. In contrast to the preceding centuries, Italians no longer possessed a monopolistic position in the trade of luxury products. Through the market of Antwerp, spices and silks reached London, reducing the English dependence on Italian merchants. The intensification of competition reduced marginal profits and therefore pushed up demand for capital, to which end investors from outside the family were attracted.[88]

Furthermore, the booming English cloth trade may have troubled Italian merchants. English exports rose fast during the fifteenth and sixteenth centuries, overshadowing the increased imports of luxury goods. Assuming that the Italians invested the money earned by importing luxury goods in the cloth trade, there are two ways in which the changing trade balance hindered Italian companies. First, if the Italian financial markets were not able to cope with the increased demand for capital, the supply of money could not match the increase of the demand for the export of cloth. Second, the relative shortage of imports means that the earnings from luxury imports fell short of enabling Italian merchants to fully benefit from the high demand for cloth. Additionally, inflationary forces increased the costs of living, leaving merchants desperate for extra capital.[89] The Italian commerce was frequently disturbed and disrupted during the sixteenth century.[90] In such unpredictable times, the struggle for capital not only resulted in partnerships with outsiders. It also meant opportunities to cut back on expenses were not ignored. This way, economic circumstances during the sixteenth century encouraged the emancipation of commercial agents. As it was very costly to maintain a network of agents abroad, a professional agent to which a company's overseas business could be outsourced was an attractive alternative. The widespread use of commissioned agents reduced the size of the Italian merchant colony considerably. At the end of the sixteenth century, the Italian community in London had virtually perished.[91]

By the time the Italian commercial settlements had developed into the efficient representation by commissioned agents, most trade networks around 1600 had yet to reach a state of maturity. During the sixteenth and the first half of the seventeenth centuries, the Scottish trade network expanded towards the north of Europe and settled in Denmark, Poland, Norway and Sweden.[92] In the case of Bergen, this expansion was for a large part driven by the Scottish demand for timber and their supply of salt.[93] During the sixteenth century, Bergen acted as the customs port for the timber trade area of Sunnhordland, south of the city, which attracted Scottish shipmasters. The Scottish merchants balanced their finances by exporting salt to Bergen. The Norwegian city thrived on their fish industry, but the domestic salt supply needed to preserve the fish fell short of demand. Therefore, Scottish salt was in dire need. During the seventeenth century French salt of better quality reduced Scottish salt exports considerably. Nonetheless, the volume of trade between Scotland and Bergen remained unaffected, suggesting that trade was mainly based on Scottish demand for Norwegian commodities. In fact, all through the sixteenth and seventeenth centuries Bergen harboured a sizeable Scottish community.[94]

A large number of the Scottish migrants kept in contact with Scotland, importing and exporting goods to and from the home country. Some of them worked as agents of merchants in Scotland. Others traded on their own behalf.

The latter type of merchants' business was not conducted exclusively with Scotland. The Scottish community in Gothenburg, for example, housed several independent merchants who had expanded the scope of their operations beyond exchange with the motherland and traded with countries other than Scotland as well. This model of business applied to the major Scottish families in Gothenburg that seem to have traded mostly on account of their own. Examples of countries with which such independent Scottish merchants in Sweden traded are England, the Dutch Republic and Baltic ports.[95] Even so, these destinations were usually in addition to their trade with Scotland and the ties between Scottish tradesmen settled abroad and their motherland remained typically strong. In the course of the seventeenth century trade between Sweden and Scotland increased significantly as a consequence of Scottish settlement in ports like Gothenburg and Stockholm, a development reflected by the fact that Gothenburg's largest iron exporter was a Scottish factor.[96]

Towards the end of the seventeenth century, the Scottish orientation shifted towards Ireland as well as the Americas, and migration to Scandinavian countries dropped to 'an unsubstantial trickle'.[97] Yet some settlements, such as the merchant colony in Gothenburg, persisted well into the nineteenth century, perhaps in even higher numbers than is documented as Scottish settlers were not obliged to register themselves and, therefore, remain outside the scope of historical research.[98] Those who did apply for Swedish citizenship, i.e. became Swedish themselves, often married natives and eventually blended into the wider community of merchants.[99] Or, approached from the opposite direction, the size of the Scottish community was maintained by mixing with Swedish families, thereby reducing the number of first generation migrants. Although not explicitly mentioned in the literature, the emancipation of Scottish merchants in Sweden as independent tradesmen appears to have contributed to the continuity of the colony during the mercantilist eighteenth century.

Conclusion

In contrast to what Veluwenkamp in his article on Dutch merchant colonies suggested, merchant colonies were not a unique Dutch trademark. But there is no doubt that merchant colonies featured prominently in the development of international trade. As is evident from this and the other chapters of this volume, other countries founded their own merchant colonies, too. Subsequently, we noted that these other colonies, just like the Dutch, emerged, grew in size, and, over time, tended to deteriorate. In an attempt to understand this broad pattern of rise and decline, we used modern business-network theories, which explain commercial settlements from the need to overcome barriers to trade. Inevitably, the expansion of trade networks into hitherto unfamiliar areas is frustrated by obstacles, for example the lack of trust between agents of domestic and foreign markets or difficulties with regard to communication. Such barriers to trade are overcome by sending representatives of domestic firms or trade companies abroad, ensuring reliable lines of communication. These informal institutional barriers can be conquered over time. As foreign markets become familiar, trust as well as communication issues are gradually solved. With the breaking down of such informal barriers, the need for merchant colonies dissolves, leading to a decline of commercial settlements.

This pattern roughly applies to the English merchant colonies in the early modern period, as the case of Stockholm clearly shows. At the end of the sixteenth century the English trade network expanded and merchant colonies were founded in many European ports. Until at least the turn of the eighteenth century, these settlements remained in place, signifying the persistence of barriers. Apparently, the cycle of rise and decline was a slow process and, in historical reality, new barriers were constantly encountered, stimulating the continuity of the merchant colonies. For instance, when the orientation of English trade shifted towards re-exporting colonial goods, the supply and demand structure of respectively domestic and foreign markets changed as well, presenting new challenges for domestic agents abroad. Also, the persistence of the Navigation Codes prevented the decline of merchant colonies in the Dutch Republic, especially Rotterdam.

So, although the first part of the cycle as described by business-network theories fits with the historical evidence, the picture is much less distinct in the case of the disappearance of merchant colonies. For instance, even in the eighteenth century, when commercial settlements elsewhere deteriorated, the English chose to stay in the Levant. It remains difficult to explain the continuity of colonies in the Levant. In contrast, in the case of Rotterdam, it is clear that formal institutional barriers forced the merchant colony to remain in place much longer than was necessary to simply overcome communication issues. The persistence of the English colony in Rotterdam during the eighteenth century was not so much driven by a lack of understanding between English and Dutch merchants. Rather, policy required the prolonged presence of English agents in Rotterdam. In contrast to informal institutional barriers, formal institutional barriers do not wear with time. As commercial networks face both forms of trade obstructions, it is perhaps not that surprising to see merchant colonies survive for long periods of time.

2 GERMAN AND ITALIAN MERCHANT COLONIES IN EARLY MODERN ENGLAND

Beverly A. Dougherty

In early modern England, inspiration for commercial organization, growth and development was drawn from the practices and experiences of the late fifteenth century.[1] In this earlier period, England was largely an agricultural country but the fact that she was strategically located and produced the finest wool in Europe made her a magnet for many foreign merchants. Merchants arrived from all over but the largest number came from the northern German cities and from many of the larger Italian cities such as Venice, Milan and Genoa. Merchants from Portugal, Ragusa, Brittany, Spain, France, Poland, Scandinavia and the Low Countries were also part of the English international trading scene.[2] Given this intense interest, England became an international centre for trade that was both prolific and profitable by the early modern period.

England basically sold wool and cloth and in return purchased a great variety of needed goods from foreign merchants. Of the many foreigners that traded with England, the Germans and Italians were the most influential because they came in large numbers and with royal permission stayed and formed separate colonies. Each colony possessed individual qualities that required creative strategies to maximize profits while coexisting with the requirements of the host country. The Germans came from a collection of profit- seeking Baltic cities that were given special privileges in London including the right to administer a city-like zone called the Steelyard. The Italians, highly individualistic and true to their derivative cities, formed a tightly closed society in a section of London, allowing no others to penetrate.

The Germans and Italians first arrived in England between the twelfth and thirteenth centuries and found a generally receptive environment. From the time of Magna Carta, England welcomed foreign merchants and assured them of treatment that was both fair and hospitable.[3] The English kings also encouraged foreign merchants with special privileges. By the early modern period, the German and Italian merchants had long been part of the English business world and especially the London landscape.[4] During this associative period, in what evolved as a most productive association, the German and Italian merchants formed colonies thereby becoming occupiers, suppliers and facilitators on English soil. They were occupiers in that they lived on English soil, suppliers because they provided products otherwise unavailable and facilitators because they created a distinct space of time whereby the English, by association and observation, eventually adopted or adapted some of the more successful characteristics of the colonies, making their own trade internationally competitive. The foreigners exemplified what could be accomplished with a strong commercial focus, strategic planning and national support. The English resented their success but in reality, their commercial efforts were carefully calculated to replicate that same success. This is clear because once the English developed their own commercial potential by using similar techniques, foreign colonies were no longer needed and, therefore, no longer existed.

The trade relationship between England and colonies was multifaceted. Their interaction revealed sales shaped by a variety of creative practices within town and country. The English preferred the Germans and Italians sold wholesale, as indicated in a number of laws, but other types of sales were also widely used depending on the goods, customers and environment. They sold wholesale, retail, exchanged at fairs and markets, operated through middlemen, sold to individuals and consortiums, presented privately to the rich and royal, and if certain subtle conditions surfaced, neither foreigner nor English were opposed to collaborative illegal partnerships for personal profit.[5] It was leverage, derived from power, money and influence, that was the most compelling factor throughout this period. In the earliest period, foreigners operated from such a position of power. By the seventeenth century, this power had passed to the English.

In order to examine the relationship and interaction between merchant colonies and host country, it is necessary to establish a few general characteristics about the colonies and the merchants who were so successful in this period. A merchant colony was an association or unit of merchants who shared a similar background and provided each other with any cooperative assistance needed in their foreign environment.[6] Individual colonies shared similar characteristics but also exhibited individuality. Subrahmanyam Sanjay presents a view of merchants and their colonies that is brief but relevant.[7] He describes merchants as individuals who understood the business environment and the successes and failures they might encounter. Foreign merchants wanted access to profitable markets and so needed to establish a rapport with their hosts. Merchants knew that the trading experience had to also encompass diplomatic qualities because if economic conditions changed or rivals gained more favour, all might be lost. The core of a colony included trusted family members who carried out the directives and financial goals set by the home office. This core consisted of sons or relatives of the director or persons connected by marriage or ethnicity. Persons outside the family circle were employed if necessary but with great caution. In this way, successful business operations were usually the result of home office directives and an effective connecting network. Colonies always balanced a dual role as they had to obey local administrative laws and also be cognizant of directives from their own country. For their home countries they provided on-site representation and established personal relationships with the English so that they were able to transact business expeditiously. Merchants were always aware of local political trends but tried not to participate in any way that might deter their business goals. They wanted staying power. Merchants were intelligent on many levels but usually never promoted themselves as such. For this reason, in this period, writers started to publicize the merchants' many fine qualities because they so often went unrecognized.[8] In all, the German and Italian merchants who populated the colonies in late medieval and early modern England were intelligent, knew their merchandise and markets, and derived strength from their home base. They grouped together, depended on family ties, used an internal organization to provide order to their operations and, in the end, tried to establish relationships with the host country that were cordial, long lasting, and profitable. All of these qualities were best accomplished if they were residents in the land of their business.

Germans and Italians interacted with the English but all three exhibited individual personalities. The colonies' characteristics stemmed from their derivative home, the type of products they sold and the privileges they acquired from the host country. The Germans represented the commercial interests of a league of northern cities, approximately 180–200, from Wendish, Pomeranian, Saxon, Westphalian and Prussian towns.[9] Basically, the Germans brought useful products such as hemp, flax, pitch, cordage, timber, corn, fish, salt, wax, potash and furs.[10] These products served English industries such as shipbuilding, domestic building, military (bow staves), food and cloth production. In return, the Germans purchased wool and cloth and received special privileges: an area for their colony, the privilege of attending markets and fairs, freedom to sell retail as well as wholesale and were fortunate to receive many other privileges.[11] Some of their privileges were beyond those given to English merchants. The Germans established solid commercial ties but made it known that they would protect their commercial interests with naval power if necessary. In opposition, the Italians, representing their individual home cities of Venice, Milan, Genoa, Florence, Lucca, etc. did not possess naval power. They made themselves indispensable by employing superior commercial abilities, providing luxuries for the rich and royal, products necessary for cloth production, offering loans to the king and financial services that the English found convenient and easy to use.[12] However, they never received the same sweeping privileges as the Germans. The goods they brought came from a vast array of sources: some from across two continents, some from Italy and some from just across the Channel.[13] Their offerings included an endless number of luxurious and exotic products such as spices, silks, carpets, medicinal plants for the apothecaries, perfumes, jewels, gold, cotton, sweet wines, velvet, satin, damask, armour, weapons, ecclesiastical vestments, writing paper, books, furs and even exotic animals for pets. Their instinctive commercial abilities earned them both riches and resentment. In opposition to both colonies, England, the host, was a centralized country with a system of laws, courts and a parliament. They used legal enactments to promote and control trade so that trade and state were interrelated.[14] Sometimes the king overrode English law for his own benefit. This action was used when the king needed financial help or favours from the foreigners.[15] However, the colonies existed by the king's permission and while their relationships were not always smooth, the goal of profit and convenience encouraged all three to remain hospitable and to work out any problems as they occurred.

The main goals for the Germans, Italians and English were profit and product availability. This made the foreign colonies welcome because they filled these exact needs.[16] Most of these needs were derived from the fact that the Germans and Italians protected their sources thereby making both their products and services only available through their trade. This fact contributed to an underlying resentment on the part of the English as they constantly pressed for reciprocal commercial privileges but were always denied. However, at this time, it was convenient for the English to have ready buyers and convenient financial services available. For the colonies, English wool and cloth fuelled their home industries and exports.[17] The colonies were important to England but these were not the largest or most important for the Germans or the Italians. Both had larger commercial operations in other countries.[18]

For the most part, relations between the English and colonies were amicable but there were periods of conflict. Conflict usually came when the English dealt with the issue of reciprocity or if there was a downturn in the economy. The English wished to be equally competitive but in the earlier stages their commercial operations were not as developed as those of the foreigner. In reality, fifteenth-century England was more like a rural area as compared to the cultural sophistication of many European cities.[19] The English had fewer financial resources, lower profit margins, lacked product diversification and distant markets. At this time, they were not quite ready to interact on the same competitive level as the foreigners. While the English and colonies had a profitable, if uneven, interdependent relationship, the colonies must be seen as coexisting with the established English legal and economic system.[20]

Economically, during the late Middle Ages and early modern period, England was in a much better position than earlier. After a mid-fifteenth-century slump, there was a welcome economic expansion during the last quarter of the century.[21] Wool was still exported but now cloth had become an even bigger export thereby producing more jobs in England. Other smaller industries such as tin, iron and hides were also experiencing growth but nothing as spectacular as that of wool and cloth. Also, now, many families such as the Celys and Pastons became involved in the wool and cloth industry thereby competing with the large-scale contracts sought by foreign merchants.[22] The Merchant Adventurers, the Staple, and middleman dealers became important connections between the wool and cloth producers and buyers.[23]

The English always had a system by which wool and cloth were produced, distributed and sold but by the fourteenth century they developed a more formalized operation.[24] This operation usually considered the convenience of the buyer and the easiest way to make financial transactions. In earlier times, the Germans and Italians bought wool directly from the countryside but gradually the English established a system that streamlined the production of wool and cloth and the places of sale so that the proper amount of tax could be assessed, recorded and collected. Many of these directives were accomplished by enacted law whereby the English hoped to achieve a competitive advantage.

One major location for the collection, presentation and sales of wool and cloth was Blackwell Hall, built in 1397 in the City of London. The system started with entrepreneur, clothier or middleman who organized the manufacture and marketing of the cloth. He bought the wool, took it to the manufacturer and then delivered the finished product to Blackwell Hall in order to connect with buyers. There it was placed for sale between Thursday and Saturday. Once sold, it was transferred to the merchant's warehouse. When the merchant was ready, porters loaded the goods on lighters at quayside and then took them downstream to ships set for sailing. On the way back, the lighters carried goods from the ship destined for sale in England. This system involved a great number of record keepers and records, many of which are now lost or incomplete. This was the general system for the sales of cloth to foreigners but additional sales were transacted in other cities throughout England. However, London, located on the Thames, was the most active and important centre for cloth sales for the Germans and Italians.

The Italian merchants represented and worked for their individual cities such as Venice, Milan, Florence and Genoa but they were most often referred to as 'Lombards' or 'Italians'. These merchants were some of the most knowledgeable, socially prominent and ambitious foreign merchants in England.[25] They were rich, financially confident and willing to pay high prices for wool and cloth and enjoyed the reputation of importing the greatest variety of luxury goods. Initially, the Italians conducted business for themselves and also handled some papal transactions.[26] They regularly purchased large amounts of wool directly from monastic houses and wealthy landowners, usually years in advance. This type of direct buying was very profitable but was gradually altered by the use of middlemen and the required use of designated areas for the sale of wool. These requirements were often eased when the king requested loans or other favours from the Italians.[27] To pay his debt, the king granted the Italians special licenses allowing them to ship their English goods directly to the Mediterranean and not pay customs and subsidies. This was easiest for the king and beneficial for the Italians. In return, they purchased volumes of English goods and, depending on the size of the sale, they bought on credit or paid cash.[28]

Italian goods and services were eagerly sought by many buyers but especially the rich and royal who purchased fine Italian products because their opulence and luxury exemplified and enhanced their regal lifestyle.[29] From the records, it appears the Italians carried out regular sales but also took advantage of almost any commercial opportunity, legal or otherwise, and made it a success.[30] For this reason, the Italians were often restricted in their contact with the locals because they had so many capabilities that the English feared that their services might be preferred to their own. However, their luxury trade in England was the most profitable. In the thirteenth and fourteenth centuries, the wealthy had 'wardrobe houses' in London for the express purpose of buying and selling expensive goods. While designed for purchasing, these houses also served as storehouses or financial centres.[31] In addition, the king and other wealthy individuals had factors or managers who served as contacts with the Italians. These types of sales by the wealthy continued well into the sixteenth century. Given the obvious relationship between the Italians and the rich and the fact that they brought their own servants from Italy to serve their colony, the general English population had little tolerance for them.

Overall, the Italians possessed outstanding commercial and financial abilities and this was amply illustrated by their wide range of contacts, extensive business operations, numbers, knowledge of the host country and professional attitude.[32] In terms of the operation of their colony in England, the Italians, numbering about sixty to one hundred, were composed of firms as well as individual factors. With firms, the top family members were the partners. The rest were close relations and these families sometimes remained for generations.[33] Within these family units there were also smaller family groups that performed specialized tasks for the full operation. Their closeness was fostered by living in a foreign environment and success was ensured because their goals were identical: they wanted to consolidate and increase profits. Sons and relatives were most favoured but if one committed a business mistake or lacked good judgement, the family member would not be turned out but transferred to a position that carried less risk and definite supervision. Other participants were comprised of agents, smaller partnerships, independents, and those offering brokerage and moneylending services.[34]

The Italians operated in separate groups according to the area they repre-sented. For example, the Venetians first came in 1319 (last fleets in 1553) and brought the most luxurious and valuable goods by state galleys.[35] These goods were handled by their London Consul and council of twelve who were responsi-ble for business matters.[36] The Florentines came in the early fifteenth century and conducted business on a smaller scale. They brought alum and other goods for the cloth industry and also came with their own fleets. The Genoese ships first came in 1278.[37] Each group operated individually but if they had a problem, they preferred to ship cooperatively with other Italians than consort with non-Italians. There were also many Italian merchants who remained in Italy and worked through commis-sion agents and factors who were also part of the Italian colony in England.

For safety and flexibility, the Italians had two main colonies, London and Southampton. London was their premier location for the luxury trade but South-ampton had advantages too. It was easily reached, had a good, deep port, good distribution points and the Italians experienced less local animosity.[38] The differ-ence in attitude was based on the fact that in London the Italians were in direct competition with English merchants but in Southampton they were considered clients that provided a great deal of employment for the area such as housing, loading and unloading, distribution, etc.[39] While the people of Southampton welcomed them they also had specific rules that showed that they were grateful for their business but were not willing to outsource their local work to the Ital-ians. On occasion, anti-alien riots and discriminatory acts in London made the environment hostile and, therefore, Southampton was a convenient move.[40] In the fifteenth century, the Italians were subjected to hosting regulations whereby upon arrival in England they had to register with the mayors's court and reside with an English 'host' who was to oversee their stay and business transactions.[41] This was irritating for the Italians as the Germans were never subjected to these arrangements based on their ancient privileges. There were other incidents too. As happened on one occasion, the Italians were fined in London because Eng-lish ships trying to reach the Mediterranean had been attacked by other Italians. Although the Italians in London were not responsible they were still required to pay a considerable fine.[42] When all was considered, the Italians found it much more practical to pay the fine than to give up the lucrative trade. Another time, because of poor treatment, the Italians threatened to move out of London com-pletely. The fact that they controlled the money market which the English needed, they were asked to reconsider.[43] They stayed. Overall, the Italians showed them-selves to be practical, flexible and firmly focused on profitable survival.

Many Englishmen greatly resented and envied the success of the Italians and in retaliation often suggested that the Italians were guilty of improprieties such as cheating or corrupting their way of life with unnecessary, frivolous goods. These feelings found their way into popular expression with the famous poems

The Libell of English Policy and *On England's Commercial Policy* highlighting
how the English felt about the foreigners, exaggerated or not.[44] The real problem was that the Italians' business and financial techniques were beyond those
practised by the English. In reality, the Italians earned higher profits reselling
most English goods to foreign markets than the English were able to realize on
their own. It has been estimated that the Italians were earning profits of 25 per
cent to 33 per cent on their sales of wool and cloth, and sometimes up to 51 per
cent on tin. Likewise, the partners of the Medici's bank often earned as much as
25 per cent profit for their financial efforts.[45] This was far more than the English realized and it made them see themselves as they were at that time: raising
and producing very profitable products but not quite able to favourably capitalize on them in this aggressive economic environment. There were other foreign
merchants in England but the Italians seemed to be the target of choice. This
resentment continued and showed itself in terms of damage and piracy to their
ships and the eruption of anti-alien riots when serious damage was inflicted.[46]
When these aggressive conflicts occurred, the king and local officials were stern
with the English agitators and ordered punishment if they were found at fault.[47]
In other words, destructive actions by the general English populace were not
ignored by the government because the king wanted the benefits of foreign
imports. The way the Italians handled resentment was to conduct their business as usual, keep a low profile, treat each incident with good judgment but
not tolerate unfair treatment.[48] Since the king favoured their business, products
and assistance, he often came to their aid.[49] Resentment of this favouritism was
also reflected in the statutes. One of the more scathing statutes directed towards
aliens, mostly Italians, was 1 Richard III c. 9 (1484) where lawmakers listed what
they perceived as unacceptable practices by the Italians and requested parliament put an end to them.[50] It was stated in the statute that the Italians filled
their warehouses with fine goods and only sold when the prices were high; they
sold to anyone including other foreign merchants, made clothes for sale with
English cloth in England, made secret contracts to buy goods at lower prices,
sold retail, often bought English products and then sold them back to the English at a profit and took in other aliens or craftsmen as they were not supposed
to do. This statute was probably passed to pacify business people who sent their
representatives to parliament to express their dissatisfaction. However, as soon
as Henry VII (1485) was crowned, he was approached by the Italians and the
statute was revoked except for a few fines.[51] Such favours were granted when the
king needed money and this was the case with Henry VII.

At the beginning of the sixteenth century, the Italians still claimed a strong
share of exports and continued to trade as they had earlier. However, it was during the third quarter of the sixteenth century that the Italian mercantile colony in
London essentially ceased to be a vital organization and some of this was due to

the fact that the English had now learned a number of important business techniques used by the Italians.[52] For example, important points about financing, the best use of credit or cash and how to organize their business. The Italians, however, still shipped large amounts of English cloth, were looked to for luxuries and their banking system was used until well after Queen Elizabeth I's reign.[53] The family nucleus continued to be important as they devoted themselves to existing business affairs. However, as the century wore on, the Italian staff in London started to diminish even though they continued to conduct a regular business. Other merchants, including the English, began to cut into their monopoly and the Italian share of trade diminished. The Italians were also weakened by domestic conflicts, mature economies that were not responding to contemporary needs, war with foreign countries and the need to find new markets.[54] Now, they also had to deal with many more regulations and restrictions established by England. These troublesome regulations made trade less profitable than earlier. Gradually, the Italians were more willing to establish partnerships and to seek new forms of investment outside the family. Some remained in England, married, became denizens and made themselves useful to the government as well as continuing their business interests and acting as agents for other clients. A number were appointed to prominent political offices.[55] Others simply went home or were not replaced. The Italians continued to do business with England but by the end of the sixteenth century the dynamics had changed. The same will be seen with the Germans.

The operations of the German merchants differed in style from the Italians but they also carried on a complex, varied trade with the English. Merchants from Cologne were the first to come and by the twelfth and thirteenth centuries others followed. By the mid-fourteenth century the northern Germans had grouped together as a 'Hanse of Towns' for the purposes of protection, economic advantage and military strength. These Germans became popularly known as Hansards.[56] The Hansards represented a number of northern European towns and were led by Lübeck and Hamburg. The composition of the Hanse was fluid and therefore not a state in the traditional sense. Their trading environment encompassed many cities but their main operations were located in Bruges, Bergen, Novgorod and London. England was happy to receive them and early on awarded special recognition and privileges. In 1157 Henry II granted permission to the people of Cologne to sell wine in England and promised protection for the merchants as well as for their house in London. In addition, he stipulated that they would not suffer any new taxes.[57] In 1340, Edward III offered Dortmunders his affection and his permission to keep all the customs and subsidies due on their English goods as way to repay money they loaned to the king.[58] However, relations were not always smooth as there were also records of German and English complaints about each other.[59] In all, the Germans were strong, focused and exemplified the concept that privilege, protectionism and power can be profitable. Strong political connections and a regular supply of well-placed gifts kept the German commercial position strong.[60] The English tried not to offend them.

German goods, practical and necessary, did not have the same dazzle of Italian goods. However, while their internal organization was more structured than that of the Italians, they still shared some similarities.[61] Their colony of eighty or more people was well managed, depended on extended German families, groups that operated as firms and individuals that represented clients for commissions. The colony was located in an area of London referred to as the Steelyard. This was the most important German colony in England. Many Germans settled in other cities such as Ipswich, Yarmouth, Lynn, Boston, etc. and drew products from all over England. However, London always remained the focal point of leadership.[62] The Steelyard was favourably located along the Thames complete with homes, warehouses, a courtyard, an area for weighing and assessing goods, and even a small tavern-like structure for socializing. They were allowed free movement and the privileges to sell wholesale, retail, to cloth producers, cloth merchants and directly to individual customers. These privileges were confirmed by the English kings.[63] It was understood by the Londoners that they had to accept this privileged position even though they and most other foreigners were not accorded the same.[64] The internal authority of the colony was divided between three groups: men from Cologne, Westphalia and Prussia. They were selected to oversee the organization and important business operations. The Germans also had their own court, aldermen, secretaries, clerks, and judges to settle disputes. These officials were above English law. The alderman oversaw any commercial or civil issues that touched the Hansards and the host country.[65] They also had a special English justice to hear their pleas.[66] For example, if German ships were damaged or vandalized in the process of conducting trade they received quick attention and compensation. They were exempt from hosting and always assured of pardons from various assessments in accordance with their ancient rights. This last right was repeated regularly in the legal literature of the period.[67]

The Germans drew their products from a vast but compact area. Their trading routes followed direct routes in the north-east and north-west area of Europe in contrast to the far-reaching markets of the Italians. However, they too kept a nucleus of family or close business members in England to oversee their operations. Their financial capabilities were very basic and often they preferred to deal directly in cash as compared to the Italians who regularly and skilfully used credit. Cash transactions were not really a hindrance because the type of products and the amount of business they were conducting did not require extensive financial arrangements.[68] In addition, if the Germans felt challenged or wronged, they had no fear protecting themselves by the use of force, boycotts, blockage or privateering.[69] However, they kept their early privileges, and also found some favouritism among the English people. In one instance, when some

Germans were imprisoned for political reasons, the English petitioned the king to let them go as it was very bad for their business which was long-standing.[70] There were other times when the English felt great resentment and petitioned to limit their privileges but usually it was of little avail. It was not until the late fifteenth century and especially after the commercial conflict and naval warfare of 1468–74 that the Germans began to feel a weaker grip on English trade.[71] However, while they experienced conflict, trade between the two did not completely disappear. The outcome of the conflict appeared to end favourably for the Germans when Edward IV made peace and restored their ancient rights. Actually, Edward IV was about to go to war with France and did not wish to deal with any other conflict either on the sea or elsewhere. He also made peace with a number of other countries for the same reason.[72] However, the Germans were pleased with their treaty, the Treaty of Utrecht (1474).[73] These privileges were confirmed many times such as by Richard III (18 July 1484), Henry VII (29 March 1486) and later by Henry VIII (20 February 1510).[74] Often, this treaty is assessed as a great loss for England because the English did not get the promised reciprocity but some historians believe that this one aspect did not destroy the value of the whole treaty.[75] The Germans continued to hold their grip on English trade but strains in the relationship were becoming obvious. In 1552, German rights were abolished only to be reinstated in 1560. However, by this time they were restricted to the same privileges as the English merchants. The Germans eventually lost their hold on English trade as the English became less accepting and pressed for more competitive and direct contacts within their territory. Also, some of the Germans' failure is blamed on the brittle attitude of those at the head of the Hanse. They lacked flexibility in the face of a changing economic environment thereby giving the English and others a chance to establish economic partnerships in their coveted areas.[76] The English expressed their displeasure in a number of ways but none more intense than attacks on the colony.[77] Gradually, the English monarchs saw their own merchants becoming more competitive and able to provide the financial and political advantages long provided by the foreigners. English merchants were now encouraged by the government and received more supportive and enhanced privileges. In 1598, Queen Elizabeth I brought the German colony to an end. They were asked to leave and the Steelyard was closed.[78]

There were a number of advantages the English gained from their experiences with the Italian and German colonies but they preferred to overlook these sources.[79] The Italians bought large amounts of wool and cloth at high prices stimulating the English cloth industry. The Germans also bought large amounts of finished cloth even though guided by the lowest prices and taxes. English products were distributed far and wide so that they were known beyond the areas that English merchants were able to reach at that time. Also, both provided materials necessary for the English cloth industry and infused the country with money paid for services while in England. The Italians and Germans were facilitators because they contributed to the economy and were good examples of successful economic and financial operations. They had high quality products, diverse markets, financial instruments, flexibility and strategic planning. It was during the sixteenth century that the English adopted and adapted a number of foreign techniques making their economic and financial systems much more resilient.[80]

The English had outstanding wool and a growing cloth industry but in their traditional way used parliamentary legislation and proclamations to facilitate their trading operations. These legal actions defined privileges and limitations they believed necessary for the success of their business relationships. The issues that concerned the English most were the king's income and opportunities for English traders. While these were the primary issues, they also recognized that if they did not deal fairly with the foreign merchants, those trading opportunities might disappear. Therefore, laws were enacted to protect the personal safety and the working environment of both English and foreign merchants. They also established guidelines for the quality of English goods, and made regular efforts to keep the places of trade open.[81] Imported finished goods were restricted to save English jobs and the king commanded that goods should only be shipped from assigned points so that they were properly searched for quality, size and price.[82] Strict fines were imposed on anyone who tried to cheat the system. Still, piracy was prevalent and profitable but if caught, restitution was required or punishment assured.

For the English merchants, the early modern period was one of growth, transition and expansion. Their growth was due to a combination of factors: determination, established trading experiences and their multifaceted association with the German and Italian colonies.[83] English merchants had been involved in trade for centuries but during the earlier period, they were not as sophisticated as the continental powers. The English tried to cut into the rich preserves of the Italians and Germans but were always repelled. They had a number of foreign ports where they sold and exchanged goods but this trade was small in size. What they needed was a systematic approach encompassing strategy and experience whereby they were able to take on an expanded role.[84] England had long extended privileges and advantages to foreigners on her soil but wanted to compete as a major commercial power in her own right. The English tried through repeated trips and negotiations to move forward but it was not until the mid-sixteenth century that progress was within reach.[85] The fact that the most ambitious foreign countries of continental Europe were now experiencing distractions such as war, domestic conflict, struggling economies and political pressure allowed the English to move forward and to make their commercial goals a reality.[86] In addition, financial techniques and bookkeeping procedures, long the preserve of the Italians, were now disseminated throughout Europe and England was also reaping its benefits.[87] Gradually, the influence of the German and Italian colonies began to weaken. However, the English had to know that they benefited from a number of years of high-level interaction with the colonies even when they were not yet fully ready to compete. Over this period, England developed and sharpened her business techniques and became ready for the much larger commercial scene that was now there for the taking. Antwerp was just one area in the sixteenth century that offered a profitable, open market for England. There was an Italian dominance in Antwerp early in the sixteenth century but the English did their best to make trade matters favourable for themselves while making the purchase of English goods more difficult for the Italians. However, while England's early relationship with Antwerp was very successful it was also about to reinforce a difficult lesson.[88] Antwerp, because of financial and political conflicts, closed its markets (1563) to England thereby causing great consternation as Antwerp was England's main commercial outlet. With markets closed, England's limitations were obvious. Lack of diversification and access to broad markets proved inconvenient and costly. Direct trade with the Mediterranean and Baltic was not an option at this time because of the unrest in those areas. However, England was ready to remedy these limitations. By 1573, the conflict between Venice and the Turks came to an end and now England records its first ship to Leghorn (Livorno). Earlier, England attempted to establish relationships with Pisa, Danzig and Riga but they were short-lived. Now, opportunities were more promising with more contacts to follow. There were developments such as the Eastland Company (1579), The Muscovy Company (1553), the English Levant Company (1581) and simply more direct contacts with lucrative foreign markets.[89] By the seventeenth century, the English were participating in a much broader and more profitable trading environment. London, always a busy city, now became the most important focal point in England in terms of international trade and financial transactions.[90]

In sum, the existence of German and Italian colonies on English soil in the late medieval and early modern period illustrates the challenges and the impact that foreign colonies can have on the development and commercialization of a host country. In the early part of this period, the level of commercialization of host and colonies was uneven with the greatest commercial advantage belonging to the colonies. They had well-developed operations and protected their extensive sources of goods. This was advantageous for them because their products were desired by the English and therefore eagerly purchased. However, the colonies also had the advantage of being conveniently located on English soil where they were able to regularly purchase large amounts of English wool and cloth. These purchased products were absolutely essential for their domestic and foreign markets. Colonies and host benefited by their trading relationship but initially the colonies profited most. The English, in the early stages, were not prepared for large scale commerce. However, what they did have was a growing body of trading experiences, a strong sense of determination and a government that supported their economic policies. Gradually, as the foreigners' privileges and strength remained an obstruction to their advancement, English anger grew. In this sense, the foreigners challenged and encouraged the English to seek more. By the sixteenth century, the unequal trading system was no longer acceptable to the English. Fortunately, at this time, the Germans and the Italians were distracted by troubling issues at home and within their commercial networks. This gave the English the opportunity they sought.

The English now stepped out onto the larger international economic scene having overcome previous difficulties. Their goal to deal directly with customers nearby and long range was facilitated by their experience and long association with the merchant colonies. They may not have approved or appreciated the foreigners' privileged positions and policies of protectionism but they were able to watch and learn that privilege and strength were profitable assets. The English did not imitate the Germans or Italians exactly but in their own way they drew on those financial, organizational, political and practical practices that were most beneficial to them. They observed and learned some other important lessons: it is necessary to develop diverse products, have access to a broad selection of markets, to deal directly rather than through a middleman and to develop good diplomatic relations with their trading partners. However, if diplomacy failed, they understood that they must be militarily prepared to enforce their rights. By the seventeenth century, the English built on their many experiences with the merchant colonies and in their own style established a strong economic position.

3 DYNAMISM AND INTEGRATION OF THE NORTH EUROPEAN MERCHANT COMMUNITIES IN FRENCH PORTS IN THE EIGHTEENTH CENTURY

Pierrick Pourchasse

The large commercial areas of the *Ancien Régime*, in particular the major ports, attracted capital as well as people and became the driving force of economic activity in western Europe. The migrants were first of all the inhabitants of near regions who came looking for work and better living conditions. Then, with the development of international exchanges, populations from afar, attracted by the desire to speculate and to make their fortune in commerce and trade, arrived in great number. Among these, the group of foreigners made itself noticed by its dynamism and its stimulating role in commerce in their adopted towns.

'Cosmopolitanism seems to be a characteristic feature of all international emporium,'[1] and the foreign merchants contributed to running the economic activity in the large French ports. The importance of a commercial centre could be measured by the size of the presence of the merchant communities from different European countries. This contribution was very dynamic and, apart from the people who settled for a more or less long period, maybe even finally in their host port, the circulation of these men was the second feature of this group of foreigners. According to the historian Jean Meyer: 'The Atlantic front of Europe from Copenhagen to Cadiz was being covered by a ceaseless flow of merchants, young people: cousins (male and female) trainee merchants who created both friendships and often even marriage.'[2]

At the end of the Middle Ages, the ships from northern Europe, Hanseatic and Dutch, came in great numbers to look for salt in the salt fields at the mouth of the Loire. The *Baiensolt*, the salt from the bay of Bourgneuf in Brittany, became the name of all kinds of French salt, even of salt from Spain.[3] The dukes of Brittany, who wanted to develop trade in their area favourably, welcomed these foreigners by giving them privileges. Treaties were signed with the inhabitants of Friesland and Holland so that they could trade freely with Breton

merchants. The French kingdom had a similar policy in order to attract merchants from the north. The king thus gave up the *droit d'aubaine*, the right to
take the assets of the foreigners who died in France and granted them complete
freedom to trade in France.[4]

Under the *Ancien Régime* the settlement of foreign communities from the
north being Dutch or German followed a parallel chronology. In the sixteenth
century, small colonies formed in the large commercial centres. These groups
of foreigners developed at the beginning of the seventeenth century spurred on
by Henri IV and Sully. The foreigners from the north set up in large ports such
as Nantes and Bordeaux as well as in the salt ports. At the Revocation of the
Edict of Nantes a large number of foreign merchants, of whom a major part had
become French citizens, left France and returned to their own countries. It seems
that among those who abjured and stayed, the number of Germans was higher
than the number of Dutch.[5]

In the eighteenth century after the death of Louis XIV new colonies
reformed. These colonies had very different features from the old communities
at the level of their activities, their importance and their integration into society. This study presents the foreign merchant communities which set up in the
kingdom of France in the eighteenth century, by explaining the reasons for their
installation, their origins, their activities as well as their progressive integration
into French society.

The New Conditions of Trade and the Presence of
Foreign Communities in French Ports

French trade with the north of Europe became important from the seventeenth
century on and in the eighteenth century, and many national activities were
linked to these exchanges. The arsenals of Brest, Lorient, Rochefort or Toulon,
and also private builders, needed planks from Prussia, masts from Riga, tar from
Finland and hemp from Russia. The manufacturing of barrels depended on oak
planks from Pomerania and from Poland. Stockfish from Norway, bait of first
quality, was essential to the fishermen who fished for sardines. Linen production imported seeds from Courlande in order to renew local seeds which tended
to degenerate. The steel industry could not do without Swedish iron bars to
produce steel of good quality. Finally during cereal crises, Poland supplied the
necessary grain in order to satisfy the needs of the population.[6]

If France was an important market for the north, it was an exception in western Europe because the exports were higher than imports. The positive aspect
of the balance of trade with the north came from the traditional exports, for
example wine products (wine and brandy) and salt as well as the new colonial
goods: sugar, coffee, indigo and other products from India. The importance of

these exchanges with northern Europe meant that emigration to French ports increased. Whereas in the sixteenth century and at the beginning of the seventeenth century the number of Spanish, Portuguese and Italian colonies was the highest, the Dutch and Hanseatic colony got the upper hand from the 1650s. The Irish also arrived in great numbers but their migration was mainly for political and religious reasons. They were in favour of the Stuarts and arrived in several waves from 1640 to the middle of the eighteenth century and settled mostly in Nantes and Saint-Malo. Parallel to this evolution of the migration movement, the activity of the traders changed.

In the sixteenth and up to the seventeenth century, most of the commercial operations were done through factors, for example individuals who received a salary for executing a commercial deal. Often when a merchant wanted to conduct a certain deal he sent one of his employees to make the transaction in the foreign port.[7] These factors could have very different statuses. Some were appointed to a merchant and moved according to the place where their employer's business took place whereas others could be both hoteliers, brokers, translators and even merchants working for their countrymen. Their margin of initiative varied much from simple executants to a role of real authorized representative.

This system was not very successful and no longer corresponded to the development in commercial exchanges. In the eighteenth century the commercial procedures were both simplified and accelerated in order to support the growth in the exchanges. Operations were now carried out through agents and correspondence replaced the factors' travelling. The Nordic merchants thus did not need to send individuals to foreign countries in order to do business for them.

In general, Nordic trade was done on commission, for example by 'a contract by which a person named commissionaires was promised to be paid a certain sum that another person called principal agreed to pay him to execute for this principal one or several commercial operations'.[8] These commissionaires were in charge of both finding outlets (sales commission) and buying products (buying commission) on behalf of their principals.

A commissionaire might have high financial availability. In fact, when a buying commission took place, 'because of the delays in transport and in the selling of products, a large financial deficit always existed between the moment when the commissionaire had registered the principal's purchase and that when the purchase was made ... and the moment when the amount of the purchase was settled by his correspondent'.[9] On the other hand, when a sales commission took place he could sometimes advance the amount of the sales to his principal and this would give him a supplementary income.

The relation between a principal and a commissionaire presented the features of an 'agency relationship' such as is defined in the science of economics, for example a contract by which one (or several) person(s) (the principal) takes on another person (the agent) in order to execute some tasks in his name which involve a certain power of decision on the part of the agent.[10] In this relationship, the principal trusts the commissionaire (the agent) to give him the best service so that his transaction will be as profitable as possible. The two parties have contradictory interests as the principal is looking for the lowest costs whereas the commissionaire is paid on commission and hopes that these will be as high as possible.

These contracts took place in a context of asymmetry of information. The commissionaire who was close to the market had information that the principal did not have and could be tempted to use it for personal use and not at the service of the principal. On the other hand, the considerable geographic distances and the slow flow of communication between the contracting parties made it difficult for the principal to survey the transaction. The problem really existed as a book from 1702 describes straightforwardly:

> 'The essentials of a good merchant who wants to negotiate with foreign countries are to make the right choice of a good and loyal commissionaire to whom he can entrust his assets safely. There are surely some but they are phoenixes with whom it is difficult to meet because, normally, they see to their own interests rather than that of their principals. They pay so much more attention to their own business that this makes them negligent of the business with which they have been entrusted, and often they let their trainees or office clerks, who do not have the capacity of managing purchases and sales, execute the orders of their correspondents. However, apart from this negligence, which is often very harmful, and the large commissions they take, the problem is often that they buy beyond the real and natural price. This shows that they have little respect for human laws and even less conscience.'[11]

For every merchant it was vital to have total confidence in his agent and therefore to choose him wisely so that he could undertake to do business in ideal conditions.[12] Without being a specialist, the latter had to be able to judge the quality and price of the goods he was required to purchase. He had to provide all the information necessary to enable his principal to know the market opportunities. 'In unbalanced economies where transportation is slow, the quality of information networks is an important factor in discriminating between the companies first to be informed of the movement in the rates for raw materials, consumer tendencies in the market or accidents, such as the collapse of businesses, public borrowing or war ...'[13] A trustworthy network of agents will assure good knowledge of trade opportunities and will guarantee fruitful profits.[14]

Business correspondence continually conveyed this concern regarding information. In their letters to their correspondents in Marseille, Pierre His and Pierre Boué of Hamburg 'are finding out about the forecasts for the harvest, quantities in stock and are on the lookout for the slightest variation in prices'.[15] The merchant made his profit from these differences in prices which often fluctuated greatly between markets, 'the winner is the one most quickly informed of the situation that is, the one with the best information network'.[16] The *Société d'Agriculture de Bretagne* (the Breton Agricultural Society) gave as an example the information systems of Britain, Holland and the northern countries who 'are notified as soon as wheat is in short supply in Portugal, Spain or Italy and shipments are made at once'.[17]

On the basis of these findings, various strategies were set up. As one mistrusts foreigners more than one's fellows, the northern merchants sent their compatriots to the towns where they did business. The Dutch Republic blazed the trail. Dutch merchants avoided local agents and all forms of indirect contact and counted on their own postal networks.[18] Often members of the merchant dynasties of the countries concerned were sent out from the Republic.[19] In France, following the Dutch, the Germans arrived in great numbers. The Scandinavians settled less often but their consular system ensured a well-structured network of agents in the ports of interest to them.

The Swedes set up an organization to concentrate the original export of the kingdom in the hands of a few traders. For the *Kommerskollegiet* (college of commerce) in Stockholm, it was preferable to focus the sale of Swedish products through one company rather than to divide commissions among multiple agents, who were mostly foreigners. To do this, the system gave exemption from consular fees, if the consul at the port of destination was responsible for the commission of the cargo. If the goods were addressed to an agent other than the consul, the settlement of rights became mandatory. To avoid double payment, the majority of traders naturally chose to ship their goods to the order of the consul.[20] On the other hand, as the authorities in Stockholm required that the consuls of Sweden speak and write in Swedish, a number of positions could not be filled and the subjects of the kingdom chose to migrate to the western ports to fill consular functions.

The French were mainly interested in colonial trade and the lack of interest they had in seagoing navigation to northern Europe favoured the settlement of these communities. By a consistent sharing of tasks, foreigners, supported by networks and family ties, were taking control of the European trade whose practices they knew best.[21] The legal situation of foreigners in France was in their favour. When they arrived in a port, they could rent premises without any formalities in particular. Only after a year of residence they were recorded in the local tax books and they could pay taxes (*capitation*, *dixième* and *vingtième*). They were subject to the same laws as other merchants. They participated in local meetings but had no vote in the Chamber of Commerce. Until the second generation, they were foreigners, while the third generation was considered French if it adopted the Catholic religion.[22]

Foreign Merchant Communities in French Ports

In the eighteenth century, foreign commissionaires arrived in the French ports. Their number is difficult to determine because it is not possible to identify them in the archives if they did not require letters of naturalization. These documents granted by the king but registered by the *Chambre des Comptes* (Chamber of Accounts) of the province allowed people to obtain French nationality. Also, communities were constantly changing, departures and arrivals were continuing and the number of migrants varied constantly. Many contemporaries had exaggerated the size of this immigration. In 1725, in Nantes, a statement of wealth identifies fifteen names from northern Europe, for example 6.5 per cent of all traders.[23] The capitation rolls (poll tax) give higher figures, though did not exceed thirty-five individuals for the entire century (Table 3.1).

Table 3.1: The number of Dutch and Germans in Nantes.[24]

Years	Dutch	German
1710	6	
1720	14	
1731	21	4
1733	21	3
1739	22	3
1742	24	3
1743	22	4
1750	16	6
1754	19	6
1762	24	10
1763	23	9
1764	25	9
1789	21	14

Source: Archives Municipales Nantes, série CC, rôles de capitation.

All foreigners did not pay the poll tax. In his thesis on the Breton port, the German historian Gerhard Treutlein identified fifty-one names from the late seventeenth century and the first half of the eighteenth century (Table 3.4, page 58).[25] The oldest were naturalized French, but others, such as Hamburg Vanherzelle (or Van Harzelle), had temporarily left France at the revocation of the Edict of Nantes. Most were commissioners, for example families like Sengstack and Van Keulen who controlled most of the trade with Sweden, Hamburg, Danzig, Norway and Riga during the first half of the century. The poll tax rolls as religious sources[26] suggest that the Dutch community was stable, but the number of Germans was constantly increasing.

Bordeaux had a German colony from the late seventeenth century.[27] In 1715, the intendant made a census of, besides sixteen Dutch, sixteen other traders from the north of Europe: ten from Hamburg, two from Bremen, one from Danzig, one from Lübeck, one from Hannover and Brandenburg.[28] The group was characterized by its youth, the average age being around 28. Most young Germans remained in Bordeaux after a few years of training in trade.[29] This first wave of immigration specialized in the wine trade or as merchants or trade assistants. In the beginning of this new century, the Dutch were always essential intermediaries in the trade of wine products to northern Europe, but for buyers from Hamburg and the Baltic, the setting up of German advisers in these markets allowed for much better knowledge of markets.[30]

As from 1730, a second wave of German immigration arrived on the banks of the Gironde. These newcomers were involved not only in the wine business, but especially in the export of colonial goods to northern Europe,[31] a commerce which was in the hands of Huguenot merchants settled in Hamburg. They were much more active than their predecessors, 'who had prepared the ground' by providing the information needed to create a commercial activity. In 1742–4, thirty-seven German merchants have been identified in Bordeaux. The Hamburg merchants dominated the group with nearly 60 per cent of the members.

The German colony of Bordeaux had been growing since the Seven Years' War, as had the development of trade with the north. One last major wave of immigration arrived after the war in America. It is difficult to know the exact number of individuals because of retirements, deaths, temporary settlement, errors and omissions in official documents etc. In the 1780s, the number of German immigrants on the banks of the Gironde can be estimated at approximately one 150 persons according to the German historian Wolfgang Henninger, while Paul Butel indicates a much lower figure, since he considers that the group is likely to be of sixty to seventy merchants.[32] The most recent study, that of Klaus Weber, listed 230 German merchants as having lived in Bordeaux during the period 1680–1830.

Table 3.2: Growth in the number of German merchants in Bordeaux, 1700–99.

Years	Arrival of immigrants	Foreign immigrants born in Bordeaux
1700–9	8	2
1710–19	10	2
1720–9	6	3
1730–9	20	3
1740–9	17	1
1750–9	22	1
1760–9	33	2
1770–9	36	
1780–9	53	
1790–9	5	

Source: K. Weber, 'Deutsche Kaufmannsfamilien im atlantischen Manufaktur- und Kolonial-warenhandel: Netzwerke zwischen Hamburg, Cádiz und Bordeaux (1715–1830)', (PhD dissertation, University of Hamburg, 2001), p. 181.

In other French ports, the presence of northern commissionaires was less important but they were present in all places that did business with northern Europe. Take the example of Brittany. In Le Croisic, the Swedish salt merchant Charles Oller was the consul for Denmark whereas his compatriot Eric Gardeman, also in the salt trade, represented Sweden. Also in Le Croisic, Daniel Hintz Goddefroy from Lübeck was interested in the salt shipments to the north. During the 1770s he declared a more or less fraudulent bankruptcy and one of his associates said he was 'a man of the Augsburg Confession, who would never have had any scruples in deceiving the Catholics'.[33] In Lorient, the names of John Leonard Puchelberg of Regensburg, Elijah-Jacques Salomon of Erfurt and Jean Boniface Schmaltz of Speyer are identified among merchants in the city.[34] Also in Lorient, merchants of Nantes originating from the north traded very actively with the French East India Company and set up one of their compatriots called André Vanderheyde, native of Flanders, to take the place of a French interpreter who, according to the documents, was lacking in skills. Sometime later, when Vanderheyde became Vice-Consul of Sweden, he had problems with a Swede called Backman who claimed to be Swedish Consul and tried to obtain commissions on Nordic ships.[35] In 1787, in Quimper, a Fleming named Grooters was Vice-Consul of Denmark. In Morlaix, the merchant Cruypenningk dominated sales made during the War of the Austrian Succession. He had dealings with his compatriot Goossens in Paris who, at the turn of the century, was a leading supplier to the French navy. The activity of the small port of Morlaix was heavily involved in the trade with the north because of the tobacco factory. Until the American war, the Dutch ensured the supply of tobacco leaves and, in 1788, 33.3 per cent of re-exports of the processed product were directed to Amsterdam and Hamburg.[36] Saint-Malo was a particular case, the merchant middle class was generally native and very Catholic,[37] but some names of dealers from the north did, however, appear such as the Germans Amsinck & Meckenhausen who also had a branch in Nantes or Abraham Theodore Nordingh who, in 1781, was Vice-Consul of Denmark.

If the majority of these foreigners carried out the activity of commissionaires, others were brokers, charterers or interpreters. Van Neunen from Nantes specialized in chartering vessels for the north, while Vanderheyde from Lorient was broker and interpreter. The growth of maritime activity in the eighteenth century encouraged those who had more resources to participate in major trade. In Nantes, Lüttman & Von Bobart, arriving from Hamburg in 1719, were investing in business in Santo Domingo from 1725, while others were involved in slave trade expeditions to Africa, for example the Deurbroucq or Schweighauser. When business was successful, they dropped out of the commission activity and became merchants working on their own, often with northern Europe where they had an excellent knowledge of markets. Thus Sengstack became a major trading name in Nantes. He had vessels in Amsterdam, where his family-in-law was in business, to avoid French legislation, just as Van Voorn[38] or Vanherzelle.[39] Some foreign firms set up here were investing in the north where they created branches: Stierling and Gullmann ran their business in Hamburg from Nantes.

In case of conflict, the trader was a man who ignored 'considerations or the patriotic theory of nationalists', as the historian Violet Barbour wrote for Amsterdammers in the seventeenth century.[40] The many family ties in European ports allowed trade to continue and wartime was often a time for doing good business. The networks played a vital role in unlawful trade from the Caribbean. Supplies from the French navy were fetched through complex circuits or English merchants who were at the forefront. Finally, it was possible to change the flag, which was very common and, in this case, it was useful to belong to an international network. During the 1720s, the Dutch shipowners were interested in the French flag for their trade with Spain. In 1724, the French Consulate in Amsterdam noticed the purchase of a Dutch frigate named the *Wolfgang Galère* on behalf of Mr. Pierre Lejeune, merchant in Nantes, who gave me the contract to be legalized in order to obtain their shipments to Nantes. I do not know if it is a simulated sale, but it seems so'.[41] The Dutch quickly resolved the problem, Jacob Hartman became Jacques Harteman, resident of Dunkirk, and his ship became *Le Triomphant* to make it all the more national. The Admiralty in Nantes issued an official document to go from Amsterdam to Cadiz and the vessel immediately went out to sea. On the same date another ship, *La Reine de Saba*, purchased in the great Dutch port on behalf of Mr. Van Robais received a document from the Admiralty in Saint-Valéry. It appeared in the consulate that Captain Joseph Graffard 'who is still young, is not really the master of his ship, but a Dutch employee that has been hired as sailor in the deck crew'.[42]

The arrival of foreign communities in the French ports gave rise to a group of businessmen investing in all areas while putting in place networks of traders across western Europe and beyond. This family presence in various European ports gave birth to cross-border companies, the true eighteenth century multinationals.

The Integration of Northern Merchants

In the French ports, the freedom of settling was the rule. The establishment of an administration of trade and the development of regulations did not limit the settlement of foreign communities.[43] In Nantes, you could become bourgeois of the city by naturalization (for example asking for a letter of naturalization) or by a sojourn of twelve consecutive years. All dealers did not, though, seek to acquire French nationality, particularly for religious reasons.

Success in business promoted integration into French society. For foreigners, as for the negotiating world in general, diversity was the rule. Most remained small commissionaires specializing in business with the north, as this activity limited risks compared to the colonial trade. Others were present in all trades of large retailers and boasted vast fortunes, as in Nantes: Vanherzelle in 1720s or Deurbroucq at the end of the century. In 1785, upon his death, Francis of Tollenare, another merchant in Nantes of Flemish origin, had 1,521,000 French pounds, of which 91.7 per cent were outstanding debts and 6 per cent was cash.[44] The report in 1725 shows that the fortunes of foreign merchants were on average larger than that of local traders.

Table 3.3: Report of fortunes in Nantes in 1725.

Fortunes in *livres* (French pounds)	Foreign merchants	Number (total)	Total (French pounds)
600,000		1	600,000
400,000	Van Harzelle	2	800,000
350,000		1	350,000
300,000		8	2 400,000
250,000		2	500,000
200,000		10	2,000,000
150,000		7	1,050,000
140,000		1	140,000
130,000		4	520,000
120,000	Van Hamel Van Voorn	5	600,000
100,000	Struyckman Van den Hoeck	22	2,200,000
80,000		26	2,080,000
70,000		5	350,000
60,000	Van den Bosch Deurbroucq	26	1,560,000
50,000	Van Berchem D'Haveloose	29	1,450,000
40,000	Sengstack Jean Albert Sengstack Pierre Belloc	26	1,040,000
30,000	Conninck Van Doorn	21	630,000
25,000		2	50,000
20,000	Vanasse Guillaume	15	300,000
15,000		8	120,000
12,000		6	72,000
10,000		3	30,000
		230	18,842,000

Foreigners from the north: 15 out of 230 or 6.5%
Fortune: 2,110,000 out of 18,842,000 pounds or 11.2%

Source: Archives Municipales Nantes, CC 484.

Religion did not generally cause any problems. Municipalities showed a lenient approach to foreign Protestants and the pressure to convert seems limited. There were also many common interests between merchants and a too-strict application of the law would have been disastrous for the economic activity of the port[45]. In Bordeaux, the German immigrants were 90 per cent Protestant and kept their religion. With the arrangement of the Edict of Fontainebleau in 1685,[46] naturalization was impossible and most of them kept their status as foreigners. Hinrich Luetkens, a German trader based in Bordeaux, did not become French although he spent twenty-six years in France and was married to a French woman with whom he had five children.[47] Protestants remained discreet and did not display their belief. In 1715, a paper on Mr. Struyckman said '... it is certain that he does not practise the religion. He is a merchant who for some years has been in charge of the Bishop of Nantes' interest in his farm, who seems to want to save him ...'[48] However, at the death of his son, the Protestant records indicate that he had always lived by the reformed religion. Only one departure because of religious problems is noteworthy and it is that of Vanherzelle, the second largest fortune in Nantes; he left the city in 1730 but he came back later to the Breton port to be naturalized in 1745.[49] In general, conversions were numerous, especially when circumstances so required. Albert Sengstack abjured on 7 January 1727, just days before his wedding (17 February) with Elisabeth Bertrand de Coeuvres.

Upon their arrival, foreigners naturally tended to gather in the same neighbourhoods even thought they did not have an organization like the 'nations'. Thus, in the early eighteenth century in Nantes, foreigners from the north mainly lived on the islands of the Loire and Pirmil, south of the river. Then they migrated to the centre and concentrated in the new district of the island Feydeau around the square of the 'little Holland'. This grouping in certain neighbourhoods did not help the integration of communities in the local population. According to Mathorez, in the sixteenth and seventeenth centuries, the communities formed separate colonies and had little contact with the locals, with whom relations were generally tense.[50] A change took place in the eighteenth century when relations with foreigners 'became courteous and instead of tearing each other apart as in the past, the Nantais and the Dutch united their efforts'.[51] We find the same attitude in many ports. In Roscoff 'observers note that there was great sympathy between the Germans and the Bretons'.[52]

Once settled, the quality of foreign trader was, as Pierre Jeannin writes, 'a transient state'[53] in a process of integration into local society by some particular moments. The first stage consisted in matrimonial alliances. The first generation of families united with merchant families,[54] often foreigners, for example Pierre Sengstack from Nantes who married his cousin Marie-Marguerite Van Keulen, and his sister Christine Marguerite who married Antoine Houckhaert. Later generations will in general marry into French families. In Bordeaux, among the

226 names of German traders found by Klaus Weber between 1650 and 1830, sixty-three marriages are known, and at least thirty-eight were with a French person and only eighteen traders were married to German women. This rapid integration is facilitated by the strong presence of Huguenots in the south-west of France. The unions were strongly influenced by endogamy: the marriages are organized in the circle of shipowners and bankers of the city.[55]

When business was successful, the major trading families sought to unite in order to assert their power. In Nantes, the wealthy shipowner Dominique Deurbroucq married the rich Marguerite Sengstack. From the next genera-tions, merchants were looking to unite with noble families, often issued from the world of trading, like Albert Sengstack who married Elizabeth Bertrand de Cœuvres, or one of Simon Deurbroucq's daughters who married a Chaurand de Chaffault. Sometimes alliances were made with older nobility. Elizabeth Seng-stack married Etienne de Levy, who might profit from the dowry of his wife as he became Secretary of Chancery of Brittany the year after. Two other of Simon Deurbroucq's daughters married advisers at the *Chambre des Comptes*: Jacques François de Gourtière and Jacques-Louis Panou de Faymoreau.

These marriages were used to reinforce local industrial relations, which is under-standable because of the importance of business taking place. However, alliances in other European markets were just as necessary to build strong international net-works and all major trading families had family ties in the major European ports such as Bordeaux, Nantes, Amsterdam, Hamburg, London, Cadiz, etc.

The dealers created a truly international network by these family alliances where there was very often the Huguenot diaspora. Jean-Georges Streckeysen, a Bordeaux specialist merchant of German origin in the trade of copper, married off his two daughters to two bankers from Berlin. His cousin, Emmanuel Streck-eysen, was linked in Amsterdam with Jean Texier, who himself was linked with the house Baril & Texier in London[56] and Bernard Texier & Co. in Hamburg. The Lüttman family, a merchant from Nantes, lived in all major ports where trading took place: in addition to Hamburg, his sister Catherine was the wife of Cornelis de Neyer of Amsterdam, his other sister Hanna was married to the merchant Andreas Heidritter of London where his brother Johannes had also set up as merchant.[57] The Sengstack family was related to Van Keulen of Amster-dam, Von Schoenven of Rotterdam and it was probably related to Sengstack of Bremen.[58] In Marseilles, Jean-Antoine Butini from Geneva, consul of Sweden, married his daughters off to merchants Jean-Robert Rilliet, his own nephew whose family had trading houses in Lyon and Paris, Jacques-Henri Fölsch, mer-chant from Hamburg, Pierre Kiel from Altona (Denmark), merchant in Nantes. Out of these alliances the company Butini, Fölsch & Rilliet was set up in Mar-seilles, and in Nantes the association between Peter Kiel and Robert Rilliet, another of Butini's nephews.[59]

Foreigners did not look down on the public responsibilities even though they remained under-represented compared to local traders. In Nantes, the Van Berchems, Van Neunens, d'Havelooses had consuls and principal county magistrates in their families.[60] The Van Voorns and Mertens were among the captains of the bourgeois militia of the city. Dobrée, a poor young man, who had entered the world of business by marrying the daughter of his employer, a Schweighauser, a family of German origin, became mayor of Nantes under the Empire.

If the cultural model of the bourgeoisie was very much present in the importance attached to work and success in business, the world of trade was attracted by the nobility, the culmination of their desire for social recognition. The merchants sought to enter the second order by the purchase of public service. Dominique Deurbroucq thus has made the acquisition of an office of advisor secretary to the king in his Chancery near the Parliament of Brittany. In 1777, a member of the family Sengstack was former controller of the *Talion et gendarmerie* of Brittany.

The second step into local integration was the acquisition of buildings. In Morlaix the merchant Cruypenninck, of Dutch origin, owned the town house Coetlosquet on the wharf of Tréguier, one of the most beautiful buildings in the city. Dominique Deurbroucq built a mansion on the island Gloriette in Nantes estimated at 300,000 pounds in 1784, then in 1791 his son acquired the marquisate of Goulaine with all its dependencies for the sum of 420,000 pounds.[61] Even the company Belloc and Collar, one of the smallest companies in Nantes, owned two houses at their bankruptcy in 1735.[62]

The integration of foreign traders in the national community did not cut the relations they have with their country. The contacts to the family who remained in the country of origin are maintained and the education of sons usually takes place in the northern ports. Vanherzelle said in 1715 'being a trader, he had judged it necessary to leave his sons a few years in Holland in order to give them an education in trade and then take them back to France'.[63] Stierling's eldest son from Nantes was 'since the last four years to study his humanities at Frankfurt-am-Main' and he hoped that 'it pleases the king and the sublime Senate to call him for the service of the Royal College of trade as a student'.[64] Johann Jakob von Bethmann married his daughter and sole heir to Frankfurt. Wills show the commitment to their country. Jean-Philipp Weltner bequeathed 100,000 pounds to his nephew of Lübeck and 10,000 pounds to the poor of the Hanseatic city.

Conclusion

According to Pierre Jeannin, when immigrant traders ceased to work as merchants, part of the substance of the foreign colony finally was dissolved into the host society. A distinctive feature of the merchant colonies in northern Europe, however, was to stay longer in the business than other foreigners and to stay very bound to their homeland.

From the second generation, the question may be asked whether we can still consider these families, who have been established here for several decades or even generations, as foreign families. The desire for integration suggests the opposite. On the other hand, despite their integration, the contemporary citizens still see these men as foreigners. The commercial rivalry and the spectacular successes of some families gave rise to xenophobia, something common in the societies of the *Ancien Régime*. Thus, according to Jean Meyer: 'Prejudice is still stronger than reality. One is easily described as a foreigner in the eighteenth century....'[65]

Table 3.4: Nantes' merchants from northern Europe (first part of the eighteenth century).

	Name	Origin	Arrival
	Witvoet		1720
	Van Witemberg	Flanders	1720
	Wynants	Flanders	1692
	D'Haveloose	Courtrai	1700
	De Wisch	Ostend	1694
	De Witte	Ghent	1673
	Stalpaert	Antwerp	1715
	Buitendick	Ostend	1723
Flanders	De Tollenare	Antwerp	1684
	Van den Bosch	Ostend	1732
	Vanderheyde	Ostend	1726
	Van den Mocke	Nieuport/Ypres	1735
	Van Haute	Ghent	1730
	Van Neunen		1687
	Vlieghe		1712
	De Waele		1707
	Deurbroucq		
	Vanasse	Roermond	1681
	Vanderbucken	Aachen (Aix-la-Chapelle)	1679
Westphalia	Van Sambeck		1676
	Lemlein	Gennep/Kleve Terburg/Bocholt	1697
	Van Keulen	Holland	1673
	Van Hamel	Leiden	1684
	Van Berchem	Holland	1688
Holland	Van Voorn	Holland	1714
	Vanysendoorn	Dordrecht	1741
	Woor	Dordrecht	1732
	Connink (Abraham)	Rotterdam	1720
	Onderdelinde	Dordrecht	1731

	Name	Origin	Arrival
Hamburg	Sengstack	Hamburg	1680
	Van Harzelle	Hamburg (Bois-le-Duc)	1671
	Lüttman	Hamburg	1719
	Von Bobart	Hamburg	1719
	Keill	Altona (Denmark)	1756
Germany & Switzerland	Amsinck & Meckenhausen	(Saint-Malo)	
	Seewalt	Nuremberg	1737
	Stierling	Memmingen	1736
	Gullmann	Frankfurt	1737
	Wilfesheim	Swabia	1741
	Hartmann (Jean)	Leipzig	1741
	Schweighauser-Battier	Basle	1742
	Amy Gampere	Geneva	
Unknown	Struykman	Marseille (?)	1696
	Van Bredenbec	St Nizier or Lyon (?)	1726
	Houckhaert		1702
	Gloye		1737
	Classen (Clas)		1734
	Helmcke		1737
	Muller		1741
	Schultz		1720
	Deuscher		
	Cropp		
	Mertens		

Source: G. Treutlein, 'Schifffahrt und Handel zwischen Nantes und dem europäischen Norden von 1714 bis 1744' (PhD dissertation, University of Heidelberg, 1970), pp. 250–1.

4 OPPORTUNITY AND LEGISLATION: HOW THE ARMENIANS ENTERED TRADE IN THREE MEDITERRANEAN PORTS

Ina Baghdiantz McCabe

'The whole country between Erevan and Tabriz was ruined by Shah Abbas ... he wanted to make the country a desert and took the inhabitants of Julfa and its vicinity, young and old, fathers, mothers, children, with whom he made diverse colonies in his kingdom. He sent up to twenty seven thousand families to the Province of Guilan, where silk is made, the terrible climate there killed many of these people accustomed to a gentler climate. The most important [of the region of Julfa] were sent to Ispahan, where the king pushed them to trade, he advanced them the raw silk, which they paid on their return, which quickly made them thrive. The king gave them grand privileges, among others they had their own Chief, their own Judges without depending on the justice of Persia ... there they built the town of Julfa, which they call Julfa the New.'

Jean Baptiste Tavernier [1]

Free ports and favourable legislation were the open doors through which the Armenians and other foreign merchants settled in several ports in the Mediterranean. Arriving mostly from the Ottoman Empire's markets of Smyrna and Aleppo, which were crucial to their silk trade, but many were not Ottoman Armenians, but New Jufan American merchants, who had their trading centre in Iran. Although they had a presence in other Mediterranean ports, the three major settlements for both the Julfan and Ottoman Armenians were Venice, Livorno and Marseille.[2] The same Armenian merchants sometimes left one port for another, their departure more often than not prompted by local legislation that made their commerce unfavourable or more favourable elsewhere. For example, one of their favoured ports of commerce in the Mediterranean was Livorno, where they became a real presence after Richelieu, prompted by the demands of the merchants of Marseille, passed legislation in 1622 that chased them out of Marseille.[3] Given the vast number of ports in which the Armenian merchants were present at one time or another, the focus here will be on these three European ports of the Mediterranean in the seventeenth century, with the largest focus on Marseille.

Some fascinating work has been done on the Sephardic Jews and the many other foreign merchants of Livorno by Francesca Trivellato: *The Familiarity of Strangers*,[4] in which she compounds the numbers given for the Armenians in Livorno from several sources and devotes a passage to them. At the origin of the large merchant population of Livorno/Leghorn by foreign merchants is the emanation of the 'Livornine' laws and constitution by the Grand Duke of Tuscany Ferdinand I de Medici between 1590 and 1603. These new laws made Leghorn a free port and therefore a duty-free zone of commercial activity. This legislation, meant initially for the Jews, attracted a great number of diverse foreign merchants who were granted freedom of religion and amnesty. She shows that if the 1593 constitution was addressed specifically to Jews, its effects attracted other merchants to the free port, the Armenians among many other mostly European trading groups. As early as 1549, Livorno had invited and accepted Portuguese Jews, but there is no trace of the Armenians at such an early date. Trivellato's focus is on the Iberian Jews but she does look at many other groups. One look at the consequences of this legislation meant for the Jews and it is clear that the Armenians should not be studied in isolation. Therefore this article will not simply be about the Armenians, although they are the focus of it, but will also look at legislation meant specifically for Jewish or Ottoman merchants. Whether in France or in Italian ports this legislation was key to the history of Armenian commercial presence or absence in some of the Mediterranean ports. In fact I will demonstrate that Armenian presence was so closely tied to Jewish presence in these three ports that the former cannot be understood without the latter, as Marseille's legislation discussed further in this article demonstrates.

As in Livorno, French legislation in Marseille was addressed specifically to Jewish merchants although the Armenians were often mentioned in conjunction. It affected the presence of 'Levantine' or New Julfan Armenians in the port often seen as one group. In my previous work in 1999, *The Shah's Silk for Europe's Silver*, I covered the relationship of the New Julfan Armenians with France in some detail. A new work on the history of the port of Marseille[5] will help me explore things further along with ground-breaking work done by Olivier Raveux[6] on the Armenian presence in the archives of Marseille which permits a more in-depth analysis of the origins of the Armenian merchant population of the port. The Armenians in Livorno and Venice have been notably studied by Armenian ecclesiastics; Father Alishan studied Venice while Father Mesrop Ughurlean concentrated on Livorno.[7] The fact that these authors are ecclesiastics is not a coincidence, as the construction of a church and the presence of priests signified a true settlement, just as it did for the Greeks in Venice and elsewhere. We will discuss that the group of Armenians more prominently present in all three ports was Julfan. While Raveux finds the term '*Choffelin*' for the Julfans in the French

archives, we will also uncover why they are often called 'Levantine' by the French
at a date when they are already living in New Julfa, their centre in Iran.

I warned in 1999 that the 'Armenians' should not be studied as a unit, be it
those of the small town of Julfa, so famous for their silk trade. As this paper will
show foreign legislation addressed them as a unit, as foreign merchants under
the general word 'Armenian', but nevertheless one should realize that they were
from different regions and had several origins, which they used to identify themselves, such as Jughaetsi (Julfan) and Tabrizi (from Tabriz). The original city of
their forefathers remained important for their network formations.[8] The Julfans
came from one town, old Julfa, on the border of Iran on the river Araxe, and
often they are called Persians in the European sources. Nevertheless one should
not forget that if they were under Persian rule in the seventeenth century, it was
recent, before that conquest they were considered Ottoman merchants. The Julfan Armenians lived under Ottoman rule and as we will discuss below fall into
the category of Ottoman merchants for legislative purposes, and not only until
the Persian conquest of the Caucasus. Beyond that conquest, even much later,
some of the Julfans established themselves for trade purposes in Ottoman towns.
Some stayed there for over a decade, as we will examine later, in order to gain
some privileges in European ports where the capitulations gave them advantages.

A few words about the Julfans/New Julfans is in order. It is within the early
seventeenth-century context of waning Portuguese supremacy and the nascent
power of the English and Dutch East India Companies that the less well-known
commercial presence of the New Julfan Armenian merchants was to establish
itself prominently on a global scale. Their markets in the Ottoman Empire and
their prominence in the silk trade predates this period.[9] When they were still
based in old Julfa, they successfully competed with the Italians and especially
the French in the Ottoman markets in the sixteenth century before the English
or the Dutch entered these markets. In the Levant trade the Armenians soon
emerged as a serious trading force. By the 1550s a large group of silk merchants
from Julfa, in historic Armenia on the river Araxe/Aras (since the Soviet period
part of Azerbaijan), had settled in Aleppo and quasi-monopolized the transit
of Iranian silk which they sold in the Ottoman Empire to the Europeans.[10] In
fact, documents in European archives indicate that the Julfan Armenians acted
as agents for the Persian shah before they were deported to Iran in 1604 and settled in a suburb named New Julfa after their original town.[11] So the dichotomy
of Ottoman Armenian/ New Julfan under Persian rule is often blurred in reality.
The region of Julfa was a war zone where power was long contested. As we will
discuss merchants could and did take advantage of Armenian presence in both
Ottoman markets and Iran when they needed a stepping stone to Europe.

Their deportation from Old Julfa marks a turning point, when in 1605 in the
capital of Iran, Isfahan, the Julfans were granted the privileges of autonomous

administration and religious freedom and were gifted the land where they settled. The suburb was a closed settlement for the use of wealthy merchants from old Julfa; it is often called an Armenian suburb, a fact that hides both the origin and class of its inhabitants. Only the very wealthy lived in New Julfa. They owned the land of New Julfa which was granted to them by Shah Abbas I (1587–1629).[12] The land grant dates to the silk auction of 1619, where the Armenians outbid the Europeans for the international commerce of the king's recently monopolized silk. At the auction held by Shah Abbas the English East India Company competed with the Armenians for the privilege of carrying his Persian raw silk to Europe and lost the bidding. The integration of the Julfan Armenians in Iran was very important to the Iranian court and the revenues of New Julfa taxes were for the use of the queen mother's household. Merchant collaboration from the New Julfans and their powerful provost with converted Armenians and Georgians, who became high officials in the Iranian administration, became the linchpin of their success in the Iranian silk trade. Many of these converted administrators held the key posts in the silk distribution and in the mints. When this collaboration subsided after 1646 and their position within the Iranian administration diminished, their international trade of silk for silver actually took off with more liberty instead of being harmed.[13] They still benefited from enough state protection to carry their trade, especially since many converted Caucasian officials rose as high as grand vizier in the administration even after the New Julfan merchant elite, specifically its provost and ruler, was excluded from the court's administrative system. Even in the more conflicted eras that succeeded, their trade was very successful well into the eighteenth century. As Jonathan Israel has argued for the Sephardic Jews, much like Israel does for the Jews, I have argued in 1999 in the book *The Shah's Silk for Europe's Silver* that Armenian success in the first half of the seventeenth century should be understood within the framework of state protection and their extraordinary privileges that were of mutual benefit both to the Persian court and to themselves. The extent of this state protection fluctuated in Iran as it would elsewhere.[14]

The issue of trust in their network would benefit from more work, yet in a joint work, the usual clichés of ethnic cohesion and imagined fraternity were discarded by us to adopt Geoffrey Jones's ideas on success being based on 'soft skills', not the least of them the control of the flow of information within the group, other trading groups and different societies.[15] There is some work on the mode of letter-writing within the New Julfan network.[16] This correspondence has much in common with other family-based early modern networks, however, as it has been demonstrated by Levon Khachikian in 1969, their language was a specific Persianized form of Armenian, impenetrable to others.[17] The adaptation and flexibility of the Julfan/New Julfan (in Iran after 1604) Armenians was also key to their success in several societies and should warn against essentialist approaches to their multiple and fluctuating identities. Even the unit of 'Julfan' or 'New Julfan' has to be resorted to only as a label in order to remain clear. It denotes their origin, but they changed their names and sometimes their religion when residing in places beyond New Julfa. They often married non-Armenians in Europe. Their identities within the network depended on this town origin, but in their own trading lives they adapted and changed. The best way to look at Armenian trade in the ports we are discussing is to proceed by studying it port by port, just as is done with Greek trade, even though so much more research still needs to be done on the many ports where the New Julfans were present. Some merchants adapted so well they became citizens and in some ports, such as Marseille, there was the possibility of citizenship in fewer than five years. Therefore, names and identities in the archives could change very quickly, leaving historians no trace of the initial origins. Names are Francizised and Italianized and intermarriage in Europe was not rare; this obscures their presence in Europe. In addition, as will be discussed below, some Julfans and later New Julfans would live in Ottoman towns sometimes for over a decade, then be seen as Levantine and Ottoman in Europe.

Only during a brief period did the Armenians have a port of their own on the Mediterranean. Armenia was landlocked for most of history, save during its brief empire in the first century BC and once again for three centuries in the Middle Ages when the crusading Kingdom of Cilicia existed from 1080 to 1375. The Kingdom of Cilicia, often called Little Armenia, was located in Anatolia on the Aegean coast and featured Ayas as its commercial heart, a very busy international port of commerce for the Mediterranean trade. The port is best remembered by being the starting point of Marco Polo's trip to China. Indeed, most of its trade was with the Venetians, the Genoese and the French although contacts with them are not continuous. From the sixteenth century onward, it is once again with the Italians and the French that the Armenians traded most on the Ottoman markets.[18] This trade, selling raw Iranian silk against cash, was crucial for their silver trade to Iran and to India.[19] It is only after tax exemptions given by Louis XIII in the early century that one finds Armenians documented as settled in France.[20]

Legislation and treaties are clearly a sine qua non to merchant presence in European ports and are therefore at the centre of our argument. As Molly Greene argues well for the Greeks, one should look at the capitulations of the Italian cities with the Ottoman sultan to understand the presence of Ottoman merchants in Venice and other Mediterranean ports. She argues that the circulation of Europeans on the main Ottoman markets and the Black Sea has been more visible than the fact that those capitulations should be read as mutual and important to opening the door to Ottoman merchants settling in European ports.[21] Rights to 'Ottoman merchants' included Greek, Armenian and Muslim merchants as no difference was made in the capitulations. What she argues for the Greeks holds true for the Armenians. As I have argued elsewhere, France was the first state to sign capitulations with the Ottomans in 1535 and it had very important consequences within France.[22] So whether in France or in Venice the capitulations allowed for the free circulation of the Armenians. The capitulations remain an important part of their liberty of commerce but they do not seem to offer explanation enough to account for their settlement: free ports or specific exemptions from taxation are at the inception of all three communities in Venice, Livorno and Marseille.

If, because of their Christianity, the Armenians viewed themselves as close to Europe because they were Christians living in a Muslim world, conversely Europe saw them as 'Levantines', 'Ottomans' and 'Persians'. As for the Pope and the Catholic Church, they had little use for Apostolic Christianity. As Greene argues for the Greeks who suffered from Catholic pressure and even from piracy, the Armenians were also under tremendous pressure from Catholicism. There were never any objections to the settlement of Armenian merchants in Amsterdam, refuge to the Marano Jews of Spain and Portugal and to the French Huguenots alike. France and Italy were Catholic and thus more problematic. Their Christianity was no help at all. In 1630, for example, the *kalântar* (provost and alderman) of New Julfa, Khwâja Nazar, requested formal permission from the Vatican for the establishment of Armenian factories in Italy, either through construction or renovation of existing houses. This permission was granted if they were Catholics or willing to convert to Catholicism.[23] Yet, despite this, somehow there seems to have been no great obstacle to their establishment in Italy, for if any port had opened its doors to foreign merchants, in these cases to the Jews, it was open to the Armenians as well. In the middle of the century, a Jesuit from Smyrna sent recommendations to the papacy that they should not let any Armenian commerce in Catholic territories without an express patent from the pope. In consequence, the Armenian priests were forbidden to say mass and were supplanted by Catholic priests who would recite the mass in Latin.[24]

The Armenians of New Julfa also had to be extremely careful in their contacts with the local Catholic missions in Iran. The shah was a jealous protector and saw conversion to Catholicism as an intervention on the part of foreign powers.[25] There was, however, a prominent Armenian Catholic family from old Julfa, the Shahrimanians,[26] who were one of the four main trading families of the wealthy suburb of New Julfa and soon became the most prominent trading family for the Julfan Armenians in Venice. There were other Armenian Catholics in New Julfa and although their numbers are not clear, they all lived in the same neighbourhood of New Julfa at the gate of the Shahrimanians, apart from the other Armenians.[27] In the case of the Shahrimanians their Catholicism did help them settle in Venice but it is legislation and tax exemption that is key to New Julfan commerce in these ports, rather than religion.

Venice

Venice is remarkable for the presence of Catholic Armenians. Armenians, not all of them Catholic, had been present there since the twelfth century because of the trading relations of the Kingdom of Cilicia with the Italian cities. There were Armenian printing presses in Venice, Marseille and Amsterdam by the end of the seventeenth century. The Armenian quarter with the church of Santa Croce is still there next to the Ferrali Bridge; it was there that the first Armenian books published in Venice were produced.[28] The earliest printed Armenian book, 'Friday Book' dates to 1511 or 1512 and was printed on the first Armenian printing press in the world, in Venice. It was a prayer book for the sick but several books, calendars, horoscopes and grammars in Armenian were also printed in Venice in the early period.[29] The printing presses were often tied to merchants and their trade in Europe.[30] Their existence depended on merchant money.[31] Alishan's work documents a hospice built for Armenian merchants in the middle of the thirteenth century by a Venetian nobleman; the Armenian merchants used this building as a *fondaco* or entrepôt for their trade through the fifteenth century. An altar and chapel were erected on the premises of the Armenian *fondaco* in 1434 and work was done to turn it into a church until 1689 to serve a growing community of Julfan merchants.[32] There is a recent work by Father Zēkʻiean, in collaboration with Aldo Ferrari, which examines the Armenians in Venice from the arrival of the New Julfan Catholic family, the Shahrimanians, to the foundation of the Mkhitarists in San Lazzaro by Mkhitar; it focuses on Catholic Armenians.[33] The fact that Venice had a sizeable Catholic Armenian population is clear from the middle of the seventeenth century on but the settlement was an earlier one.

The number of Armenians present in Venice remains difficult to document. The number of Julfans in Venice probably increased when the Venetian Senate provided tax exemptions on the import of Iranian raw silk to its harbour. Father Alishan has studied the Senate's decree and argues that this was an agreement between Iran and Venice and that these exemptions were preceded by agreements signed in 1576 and 1589 and confirmed for the period after 1632.[34] Alishan suggests that an eighteenth-century census report from 1750 documenting seventy Armenian merchants and seventeen priests marks a period of decline for the community in Venice because several Armenian mercantile houses had left the city between 1730 and 1738. This is interesting to note because this was a period of difficulty for the Armenians, both within Iran and in some of their Indian Ocean markets. One would expect them to flock to Europe but it seems that these difficulties also made a decline of their trade in the Mediterranean, a sign that the network was connected closely. Armenian presence in Venice was at the instigation of the city of Venice itself. As we saw the Armenians' presence in Venice is early in the thirteenth century, while Cilicia (or Little Armenia) is a trading partner; the first incentive for the Armenian merchants was a gift from a powerful Venetian: in 1253 Marco Ziani, son of doge Pietro Ziani and nephew of doge Sebastiano Ziani, donated a house to the Armenian merchants in the quarter of San Giulian (San Zulian). There was enough Armenian presence for a printing press some centuries later; the first Armenian printing press in the world functioned as early as 1511 or 1512 in Venice. The merchant population was there in the sixteenth century before the exemptions provided by agreements signed by Venice with Iran in 1576 and 1589 were continuous after 1623.[35] There were privileges that Venice offered later specifically from the Armenian traders from Iran, i.e. the New Julfans. The Venetian Senate offered the Persian silk trade great incentive by making an exception: it had decreed in 1622 (the decree was confirmed in 1646 and 1648) that the Armenians and Persians bringing in silk and other goods were exempted from taxations (*tassi dei cottimi e di bailaggi*).[36] Venetians extended their protection to this group of Armenians even further in the 1670s: the Cinque Savi issued several decrees protecting the Armenian merchants and their goods and contracts. To offer this form of state protection from Venice there are several decrees, one as early as 1661, another in 1672, a later decree of 1676 offered even more – it gave them the city's supervision of their merchandise and affairs.[37] These privileges and incentives to the New Julfan Armenians came with conditions of strict control to differentiate between Armenian merchants from Iran and those under Ottoman rule. In order to get the exemptions that the city had given Persian trade, the Armenian merchants had to stop en route either at Aleppo or Damascus and get an affidavit from the Venetian consuls posted there that they were not subjects of the Ottoman sultan, but Armenians from Iran. In addition, to tighten the control of their trade within Venice a decree of the Cinque Savi of 10 June 1662 demanded they not use their own *fondaco* but deposit their merchandise in the *fondaco dei Turchi* usually used by Ottoman subjects, but in a totally separate part of the *fondaco dei Turchi* now devoted to their silk. Another decree followed shortly, it condemned any merchants from Persia that broke this new rule to the galleys.[38] These decrees were specific to Persians and Armenians from Persia as they are described in the documents, mostly Armenians from New Julfa, but in 1613 Muslim Persians had brought the first Persian silk sent as a sample by Shah Abbas to the Venetian doge.

It was the great need for raw silk, since Venice's silk industry exported many finished goods, shoes, textiles and clothing, that created these generous incentives for the New Julfans. Yet Venice had a long history with inviting the Armenians into the republic since its early wars with the Ottomans. The Armenian church of Santa Croce still holds the remains of the most famous New Julfan trading family with some members residing in Venice, the Shahrimanians. They had long ties with several Italian city states because they were Catholic Armenians, but most memorable is their loan to the doge of Venice of 200,000 ducats, recorded by the Carmelites in Persia, to aid in the war (1684–99) against the Ottomans.[39] The last war was fought to reverse losses to Venice when the Ottomans declared war on 9 December 1714, using some transgressions of Venetian merchants as a pretext. The Ottoman fleet, numbering eighty warships under Canum Hoca, captured the last Venetian possessions in the Aegean. These conflicts were an impediment to Ottoman Armenians trading in Venice. Yet earlier it is Venice's capitulations with the Ottoman Empire that were the set of legal privileges that permitted Armenian merchants from the Ottoman Empire to trade the port as early as 1502. Capitulations/*Ahdnameshs*, were granted to Venice by the Ottomans in 1502, 1513, 1517, 1521, 1540 and 1567. Horii Yukata has studied the *ahdnamehs* closely to differentiate between those granted to subjects of the Ottomans and the rights granted to foreigners who were given safe passage in the Ottoman Empire. The Venetians fell into the second category and did not owe *haraj*/poll taxes owed by non-Muslim subjects, and maintained their trading colonies in Ottoman lands as they had in medieval times with a Bailo (a diplomat) in Istanbul to oversee all matters of trade.[40] The largest part of the *ahdnamehs* were largely devoted to merchant rights and reciprocity between Venice and the Ottomans.

Venice's wars with the Ottomans, its shipping and commerce in the sixteenth century are both well known and well studied. Greene looks at this literature to point out that the great Venetian merchant galleys abruptly drop out of use shortly after 1500. The increasing capability of the round ship combined with the decreasing availability of luxury goods rendered the galley system unworkable. This prompted a progressive turning away from the sea for the Venetian nobility, many of whom were still shipowners who started to leave the actual captaincy of their ships to others. The Venetian merchants no longer ruled the seas as they had fierce competitors in the English, Spanish, Raguseans and the Genoese who all moved on the seas. Greene notices that the very active Greek merchants seem absent from these competitors despite the fact that they moved quickly to capitalize on Venice's weakness.[41]

There was, Greene finds, important differences between the Greeks from the regions ruled by Venice and the other foreign merchants in the port of Venice.[42] These Greeks were subjects of Venice but not Venetian citizens, but by the sixteenth century Greene argues that this distinction was not enforced. The difference now was between 'foreigners' as one group, and 'Venetians', and 'subjects of Venice' as another. Therefore there was little distinction at this point between the *sudditi* (subjects) and *cittadini* (citizens).[43] The *sudditi*, Greek subjects of Venice from the islands ruled by her sea power, were sometimes described as Venetians when they lived abroad. Maria Fusaro's work on the Venetians in London finds that Greek subjects of Venice were called and seen as Venetian in England.[44] Foreign merchants, as distinct from the Greeks that came from the

islands under the rule of Venice, were often from the Ottoman Empire. Greeks
from the Ottoman Empire were not *sudditi*; they too were foreign merchants
like the Ottoman Armenians and the Ottoman Jews.

Yet Ottoman Greeks seemed to have circulated freely as well, as would have
been true for the Ottoman Armenians. Greene demonstrates that in Venice the
capitulations applied to Ottoman merchants in general without regard to religious identity covered Jewish, Christian and Muslim subjects of the Ottomans
alike. Greene argues that the capitulations created a routine through which Ottoman merchants could conduct business in Venice and Venetians could conduct
business in the Ottoman Empire without the intervention of political authorities.[45] Ottoman merchants, Jews, Armenians and Muslims alike could sell their
goods, contract debt and rent lodgings even for extended periods. Studies on
Muslim merchants in Europe are extremely rare and Cemal Kafadar's article on
the death of a Muslim Ottoman merchant in Venice is one of the rare studies
we have that illustrates that the Ottoman merchants settling in Venice were not
only Christians and Jews.[46] Greene points out that the Greek merchants in Venice
operated vastly differently and in diverse worlds and that it is very problematic to
bring them together as 'the Greek community of Venice or Greek commerce and
shipping'.[47] This certainly holds true for the Armenians found in Livorno, Venice
and Marseille, many of whom had settled in thanks to the capitulations or to the
more specific legislation meant for Jewish merchants in Livorno or for the Jews
and Armenians in France. They continued to trade in these cosmopolitan, Mediterranean ports, not only for the profit of their own network but often acting as
agents for other groups or contracting agents themselves. It is a mistake both to
look at the Armenians in isolation, or to group them as one unit.

Livorno

Venice and Ancona were the two most important destinations for Ottoman
merchants in the sixteenth century but Livorno also became an important centre. Very little has been done on Ancona. Like Venice, Ancona and Livorno
competed for foreign merchants when their commerce was in decline in hopes
of gaining prosperity for themselves against their neighbours. Again, they were
most interested in attracting Jewish merchants but this does not change the fact
that these concessions brought in other Ottoman merchants.[48] In 1532, Ancona
was incorporated into the Papal States and Clement VII was disturbed by the
large number of 'Turkish merchants in the city'. When the privileges accorded
to Jewish merchants in Ancona were revoked, the city of Pisaro tried to benefit
from Ancona's trouble and in 1555 gave a charter of commercial privileges that
was addressed to '"Turchi, Armeni, Greci and Mori", [Turkish, Armenian, Greek
and Moors] as well as "Ebrei" [Jews].[49]

The Armenians in Livorno have attracted the attention of several scholars, most of whom have been examined by Francesca Trivellato for her work on the Sephardic Jews of Livorno. She gives a very good summary of their numbers in Livorno and uses the work of Lucia Frattarelli Fischer.[50] The earliest work on Livorno, printed in 1891, remains that of Father Mesrop Ughurlean who traces the presence of the Julfan Armenians in Livorno to 1582. According to him, a merchant from old Julfa, Khwaja Gregorio di Guerak Mirman (buried in the church of Santa Croce in Venice), resided in Livorno as an agent for the Shah of Iran as a trader of Iranian silk.[51] The presence of the Julfans as agents for the Persian kings in Europe predates their deportation of 1604 to Iran and the silk auction of 1619, where they became the carriers of raw Iranian silk for Shah Abbas. This early collaboration and several royal edicts dated before the reign of Shah Abbas indicate a close collaboration even under Ottoman rule that probably instigated the deportation of merchants loyal to the Persian king to the capital of Iran, Isfahan, during the wars with the Ottomans.[52] Persian documents indicate that Armenian success in the international silk trade was closely tied to their political and social role within the Iranian court.[53] This gave them privileges that enabled their success and it is because of privileges accorded elsewhere that there is a move to the ports of the Mediterranean, either as subjects or representatives of the shahs or Ottoman subjects under the capitulations. Yet, in addition to the privileges that were directly given to the Armenians, there is another twist that goes beyond these decrees between states specific to their trade: the Armenians indirectly took advantage of legislation meant to open the ports to Jewish traders, and we will see that this holds true in Marseille, and, as Trivellato demonstrates, for Livorno. Legislation specifically addressing the trade of the Jews opened the door to the Armenians in several ports.

As Francesca Trivellato makes clear, the Livornine laws included concessions to merchants other than the Jewish merchants they originally addressed; these concessions, intended only for the Jews, included the cancellation of all that was previously accumulated outside of Tuscany and the legal validity of accounts and contracts for their commercial activity.[54] She makes clear that, similar to most laws in the old regime, the Livornine laws were not universal but designated rights and obligations only specific to the Jews. However, other foreigners could appeal to these patents in order to enhance their status. Nevertheless, it fell to the Duke of Tuscany to determine these negotiations with the merchants of many nations that had begun to settle in Livorno. There is no question that none of these merchant groups ever competed with the Sephardic Jews in demographic size or in the importance of international commercial activity.[55] The Jews in Livorno formed a *suddita nazione* (subject nation) and were subjects of the Grand Duchy of Tuscany while other merchant communities are referred to as *nazioni estere* (foreign nations).[56] This is a very important distinction because the Armenians were considered foreigners as they were also in Venice and this is in contrast with the French policy of integration towards the foreign merchants in the port of Marseille. Louis XIV had a policy of national integration, he extended rights of naturalization to foreign merchants including the Armenians. There were exceptions made for some very wealthy Armenian Catholics in Venice and in some other ports, but otherwise the Armenians were a 'foreign nation' of traders.

If the Armenians are documented to have been in Livorno as early as the middle of the sixteenth century, their numbers did not rise substantially until the end of the century and peaked in the middle of the seventeenth century where there are forty-seven Armenian merchants documented as settled in Livorno. By 1763, only fourteen Armenian households are documented.[57] The Armenian Apostolic church of Saint Gregory the Illuminator was inaugurated quite late, in 1714, but was only allowed to celebrate mass on the condition that it followed the Roman liturgy and that the Armenian patriarch never be mentioned, making it effectively into a Catholic church rather than an Apostolic one.[58]

Marseille

Some legislation instigated in 1622 by the Chamber of Commerce of Marseille had many merchants leave the French port for the port of Livorno.[59] It is not clear how many Armenians made the move. This is not the only case of mobility between ports and Levant markets and it is important to note that this population of merchants was constantly on the move. French merchants are important to the study of Armenian commerce because they were the main clients of the New Julfans on the Ottoman markets and because the French monarchy had political aims of protecting the Catholic Armenians. The relations of the Armenian merchants with the French differ in two ways from their relations with the rest of Europe: first, there was a certain amount of religious friction because of the French missions' attempts at proselytization and aims to convert Orthodox Armenians and second, the French economy, both in its structure and policies, more often than not, was closed to Armenian commerce within French territory. The French were not only the chief clients for Iranian silk on the Ottoman market, but also primary rivals who were better established in the silk trade than the English Levant Company or the Dutch at this date. The failure of Colbert's commercial companies masked the importance of the French in Asia and their failure in India and Persia was well compensated for with their activities in the Levant. The majority of the French merchants that were engaged in the Levant trade in competition with the Armenians were from Provence, and the Marseillais were among them.

Their Levant trade started with the French capitulations with the Ottoman Empire in 1535 but was rather slow to take off. It is in the seventeenth century that Marseille becomes the main port for the Levant trade, not only for the town's merchants, but also for the Ottomans, the Armenians and the Jews engaged in this trade. From 1486 to 1660, Marseille's administrative legal structure remained unchanged despite conflicts among the ruling aristocratic elite and the rising merchant families.[60] The quays of the port were constructed under Louis XII and Louis XIII and an important shipyard for galleons put in place as part of Richelieu and Louis XIII's efforts to build a French navy. In their well-documented history of the commerce of Marseille, Louis Bergasse and Gaston Rambert studied the commerce of Marseille from 1599 to 1660. They see a long decline because Marseille had everything conspiring against its growth: piracy, the wars with Spain, the wars with the rulers of the Barbary Coast, the creation of a free port in Livorno and the creation of the free port of Villefranche by the Duke of Savoy. They see a reduced activity in the Levant and commercial ties that are limited to Spain and Italy. The exchange of wheat, oils and wine were more important than the importation of exotic products from the Levant. In 1660, Italian free ports had taken away Marseille's dominance but that situation would reverse itself under the policies of Louis XIV and Jean-Baptiste Colbert.[61]

A new port was built by the king after a merchant revolt against the Crown. Louis XIV ordered the erection of the forts of St Jean and St Nicolas and built an arsenal and fleet in the Old Port for his famous galleys on which later, after 1680, Turks and Protestants suffered a terrible fate in the royal war fleet. They wintered in Marseille and at times the city became a prominent Levantine port, with the presence of Turkish galley slaves looking for other seasonal work or the foreign merchants invited in by Louis XIV to the chagrin of the citizens of Marseille.[62] As Louis XIV rose to real power in the 1660s, he aimed to achieve political control of the port of Marseille so that the Crown could profit from a newly encouraged rich commerce in oriental goods. This was not always to the liking of the local merchants and conflicts were created among those who were royalists and those who were fiercely independent. These conflicts prompted Louis XIV to travel to Provence on his way to his own wedding; his wedding procession would march on Marseille with troops and leave it in ruins before Louis met his Spanish bride.[63]

Shortly after Louis XIV assumed power in 1661, he chose a new controller-general Jean-Baptiste Colbert, who would work towards fulfilling Louis' dreams of centralization and control over French commerce. Decades earlier, fearful of losing the monopoly over the commerce of the Levant granted to them by the protectionist edict of 1622, the merchants of Marseille demanded that a tax of 20 per cent be levied on all merchandise brought into the port on foreign ships or on all merchandise belonging to a foreign merchant on a French ship. When Colbert issued an edict in 1669 that had the possible consequence of the Armenians trading in Marseille, the 20 per cent tax due from foreigners remained as the last protectionist measure to aid the Marseillais.

He wrote to the Baron d'Oppède in charge of the application of the 1669 treaty concerning the franchise of Marseille: 'I pray you should give the Armenians all the protection that the authority of your office will permit you, to preserve them from all the annoyances of the local inhabitants who do not see what constitutes the advantage of their commerce.'[64] Colbert's intentions were clear concerning the Armenians and the Jews. He did just what he would do with the East India Company: open it to foreigners with experience. A Dutchman and an Armenian were hired as directors in the hope that it would benefit France. Elsewhere, I have looked at the life of Marcara Avanchintz, naturalized by Louis XIV, engaged by Colbert in 1664, whose gem and silver trade took him first to Livorno, and to France where he was naturalized, and to India as a French agent, a director of the first French East India Company in the late seventeenth century. His post is unusual but not his itinerary. Many of the Armenian merchants in the Italian cities or Marseille stay there temporarily and are present in other ports and markets at different junctures of their trading careers.[65]

Takeda argues that this new era for Marseille and the Crown's political agenda had significant effects over both the population of Marseille and the foreign merchants who flocked to the port after 1669 when Colbert declared it a free port. The king's architectural imperialism redesigned the town and local merchants accused the Crown of changing the city for foreigners to their own detriment.[66] The elders of Marseille, the *échevins*, were completely opposed to the project of renovation because they believed it catered to the non-Marseillais.[67] These non-Marseillais were chiefly Turks, Jews, Armenians and Italian merchants, many of whom were settling in the town. Historians have used the term 'commercial humanism' to describe the ideology behind the mercantilist expansion of Louis XIV and Colbert. Many writers argued that the merchants were citizens dedicated to the public good.[68] It is with an inquiry into whether the settlement of foreigners in Marseille would benefit the public good or not that decisions were eventually taken in 1669 to open the port as a duty-free zone to foreign merchandise.

Colbert's 1669 edict was an open invitation to foreign merchants and although it stipulated that silks from Italy, the Levant, Africa and regions ruled by the Ottomans could enter France only through Marseille or Rouen, it encouraged the Levant trade to use the southern port of Marseille. It also specified that non-French foreigners could become naturalized Frenchmen and citizens of the bourgeoisie of Marseille if they worked in Marseille or married a Marseillaise. They would have to own property or buy a house set specifically within the walls of the new expansion ordered by the king. They would have to live in a house which cost more than 10,000 *livres* (pounds) for only three years or a house that cost between

5,000 and 10,000 *livres* for five years before becoming naturalized. With no own-ership, they would have to do commerce and spend twelve consecutive years in Marseille after which Marseille's administration, the *échevin*, rendered them a par-ticipant in the civic laws of Marseille with all of its privileges and exemptions.[69] The city of Marseille was transformed by Colbert's edict. Armenians and Jews in particular, as well as Protestant merchants who were sometimes English, benefited most from Colbert's edict. This was not the first time that there was an open-door policy towards the Armenians. Earlier, Cardinal Richelieu had overridden Marseille's municipal decisions of 1620 and the 1622 edict, dictated by the Chamber of Commerce, in which the Armenians were forbidden from exporting bullion (silver and gold) out of France. A June 1636, a treaty permit-ted 'Armenian merchants to come at liberty from their countries to ports and cities in Provence and others in the kingdom with whatever quality of silk and other merchandise'. Yet it is only following Colbert's 1669 edict that Armeni-ans and Jews, merchants, priests, rabbis and artisans among them, began arriving again in Marseille to his delight. In fact, in 1671, Colbert wrote to the president of the parliament in Aix, Oppède,

'that it is a great advantage for us ... that the merchants have abandoned Leghorn [Livorno] and that the Armenians have brought silks to Marseille. He guaranteed Armenians protection from all the chicanery of the city's [administrators]. Through similar protection, an Armenian founded Marseille's first café, the first in France, in 1672. Encouraged by Colbert, Armenians founded the city's first Armenian publish-ing house in the city the same year'.[70]

A number of Marseille citizens, mainly merchants afraid of competition, reacted negatively to the arrival of the Armenians and the Jews. Takeda cites an anony-mous memoir written on behalf of the public benefit to the *échevin* describing how the Jews had grown in the French commerce and corrupted its citizens with usury, counterfeit currency, and buying at ruinous prices to the sellers. They are also accused of corrupting the virtues of Marseillais women by tempting them with fineries and trading at unfair prices. While the treaty calls for the expulsion of the Jews from the port of Marseille, Colbert rejected many arguments made against the Armenian and Jewish merchants of Marseille and in turn accused the merchants of Marseille of their lack of interest in the public good.[71] He argued 'there is nothing more advantageous for the general good of commerce than to augment the number of those who can do it; and in this regards, that which is not advantageous for the particular inhabitants of Marseille is for the general strength of the kingdom'. Colbert insisted: 'Since for religious reasons aside, we have never forbidden Jews from trading', he decreed that it is not necessary to listen to the propositions [the Marseillais] have made against these Jews.'[72]

As Takeda points out in her study, both Colbert and the French king him-self believed that the Jews and Armenians benefited the public good of France more than the local Marseillais. Due to the fact that the citizens of Marseille and their Chamber of Commerce had often resisted central control, they did not have the favour, politically, of the king. For Colbert, neither race, ethnicity nor religion were grounds for exclusion from French commerce, especially if French merchants were not cooperative. Indeed, what's very new in this period is Louis XIV's policy of naturalization of adoption of foreigners as naturalized French merchants for the good of French commerce. In my previous work in 1999, *The Shah's Silk for Europe's Silver*, I showed an extreme case of this with an Armenian named Marcara Avanchintz who was appointed by Colbert as Director of the French East India Company. An Armenian, who probably converted to Catholi-cism in Livorno where he was thrown in jail for carrying arms, he obtained the first edict that opened India to French trade as a French agent. This form of col-laboration with the Armenians was state sponsored and pushed by the court but irritated local merchants who saw their own interests as undermined. Indeed, those quarrels extended even to India, where the conflict between a French director and Marcara ruined that first effort in India for Colbert's 1664 East India company.[73] Another clear case of conflict were the coffee imports through Marseille, which was at one point in time in Ottoman and New Julfan Armenian merchants' hands.[74] Nevertheless, despite this new open policy by the Crown, there was still ground for religious conflict. This complicated but did not stop commercial relationships in Catholic ports. In New Julfa, however, the tension between Armenian Catholics and Apostolic Armenians was at its height in this period. Letters were written to Louis XIV from the Armenian patriarch of New Julfa who, convinced that it was the only solution, offered the conversion of his entire flock to Catholicism in return for the king's protection. Similar letters were addressed to the Pope as well.

> After several conferences it was resolved that the patriarch would write to the Pope, to the de Propaganda fide and to the King of France, and to the father confessor, all of which was executed a few days after. The Patriarch's letters were very urgent, and moving. He therein set forth in very plain terms that he acknowledged the Pope's Monarchy, and submitted his Person, and his Flock, to the Authority of the Roman Church; but begged in the name of God, that speedy and effectual Secours might be procur'd him. The Deputation procured nothing for the *Armenians*; for the *Augustins* and the *Carms*, being jealous and provoked that they had no Share within, writ to Rome, that they could perceive nothing but human Motives in this Contrivance.[75]

Upon learning of the negotiations with the Pope, the prosperous merchants of New Julfa were quite opposed to them and very afraid of their consequences.[76] The wealthy, sedentary merchants in New Julfa were conservative and anti-Catholic for fear of their position with the shahs and concern of reforms within their own Apostolic Church. The church often served as a centre for merchant affairs. A certificate obtained by the Provost of New Julfa and signed by the local merchant assembly and local clergy was handed by the Apostolic Church to a French Capuchin and served as the trial of the French Armenian director Marcara. This was a certificate to attest the noble birth of Marcara Avanchintz, a director of the French East India Company, who was now in prison and on trial in Paris for being sued by the French East India Company that he had represented. Considering the church was a centre of affairs, a conversion to Catholicism would have been of immense importance politically.[77]

The man responsible for some of the trouble for Marcara was François Caron, a Dutchman in the service of the French East India Company who was hired as a foreigner by Colbert at the same date as the Armenian Marcara. In a letter by François Caron[78] it is clearly explained that the Catholics were not well received in Japan because of the Portuguese and that the French East India Company should send exclusively merchants of the Reformed faith to the eastern powers. Both Caron and Marcara had converted to Catholicism and been naturalized citizens by Louis XIV before becoming trading agents for the French company. Like Japan, the Persian court did not react pleasantly to any rumours or suggestions of the Armenians converting because they considered it interference by a foreign power, machinations by foreign powers to subvert the Armenians and make them their own subjects.[79]

It is, however, misguided to believe that the many edicts forbidding Armenians to trade in France in the late seventeenth century had anything to do with these bitter religious differences. When, after 1622, the Armenians went to Livorno[80] it was not a religious issue, but caused by the demands of the merchants of Marseille. France maintained a very protectionist economic policy. Contrary to England where Persian silks were a very important imported good, France was trying to keep Persian and Italian silks out because it had a silk industry of its own. The first decree against the Armenians dates from the time of Richelieu. The decree of 10 December 1622 was a direct consequence of the demands of the merchants of the port of Marseille where many Armenians were already trading. There was nothing religious about these demands yet religious legislation would play a role in policy reversal in France.

After the permissive policies of the Crown in 1669 there was an abrupt change of royal policy in the 1680s. In general, this is a period wherein religious tolerance was no longer a policy in France. The revocation of the Edict of Nantes in 1685 formalized religious intolerance and had dire consequences not only for all French Protestants, but also for the foreign merchants in Marseille and elsewhere.[81] Despite the fact that Marseille had the oldest Chamber of Commerce in France since 1599 and was ruled by merchants, the Crown now had a clear hand in its affairs. Colbert now wrote to the intendant of Aix in 1681, asking him to provide the number of Jews residing in the port of Marseille 'as the King no longer allows them in the country ... you will examine secretly if the people are useful or not in Marseille'. Should it be found that they were not useful to the public good, the expulsion of the Jews was ordered. Yet he warned his intendant in Aix, Oppède, to disregard the local interests of the merchants because of commercial jealousy and to analyze whether the same commerce could ever be supplied to France by Frenchmen. Local initiatives in Marseille to expel the Jews gained force after this new initiative and inquiry.

Marseille's powerful Chamber of Commerce opened a dossier against the Jews who had begun arriving from Livorno as early as 1670. The community had prominent merchants whose elite included Abraham Attias and his brother-in-law Joseph Villeréal who were prominent in the Levant markets on the Barbary Coast and in Livorno. For a decade the Chamber of Commerce accused them of usury and corruption. It argued that the poverty of Marseille was due in large part to the 'corrupting mores' and their lawless influence. In 1682, Louis XIV expelled Marseille's Jews for illegally operating a synagogue in Villeréal's home and for conspiring with the Barbary pirates.[82] The conflict with the Barbary pirates who captured and enslaved many Frenchmen was most felt on the shores of the Mediterranean. An accusation of complicity was equivalent to a charge of treason.[83]

The issue of expelling foreign merchants from Marseille forged a very unusual alliance between Louis XIV and Marseille's Chamber of Commerce. After Colbert's death in 1683, the king developed the same exclusionary policies towards the Armenians as Colbert had wished for the Jews. Colbert's successor Pontchartrain initially continued policies of exclusion and accepted one inclusion, by enrolling young Armenians in the royal colleges as interpreters at the service of France.[84] But in 1687 Seignelay, his successor, prohibited the Armenians from trading in France in order to protect the French silk trade and on the premise that cheaper, inferior silk brought in by the Armenians – *ardasse* – had ruined the French manufacturers. This decimated the Marseille colony and the Armenians who stayed in Marseille faced prison and harassment and risked their goods being confiscated often.

Later, when Armenians like Oandjy and Ibraham Barsan disembarked in Marseille in 1716, the Chamber of Commerce and royal intendants confiscated their goods and accused them of illegally selling silk.[85] French discourse about the Jews was harsher than the one towards the Armenians. The Jews were often accused of conspiracy between the Jews of Livorno, Marseille and Algeria and of being a threat to the French state. Yet the Armenians were subject to the same laws. Because of its long tradition of posing as the protector of the Christians of the Ottoman Empire in the capitulations, France had forged close ties with the Armenians, but this mattered little. Many of them had worked as interpreters to

French consuls in the Levant. Takeda cites the example of two Armenians who in 1720 hoped that their services to the French nation in Smyrna would protect them from the exclusionary policies of the port. Like many Armenians, their father had been awarded Louis XIV's protection by the French ambassador in Constantinople through formal letters of protection. Despite all this, the Crown and the Chamber of Commerce rejected their petition.[86]

Even the naturalization policies of France were no longer as tolerant. Although the laws did not disappear, the Crown began to clamp down on absentee un-naturalized subjects by demanding the show of formal certificates of naturalization and imposing new taxes. Several new ordinances between 1681 and as late as 1725 called for naturalized subjects, now citizens of Marseille, to complete two- to three-month apprenticeships, serve on a ship belonging to His Majesty or serve a minimum of five years on a French merchant ship before becoming captains and pilots. Takeda concludes that France's commerce spawned both inclusive and exclusionist policies during Louis XIV's reign but that when the 'foreign' made inroads into France itself, exclusionary arguments took over. 'Ottomans were untrustworthy, Jews were usurers, Armenians were deceptive.'[87]

In 1686 Seignelay, Colbert's oldest son, hopes to continue his father's policy of protecting foreigners and Armenian commerce. Yet in 1687 he began to be annoyed at the advantages that the English were gaining by conducting commerce through the Armenian houses established in Marseille. An edict of 21 October 1687 forbade the Armenians from engaging themselves in the silk trade in the city of Marseille. The treaty names the Armenians of the Ottoman Empire, not the Persian Armenians.[88] In 1694, there was a formal request from the Armenians for permission to settle in Marseille. It met with the strong opposition of the Chamber of Commerce of Marseille:

> 'You cannot compare the situation of Marseilles to Livorno, because the Italians do not do the sea transportation and all the sea transportation is done by foreigners; In Marseilles the commerce with the Levant was done by the *Marseillais*; to give Marseilles a franchise would be to ruin French navigation, in Livorno the Italians have to resort to foreigners to arm a ship for the Levant.'[89]

The Levant was the main market for the French but the word 'Levantine' or *Levantin* used for the Armenians is very confusing. The recent research of Olivier Raveux has elucidated the fact that most of the Armenian merchants living in the port of Marseille were indeed New Julfans or *Choffelins*. Raveux believes that the term is a French translation of the Italian *Ciolfalini*.[90] Raveux completes Tékéian's work on Marseille and seems to find smaller numbers of merchants in the south of France than initially indicated by Tékéian.[91] He has studied the Armenian colony of Marseille during the last part of the seventeenth century when it was at its height as a result of the policies inaugurated by Colbert. In an annex to his latest article, he gives a list of names but cautions that it is not an exhaustive survey.[92] His previous work also showed the importance of Armenian artisans in Marseille and demonstrated that the community was not simply a community of merchants. Olivier Raveux has demonstrated the agency of the Armenians in the transmission of the technique of calico printing to Marseille.[93] The confusion about the word 'Levantine' might be elucidated by his recent work on the languages and education of these merchants as it shows their itineraries.

In his most recent article, Raveux examines the great diversity of roles played by the Armenian merchants settled in Marseille. His work on the notarial archives of Marseille demonstrates a double function of interpreter and representative played by lesser merchants for important merchants or the wealthier *négociants*. He gives the names of at least fifty-two Armenian merchants at the service of two wealthy merchants, Melchion de Nazar and de Zacharie de Georges.[94] What is very interesting in this latest study are his efforts to look at the use of languages in the Marseille colony. He asks the question: is the linguistic formation and education available to New Julfan merchants different from the one offered to European merchants of the same period?

Raveux argues that with superior linguistic ability the Julfans seemed to have an advantage over many merchant communities. He cites a passage in Antoine Galland that referred to their language acquisition in the city of Smyrna. According to Galland, they remained in Smyrna for about ten years to acquire familiarity with European languages in order to be able to negotiate in Europe. Antoine Galland tells us that they learned the *langue franque*, a 'lingua franca', a mixed language that permits commerce in the ports of the Mediterranean.[95] A great majority of the Iranian New Julfan Armenian merchants of Marseille spent ten years in Smyrna, then a sojourn in an Italian port, before arriving in France. Reading Raveux quote Galland, it becomes clear why after a ten-year sojourn in Smyrna they could be called Ottoman merchants, 'Levantines' in France, even if initially they were *choffelins* or from New Julfa. Nevertheless their origin is not always clear. What he does not say but is clear from examining legislation is that this offers them a chance to take advantage of the Ottoman capitulations with the Italian ports. Even if they are New Julfan they can come in as Ottomans in France or Venice.

We know from the narrations of several merchants that Melchion de Nazar and Paul de Serquis in Marseille came from Venice while Serquis de Jean and Raphaël Ruply de Livourne came from Livorno.[96] Raveux finds that many Armenians in Marseille would sign their names in Italian such as '*Nazar di Ovan*'. He finds that the New Julfans not only speak Italian, but that many of them in Marseille are proficient and literate in French as well. When they arrive they all use interpreters but within two years they no longer need them. According to Raveux, this signifies that they can at least speak French, Italian and the lingua franca. He also finds a difference in the need of interpreters between those merchants that have come directly from the Ottoman markets and those that stay several years. He cites the case of a merchant from Trebizond, Jean Cheleby de Amirat, who still needs an interpreter after ten years in Marseille, despite the fact that he was naturalized in 1694.[97] It could very well be that he was one of those absentee naturalized Armenian merchants of Marseille that the French were beginning to crack down on.

The French merchant of Marseille, Etienne Guirard, was proficient in Armenian and did the majority of his own trade with the Armenians whom he also hosted regularly. Most interpreters simply do sporadic negotiations to render a service and the only exception that Raveux finds is that of the clock maker Estienne Provance, who learned Turkish in a clock-making workshop in Istanbul. Turkish, he finds, is more often used as a language of negotiation than Armenian. Estienne Provance is so omnipresent in the notarial archives of the 1670s, studied by Raveux, that he calls himself *trouchemente des Armeniens* from the word '*Tarjuman*' (interpreter) in Turkish.[98] From 1666 to 1672, Estienne Provance was also the representative in the port of Marseille for all the affairs of Antonio Boghos, a customs official in Smyrna and the principal Armenian merchant in Livorno.[99] Etienne Guirard's knowledge of Armenian is a rare skill. One of the most interesting conclusions that Raveux comes to is that the Armenians in Marseille not only helped the New Julfans, but also become interpreters for Greeks, Syriacs and especially for Maronite and Turkish merchants who are either living in Marseille or are going through its port.[100] This indicates the kind of collaboration between networks that needs further research.

In 1672, investment in Oscan's printing press by the Marseille merchants demonstrates their network's need to publish books on languages and techniques. The books published covered such themes as mathematics, accounting and climate. As in Venice, their network also carried the books to the Levant and to Iran.[101]

In Marseille, even when legislation did not favour the Armenian merchants, the protectionist tax of 20 per cent was for the most part bypassed by fraudulent means. It seems the Armenian merchants found a way of avoiding the problem: French merchants enter their silk in their own names, for example. Fraud seems to have been widespread and very detrimental to the newly augmented French silk industry.[102] There were more than fifteen hundred bales of *ardasse* silk entering Marseille, despite these strict protectionist efforts.[103]

It is clear that the Armenians, save for one exception, Marcara Avanchintz, had no commerce with the French East India Company at this date. However it must be remembered that in 1664, Tavernier wrote that the French merchants were the customers the merchants of New Julfa preferred in Turkey. It is with non-Company merchants that Armenians of New Julfa conducted commerce and were paid in cash.[104] The prohibition of Richelieu's edict still stood and the

Armenians could not directly export gold or silver from France. Yet the silk trade with the French took place in Aleppo and Smyrna and the cash was carried there by French merchants. The Armenians then carried it from the Levant markets to either Iran or India.

Conclusion

As we saw, legislation in these three ports never addressed the Armenians alone or even specifically. Only in the edicts of Colbert are the Jews and Armenians both addressed specifically, but the Livornine laws were only specifically addressed to the Jews. Yet they served the Armenians. In Venice and Ancona the legislation was meant for all Ottoman merchants, Armenians, Greeks, and Jews alike. A close study of names would surely find great mobility from port to port, often the same merchants living first in Ottoman cities, Italian ports of Livorno and Venice, Marseille and even Amsterdam. While favourable legislation and state privileges and protection are key, other aspects of their contacts in these ports become clear. As discussed, the Armenians interpreted for other groups in Marseille signifying that collaboration and trade were often intertwined. Collaboration between networks, a very important element of success for merchant networks, is often forgotten in studies that concentrate on one ethnic group alone. Gelina Harlaftis and I are collaborating on a work about the expedition of a Greek and an Armenian merchant in their joint venture to go to China. The future of this field depends on examining the many cosmopolitan aspects involved in the astounding success of a small group of merchants like the Julfan Armenians.

This collaboration between different groups could be treaties or contracts not only among diaspora networks, but also with European carriers that had navies. As I have discussed elsewhere, much of the trade the Armenians carried to the Mediterranean was carried there on English and Dutch ships,[105] a fact that did not escape Colbert or his son Seignelay. Colbert argued that the freedom of trade given to the Armenians in the last part of the seventeenth century was of great profit to the English. Even much later, the Dutch and the English were the carriers of Armenian trade, be it silk, gems or coffee.[106] Daniel Panzac has shown that most of the ships carrying Ottoman trade to the Mediterranean and Indian Ocean were European ships and very few of them flew the Ottoman flag. He has found that the Ottoman trade to the Indian Ocean was in Armenian hands, a sizable portion of it was carried on European ships from Basrah, the main port of this Indian Ocean trade. Panzac cites a 1785 document that valued the annual import of the Armenians from India to Istanbul to five million *piastres* of which two thirds went to the purchase of muslin. This Indian Ocean trade was closely linked to the Mediterranean and to the Atlantic. In 1768, three fourths of the cargo loaded in Smyrna onto Dutch ships was bound for Amsterdam and belonged to Ottoman minorities such as the Greeks and the Armenians.[107] A few more studies, such as Daniel Panzac's on the main Ottoman ports and the ships leaving them, should be key for elucidating Julfan Armenian maritime trade in the Mediterranean.

To understand global success one should look at the ties of the Julfan and Ottoman Armenians to other groups of merchants. In the latter part of the century the New Julfans sought treaties with the Russian tsar and the Russian route became key to their trade.[108] A new study highlights New Julfan collaboration with the Greeks in Russia. Iannis Carras has ample evidence of collaboration of Greeks with Julfan Armenians via Astrakhan from the archive of the Greek community in Nizhen.[109] A slew of studies highlighting collaboration are necessary to elucidate the ties the Armenians had with other merchant networks. The Armenians, the Greeks and the Jews are often essentialized as solid groups with one identity. Trust is often essentialized as an eternal, unchanging, close-knit fraternity based on kinship and ethnicity. Looking at these groups together with new studies on collaboration would put the idea of closed ethnic networks, working in isolation within internal trust networks, to rest. No one denies that there were family firms and even larger organized relationships often based on ethnicity, networks based on towns of origin, but taking the national lens to the cosmopolitan circuits of trade in early modern times is a distortion.

5 RUSSIAN MERCHANT COLONIES IN SEVENTEENTH-CENTURY SWEDEN

Jarmo Kotilaine

The centuries-long confrontation between Russia and Sweden – which by the late sixteenth century had clearly grown into a broader fight for supremacy in the Baltic space – has tended to eclipse the underappreciated reality of intensive commercial ties between the two rivals. Yet such relations were not only of very long standing but had centuries earlier effectively given rise to Russian statehood in the era of Kievan Rus'. Even in the early modern era, they continued to be of considerable importance for both countries, both at the level of the adjacent border regions and the broader context of the national economies. In spite of laudable efforts by writers such as Artur Attman, Helmut Piirimäe, and Igor' Shaskol'skii, even the historiography of early modern Russian foreign trade has tended to dwell above all on White Sea trade, which was triggered by the English Muscovy Company in the sixteenth century. Naturally, it was undoubtedly the Dutch commercial superpower of the era – assisted by north German and English merchants – that paved the way for Russia's economic integration in the broader European economy. Nonetheless, this remarkable success story never undermined or substituted for Russia's long-standing commercial relations with its geographic neighbours. While the remarkable rise of Arkhangelsk inevitably led to a decline in the relative importance of trade in the Baltic, trade with the ascendant Swedish realm constituted an important aspect of Russian trade policy throughout the seventeenth century.[1]

Sustained, large-scale commercial activity anywhere inevitably gives rise to a significant infrastructure of transport vehicles, dwellings, and storage facilities which almost invariably translated into a permanent presence on the ground at various points along the trade routes. The famous 'German Quarter' (*nemetskaia sloboda*) in Moscow was one particularly well-known case in point but similar colonies arose in all the towns regularly involved in Russia's commercial interaction with the rest of the world. But just as much as merchant colonies could be a by-product of regular commercial exchange, the causality can run in the opposite direction as well. The commercial relationship between Muscovy and

Sweden offered instances of both types of colonies, in no small measure because of the periodic redrawing of boundaries which, during the period of Swedish expansion in the seventeenth century, left Russia – or at least Russian Orthodox – populations 'captive' on the Swedish side of the border. If we define merchant colonies as at least partially permanent populations actively engaged in trade, we can identify three main categories of Russian merchant communities in Sweden during the era of her regional supremacy.

The 'Swedish Russians'

The decades following the Livonian war were marked by a steady eastward push of Sweden into Karelia and the eastern Baltic. Most importantly, the Stolbovo peace treaty of 1617 led to a number of historically and ethnically Russian set-tlements coming under Swedish control. Of particular importance in this regard were the provinces of Ingria (Swedish: Ingermanland; Russian: Izhorskaia zemlia) and Kexholm (Russian: Korela; Finnish: Käkisalmi) that enveloped the eastern tip of the Gulf of Finland from the Estonian border to the Kare-lian Isthmus and Lake Ladoga. While many people fled the invading Swedish forces and the Time of Troubles exacted a considerable demographic toll on Novgorod's erstwhile north-western borderlands, substantial numbers of Rus-sians nonetheless stayed behind in the now Swedish-controlled territories. In some cases, their presence was actively encouraged by the new overlords eager to avoid the depopulation of strategically sensitive border areas while ensuring that they would continue to play a pivotal role in trade with Russia. In spite of subse-quent efforts to populate these territories with migrants from Finland, Sweden and elsewhere, in part through projects to charter new cities, these two Swedish provinces remained ethnically mixed until the Russians regained them in the eighteenth century and beyond.

'Russian Relatives'

Many of the Russian subjects of the Swedish Crown maintained relations with their relatives and acquaintances across the border, which since 1617 cut across or at least close to the Novgorodian heartlands. The Swedish realm now extended close to some of the leading and most ancient settlements of north-western Russia, ranging from Pskov and Novgorod in the south to Tikhvin, Ladoga and Olonets further north. The new political boundaries inevitably paid little heed to the structure and internal dynamics of the region's established ethnic communities. After the Stolbovo treaty, both sides of the border were settled by Russian Orthodox Karelians in eastern and south-eastern Finland and by a variety of (Orthodox) Finnic tribes and ethnic Russians in Ingria. These populations, in spite of the political division, continued to share their linguistic, cultural and religious communalities. During periods of relative political stability, which even during the bellicose century remained the norm, they continued to interact with each other across the border, as if nothing had changed, often disregarding the regulations imposed by their new overlords and sometimes forcing changes in them. This was made all the easier by the slow and often tentative imposition of Swedish administration and border control in the newly acquired territories. Merchants continued to frequent fairs and markets on both sides of the border and many of them led itinerant lives in the relatively sparsely populated areas, especially along the northern portions of the Swedish-Russian border. With time, even some of the new settlers from Finland and Sweden were drawn into these networks in a region where cross-border trade represented an important source of livelihood. This interaction, while it involved frequent visits, only gave rise to colonies in the loosest sense of the word. Rather, the largely virtual community it created should be viewed as an element of overlap between the now-divided but still culturally unified population inhabiting the region. The presence of friends and relatives on both sides of the border enabled lengthy stays as well as the consolidation of relationships through intermarriage.[2] Muscovite relatives hence became a way of bolstering, temporarily or permanently, the existing Russian Orthodox communities on the Swedish side of the border.

Russian Satellite Colonies

As Attman[3] in particular has argued, the Swedish great power built its economic might to a large extent by exploiting the strategic commercial advantages of the eastern Baltic coastal settlements that would continue to serve their geographic hinterlands regardless of political boundaries. This was particularly obvious in the case of Ingria where the river system flowing into the Gulf of Finland through Narva made the Pskov and Novgorod regions the natural hinterland of the newly Swedish-controlled littoral. The new foundation of Nyenskans/Nyen in the Neva estuary sought to replicate this model with respect to the Neva water system stretching from Karelia down the Volkhov and covering much of the old Novgorodian lands. But Sweden also actively sought to encourage regular Russian trade in other important cities, most notably the capital Stockholm, the Estonian capital Reval (Tallinn), and the Livonian emporium Riga.

The political aspirations underpinning this trade found a formal reflection in periodic treaties between the two neighbours and led to the creation of a physical infrastructure in the form of guest houses for Muscovite visitors, a policy that was broadly reciprocated in the Russian border towns. Government-sponsored facilities in the eastern Baltic ports were the earliest and the most salient cases of this. But ultimately, the single most impressive success story was the creation of the 'Russian Yard'(Ryssgården) in the royal capital Stockholm. This served boatmen from a number of leading north-western Russian settlements, most importantly Novgorod, Olonets, Tikhvin and Ladoga.

The creation of these facilities in turn enabled Russian visitors to establish an increasingly permanent presence in the leading Swedish commercial centres. Even though the residents of the guest houses varied over time, the large family ventures engaged in this trade often ensured that some of their representatives would reside in Sweden virtually all the time, albeit typically under fairly carefully controlled circumstances. By contrast, the presence of the vast majority of Russian visitors followed a seasonal pattern. This was particularly obvious in Stockholm where trade relied on shipping along the Gulf of Finland during the ice-free months of the spring, summer, and autumn.[4] In the sparsely populated north in Finland and Sweden, elaborate networks of rivers and lakes allowed Russian and Karelian pedlars to operate across a large territory in a way that paid little heed to political boundaries.[5]

The Ingrian Settlements

The Swedish expansion into Ingria during the Time of Troubles was accompanied by devastating destruction. However, in one important instance, namely Ivangorod, it left the conquerors in control of an important established urban and commercial centre. The Russian fortress in the Narova estuary had originally been established by the Muscovite Grand Duke Ivan III (who also lent it his name) in 1492 as a Russian alternative and rival to the Teutonic Narva which faced the Russian fort on the west bank of the river. This western bulwark of Muscovy received an important boost to its standing when Ivan IV – 'the Terrible' – sought to exploit the vacuum created by the disintegrating Livonian Order and in 1559 made the newly conquered Rugodiv – as he renamed Narva – a centre of Russian trade in the Baltic.[6] During the subsequent decades, the Narva-Ivangorod twin cities experienced dramatically changing fortunes without, however, ever really living up to the expectations of the alternating Russian and Swedish masters.

Throughout this era of at times extreme instability, Ivangorod remained a fairly modest settlement. Nonetheless, the 1617 census found that its population of 178 tax-paying citizens and thirty widows exceeded that of Narva.[7] Ivangorod's weight was further amplified by its position as a natural candidate to play a key role in the Swedish government's 'derivation' programme of diverting much Muscovite export trade to the Swedish-controlled eastern Baltic ports. Given Sweden's still-tenuous control over the region, as well as its modest fiscal resources (which the expected renaissance of Baltic trade was expected to rectify), the Russian-speaking residents of Ivangorod were naturally ideally suited for a key role in channelling and fuelling this commerce. A number of

Ivangorod's residents had relatives in the Novgorod region and especially in Pskov which enjoyed a convenient waterway connection with Narva through the Narova River and Lake Peipus. The main hurdle to realizing this undeniable potential was presented by Narva's open hostility towards its eastern twin from which it hoped to wrest this key responsibility. Moreover, many policy makers in Stockholm instinctively preferred to place their faith in a culturally and ethnically 'western' city, a tendency that gained currency after the conflicts of the mid-century when many Ivangorod citizens came to be viewed as traitors.[8]

This uneasy marriage – a fairly mature but culturally and ethnically Russian city flanked by one of the centres of the Swedish government's imperial aspirations – was virtually guaranteed to make for a tense relationship between the two neighbouring fortresses. Initially, Ivangorod enjoyed the support and sympathy of the central government which was not only eager to prevent further depopulation of the war-ravaged province, but in fact appears to have held a fairly favourable view of the abilities and potential of the local Russian population as agents of the derivation policy. Some leading policy makers in Stockholm in fact suggested that the Ingrian Russians might prove more useful to Sweden than the burghers of Narva. Urged on by the ever-pragmatic King Gustavus II Adolphus, formal measures were taken to protect the traditional rights and privileges of the Ingrian Russians.[9]

In terms of the legal standing of the two cities, the Swedish government's initial post-Stolbovo policy nonetheless represented a rather awkward compromise designed to cater to the needs and expectations of both Narva and Ivangorod, albeit without ultimately fully satisfying either. While Narva was granted the right of emporium vis-à-vis visiting western merchants, Ivangorod was to retain monopoly rights over trade with Russia. Naturally, without Russian trade, there would be no western visitors and, to an extent, vice versa. Thus, even if Narva could hope to better its fortunes by claiming a greater share of the trade flows passing down the Narova, it could only legally to do so if Ivangorod was allowed to prosper. Under the circumstances, establishing Narva's regional supremacy became a near-impossible task. The twins, if they were to succeed, had to do so together. Narva's challenge was further complicated by the reality of depressed trade flows in the wake of the Time of Troubles, which had wreaked considerable havoc on both sides of the border but especially on the economic heartland of the Novgorod region. By seventeenth-century standards, the era between the Time of Troubles and the Second Northern War was by far the worst for Russian-Swedish trade, a period marked by low trade volumes and at best very gradual normalization. However, key members of the Swedish administration still continued to feel sympathetic to Ivangorod. Governor General Bengt Oxenstierna of Livonia in 1637 suggested that no distinction should be drawn between 'Jews and Greeks' and characterized Ivangorodians as 'energetic and careful merchants'.[10]

As the century wore on, however, the mood in Stockholm began to shift, much to the delight of Narva and Reval alike, both of them determined to boost their standing at Ivangorod's expense, still convinced in the expectation that the derivation strategy would ultimately deliver handsome returns. The increasingly widely shared desire to foster the development of Narva, which some even envisioned as a second capital for the Swedish realm, fuelled steadily more predatory attitudes towards the Russian side of the river. Paradoxically, one of Ivangorod's chief liabilities in the eyes of Narva's political and commercial establishment was its relatively prosperous merchant community. In the first half of the century, Ivangorod had seven merchants with annual tax payments of 100–20 *Reichsthaler*. The corresponding figure in Narva was only four. The three Belousov brothers – Iakov, Pavel, and Petr – were of particular importance and had fortunes of several thousand roubles. The obviously unparalleled ability of Ivangorod's leading merchants to capitalize on their eastern ties further contributed to the mounting tensions. Incorporating this potential in Narva's own designs, or eliminating the competition it represented, was widely seen as a precondition for the city's eagerly anticipated economic take-off.[11]

Supported by the shift in the sentiment in Stockholm and having largely failed in its economic quest, Narva resorted to politics as the main weapon in its struggle for local supremacy. By the 1640s, Narva had launched a concerted push to make itself the sole centre of foreign trade in the Narova estuary. In 1640, the Narva City Council in fact received authorization to build a guest house for visiting Russian merchants, which blatantly violated the existing division of labour between the two neighbours. This concession effectively created the institutional basis for Narva supplanting its eastern neighbour and becoming the sole centre of international trade in the area. But this naturally still failed to properly address the awkward question of Ivangorod's statutory independence which had been previously guaranteed.[12]

The generally anti-Russian administration of Queen Christina increasingly willingly acquiesced to Narva's design to fully absorb its neighbour. A formal decision to unite Narva with Ivangorod was taken in December 1645 after a concerted campaign to assure Ivangorod's Russians that they would enjoy full citizenship rights in Narva.[13] But the stroke of a quill in Stockholm was slow to change the realities on the ground. The Ivangorodians' reaction to the new state of affairs was stubborn inaction. They stayed put, as if nothing had changed, seemingly assuming that the hitherto fickle government would once again change its position. Although the Russians were eventually given the deadline of January 1648 to move across the river, the process appears to have been belatedly completed only two years later in 1650. Even after the formalities were seemingly concluded, the de facto merger of the two communities proved extremely acrimonious. Narva's artisans flatly refused to recognize the qualifications of

their Ivangorod colleagues who were systematically marginalized and discriminated against. At the same time, the old predatory attitudes persisted with the
1655 Contribution roll including 320 Russian and only 115 other names.[14] The
end result of this unfortunate state of affairs seems to have been to erode Narva's
potential in Russian transit trade by significantly demoralizing and weakening
its key asset in this trade, i.e. Ivangorod's ethnically Russian population.

In spite of the statutory merger, hostility between the two Ingrian neighbours peaked during the 1656–8 war between Sweden and Russia when the
Muscovite rulers unsuccessfully sought to penetrate the Swedish Baltic barrier.
Against the backdrop of growing distrust of Sweden's Russian Orthodox borderland population, the eruption of an open military conflict quickly led to often
baseless accusations of many of them actively conspiring with the enemy. Many
of the Ivangorod Russians were subjected to drawn-out investigations after an
armistice was signed and, although nothing appears to have ever been proved,
the balance of power in the Ingrian twin city shifted markedly further in favour
of Narva. In spite of the growing tension and the effective disenfranchisement
of the Ivangorod Russians, Ivan III's creation received a new lease of life in 1657
when the new Russian suburb of Narva burnt down and the former Ivangorodians moved back home across the river. In spite of resistance by Narva, the
Swedish government accepted the fait accompli, undoubtedly due to the multi-
tude of more pressing priorities at a time of war.[15]

Even though the Russians of Ivangorod experienced a seemingly inexorable
decline in their influence in the second half of the century, the political climate
once again began to change in their favour after the abdication of Christina in
1654 and especially after the conclusion of peace. A confirmation of privileges
issued by King Charles XI to Narva's Russians in 1662 once again allowed them
to build houses on the Ivangorod side of the river, albeit only under the supervision of representatives of the city of Narva. Once again, however, consistency
eluded Swedish policy makers. Only four years later, the central government
once again called on the Russians to return to the northern suburb of Narva.
By that time, however, from a purely legal perspective the former Ivangorodians
appear to have been equals of the Germans and Swedes of Narva. But even as the
legal disputes eventually subsided, the years of conflict exacted a heavy toll on
the once- thriving merchant community. A 1674 report by the royal College of
Commerce in Stockholm noted that the Russians were of increasingly marginal
significance in attracting Muscovite traders to Narva, tending instead to trade
with pedlars from the adjacent Ingrian countryside. The college also demanded
that the Russians should return to their suburban plots in Narva, highlighting
the persistent difficulties of assimilating them into the urban fabric of Narva.[16]

By the time Narva embarked on its extraordinary economic renaissance in
the closing decades of the century, which for a short while turned it into one

of the leading points of Russian foreign trade, the once-so-proud and powerful merchant community of Ivangorod was a shadow of its former self. Even though Narva thus subdued its rival, the new economic – and political – climate at long last seemed to offer new opportunities even for Narva's Russians. Trade with the city's Novgorodian hinterland expanded dramatically and the economic relationship became increasingly well regulated and, at least compared with much of the preceding century, relatively tension free. Some ethnic Russians in fact now emerged as key players in Narva's economic renaissance. Thus for instance, Gerasim Kondrat'ev in 1696 set up a iuft' (also sometimes known as 'Russian leather') factory in Narva. He was granted a twenty-year monopoly of iuft' production in Narva and Ingria. Iuft' leather was one of the leading, most valuable and most sought-after exports of Narva in the seventeenth century and indeed one of the leading exports of Muscovy to Europe more generally. Iuft' exports through Narva by the 1690s could exceed 140,000 hides a year, whereas they had seldom risen to 20,000 during much of the preceding century.[17]

The story of the Neva port Nyen in many ways parallels that of Narva, although its origins were more recent and its development on the whole less impressive. The new city was established in the marshy lowlands of the Neva delta and represented one of the most ambitious elements of the Swedish government's diversion agenda. The area, contrary to the Pushkinian myth, was never deserted but rather, in spite of its somewhat inhospitable geography, consisted of a number of settlements by Finnic (but culturally Muscovite) Izhorians and Votes, as well as some Russians. By the early seventeenth century, the leading Russian settlement in the estuary was called – appropriately enough – Nevskoe ust'e, and the Swedish fortress of Nyenskans was built right next to it, at the confluence of the Neva and the Okhta, soon after the beginning of the Swedish incursion into Russia in 1611. In spite of its growing strategic significance, Nyen as a town remained a modest affair. The Swedish Mill Duty records put the total population at 294 in 1640 and 384 in 1642. Other sources provide roughly comparable estimates, although Prince Petr Ivanovich Potemkin in 1656 claimed that Nyen, taken together with its suburbs, had a population of 2,000–2,500 living in some 500 houses.[18]

The new settlement came to be known to the local and visiting Russians as 'Kantsy'. Although the city archive of Nyen has been lost, there is a great deal of evidence to suggest that the city's population not only included a number of Russians but that some of them were quite prominent members of the community. A customs roll of duties levied on merchants passing through the port in 1615 was compiled by a certain Afanasii Brazhnikov. The records reviewed by Carl von Bonsdorff for his 1891 seminal study on Nyen and Nyenskans offer little evidence of Russian names among the burghers of the young town. However, a handful of the names could well be distorted Russian names. Moreover, there are references to families such as Wenäläinen (Finnish for 'Russian') and it is possible that some of the former Muscovite subjects were listed by Finnish or Ingrian names. Records from the 1680s and 1690s contain unequivocally Russian names such as Antonij, Busbetskij, Hardeloff and Sergeioff. Igor' P. Shaskol'skii has located a total of forty-six names of Russian residents of Nyen in the second half of the century, something that compared with a total of 100 houses belonging to Swedish citizens in the town and its suburbs in 1691. Many of these seemingly Russian individuals are likely to have been former inhabitants of Nevskoe ust'e or their descendents. In generally, however, Nyen, even more than Narva, was subjected to deliberate colonization involving the arrival of people from elsewhere in the Swedish realm, most notably Finland. It is thus likely that local Russians would have been incorporated in the local elites only in relatively exceptional circumstances. The surviving two complete customs records for Swedish Nyen provide no conclusive evidence of local Russians being engaged in trade.[19] Although Nyen had a Russian population and, moreover, was flanked by a number of at least culturally Russian settlements, it seems certain that its ethnically Russian community was never comparable to that of Narva-Ivangorod. Nyen was a new foundation, an instrument of deliberate colonization policy in an area that was relatively sparsely populated, at least compared to the more established Novgorodian settlements further east and south. In fact, Nyen had a number of similarities with the other eastern Baltic port towns in as much as the concrete Russian presence was more due to visitors from the north-western Russian interior than the local population. Indeed, Nyen, as its eastern Baltic peers, over time created an infrastructure of warehouses for its Russian visitors who, over time, came to be quite numerous due to the growing importance of the Stockholm axis.

The Karelian Borderlands

The previously Russian settlements in the Swedish-controlled Kexholm province were significantly smaller than the Ingrian port towns. Korela-Kexholm (known nowadays as Priozersk) was the only truly historic city with proper fortifications at the time of the Swedish conquest. In spite of its strategic significance at the point where the Vuoksen (Finnish: Vuoksi; Russian: Vuoksa) River emptied its waters into Lake Ladoga, it was a modest settlement with an estimated population of perhaps 1,000, with some 150 burghers and 125 others recorded in 1697. The Kexholm province as a whole had some 45,000 residents after the conclusion of the Stolbovo peace treaty. Most of them were clearly ethically or culturally Russian. However, the Swedish assimilation and colonization policy was applied just as enthusiastically in the old Korela lands as it was in Ingria. Its most concrete, and on the whole lasting, expression involved a number of attempts to charter regional towns as centres for trade and handicrafts.

Sordavala in the north-western corner of Lake Ladoga was the most notable and successful of these ventures. Most of the new settlements tended to be popu- lated by migrants from Finland and Sweden, although they naturally adapted to the ethnically and culturally mixed area in spite of the steady progress of the ethno-cultural transformation. In fact, cross-border trade with Russia eventually received a major impetus from the emigration of some of the Kexholm Province's Russian residents to Muscovy during times of conflict. Many of them continued to trade with their contacts on the Swedish side of the border.[20]

There were few other substantial settlements on the Swedish side of the border that cut through Lake Ladoga, leaving its north-eastern corner under Muscovite control. This Russian quarter, however, was home to Olonets (Finn- ish/Karelian: Aunus), a rapidly developing centre of commerce and handicrafts. Located close to the Swedish border on the northern shore of Lake Ladoga, it had long-standing ties with the Korela lands. The role of Olonets was boosted significantly by the construction in 1649 of a border fortress to protect the area from a possible Swedish attack. By the 1670s, Olonets – along with its suburbs – is estimated to have had over 700 houses. An estimate from 1700 puts the figure at some 600. The city's total population is thought to have been around 4,000. It was thus a sizeable regional centre, not only by Russian standards but also as compared to the towns on the Swedish side of the border. Olonets had a number of prosperous townsmen who frequented fairs across northern and even central Russia and thus could competitively supply their clients and business partners in Swedish-controlled Karelia with a wide range of goods. For many of them, Olo- nets was of greater economic importance than the Swedish Karelian regional centres, whether Kexholm, Viborg, or others. Olonets also became an increas- ingly important player in the trade with Stockholm.[21]

But with time, the influence of these Russians waned in Swedish-controlled Karelia, much as it did in Narva-Ivangorod. Following the outbreak of war in 1656, the Orthodox population of the Kexholm Province in many cases wel- comed the Muscovite armies as liberators from religious oppression and actively supported them during the campaigns in the Karelian Isthmus and on the north- ern shores of Lake Ladoga. There were some rebellions even further inland. A large-scale exodus of Orthodox Karelians eventually accompanied the retreating Russian armies and many of them settled in the Tver' region, never to return. A dialect of the Karelian language survives in these communities to this day. The abandoned areas were resettled by Finns, who naturally lacked kinship rela- tions in Russia. However, as much as this may have hurt cross-border trade in the immediate post-war era, the newcomers seem to have quickly recognized the economic opportunities offered by trade, a process much facilitated by lack of linguistic differentiation in the largely Karelian-speaking region.[22]

Also Sweden's oldest bulwark in the east, Viborg (Finnish: Viipuri; Russian: Vyborg) was an active participant in Russian trade even if commerce with its erstwhile Novgorodian hinterland was virtually entirely diverted to Narva and Nyen. Nonetheless, there is sporadic evidence to suggest that Russian goods continued to the flow to the city. Moreover, it received at least a small number of visiting Russian merchants virtually every year, although quite probably not enough to create the basis for even a temporary Russian settlement in the city.[23] More generally, the fairs of eastern Finland were regularly frequented by Russian visitors, some of them from as far away as Arkhangelsk.[24]

The northernmost parts of the Swedish realm remained very sparsely populated throughout the century but even there the government did undertake some strategically important ventures to foster settlement and to stimulate and better organize regional trade. The most important urban settlements were Torneå (Tornio), Uleåborg (Oulu) and Kajaneborg (Kajaani). Uleåborg was the oldest and most important of these foundations, having been chartered in 1605. Torneå followed in 1621 and Kajaneborg in 1651. It is unlikely that any of them ever had full-time Russian inhabitants. Indeed, the local authorities fairly consistently took pains to keep Muscovite visitors out for security reasons as well as in order to protect the privileges of their fledgling bourgeoisie who took decades to properly establish themselves. It is evident, however, that Russian and Karelian merchants regularly travelled across northern Finland and even Sweden. They were almost invariably seen at annual fairs of the region's towns. In fact some regional administrators, most notably Count Per Brahe, made active efforts to attract Russian merchants to these events. For some of the new towns in the Finnish interior, visiting Russian merchants were seen as a means of reducing their dependency on the burghers of the more prosperous coastal towns, especially Uleåborg. However, Swedish policy, much as in the eastern Baltic, frequently vacillated between liberal tendencies and protectionism, as a result of which the Russian presence grew gradually over time but never really flourished to its true potential.[25]

Much of Finnish Ostrobothnia and Lapland is naturally linked with Russian Karelia. The cities of Torneå and Uleåborg are located at the estuaries of important river systems originating in the eastern borderlands of the Swedish realm. They hence offered easy transportation opportunities for the itinerant Russian trader. In the context of the small northern towns and rural settlements, these eastern pedlars were often of critical importance for the local economy, something that allowed this tradition to continue into the twentieth century. There is little to suggest that the scale or structure of this commerce evolved much over the centuries. As modest as the scale of their business was, the Russian travellers effectively tied the small fledgling settlements of northern Finland into Arkhangelsk's sphere of influence. Even west European goods, brought to the White Sea by the Dutch and the English, were regularly found in the bags of these visitors.[26] Whatever permanent presence these merchants had in Finland is unlikely to have extended beyond the immediate border region and the occasional marriages, not enough to call them a merchant colony, except in a temporary sense due to the regular annual cycle of their travels.

Russians Beyond the Borderlands

The above discussion has demonstrated that the history of Russian communities in seventeenth-century Sweden was by and large a story of gradual but seemingly inexorable decline. Active discrimination and deliberate assimilation policies made it increasingly difficult for Ingrian and Karelian Russians to remain competitive against their increasingly numerous Swedish neighbours. The wars of the mid-century were in all cases used as an attempt to further disenfranchise the community through allegations of treason and subsequent investigations. The deliberate colonization of the newly acquired territories, if anything, made it even more difficult for the Russians to maintain a competitive advantage in the rapidly evolving commercial landscape. Increasingly, therefore, the Russian presence in Sweden came to be linked to institutional and regulatory drivers, deliberate attempts on the part of the Swedish authorities to use economic policy as a way of attracting Muscovite visitors to the kingdom. The attitude towards the Russians, while almost never fully consistent, was dramatically different when it was dictated by commercial, as opposed to security, policy.

Outside of the ethnically mixed border regions, attempts to attract a steady influx of Russian visitors were particularly notable in the cases of Reval,[27] where they were increasingly frustrated over time, and Riga where some progress did ultimately materialize albeit after a lengthy period of stagnation and largely independently of the policy measures undertaken by the Swedish authorities.[28] The Russians were naturally drawn to the Düna/Dvina estuary by its unparalleled stature as a leading centre of international trade in the Swedish realm. However, until the closing decades of the century, they tended to be almost exclusively overland travellers from Pskov. Their numbers were limited by the modest facilities for trade and the inauspicious conditions created by the Livonian merchants and the Swedish administrators alike.[29] It is unlikely that much more than twenty Russians stayed in Riga at any one time and probably never more than fifty during a given season. Attempts to formalize trade with Pskov were made in the second half of the century, particularly under a project by Riga burgher Adolf Lüders and Friedrich Wesseling which was approved in 1676. Under the arrangement Lüders spent a decade in Pskov to manage the trade which never really delivered on the expectations placed on it.[30]

The closing decades of the seventeenth century, however, at long last came to see a dramatic shift in the orientation of Riga's Russian trade. The role of

Pskov became secondary, partly because the city oriented its external commercial interaction increasingly to Narva. By contrast, a new opportunity for Riga's trade with Russia emerged with the return of the Smolensk region under Russian control in the 1660s. The Principality of Smolensk was a nationally important producer of hemp and timber which had historically found their leading export market in Riga. Logically, the Russian government made deliberate attempts in the closing decades of the century to foster the development of the region by fostering its exports of these key naval stores to the Baltic coast. Shipping to Riga became regularized by the 1670s. The scale and logistics of the trade increasingly necessitated protracted stays by visiting Russians in Riga and it is likely that a semi-permanent community emerged by the end of the century. However, its overall size is unlikely to have been much more than a handful of people and its membership at least to a large extent revolving and seasonal. By the 1690s, Russian barges accounted for 5–10 per cent of total shipping on the lower Düna.[31]

The history of Ryssgården in Stockholm – the cluster of guest houses deliberately built for visiting Muscovite merchants – represents one of the most impressive successes of the political diversion agenda. Russian merchants were brought to the Swedish capital by a combination of regulation and demand, not by any obvious geographic advantage or kinship ties. The eventual creation of the 'Russian Yard' in the late 1630s was part of the general progress of institutionalizing commercial exchange on the basis of formal agreements entered into in peace treaties.[32] Relatively soon, Stockholm was attracting a steadily growing stream of visiting boatmen from Novgorod, Tikhvin, Olonets, Ladoga and other smaller settlements. Eventually even some central Russian merchants from Iaroslavl', Moscow, and smaller towns eventually joined in on these trips.[33]

It was quite obviously the scale of the commercial exchange, the distances involved and the accommodation as well as storage facilities that eventually allowed the visiting north-western Russian merchants to operate in the Swedish capital on a more or less permanent basis. One of the regular Stockholm travellers, a Novgorod merchant by the name of Semen Stoianov, claimed that total customs duties paid by Russian visitors in 1645 totalled 5,000 roubles. By April 1648, some fifteen Novgorod merchants were said to be trading in the Swedish capital on a regular basis. Many of them travelled with massive cargoes worth 2,000–4,000 roubles, which almost certainly necessitated a semi-permanent local presence of agents.[34] Stockholm was a particularly attractive venue for trade because it gave the visitors access to the exceptional mineral wealth of central Sweden, most notably its iron and copper which found a ready market in Muscovy that had effectively no metal mining of its own at the time. The strategic significance of these purchases was amplified by the strong demand for them on the part of Russia's military industry.[35]

Russian operations in Stockholm continued their steady expansion towards the end of the century. A June 1661 report puts the number of Novgorod merchants active in the Swedish capital at twenty-two. The number of their Tikhvin counterparts was a comparable twenty-one in 1662. Twenty Tikhvin merchants journeyed to the Swedish capital in 1685, thirty-one in 1687, forty in 1688, and thirty-four in 1690. According to a June 1663 account by visiting Olonets merchants, twenty-five of them had at least occasional contact with Stockholm. A customs official, Ivan Dolgii, in 1690 reported that Olonets merchants annually exported 200,000 roubles' worth (almost certainly a significant exaggeration) of various goods to Sweden on at least twenty vessels.[36] The extraordinary dimensions that Russian trade with Stockholm eventually attained become evident from a September 1700 report by a Russian resident in Sweden, Prince Andrei Khilkov. According to him, there were 150 Russian merchants, with total cargoes valued at some 100,000 roubles, waiting to get royal passes for their return trips to Russia. Another 150 merchants on 16 vessels had already left earlier during the season carrying goods worth 200,000 roubles. Olonets merchants Ananii Shablin and Lazar Anan'ev claimed that the value of the wares confiscated by the Swedish authorities totalled some 300,000 roubles.[37] These were large sums, comparable to the total volume of trade in Arkhangelsk in the second half of the century and, even allowing for some inaccuracy, suggest that the Russian commercial presence in the Swedish capital had reached large proportions and a high degree of sophistication.

Drivers of Russian Presence

The Russian presence in Ingria and Karelia was due to geographic and historical factors. Swedish policy, with some exceptions, sought to contain these culturally 'divergent' border communities and concerted efforts were made to better incorporate the annexed territories in the Swedish realm and to assimilate them through active discrimination and colonization. The result of these actions was the same everywhere: the Russian presence declined in relative – probably also absolute – numbers and above all in influence. Both the Time of Troubles and the wars of the 1650s resulted in the permanent departure of large numbers of Russians, most of whom never returned. In spite of these negative tendencies, however, the Russian communities never disappeared altogether. The Swedish borderlands remained ethnically mixed and, of course, the balance was ultimately reversed to a degree after the reincorporation of these territories in the Russian Empire.

Beyond the borderlands, the Russian presence was inevitably conditional on regulatory and institutional factors that made it possible for Russian merchants to safely and profitably operate in the Swedish interior. While derivation was an overriding theme in Swedish commercial policy throughout the century, the practical aspects of the Swedish treatment of visiting Russian merchants varied a great deal in the course of this turbulent century. As much as Swedish-Russian diplomatic negotiations consistently recognized the need for appropriate regulation and suitable accommodation and storage facilities, the implementation of these aspirations was often slow and inconsistent. The end result of such prevarication and inconsistency, whose effects were amplified by periodic open conflict between the two countries, was a relatively limited and even discontinuous Russian presence in the main commercial centres of the Swedish realm. Positive trends were seen during periods of early modern 'détente', most notably during the 'First Baltic Boom' of the 1640s and early 1650s and again in the closing decades of the century. But there were times when Swedish or local Baltic German hostility and a lack of appropriate infrastructure quickly reversed this momentum. Nonetheless, as reflected by the broader ambitions of the Swedish derivation policy, the arguments for such trade were compelling and this ultimately made it remarkably resilient in the face of adversity. As much as periods of decline and growth alternated, the regular flow of goods and the emergence of commercial networks were never completely interrupted.

One of the most concrete expressions of the derivation ambitions was the mutual commitment made at the Stolbovo peace talks to actively foster trade through the establishment of proper guest houses in all the important border points in Sweden and Russia alike.[38] This reality repeated itself in the 1650s and early 1660s in Valiesaar and Kardis.[39] However, progress always proved very slow, in reflection, to be sure, of the invariably very gradual post-war recovery and the limited resources of the Swedish and Russian treasuries. But it was also clear that the notion of semi-permanent communities of visiting merchants from a potentially hostile neighbour was not welcome to all, not least due to security considerations. Using merchants as spies was a common activity in the early modern era, and indeed thereafter.

A revealing example of the inconsistencies of Swedish policies was the Livonian port of Riga which, although it was only conquered by the Swedes in 1621, was the pre-eminent port of the kingdom for much of the seventeenth century. At least in principle, therefore, Riga constituted a major magnet for merchants from north-western Russia, a city where they could expect strong demand for their wares and – at least by regional standards – ample availability of credit. In practice, however, the process of enabling Russian visitors to operate in Riga proved slow and cumbersome. Although the Riga Magistrate had made it possible for Muscovite visitors to stay with individual burghers as early as 1612, the plans to create a proper guest house for them dragged on. The first mention of such a house dates from 1642 and it may have begun operations as late as 1648. However, it was a very modest facility and located outside of the city walls, which in practice made it very difficult for Russians to visit the city to claim outstanding debts etc. The housemaster Jürgen Strieß seems to have been almost legendary for his high-handed behaviour with repeated charges of ill treatment of the Russian visitors.[40] As was noted above, a proper take-off in Riga's trade with Muscovy had to await the closing decades of the century, by which time it had little to do with the Muscovite House.

Attempts to replicate this model in Reval resulted in minimal and very discontinuous progress during the century and Russian trade in the Estonian capital would typically only thrive when government policy actively discriminated against Narva or security considerations made it difficult to operate there. During the closing years of the century, Reval benefited from some spillover of Narva's trade. The only other guest house venture of significance was Ryssgården in Stockholm. The idea of creating a Russian commercial hub in the Swedish capital was endorsed in the 1617 Stolbovo peace treaty but its implementation had to await a renewed plea by Tsar Mikhail Feodorovich in 1635. The new Russian Yard, in the guise of twenty-one temporary wooden huts only opened its doors two decades after the initial agreement in 1641. Although its inception was significantly delayed, its evolution proved much more remarkable than that of its inadequate counterparts elsewhere in the realm. From the beginning, Ryssgården was fairly impressive by the standards of the time, clearly larger than the guest houses established at other border points, whether in Russia or in Sweden. It was composed of twenty permanent cabins and twelve wooden ones but the numbers steadily increased to seventy-four by 1654. Over time, the facility was restructured and rebuilt a number of times. Also the location of the yard was enviable, right across a narrow sound from the main city island in Stockholm on the northern shore of the suburb of Södermalm.[41] If trade on the Nyen-Stockholm axis ultimately evolved into one of the great success stories of the Swedish derivation policy, this was at least in large measure because Stockholm was the only major city in the kingdom to possess an adequate infrastructure for this trade.

Conclusion

The history of Russians in seventeenth-century Sweden is a story that proceeded in fits and starts as a result of inconsistent and even conflicting policy impulses and priorities in Stockholm and among the regional administrators. The ambitious derivation policy logically sought to actively foster the numbers of Russian visitors and, for this reason, to improve the infrastructure supporting them. The triumph of reason over inertia and short-term opportunism was, however, far from convincing and, moreover, frequently reversed. Ultimately this meant that the Russian presence in Sweden underwent a considerable structural transformation in the course of the seventeenth century. At the beginning of the century, the Russians of the newly conquered territories of Ingria and Karelia constituted a bridge – indeed the key connection – to their friends, relatives and business partners in the Novgrodian lands and the Pskov region.

Over time, however, the numbers and importance of these 'indigenous' Russians declined and Swedish-Russian commercial interaction came to depend more and more heavily on the government's trade policy and the facilities created for Muscovite Russian visitors in Riga, Stockholm and Narva. The economic renaissance of the Novgorod lands contributed to this process by giving Russian merchants the means to operate over longer distances and on a grander scale. By contrast, the German, Swedish and English burghers of Narva supplanted their once-so-important Russian brethren in Ivangorod as the key counterparties of Russian merchants in south-western Ingria. A similar pattern played out in Nyen which was one of the leading lights of the Swedish colonization and derivation policies alike. Riga's revival in Russian trade was above all driven be the reincorporation of the Smolensk lands into Muscovy and the dramatic take-off of hemp and timber trade on the Düna/Dvina route. However, the ultimate success of this trade had little to do with the largely unsuccessful earlier efforts to attract Pskov merchants to Riga.

But as much as the derivation policy ultimately triumphed, only to be reduced to nothing by the onset of the Great Northern War, it made the economically most significant Russian communities in Sweden into carefully controlled enclaves of recurrent visitors. Even though the scale of these colonies was such that a number of their representatives would spend extended periods in Sweden, there was no realistic prospect of integration. These Russians remained foreigners, some of them very familiar with Sweden, but never allowed to properly settle there. The religious differences alone, which tended to be strictly enforced, offered no opportunity for even marginal integration. Ultimately, the two categories of Russian presence in Sweden converged: the borderland communities of ethnic Russians became enfeebled and disenfranchised as their numbers dwindled and economic standing declined. The clusters of visiting merchants grew, but never attained a significant scale or truly permanent nature.

6 FOREIGN MERCHANT COMMUNITIES IN EIGHTEENTH-CENTURY RUSSIA

Victor N. Zakharov

Introduction

It is well known that in early modern time so-called colonies of foreign merchants developed in different parts of the world market and played a great role in organizing trade ties between west European countries and other regions of Europe. Russia was no exception to this process. In the Middle Ages Hanseatic merchants operated in Novgorod, while in fourteenth-century Moscow there appeared a corporation of *gosti-surozhane* (Surozh merchants), which included merchants of Greek and Italian origin.[1] When the northern port of Arkhangelsk was founded in the sixteenth century, English, Dutch and Hamburg merchants used it to access the Russian market. Besides, Russia had long-standing trade relations with its neighbours in the south-west, south and south-east, causing groups of merchants to form from Balkan countries, the Middle East, central and south Asia in different towns and regions of Russia. There were Indians in Astrakhan', Bukhara traders in south-western Siberia and Astrakhan', as well as Greeks, the most numerous colonies of whom were in Nezhin (Ukraine), and Armenians trading in many places such as Astrakhan', Moscow, Arkhangelsk and Taganrog.

What would we call these groups of foreign merchants? In western European tradition such associations of tradesmen far away from their native land are usually called 'colonies'. In Russian sources and historiography, this term is rarely used in relation to foreigners living in Russia. Moreover in modern Russian, colonies are countries incorporated into empires and depending on other states. For example, India, Kenya, Nigeria and many other nations used to be British colonies; Brazil was a Portuguese colony and Indonesia was a colony of the Netherlands.

If groups of foreigners in this or that country are called colonies, it means a restricted and homogeneous character of their outer and inner relations. However in due course this restricted character of the ties became loose and along with homogeneous relations, heterogeneous ones were also inevitably established, together with various degrees of assimilation into the country of residence. The focus of this paper is the foreign merchants trading in Russia in the eighteenth century, the time when these processes were under way. Hence the term 'colony' in reference to the mentioned foreign merchants is not quite correct. The term more preferable to us seems 'community' (*obschina*) which to a greater degree corresponds to Russian terminology and better describes the inner organization and outer contacts of foreign traders in Russia.

While this introduction to the discussion of foreign communities in Russia concerns mainly terminology, the main task of the paper is to investigate the organization and status of foreign merchants in eighteenth-century Russia, addressing the organizational and legal status of their groupings and differences in organization and degree of unity of different national groupings of merchants. It is also important to consider how the principles of organization of foreign communities had changed in comparison with earlier times. The final focus of our attention will be on the composition of communities, examining their homogeneous or heterogeneous character from the angle of their kinship ties, ethnicity and contacts with the native land and world market.

It is natural that groups of foreign merchants in Russia, as in other countries, were formed on the homeland basis, i.e. these were the communities of compatriot merchants of identical national origin. This study is concerned with the western European merchants who played the principal role in providing the necessary ties for Russia's sea trade in the west, which was the most significant economically and in turnover for the country in the period.

Foreign Trade Communities in Russia in the Middle Ages and Early Modern Times (Twelfth–Sixteenth Centuries)

Russia has been involved in world trade since the earliest times, not only through Russian merchants called *gosti* – literally, 'guests' – who travelled abroad, but also through foreign merchants trading in Russian territory and uniting, as a rule, in special groups depending on their origin. Such groups emerged for a number of reasons. Firstly, foreigners were far from their homeland and needed security, legalization of their abode in another country and guaranteed rights to trade. This was achieved by agreement with local authorities who, in their turn, preferred to deal with an organization and not with individual merchants. To serve the same purpose treaties could be concluded between the governments of the country of origin and the country of residence of a trade corporation, which also influenced its status. Secondly, in a foreign country merchants might not find the forms and means of organizing trade activity to which they were accustomed because often the market was less developed than in their own country. Thus, within their corporations foreigners would often use the traditional customs, trade practices and the legal norms of their countries. Thirdly, foreign merchants incorporated into communities maintained close ties with their mother country, being the 'vanguard' of its business world and stimulating its trade development and advance to other states and continents. The last circumstance acquired special significance in early modern history when the trading capitals of some European countries (first of all the Netherlands) succeeded in extending their activity and exploring more and more new markets, an issue of special interest in present-day historiography, notably in the works of Jan Willem Veluwenkamp.[2]

Thus, foreign merchants in Russia acted, as a rule, within the limits of a certain corporation that had its structure and legal status. In the Middle Ages and early modern times the structure and legal status of a foreign corporation were very clearly fixed. A good example is the Hanseatic League trading in Russia between the twelfth and fifteenth centuries, mainly in Novgorod, where the Hanseatic office (*Kontor*) was located. Hanseatic activity was regulated by a special charter known as *Skra*, resolutions of Hanseatic meetings and trade treaties between Novgorod and Hanse. It was strictly prohibited for Hanseatic merchants to join Dutch, Flemish and Danish companies.[3] German merchants arriving in Novgorod were housed in specially built yards (German and Gott) surrounded by a tall, solid-timbered wall. Up to 100 and more German merchants arrived in Novgorod annually. All of them constituted a community with a fairly well-developed and complex structure of governance. The most important issues affecting the community were discussed at the general meeting of all merchants and the decisions taken were recorded in a special book. The community was headed by *oldermen* (seniors or aldermen) of the German yard, elected by the merchants themselves or appointed by the commissioners of the Hanseatic League cities. The *oldermen* ensured the observance of the established order, collected fines in case of its breakage, judged quarrels between German merchants, contacted, if necessary, the Novgorod authorities and took care of common interests. The community was also kept united by religion: the centre of religious life of Hanseatic merchants in Novgorod was St Peter's Church in the German yard.

Although all Hanseatic merchants in Novgorod acted as members of one corporation, each traded for his own profit. Thus, the Hanseatic merchant community was by no means a trade company; rather, it was a union of independent traders.

Hanseatic merchants in Novgorod maintained contacts with their home cities. They did not really live in Russia but visited in summer to negotiate deals and then returned home. Thus, correspondingly, corporations of merchants in continual contact with Novgorod appeared in some Hanseatic cities. The most famous of these was in the main Hanseatic city of Lübeck where the merchants who traded with Russia constituted a group named *Novgorodfahrer* (literally, 'the ones travelling to Novgorod').

The sixteenth century was a time of great change in the western direction of Russian trade. Hanse's trade was in decline and its merchants had to surrender to their competitors, who were mainly Dutch and English. Here the role of the comparatively new port of Narva acquired a special significance in the development of Russia's trading ties via the Baltic Sea. Since Narva was not part of the Hanseatic League, it was chosen by the English and Dutch as the main platform for their trading activity in the east Baltic region. In the second half of the sixteenth century Russia also began to trade with west European countries across the White Sea, mostly with the Dutch, English and then Hamburg merchants. It should be noted that though Hamburg was a member of the Hanseatic League, its representatives were not very active in trading with Novgorod across the Baltic Sea. In the sixteenth century when the Hanseatic League became weak they began to act independently in northern Russia.

Thus, new groups of foreign merchants appeared in Russia, notably English, Dutch and Hamburg traders. They constituted their own communities or corporations, though with different processes. English merchants, for example, set up a separate company with a degree of formal status in England in the mid-sixteenth century. It united the merchants trading with Russia and was first entitled the Muscovy Company and then the Russian Company. Unlike the community of Hanseatic merchants trading in the Middle Ages in Novgorod, the English Muscovy Company was a joint-stock company whose members contributed their shares to the cumulative capital of the company. Like a number of other companies formed in England in that time for the purpose of trading in different regions of the world, the Muscovy Company obtained a monopoly on trade between England and Russia. The company was chartered on 6 February 1555, by King Phillip and Queen Mary.[4]

The charter decreed that to ship goods to Russia, English merchants must join the company. Should anybody dare to trade with Russia without membership, his goods and ships would be confiscated, half the confiscated property becoming the income of none other than the Muscovy Company. The Muscovy Company was well structured, being headed by a board or council consisting of two governors, four consuls and twenty-four assistants. The Council developed the company charter, while sergeants executed its decisions and controlled the observance of the company's rights of and its privileges.[5]

The right of the Muscovy Company to trade in Russia was also guaranteed by the Moscow government in charters granted to the company on behalf of Russian tsars. Ivan Groznyi was the first who gave this kind of permission; subsequently these charters were invariably confirmed during the reigns of Feodor Ioannovich, Boris Godunov and Michael Feodorovich. Of course, the representatives of other countries could also trade in Russia, but among English merchants only the members of the Muscovy Company had this right. The charters granted by Russian tsars to the English company guaranteed its members a variety of trading privileges. English merchants could trade both in the seaport of Arkhangelsk and in internal Russian cities, which they profited from actively, having arranged their yards in Moscow, Yaroslavl, as well as in Vologda, where they had obtained a permit to build a rope factory. Members of the company were released from duty payments.

Unlike England, the Netherlands had no agreements with Russia about privileges for their merchants acting on the Russian market. There was no company in the Netherlands that had been especially created for trade with Russia and possessing monopoly rights. Any local merchant could travel to Russia on business, but to penetrate the Russian home market individual merchants had to obtain a personal charter from the Russian tsar. Merchants from Hamburg penetrating into the Russian market shared the same opportunities and challenges.

Under such circumstances, it was difficult for individuals to run their business, which is why they established regular contacts within their community. These could be constant relations of partnership, kinship and other mutual relations of a private nature. Jan Willem Veluwenkamp attributes much of the Dutch merchants' success in Russia at the time to this stability of individual and family contacts.[6] In many families the business passed from generation to generation, resulting in a long and stable existence for the company. For nearly two centuries representatives of several generations of the same Dutch families acted in Russia. These were the Houtmans (three generations), Swellengrebels (four generations) and de Boes (five generations), etc.[7]

Thus, at the beginning of the early modern times, there were two basic types of organizations of foreign merchant communities in Russia. The first type retained many medieval features and included the British Russian Company, an organization in which it is easy to trace some characteristics typical of the corporation of Hanseatic merchants operating in Novgorod in the twelfth to fifteenth centuries. These characteristics are as follows: detailed regulation of activity on the basis of the companies' inner charters, statutory acts of the mother countries and governmental agreements with Russian authorities; accurate criteria of belonging to a community that was caused first of all by an affiliation with the trading world of this or that country; exclusive (up to monopoly) trading rights in Russia.

The Dutch and Hamburg merchants beginning to penetrate into Russia in late sixteenth and early seventeenth centuries were organized in somewhat different ways. This type of organization was characterized by the absence of any formal associations or defined legal status but is compensated for by the presence of fairly strong informal family relations and business ties within the community.

What was to be the destiny of the two types of organizations and forms of foreign commercial activity in Russia in the eighteenth century, when the country's foreign trade had considerably expended and undergone essential modernization?

Russian (Muscovy) Company of English Merchants in Eighteenth-Century Russia

It is evident that the exclusive position of English merchants displeased other foreign businessmen as well as Russian large-scale business merchants who repeatedly complained to the government about abuses suffered in dealings with members of the Muscovy Company. These complaints had an effect from the middle of the seventeenth century.

In 1650 having yielded to the Russian merchants' insistent requests, and on the pretext of the execution of Charles I, the government of Tsar Alexey Mikhailovich deprived English merchants of their privileges. They had to leave Moscow and other inland Russian cities to trade only in border ports, of which Arkhangelsk was the only one.[8] As a result, in the second half of the seventeenth century English trade in Russia fell into decay and membership of the British Russian Company sharply declined. But, as previously, still no other foreign merchants had the same statutory right to trade in Russia. This situation lasted until the end of the seventeenth century. England's participation in the War of the Spanish Succession and her demand for naval stores stimulated the commercial activities of English merchants in Russia. In 1698 the English Parliament passed a bill to simplify the access to the British Russian Company. It was enough to pay £5 to become a member.[9]

By this time, the company had completely lost its status of a closed exclusive association and turned into an open society of businessmen accessible to all interested persons. It wasn't the company on an equal footing (later to be called a joint-stock company). Since then it has been characterized in historical literature as regular company, which means an association of independently operating businessmen or trading firms consisting of two or three partners.[10] The only company requirement remaining as defined as early as the mid-sixteenth century was the condition that access to trade with Russia remained exclusive to members of the company. On the Russian side, the privileges granted to members in the sixteenth century by the Russian government were no longer valid. However, one should not forget that the English had an important advantage when competing with other foreigners. This was Cromwell's Navigation Act of 1651, which continued until the mid-nineteenth century. On the basis of this Act, goods could be delivered to England from other countries only on British ships or on the ships of those countries where these goods originated. As Russia did not own a merchant fleet, it could trade with England only by using English merchant ships. This severely restricted the opportunities of Dutch and Hamburg merchants, who were mainly occupied with delivering goods made in the third party countries.

Thus, the opening of access to the British Russian Company to practically all comers under the conditions of the 1651 Navigation Act considerably increased the number of British businessmen in Russia during the reign of Peter I. In 1693 in Arkhangelsk there were no English merchants at all, though some of them traded through Narva. There is evidence of as many as fourteen British merchants trading in Arkhangelsk in 1710 and twenty-three – both in Arkhangelsk and newly built St Petersburg – in 1719.[11]

Simultaneously the goods turnover of English merchants grew rapidly. According to Walter Kirchner's estimates, during the period from 1695 to 1735, it multiplied six times over, surpassing the total turnover of English merchants from other countries.[12] It is important to underline that this advantage was reached by Englishmen in the absence of any privileges granted by the Russian government. But as early as the second third of the eighteenth century British diplomacy was actively striving to regain the grant of privileges for their merchants in Russia – and succeeding.

In 1734 a trade treaty between Russia and Great Britain also gave English merchants in Russia considerable benefits in comparison to other merchants. They could pay duties not in foreign but in Russian currency. The duty for the English traders importing the most important of English goods – cloth – was reduced by a third. They fell under the jurisdiction of the Collegium of Commerce (*Commertz collegia*), while other foreign merchants were under the supervision of municipal administrative bodies where judicial cases were considered for lengthy periods – and mostly decided in favour of Russian merchants, as the latter were very influential in such bodies.

The 1734 treaty also granted British merchants the right to trade with Iran via Russian territory.[13] Most of these privileges (except the right to trade with Iran) were confirmed by subsequent agreements between Russia and England during the whole of the eighteenth century. Yet these privileges, of course, were not as great as those granted to English merchants in the sixteenth century, which had been typical of the Middle Ages and the early modern times when it was important for foreign businessmen to settle themselves in new markets and maintain and develop trade in unusual conditions. Excluding the soon-to-be-abolished right of transit trade with Iran, these later privileges were mostly concessions in taxation to enable a decrease in trading costs and increase in profits in accordance with an age where monetary principles predominated.

It should also be noted that the idea of 'most favoured nations' became one of the basic in the Russian–British agreement of 1734. Article 28 of the agreement says: 'It is understood between the High Contracting Parties, that the subjects of each shall always be considered and treated as the most favoured nation ... '.[14] It was a new principle of mutual relations between the states first formulated in the agreement between England and Spain in 1715, though this did not address customs regulation directly.[15] At the heart of the 'most favoured nations' idea lies the principle of mutually advantageous relations between the countries. In fact, the activity of English merchants benefited Russians more than dealers from other countries. The English purchased Russian goods in great amounts, giving Russia a positive balance of foreign trade. In the 1730s exports from England to Russia averaged £49,000 sterling a year, while exports from Russia to England constituted £283,000 sterling a year.[16] As a result, more than £200,000 sterling annually arrived on the Russian capital markets. England particularly needed iron and 'naval stores' from Russia. Hence, both parties were eager to give preference to the other in the foreign trade policy, leading to the Russian government considering England as a 'favoured nation' and granting its merchants corresponding privileges. Similar privileges would have been granted to Russian merchants in England, but, in fact, few of them were there. In any case, the rights guaranteed to the members of the British Russian Company under the Act of 1734 distinguished them favourably from other foreign businessmen. It strengthened the special status of the British merchants in Russia, making company membership attractive.

Who were the members of this company in Russia? Obviously, those British citizens who paid the entrance fee and acquired the right to conduct trading operations in the Russian market. Early eighteenth-century Russian sources reported about the 'English Company' which supposedly included all merchants who had British citizenship. The administration of the company resided in London.

Any special branch of this organization in Russia probably did not exist. Our scant knowledge concerns only the functioning of the so-called *poverennyi* (confidant or attorney) of the company who, representing the interests of all members of the community, could represent their interests to Russian authorities. The activity of the British Russian Company in Russia was also under diplomatic protection. According to the practice established in the eighteenth century, caring for the interests of compatriot-businessmen had become the main task of diplomats of consular rank in many countries, particularly in large foreign trade ports. Businessman Charles Goodfellow, the agent of the Tobacco Company organized in 1698 to trade Virginia tobacco in Russia, became the first consul in Russia in 1699. In 1714 Goodfellow returned home to Britain and after his death in 1728 he was succeeded by Thomas Ward, also a merchant of the British Russian Company. However, Ward died in 1731 and the duties of the consul were assigned to Claudius Rondeau, the head of the British diplomatic mission in Russia. After Rondeau died in 1739, nobody performed the consul's duties until 1744. These were the years when the role of *poverennyi* of the company performing the duties of the consul as a representative of the company increased. In 1744 the office of the consul was taken by Jacob Wolff, one of the most influential members of the British Russian Company. Later, in the middle and second half of the eighteenth century, other particularly active businessmen from the British Russian Company received the rank and powers of the British consul. Among them were: Thomas Wroughton, Walter Shairp, Samuel Swallow, John Cayley and Stephen Shairp.[17]

We can gain some insight into the nature of this English community in the middle of the eighteenth century through a list presented to the Collegium of Commerce by the *poverennyi* of the community of John Edwards in 1743.[18] The list includes the merchants who had commercial activity in St Petersburg, which had become by that time the centre of English foreign trade. There are forty-four merchants on the list. Far from all of them are English by birth. Indeed according to our calculations there are twelve merchants of German origin. Jacob Wolff and Henry Schiffner are from the east Baltic. Ernst Bardevik came from Oldenburg. Gottfried Weockel was a Prussian merchant from Berlin. Meyer and Sanders in the 1720s were known as merchants from Hamburg.[19] Practically all of them had long-standing ties with the Russian market and Russian merchants, so were quite experienced in the specific character of Russian trade. That is why they were prospective partners for English merchants, especially for those who were interested in the development of contacts with St Petersburg. On the other hand, German merchants could have expanded considerably the scale of their trade operations if they had managed to trade with Russia and England. To achieve this goal, one would have had to become a member of the British Russian Company and a citizen of Great Britain.

The reorganization of the company made it possible to enlarge its membership by inviting foreigners. It was mainly merchants from Germanic countries who compromised the majority of foreigners joining the British Russian Company in the eighteenth century. According to Margrit Schulte Beerbühl, in the period 1725 to 1734, the Russian Company in England included fifteen German merchants, one Dutchman and three Frenchmen; and from 1735 to 1744, six Germans, three Dutchmen and two Frenchmen.[20]

No French merchant can be noted among the members of the British Russian Company in St Petersburg in 1743, though there was a Dutch merchant – Peter Svellengrebel. He belonged to a trading family which had operated in Russia since the middle of the seventeenth century. It is also known that Hermann Meyer, one of the most influential Dutch merchants on the Russian market in the early eighteenth century, was a member of the British Russian Company.[21]

The descendants of German Ostseatic merchants appeared among the members of the English community in Russia in subsequent years. In the period from the early 1760s to the late 1770s Ritter, Thornton & Cayley became one of the leading English firms in St Petersburg. The membership and logistics of the company are typical of the largest British corporations on the Russian market. Ritter descended from German merchants in Narva and his relationship with Jacob Wolff led to him being the executor of Wolff's will.[22] John Cayley was with Ritter in St Petersburg. Godfrey Thornton belonged to one of the most powerful trading families in London and was a member of the board of the Bank of England as well as one of the leaders of the Russian Company.[23] Thus Thornton organized his firm's operations in England, while his partners in St Petersburg received goods from London, bought products for their company in Russia, etc. The fact that one of the partners was an Englishman and the other was a German from Baltic merchants broadened the company's circle of ties on the Russian market both among Russian and foreign merchants.

In 1764 the government once more required data on English merchants in Russia. This time it was presented by the consul Samuel Swallow. According to Swallow's list, in 1764 there were forty-seven members of the British Russian Company in St Petersburg (see pp. 125–6). Of these, eleven people, judging by their names and other particulars, were not native-born English.[24] These were nine Germans, including Lawrence Bastian Ritter, a Dutchman Peter-Konraad Svellengrebel and a French-Huguenot Jean-David Vernesobre. Nevertheless, the author of the list particularly noted that all persons mentioned were citizens of Great Britain. Hence, British citizenship remained a necessary requirement for access to the British Russian Company and its privileges. Besides the merchants staying in St Petersburg, Swallow listed the names of the compatriot-businessmen resident in Moscow (ten in all), Kronstadt (three), Arkhangelsk (four), Onega (four) and Riga (thirteen). Thus, the number of British merchants in St Petersburg had scarcely increased, while smaller quite stable groups appeared in other cities, with the majority of them being native-born Englishmen. Only Henry Bardevik was mentioned as being in Riga. Thus, in the second half of the eighteenth century the process of German and other foreign merchants infiltrating the British Russian Company slowed down. Those who had already become members were assimilating into the English environment. Not without reason, the first name of the above-mentioned Bardevik was Henry and not Heinrich.

However, the inclusion of German and Dutch traders into the British merchant circle had little influence on the character of English household ties. British merchants preferred to have relatives among their own compatriots. Anthony Cross revealed the relations between the Cayley and Raikes clans who belonged to the leading British trade houses in St Petersburg. John Cayley, Ritter and Thornton's companion, British consul in St Petersburg in 1787–95, was married to Sarah Cozens, a sister of an English merchant and manufacturer, the founder of one of the first chintz manufactories in Russia.[25] Cozen's other sister Marie was married to Nicholas Cavanagh, an English merchant and the owner of a sugar manufactory in St Petersburg. Nicholas and Marie Cavanagh's daughter – also Marie – was married to Timothy Raikes. John Cayley's son – John Cayley junior – married the daughter of Timothy and Marie Raikes-Harriet.[26]

In the sixteenth century the British Russian Company presented itself as an association of businessmen acting together, rather like a joint-stock company. But from the seventeenth century onwards, it began to act as a more open society, uniting the interests of businessmen wishing to trade in Russia while allowing each of them to act independently. This did not preclude merchants grouping with each other to create trading of two or three partners, especially when one of the partners lived permanently in England and ran the business there (purchasing cargoes for Russia, receiving the goods which arrived from St Petersburg, distributing them in England, etc.). In the above-mentioned company 'Ritter, Thornton & Cayley' this role of conducting 'the English end of business'[27] belonged to Thornton. Matthew Shiffner, Jacob Wolff's partner, also lived in London. Whatever the case, both English merchants staying in Russia, and their partners living in England, would have had to be members of the Russian Company, otherwise they would not have enjoyed the old privilege granted by King Phillip and Queen Mary to trade with Russia.

Dutch and German Merchant Communities in Eighteenth-Century Russia

In the second half of the seventeenth century, the Russian Company being deprived of its privileges under the Act of 1650, the European trade balance of Russia shifted to the Dutch merchants. It has already been mentioned that in Peter the Great's reign Englishmen still managed to surpass Dutch in goods turnover. However the Dutch merchant community remained the most numerous in Russia, at least until the end of the 1720s. In 1725, the year of Peter the Great's death, the sources reported forty-eight Dutch merchants and twenty-four Englishmen on the Russian market.[28] However, in St Petersburg, which had become Russia's leading foreign trade seaport as early as in the1720s, the Dutch had no advantage from the start. The list of foreign merchants made by St Petersburg customs in 1719 reported nine Englishmen and nine Dutchmen.[29]

The peculiar feature of the Dutch merchants' activity in Russia is their close and long-established ties with Arkhangelsk, which the majority of the Dutch preferred to other Russian ports. In the eighteenth century Dutch merchants mainly concentrated on trade in Arkhangelsk, despite this northern Russian port being in the shade of quickly progressing St Petersburg. The Dutch renewed their position as the largest community of foreign merchants in Arkhangelsk. In 1741 their share in the export of Arkhangelsk amounted to 77 per cent.[30]

Thus, despite the general decline of Dutch foreign trade in the eighteenth century, Dutch merchants kept a rather strong position in the Russian market in the first quarter of the century and dominated still longer in the Russian north. But as before, the Dutch had no organization, uniting them and guaranteeing certain rights and privileges in Russia. It distinguished them both from their compatriots operating in south-east Asia as a part of the well-known VOC[31] and from English merchants in Russia, members of the Russian Company. On the other hand, Dutch merchants, continuing their trade in Russia in the eighteenth century, preserved family and business ties established as early as the seventeenth century. Thus, in the eighteenth century they kept on operating through 'household-production networks' providing considerable stability for their business.[32]

In the eighteenth century fairly branchy clans had been formed in a milieu of Dutch merchants, whose members permanently lived in the Netherlands, most often in Amsterdam, maintaining business contacts with their relatives in Russia. In the first years of the eighteenth century Jean Lups, a commercial agent of the Russian government, gained great popularity among Dutch merchants. One of his daughters, Anna, married Hermann Meyer, a Dutch merchant in Russia, the other daughter, Susanna Sofia, became the wife of an Amsterdam banker and merchant Ludwick Hovy. Susanna and Sofia's brother, Hendrik, along with his brother-in-law Ludwick Hovy, launched a trading company in Amsterdam.[33] At the same time in Russia Hermann Meyer conducted commercial activity with Jean Lups junior, who was a nephew of Jean Lups senior and a first cousin of Hermann Meyer's wife and Hendrik Lups and whose sister, Elisabeth, married a Dutch merchant Hendrick van Jever, who, like his father, traded in Moscow and Arkhangelsk in the early eighteenth century.[34]

Hendrick's younger brother Volkert van Jever moved to Amsterdam to become one of the most prosperous merchants there, maintaining regular relations with the company of his brother in Arkhangelsk. Quite often clan relationships of Dutch families extended outside the national community. This is the case with the clan of the Lups–Meyers–van Jevers. As has already been stated, Hermann Meyer became a British citizen and a member of the English trade company in Russia, also joined by Hendrik van Jever and a German merchant Hermann Boltenhagen at the beginning of the 1740s.

As late as the end of the 1780s Dutch merchants still constituted 30 per cent of foreign trade turnover of Arkhangelsk (German – 20 per cent, English – 10 per cent, Russian – 40 per cent).[35] However it should be noted that by that time nearly all Dutch merchants, who had been domineering in the Russian north, had stopped their trade in Arkhangelsk. The only Dutch company having a significant share in Arkhangelsk's trade turnover was Rutger van Brienen Sons and Anthon Mensendijk. Van Brienen's company was founded by Rutger van Brienen, a Dutchman by birth, who had lived in Hamburg before his arrival in Russia and was often identified as a Hamburg merchant. At the end of the century van Brienen became closer to the German milieu. Abraham, the elder son of Rutger, became the consul of the Habsburg Empire in St Petersburg. His elder son, Abraham II, became a Prussian consul in Arkhangelsk.[36]

In St Petersburg Dutchmen were always comparatively small in number and in the first half of the eighteenth century made close contacts with German merchants. At that time 'Limburg & Boethlink', launched by a Dutchman Abraham van Limburg and a descendant from Lübeck, Peter Boethlink, came to the fore. Jan Cruys, the son of a Dutch admiral on Russian service – Kornelius Cruys (from Norway) – became a prominent merchant. Three of Jan Cruys's daughters married the following German merchants: Jacob Stelling, Heinrich-Christian Stegelmann and Karsten Voigt.[37]

Thus, the tendency towards Dutch-German merchant cooperation became evident. It was favoured by common features of their trade organizations, transactions and, in most cases, identical national origin.

As Germany's political system of the epoch was rather complicated German merchants staying in Russia were identified mainly as representatives of separate lands and cities. In the seventeenth century Arkhangelsk was the only Russian trading port and almost all comers were German merchants from Hamburg. As a result the Hamburg community appeared, uniting the majority of German merchants even at the beginning of the eighteenth century. From the point of view of the legal status and organization of trade activity Hamburg merchants had much in common with Dutchmen, and besides, some of them were connected with the latter by birth or marital ties. The above-mentioned van Brienen can be identified both as Dutch and German merchants. Like the Dutch, Hamburg merchants had individually granted chartered permissions to act on the Russian home market. On this ground even in the eighteenth century Dutch-Hamburg merchants were often considered as a united community, as opposed to the English.

The English merchant community had a more definite status as its parts were members of the privileged Russian Company, subjects of Great Britain and acted under the protection of the British consuls usually performing the functions of mayors of the company. Dutch and German merchants were deprived of such privileges. To represent their interests before the government they elected trusted members called *burmistr*. The word '*burmistr*' goes back to German *Bürgermeister* (major) which was introduced into Russian usage during Peter the Great's reign and denoted the head of a town or rural community. The known *burmistrs* of Dutch and German communities were Giuseppe Mariotti (an Italian who arrived from Hamburg), Abraham Limburg (a Dutchman) and David

Berkhjusen (from Hamburg). In 1767 a Dutchman Gabriel Bacheracht and Simon Brumberg (from Narva) were elected *burmistrs* to represent the interests of all foreign merchants except the British.[38]

As for German merchants in particular there were two basic groups of them at the beginning of the eighteenth century. The first group included the previously mentioned Hamburg merchants operating mainly in Arkhangelsk. At the turn of the century they were not numerous but influential. The second group consisted of the merchants arriving in Russia through north-west boundaries, the dwellers of Liflandia and Estlandia cities and subjects of Sweden. Among them were, for example, Thomas Knipper who was a Swedish diplomat in Russia, Andrew Minter and some others. However the beginning of the Northern War[39] blocked the trade in this direction. Some German merchants became interned. After the capture of Narva in 1704 local merchants were moved to Vologda and other cities of northern Russia, while the trade of Hamburg merchants via Arkhangelsk continued and even prospered.

After the Northern War Russia renewed its trade in the north-west, especially when the eastern Baltic coast fell under its control. The centre of the Russian trade in the Baltic region shifted to a new capital city and seaport St Petersburg. This resulted in German trade expansion as more cities and lands sent their commercial representatives to Russia.

Alongside Hamburg merchants the representatives from other Hanseatic cities began to trade more actively, first those of Baltic origin (from Lübeck and Rostock), then from Prussia, Mecklenburg, Holstein and Saxony which had recently established political contacts with Russia. The latter were not numerous but included some distinguished personalities, such as a Prussian merchant Jean Pelloutjer who acted on behalf of the company of Berlin merchants, holding an exclusive right of supplying cloth for the Russian army in sharp competition with the British traders in the period between the 1720s and 1730s. Jean Pelloutjer belonged to a family of French Huguenots, resettled in Prussia after the revocation of the Edict of Nantes in France.[40]

Immediately after the Great Northern War Germans advanced their trade rapidly in St Petersburg and, as a result, their numerous community began to merge with the scanty Dutch. This attachment of some European merchants to the German community became apparent even earlier, in the middle of the eighteenth century. The fact is proved by a list of merchants of the 'Dutch and German Company' compiled in St Petersburg in 1743 alongside the abovementioned list of the British Russian Company. The compilers of the list were *burmistrs* of the company – a Dutchman Abraham Limburg and David Berkhjusen (from Hamburg).[41] There are sixty-eight persons on the list. The descendants from German states obviously prevail. Only eight men including Jan Cruys, Johannes van Belkamp, Abraham Limburg and Leopold Potet are undoubtedly Dutch. Stephan Lindemann, a merchant from Kopenhagen, was one of the few representatives of Danish merchants as well as Jacob Magnussen.

This Dutch-German community also included merchants from southern and south-western Europe. They were Frenchman Jean Bouzanqet and Italians Marco Boeni and Bernardo Lezzano. Thus, in the eighteenth century the so-called Dutch-German community in St Petersburg united nearly all western European merchants except the English. Some other examples of foreign merchants on the 1743 list were two merchants from Genoa, Giuseppe Mariotti and Giovanni Bustelli, who had commercial activity in Hamburg. They maintained contacts with the Russian market and in the 1720s turned up in St Petersburg, a new foreign trade harbour of Russia. In 1719 G. Mariotti was already among Hamburg merchants who traded in St Petersburg and soon became a *burmistr* of the Hamburg community.[42] Thus, an Italian-born merchant turned out to be among the Hamburg merchants in Russia.

In the middle of the seventeenth century Ludovic Molveau, who traded wine in France, came to Lübeck. Here Molveau and his descendants continued the same activity but on a broader scale, having increased the export of wine to northern European countries, including Russia. Simultaneously they penetrated into the elite milieu of merchants of the Hanseatic capital. In the 1740s Hermann Nikolas, a grandson of Ludovic Molveau, who had already been considered a Lübeck merchant, arrived in St Petersburg.[43] At the beginning of the nineteenth century his son Jakob became one of the founders and the first chairman of St Petersburg Exchange Committee and mayor of St Petersburg from 1815 to 1818.[44] In the second half of the eighteenth century the number of German merchants grew due to the descendants from many cities and lands of Germany. This led to German merchants becoming the most numerous.

The lists of foreign merchants who traded in St Petersburg in 1765 totals 297 people.[45] There are fifty-four British companies (including seven of German origin), twenty-three Lübeck merchants, fourteen Hamburg merchants, thirty-eight French, seven Swiss, one Berliner, five Danish, six 'Caesarians' (from the Habsburg Empire), four Italians, one Venetian (with a Greek surname), eleven Armenians, five Saxons, three from Rostock and forty-seven Dutch. Besides, there is a list of merchants from 'miscellaneous nations' including fifty-nine people, the origin of some of whom is specified as follows: three merchants from Gdansk, two from Nuremberg, one from Breslau, one from Kurland, three from Sweden and one from Reval. The nationality of the rest of the forty-eight foreigners is not specified, but judging by other sources they include forty-three Germans, one Swede and four Frenchmen.

Some merchants of undoubtedly German origin were mentioned in the list of Dutch merchants. It is of interest that they constitute the majority of the list – thirty-two people – while only fifteen are Dutch. The inclusion of such a large number of Germans in the Dutch list is suggestive of close business and family relations between them, enabling the Russian government to consider the Dutch and the Germans as one community.

Finally, some foreigners who had accepted Russian citizenship were mentioned among Russian merchants: twelve Germans, three Dutchmen, two Frenchmen and two Englishmen. Thus, the total number of merchants of German origin who participated in foreign trade in St Petersburg in 1765 constituted 154 people. The total number of other foreigners amounts to 143 merchants or trading companies. There is similar data for the subsequent years. Thus, applying the same method of counting, it is possible to determine that in 1792 there were 97 German merchants and trading companies, and 127 merchants from other European countries.[46] While in 1765 the number of merchants from Hanseatic cities was forty-four, in 1792 it was reduced to sixteen.

Table 6.1: Number of foreign merchants trading in St Petersburg in the second half of the eighteenth century.

Year	German	British	Dutch	French	Italian	Swiss	Danish	Swedish	Greek	Portuguese	Spanish	Armenian	Total
1765	154	49	18	44	4	7	5	4	1	–	–	11	297
1792	97	58	6	34	9	3	6	1	4	2	4	–	224

Source: A. I. Komissarenko and I. S. Sharkova (eds), *Внешняя торговля России через петербургский порт во второй половине XVIII – начале XIX в. Ведомости о составе купцов и их торговых оборотах* [Russian Foreign Trade via St Petersburg in Late 18th–Early 19th Centuries. Merchant Composition and Trade Turnover Lists] (Moscow: Academy of Sciences of USSR, Institute of History of USSR, 1981), pp. 30–50.

The dynamics of change in the number of national communities of foreign merchants in Arkhangelsk and Moscow was similar. The data of the Moscow duty census for 1795 (the so-called fifth census) testifies to 114 foreigners entering the Moscow merchant circle. Among them seventy-three were from Germany and thirty-nine from France. The representatives of Hanseatic cities were not more than five people. Among others were natives of Cologne, Freiburg, Aachen, Frankfurt, Hanau and many other parts of Prussia, Saxony, Bavaria, etc. The brothers Karl-Ludwig and Friedrich-Willhelm Amburger deserve special attention.[47] Karl Bartel, a native of Augsburg, is listed among Lübeck merchants, which means that Hanseatic cities were sometimes a transitional point for the German merchants on their way to Russia. In any case the increasing number of merchants, arriving from inland regions of Germany, resulted in Hanseatic merchants (first of all the citizens of Lübeck and Hamburg) gradually mixing with the German merchants from different lands.

Like Hanseatic cities, the cities of east Baltic provinces can also be considered transitional points on the way of German merchants' advancement to Russia. In the eighteenth century the natives of Ostseatic provinces, whose ancestors in their turn proceeded from Germany, traded in St Petersburg and Arkhangelsk, for example, both the above-mentioned Jacob Wolff who was a member of the British Russian Company, and the Roddes, who deserve further consideration, originated from Lübeck. But by the end of the eighteenth century in the milieu of foreign merchants in Russia some descendants of western European countries not belonging to local influential families had appeared, which was especially typical of German merchants who arrived from inland parts of the country – the Amburger brothers, for instance. They were quick enough to rank among the leading merchants on the Russian market, being the sons of an official who served the Solms princes.[48] One of the founders of the well-known Kuemmel & Blessig, Philippe Jakob Blessig, was a son of an innkeeper from Strasburg. Johann Joachim Mahs, the founder of the business clan, known in Russia in the eighteenth and nineteenth centuries, was a member of the family of Hamburg handicraftsmen dealing with silk fabric processing.[49]

The prevalence of German merchants made other foreigners strongly attracted to the German community. Of course, this does not concern the English, who formed a separate influential group. The German community was especially attractive for Dutch merchants, who had sharply declined in number by the end of the eighteenth century, as well as for the Swiss and Danish, who had always been scanty in Russia. Swedish merchants were also members of the group as many of them had German roots. On the other hand, some merchants from south-western and southern Europe – Italians and sometimes Frenchmen – also had close ties with the German community. This can be explained by the fact that a lot of merchants from Italy and France came to Russia via Hanseatic cities. Hamburg and Lübeck, in their turn, had contacts with Genoa, Venice, Bordeaux, Burgundy and other regions of France and Italy, playing the role of their trade mediators on the east European market.

As for household-related ties inside the German community, one can detect here a variety of clans. In the seventeenth and early eighteenth centuries it was typical for Hamburg merchants to have family relationships with the Dutch. This can be explained by the fact that since the end of the sixteenth century the representatives of many distinguished trade families from the Netherlands had been moving to Hamburg. At the beginning of the eighteenth century the most authoritative Hamburg merchants in Russia were the brothers Matthäus and Johann Poppe. Their father Lorenz Poppe, having arrived in Hamburg from Thuringia, married a daughter of François Haex, a descendant from Antwerp and influential member of the Dutch community in Hamburg. When his sons Matthäus and Johann Poppe arrived in Russia they were assisted by a relation of their mother's, a Dutchman Stepan Ellout. Soon the brothers married the daughters of an influential Dutch merchant in Russia, Daniel Hartmann.[50] As a result Matthäus Poppe inherited from D. Hartmann a right to purchase mast wood and send it abroad.[51]

The Roddes, one of the most influential trading families in Lübeck in the seventeenth and eighteenth centuries, represented local merchants on the Russian market. In the seventeenth century several members of the Roddes family performed trading activities in Ostseatic cities (east Baltic cities), such as Riga, Reval and Narva, and then arrived in Novgorod and Pskov. Kaspar Adolf Rodde and his brother Diedrich moved from Narva to Arkhangelsk during the Northern War. Thanks to the contacts of his Lübeck relatives with the religious and charitable organizations of professor A. G. Franke from Halle, K. A. Rodde organized the supply of books, medicine and other necessary goods for Peter I and his milieu. The daughter of K. A. Rodde, Margaret Elizabeth, married an associate of A. G. Franke, Pastor Christian Gottlieb Becker, who had arrived in Moscow. Their sons Samuel Gottlieb and Alexander Christian Becker became merchants in Arkhangelsk, like their grandfather. Hereinafter the relationship within the Rodde-Becker clan in Arkhangelsk became more solid. Having arrived from Reval, Kaspar Adolf and Diedrich's nephew, Berend-Johann Rodde, married one of Diedrich's daughters and launched a trading company together with the Becker brothers.[52] This clan acted in Arkhangelsk during almost the whole of the eighteenth century and had no relations with the Dutch clans there. However in the 1760s Berend-Johann Rodde established direct contacts with Hamburg and stayed there for a long time, preoccupied with the deals of his Arkhangelsk trade enterprise. Like the members of the Poppes and Roddes families, who traded in Russia and had relatives among elite merchants in their native land, Dutch merchant clans possessed the same peculiarities.

One of the major functions of foreign trading colonies or communities was maintenance of contacts between their mother countries and the Russian market. Therefore the Dutch acting in Russia and Hamburg, as well as English merchants, had permanent contacts with their partners in the homeland. As a result there appeared some associations of merchants consisting of two parts: the businessmen staying in Russia, and their partners in the mother country. These associations could be arranged differently. In the case of England it was a uniform 'Russian Company' incorporating both parts. The Dutch and German merchants had no permanent organization or a general company in Russia.

However, their partners could create organizations. The above-mentioned merchants in Lübeck were members of the *Novgorodfahrer* group. In 1702 the Northern War prompted the foundation of the Hamburg Society of merchants trading with Russia. The trading vessels sailing to Russia could be attacked by the Swedish fleet and consequently needed support of the military ships. During the war Arkhangelsk was the only port in Russia permitting foreign trade. The merchants of Hamburg trading with Arkhangelsk (*Archangelfahrer*) were obliged to install payments into the Society fund at a rate of 1.3 per cent of the cost of the cargoes shipped by them to Russia. The Society pleaded with the Admiralty of Hamburg to provide protection for the trading ships sailing back and forth between Hamburg and Arkhangelsk. Under the treaty of 1704 the Admiralty allocated for this purpose the battle ship *Wappen von Hamburg*, one voyage of which cost 10,000 thalers.[53] After the Northern War such escorts were no longer necessary, but the Society continued to operate. It was busy with organizational matters and petitioned for merchants' needs before the Hamburg authorities and the administration of St Petersburg. The Society (it survived up to the nineteenth century) reached the height of its activity in the early reign of Catherine II when the trading agreement between Russia and Hamburg was negotiated, though never signed.

The structure of the Society deserves special attention. Its members were representatives of the largest trading families of Hamburg (Kellinhuisen, Schuback), as well as the relatives of those who traded in Russia. Thus, Franz Poppe was one of the founders of the Society and its most active member in the early eighteenth century. He was the senior in the family whose members actively conducted overseas trade including operations with Russia. And Matthäus and Johann Poppe who kept the leading positions among Hamburg merchants in Russia were none other than Franz Poppe's younger brothers. In 1702 the list of Society members also included Herman Govers, Henry Pren, Arnold Ferporten, Joachim Konau – all of whom traded in Arkhangelsk – and, finally, the Rozens and van Somms, well known in the Russian market in the late seventeenth–early eighteenth centuries.

Similar organizations existed in the Netherlands. In Amsterdam the merchants trading with Russia operated under the aegis of *Directie van de Moscovische handel* ('Board of Directors for the Muscovite Trade'), formed at the end of the seventeenth century. Its responsibilities included helping to organize military escorts of trading fleets to Russia, petitioning diplomats and government for protection of the Dutch merchants' interests and other issues of mutual aid and support of the businessmen. To refund escorts and for other needs Dutch tradesmen made payments to the treasury of *Directie van de Moscovische handel*. The sum of the payments depended on the number of ships sailing to Russia and the amount of cargo loaded on them. Hence, the size of the payment, as in the Hamburg Society, was determined by the trade volume of one businessman or another.

The members of the Board of Directors for the Muscovite Trade should have been elected by merchants. From 1693 up to the beginning of the eighteenth century the list of directors numbered eighteen persons.[54] Among them were those who, then or before, stayed in Russia (Christoffel Brants, Jan Timmerman, Jacob Daniel de Vries). Besides, some directors had relatives operating in Arkhangelsk on a regular basis. They were Matthijs Romswinkel (whereas Nikolay Romzvinkel resided in Russia in the early eighteenth century) and also Willem Joseph van Brienen, belonging to the family already known to us who settled in Russia in Peter the Great's reign. Aarnout Dicx and Egbert Thesing also had permanent partners in Russia at the beginning of the eighteenth century, and Willem Willink at the end of the century. Among the members of these associations we can often find the businessmen who commuted to Russia and consequently appeared in Russian seaports.

Thus the associations of businessmen trading with Russia in Amsterdam and Hamburg rendered them necessary assistance in establishing contacts with the Russian market. The stability of such contacts was preconditioned by those 'family-industrial networks' uniting the Dutch and Hamburg merchants. The existing associations of businessmen in Amsterdam and Hamburg compensated for the lack of any companies or other formal Dutch and German organizations in Russia.

Merchants from South-Western Europe in Eighteenth-Century Russia

The growing scope of foreign trade in the eighteenth century expanded the geography of Russia's commercial communications. As a result in St Petersburg and other cities there were merchants from those countries which had scarcely, if ever, appeared in the Russian market before, such as merchants from Denmark and Sweden who were never numerous and registered in the lists of the German merchant class. Merchants from south and south-west Europe differed greatly from those of other foreign communities. They stood aloof and kept their identity. A rather small group of Italian businessmen were mainly from Genoa. French merchants appeared in Russia in Peter I's reign. But originally their trade was not of considerable size. Attempts to form trading companies for direct trade between Russia and France in the first quarter of the eighteenth century had no success.[55] And this was in spite of the fact that Russia and France had always exchanged goods. However, traditionally barter between the French and Russian market was in the hands of intermediaries, particularly to the Dutch and Hamburg merchants. It explains why individual French merchants arrived in Russia via Hamburg or Lübeck and appeared in St Petersburg as members of the German trading community. In the mid-second half of the eighteenth century foreign trade of St Petersburg was conducted by dozens of English, Dutch, German trading houses and companies and a few Frenchmen whose names were Jean Michel, Joseph Rajmbert (taking the office of the French consul) and at the end of the century Franc Noel & Grenning and Barral & Chenonnie.[56] The goods exchange between Russia and France was still mediated, which interfered with the formation of a large and influential French merchant community in St Petersburg.

However in the last quarter of the eighteenth century the number of French merchants penetrating into the sphere of small and retail business in Moscow and St Petersburg rapidly increases. To obtain the right of retail business or gain the necessary leeway in the Russian home market foreigners had to join local merchants and become Russian citizens. The archives keep dozens of cases about foreigners joining the Moscow merchant class, providing us with interesting information about their origin. Thus Jean-Marie Gautier Dufayer, who became a Moscow merchant in 1770, was a son of a judge from Saint-Quentin. The native of Lyon, Jean Simon, on arrival in Russia in 1769, became a watchmaker in a well-known Swiss company Sando & Basselier. But only in 1774 was he enrolled into Moscow merchant class. Jean Le Fort from Bley worked from 1765 to 1777 as a French teacher in different Moscow families and only after that did he became a Moscow merchant.[57] Such examples are not rare. Thus the French trade community appeared rather special. Besides two or three large trade companies in St Petersburg – first Jean Michel and Josef Raimbert and then at the end of the century Franc Noel & Grenning and Barral & Chenonnie – it incorporated a great many merchants, trading on a small and retail scale in Moscow and St Petersburg, namely the owners of bakeries, confectioneries, haberdasheries and wine cellars having the most varied class origin and eventually becoming Russian citizens.

In the eighteenth century Russia established contacts with the countries of the Iberian Peninsula, intermediary English firms dominating in trade with Portugal. In the 1720s at the initiative of Peter I an unsuccessful attempt was made to launch a Russian-Spanish trade company supported by the state treasury.[58] Only in the second half of the eighteenth century did some Spanish and Portuguese businessmen turn up in St Petersburg. The Spaniards were Phillip Shone from Bilbao, Francisco da Milans from Cadiz and Antonio Colombi from Barcelona.[59] In the 1790s the trade firm Serra & Riba[60] becomes rather prominent. Some Portuguese merchants who arrived in St Petersburg in the 1780s launched the company Velho, Araujo & Martens.[61] The Portuguese and Spanish merchants were represented by only a few foreign trade firms in St Petersburg, establishing no relations with other communities of foreign merchants.

Conclusion

The study of the composition, interrelations and status of national groups of west European merchants in eighteenth century Russia confirms the relevancy of applying the term 'community' to many of them. This term presupposes the presence of multi-level organization, including an informal one, and the absence of any juridical status. One common feature is quite sufficient. In this case it is common origin, affinity to one or other national group.

The composition and number correlation of western European merchant communities in Russia underwent considerable changes during the eighteenth century. At the beginning of the century three communities existed: Dutch, a rather influential and active one; Hamburg, inferior to the Dutch in number and influence, but similar in status; and English, though having lost its former importance but still leaning on the British Russian Company in London. At the end of the century the English community comes to the fore exceeding all others by the volume of trade and enjoying considerable privileges. It is rather closed from the point of view of household ties, but incorporating comers from other countries who accepted British citizenship.

In the second half of the eighteenth century a French community is formed, primarily in the milieu of small and retail business. Its representatives arrived from various, mostly provincial, cities of France, being descendants from non-commercial families.

The Dutch community nearly disappears, many of its members fuse with the German merchants, the latter include not only natives of Hamburg and Hanseatic cities, but many other German cities and lands. German (or even German-Dutch) community stands out by its multiplicity and branchy clans. It unites the merchants of most miscellaneous levels and different social origins, up to descendants from the families of officials and handicraftsmen. It attracts Danish, Swedish, Swiss, some French and Italian businessmen.

At the same time the informal status of the majority of west European merchant communities promoted their acquiring of a transnational character. In Russia merchants from different countries developed business and family relations with each other whereas their ties with metropolises were getting weaker.

This is obvious in the case of German merchants and their partners from other countries. The English community gained transnational character due to the privileges the members of the Russian Company enjoyed, stimulating the interested foreigners to accept British citizenship.

The transnational character of foreign merchant communities in Russia is proved by the activity of the English Club in St Petersburg. It was founded in 1770 by an English merchant Francis Gardner. But soon after it began to enroll not only English tradesmen, but also many other foreign merchants, among whom were Hendrik Bacheracht, Fredrik van Zanten and Abracham van der Fliet (Dutchmen), Colombi (an Italian), the Kondoidis (Greek), François Raimbert (a Frenchman), Johann Magnus Archjusen (a Dane) and a great number of Germans, including the above-mentioned Abraham van Brienen the senior, etc.[62]

Western European communities of merchants, trading with Russia, in many cases consisted of two types: those who stayed at the Russian seaports and the ones operating at home. The Russian Company included both types, but the associations of merchants in Amsterdam and Hamburg did not incorporate those who traded far from the native land.

Thus, in the eighteenth century the composition, role and status of foreign trade corporations and communities operating in Russia considerably changed in comparison with the Middle Ages and early modern Times (in the fifteenth and sixteenth centuries). It is obvious that the frameworks of foreign merchant organizations tend towards more flexibility, their compositions cease being homogeneous and many privileges are revoked. The compositional changes are first of all observed more and more in the multinational character of trade communities, with the factor of origin losing its crucial importance. Firstly, it results in multiplying business and matrimonial ties between merchants of different countries, whose ancestors belonged to various national corporations while residing in Russia. Secondly, it provokes partial loss or changing by many merchants of their national identities.

Finally, western European merchants can be classified as forming two communities: the English and other merchants. The English community included the British and those who acquired British citizenship to enjoy the trading privileges of the Russian Company. The other merchants fell gradually under the leadership of German businessmen. It is obvious that these groupings reflected two directions in Russian foreign trade: England and continental Europe. The latter was mainly represented by northern Germanic (earlier Hanseatic) cities and the Netherlands. These centres provided trade contacts between Russia and other European countries, attracting not only Dutch and German businessmen, but also French, Italian and Swiss. At last, the Russian government's attempts to establish direct connections with a number of the countries that had not yet developed contacts with Russia, namely Spain, Portugal, France and North America, resulted in the formation of tiny groups of businessmen from these countries in St Petersburg. They kept more or less separate, but nevertheless gravitated to one of the two big and influential segments of foreign merchant classes in Russia.

British Merchants Staying in Russia in 1764

British consul James Swallow submitted the following list to the Chamber of Commerce on 21 July 1764 (RGADA, f. 276, op. 1, d. 257, ll. 4–5).

St Petersburg: William Gomm, Godfrey Thornton, John Cayley, Jacob Riegl, Arthur Meister, Jacob Rheingold, Charles Rheingold, Lawrence Bastian Ritter, Henry Clausing, Andrew Burnet, Anthony Welden, Alexander Cook, John Dude, James Jackson, Timothy Raikes, Benjamin Cool, John Watson, Archibald Ross, William Watson, Richard Sutherland, Nicholas Cavanagh, William Glen, Gilbert Lang, James Safrey, Thomas Stevens, Randolph Meyer, John Paris, John Henry de Marin, Ernest Jacob Opitz, Christopher Leek, Richard Cozens, Edward Fowel, Robert Crump, Cornelius Gardner, Jean-David Vernisobre, John Ferguson, George Edwards, Peter Prescott, Edward Fogg, Otto Evald Setler, Peter Golsten, Peter-Konraad Svellengrebel, Everhard von Ludwig, Samuel Pomfret, Edward James Smith, William Proctor, Robert Adams.

Moscow: John Tames, John Thomson, George Thomson, James Rowand, Francis Gardner, Martin Butler, James Grief, William Marten, John Butler, Robert Dickinson.

Kronstadt: William Yung, John Booker, John Wilson.

Astrakhan': Charles Gordon.

Arkhangelsk: Henry Fraser, George Sperling, William Brown, William Hungeone.

Onega: Richard Gabris, Bartholomew Angelo, Edward Bleachendon, Phillip Geeks.

Riga: Thomas Gritted, George Cayley, William Collins, James Fraser, John Ohterloni, Patrick Renni, James Donaldson, James Cumning, Phillip Ibbetson, John Fenton, James Pearson, George Renni, Henry Bardevick.

Narva: Nicholas Langle, Robert Thorp.

Acknowledgements

The paper is prepared in the frame of the programme 'Scientific and Scientific-Pedagogical Personnel of Innovative Russia 2009–2013'. Contract P357 from 7 May 2010.

7 GREEK MERCHANT COLONIES IN CENTRAL AND SOUTH-EASTERN EUROPE IN THE EIGHTEENTH AND EARLY NINETEENTH CENTURIES

Olga Katsiardi-Hering

In recent years, the economic, administrative and social historiography of the Greek diaspora[1] has flourished, especially with regard to the Greek communities of central Europe. It has evolved as part of a vibrant methodological discourse built upon migration, network-systems[2] and colonial/postcolonial studies. The title of the volume of which this paper forms part refers to 'merchant colonies' and their importance in European international trade in the early modern period (late fifteenth–eighteenth centuries). Consequently, we will be discussing the trade undertaken by foreign merchants to and through central Europe, especially those who established themselves in that area in the eighteenth and early nineteenth centuries. We should begin by explaining the geographical and geopolitical context in this area during the period in question. The term 'colony' occupies a central place in this volume, and needs to be explained and compared with others such as 'nation' (*Nation/Γένος*), 'establishment' (*Niederlassung/paroikia*),[3] 'community' (*comunità/Gemeinde/κοινότητα*), 'confraternity' (*Confraternità/Bruderschaft/Αδελφότητα*) and 'companies' (*compagnie/Gesellschaften*).[4] The merchant colonies in central Europe, which were part of the south-eastern European Orthodox diaspora, should be examined in terms of the conflicts, as well as the convergences, between the two – and after the late eighteenth century, three – empires with territory in central Europe, and of developments in their respective economic policies.

I am using the term 'central Europe' to denote the space delimited by the city-port of Trieste and the Transylvanian lands of the Carpathians, with small 'deviations' as far as the Black Sea. During the period under examination, this space was subject to the Habsburg Monarchy, those parts of it that extended into the Danubian Principalities which, though under Ottoman rule, enjoyed a semi-autonomous status. Venice, though part of the same geographical space as Trieste, will only be taken into account indirectly, given that it remained the capital of the 'imperial' maritime *Repubblica*,[5] while the long-term settlement of non-Catholic groups in its lands was not restricted to populations involved in commerce. The Habsburg annexation of Venice in the late eighteenth century meant the city lacked prestige as a place of reception for a new commercial class. In contrast, Venice's neighbour and competitor, Trieste, continued to enjoy high status in this regard into the early twentieth century. Economically, Venice was oriented primarily towards the Adriatic and the eastern Mediterranean and less towards the geopolitical core of central Europe. This orientation resurfaced recently in the resumption of the inter-war debate on central European political and economic unity (*Mitteleuropa*).[6]

Our central Europe was bound above all else by the Danube and its tributaries, and the geomorphology of the lands on either side of it. Given that, since the Treaty of Karlowitz (1699), that part of central Europe west of the Carpathians as far as the Austrian Litorale had belonged to one empire, the Habsburg, and that part to their east, the semi-autonomous trans-Danubian Principalities of Moldavia and Wallachia, had belonged to another, the Ottoman, it would be wrong to treat the region as a single geopolitical and social entity. The inhabitants of the Hereditary Lands (*Erbländer*), and their leaderships in particular, as well as the populations of Hungary and Transylvania, who were in a comparatively less dominant position due to their administrative dependence on the relatively advanced central Hereditary Lands and because of the agricultural and artisanal nature of their communities and relative lack of urbanization,[7] comprised another factor which necessitates a non-unitary, multifaceted approach to our subject.

In the context of our analysis, the space of south-eastern and central Europe was linked – oppositionally in the sphere of politics, and complementarily in the sphere of commerce. In the period under examination, it was primarily subject – absolutely or semi-autonomously – to the Ottoman Empire. Although the Ionian islands, which were under Venetian rule until 1797, are not always included under the term 'south-eastern Europe', they indubitably form part of the broader geopolitical area of the Levant, over which the western European powers engaged in such fierce economic competition in the eighteenth and nineteenth centuries.

The geomorphology of the space is another factor to be taken into consideration. It was in the lands adjacent to the Danube that the Ottoman Empire fought its successive wars with the empires along its northern borders. The Ottoman victory at Mohács (1526), a city on the Danube, paved the way for their establishing themselves in most of Hungary and Transylvania, and for their remaining in Buda until 1699. In the late sixteenth century, the so-called long Turkish war (*der lange Türkenkrieg*)[8] of 1593–1606 would also be fought on the banks of the Danube. In 1683, the Ottomans failed to defeat the united forces of central Europe at the foot of Kahlemberg hill, again on the banks of the Danube, and had to abandon their dream of ruling central Europe as a result.[9] The treaty of Karlowitz (1699) would make them lords of the right bank of the Danube, and the river – in whose vicinity the new wars of the eighteenth and nineteenth centuries would be waged – now divided two empires. Almost all the eighteenth-century peace treaties which the Ottoman Empire signed with the Habsburg and Russian Empires would be agreed on the Ottoman side of the Danube (the treaties of: 1699 Karlowitz, north of Belgrade; 1711 Pruth, a tributary of the Danube; 1718 Passarowitz, south-east of Belgrade; 1739 Belgrade; 1774 Kutschuk Kainardji, near Silistra; 1771 Sistov; 1792 Iasi, the capital of the trans-Danubian principality of Moldavia; 1813 Bucharest, the capital of the other trans-Danubian principality of Wallachia) (see Figure 7.1). If the Danube flowed through the lands of one empire, the Habsburg between Vorarlberg, near its source, and the Habsburg fortress city of Temeswar,[10] east of Belgrade, it marked the border between the two empires or flowed through Ottoman territory in a mountainous landscape which grew increasingly precipitous after the Iron Gates (Turnu Severin) and did not lend itself to easy navigation and commercial exploitation over long stretches as it neared its end.[11] Possession of its main geo-economic crossings (around Semlin/Zemun or the Danubian island of Orsova,[12] both in Habsburg territory) was another factor that would influence the networks of those who moved between the two empires.

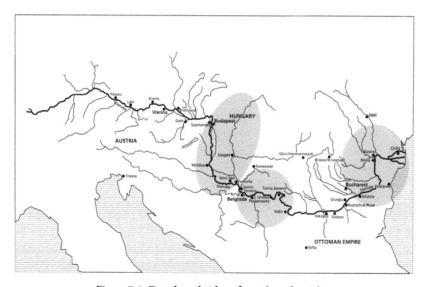

Figure 7.1: Danube: a bridge of people and articles.

It was via these crossings that the Orthodox inhabitants of south-eastern Europe headed towards Hungary in the eighteenth century, primarily via Semlin, where the Austrian emperors set up one of the empire's first sanitary facilities (*lazzaretti*),[13] and via Orsova that they crossed into Transylvania and Braşov (Kronstadt) and Sibiu (Hermannstadt), in particular. The merchants followed the commercial routes[14] through the Balkans with which they were familiar from their caravans. Beginning with the above presentation of the Danube's position in war and peace, I propose to examine the evolution of the merchant colonies in the context of the dynamic south-eastern European trade by dividing the Danube into three sections (see Figure 7.1). Chronologically, this division starts with the treaties of Karlowitz and Passarowitz when, especially after the latter, the Habsburg emperors took a series of measures to bolster their trade in a period during which the Ottoman sultans failed to orient themselves to take comparable measures to modernize their economic policies.[15] In the light of the commercial treaty of Passarowitz, and with a view to increasing their imports of raw materials for their burgeoning craft/industrial production[16] (cotton, yarn, leather, wool, tobacco, olive oil for soap production, ingredients for vegetable dyes, materials for tanning, yarn production, etc.), the Habsburg emperors declared the free navigation of the Adriatic (1717) and Trieste and Fiume (Rijeka) free ports (1719).[17] The port of Trieste developed into a crucial hub in the sea transit trade in which the city's Greek community played a leading role. The favourable tariff regime by which Ottoman subjects paid import duty of between 3.5 and 5 per cent at the border without any of the additional taxes which burdened Habsburg subjects, resulted in a gradual shift among the Orthodox subjects of the Ottoman Empire towards trading in the local markets of Transylvania, Hungary, Austria, Moldavia, Bohemia, Silesia and the Ukraine, and to their settling and organizing themselves into numerous colonies and communities.[18]

The above survey allows us to locate the following in central Europe:

the merchant colonies created by Greek Orthodox traders in Venice and Trieste, which developed in areas primarily oriented towards the sea but with an indirect commercial connection with the hinterland;

the merchant colonies in the Habsburg capital of Vienna, the Hungarian capital of Pest, and the Hungarian and Transylvanian provinces;

the merchant colonies in the Low Danube.

The first two developed between the seventeenth and nineteenth centuries, the third from the second half of the nineteenth century on, which places them beyond the ambit of this paper. According to the 'central places theory',[19] Pest could be considered the space in which the central merchant colony developed in relation to the numerous 'colonies' founded by Greek Orthodox merchants throughout Hungary.

Observing the 'triple' Danube (see Figure 7.1) and its role in trade and the growth of cities and commercial activities throughout the Danube region, and considering its first section to be that part of the river running between Vienna and Semlin, we note that the Orthodox colonies[20] are spread, within Hungary, across and around the plain between the Danube and the Tisza, its tributary, and in the area known as the Danube Knee.[21] This development was driven by its fertile soil and the ease of transport the region allowed. The Orthodox Ottoman subjects made use of the crossings at Semlin, Pancevo and Orsova to enter the Austrian and Hungarian space, meaning that the 'middle' Danube, which served as a border between the empires from Semlin to the Iron Gates, was of vital importance both economically and, of course, for the movement of people and goods, until the mid-nineteenth century. From the frontier island of Orsova, goods were disseminated to the companies of Brașov and Sibiu[22] in Transylvania. According to the 'central places theory', both Brașov and Sibiu would have served as the main reception cities for the merchant colonies of Transylvania as a whole. The settling of merchants from the Ottoman south in these cities would also facilitate and expand their trade with the Ukraine (L'vov/Lemberg, Njezin/Νίζνα)[23] and Russia. The situation would gradually change after the treaty of Kutschuk Kainardji (1774). The territorial and political changes enacted by the treaties of Iasi, Sistov and Bucharest would make the Low Danube even more important, thanks to its indirect links with the fertile areas of southern Russia (Novorossija). Until the third decade of the nineteenth century, despite the enormous efforts made by the Austrians after 1780,[24] transportation east of the Iron Gates remained in the hands of mariners who were Ottoman subjects. Due to the physical difficulties presented by the terrain, trading along the rivers and through the ports[25] of Kalafat, Ruschtschuck (Ruşe), Giurgiu,[26] Sulina, Braila[27] and Galatz was conducted with the opposite bank or at very short distances along the Danube.[28] The situation would start to improve with the projects undertaken from the 1830s at the behest of István Széchenyi to make the Danube more navigable as far as the Iron Gates, and to build bridges across it.[29] The region's grain was transported to Constantinople via Braila.[30] Flexible family-owned shipping companies, some Greek,[31] transported goods from the Black Sea via Sulina or Braila to Brașov[32] and thence to the rest of Transylvania, Wallachia or the Ukraine.

We should also view the Greek merchant colonies in central Europe in the context of:

the changing role of the European Powers in south-eastern Europe in the light of the political and economic treaties of the eighteenth century, and above all of the rise of the Habsburgs and the emergence of the Russian Empire;

the change in economic roles stemming from the increase in artisanal and industrial production;

the resultant change in behaviours and mindsets which could be summed
up in the word 'fashion', personal and domestic (Braudel's power of commerce); consumption would gradually become the new social ideal;[33]

Ottoman economic policy's delayed provision of support for major industrial change and the organization of economic companies of international
standing;[34]

local and supralocal trade, the formation of trade routes, population movements, the setting up of familial-economic networks.

The economic, taxation and administrative policies of the countries of departure
also played a key role alongside the context shaped by the multiple factors detailed
above, as did – still more significantly – those of the countries of reception. For
over half a century (late eighteenth–early nineteenth centuries), Vienna would be
the focal point for the trade in cotton and the precious red cotton yarns, and later
of their provision to the numerous artisanal and industrial units which processed
the threads in Upper and Lower Austria, Moravia and Bohemia.[35]

In this geopolitical and economic context, as used in this paper the English term 'merchant *colonies*' includes the content of *confraternities*, *communities*,
'nations', κοινοτήτων and παροικιών, in reference to the itinerant merchants' collective forms of settlement and organization, but also the content of the terms
commercial societies, *firms*, *Gesellschaften* and *ditte*. The first group refers to
the form of the administrative and collective organization of the immigrants
within their places of reception in accordance with the measures decreed by the
authorities there. The second group refers precisely to the organization of the
single-trader, family and other commercial firms which evolved as a result of
the measures decreed by the reception authorities to protect, and hence attract,
foreign merchants. The networks formed by the merchant colonies in the second group were subject to numerous laws and conventions in force both in their
places of origin and reception, and the places they moved to subsequently.

We shall examine the first group in accordance with the immigration policy
applied – in this case by the Venetians – to the reception of non-Catholic immigrants in their capital, and primarily by the Habsburgs with regard to the groups
of Venetian and Ottoman subjects who settled in their territory, especially during the eighteenth century. Within these territories, immigration policy[36] was
never applied uniformly across an entire jurisdiction or over time. Because of
their territorially fragmented *Repubblica*, the Venetians found themselves facing
the problem early on of settling populations which adhered to other denom-
inations and religions in its capital, who were chiefly, though not exclusively,
subjects of its expanding territories in the Levant. Guided primarily by its economic and political interests, and acting in accordance with the Common Law
and rules of governance, the Venetian *Repubblica*, sometimes acceding with

the wishes of the Catholic Church and sometimes clashing with it, accepted the organization of numerous *confraternità* or *sc[u]ole* which, organized along the lines of the late-Mediaeval guilds, evolved according to its interests and the needs of the new arrivals. To facilitate the settlement of Greek Orthodox merchants, their institutional *confraternità* was formed from the fifteenth century on by successive groups of refugees, *stradioti* in the service of the *Serenissima*[37] and merchants from Epirus, the Peloponnese and Crete, constituting a vigorous economic community with a host of scholars active within it, due to the activities of the Greek publishing houses[38] based in the city whose influence and production extended throughout the Balkans. From the late seventeenth century on, in particular, the network of Epirote and Peloponnesian merchants came to include Venice, where it had representatives active both in the running of the *confraternità*[39] and of the *comunità*, which it developed into after the late eighteenth century.[40] Large numbers of sailors and other groups which did not belong to the merchant class were active on the communities' fringes.[41]

The word 'privileges' conveys its literal meaning, in the case of Venice where the organization of Greek Orthodox communities in its capital may have formed the model for the establishment and organization of community of every type in those places which received arrivals from south-eastern Europe. The Habsburgs adopted mercantilist policies, especially from the late seventeenth century on and mainly during the eighteenth century. The need to attract both experienced merchant capitalists and specialized craftsmen for the empire's burgeoning industrial production was one of its chief concerns, and the central authorities' interest in both groups would continue undiminished until the 1770s and 1780s. Thus, in both Transylvania and regions of Hungary, the imperial authorities responded positively to the increasing number of Ottoman subjects arriving from the south. The migrants were also motivated to leave their places of origin by the unfavourable conditions pertaining there. Thus, after the loss of Crete (1669) and its brief rule over the Peloponnese (1685–1715), Venice's overseas territories had shrunk to the Ionian islands, while in the Ottoman Empire, the increase in the number of large landowners (*çiftliks*), which led to new conditions of tax dependence for Ottoman subjects, and hence to increased taxes, successive wars and the resulting destruction of cities (the fate of the once-flourishing Moschopolis, now Voskopolje),[42] and commercial competition from the European powers, especially in the eastern Mediterranean – coupled with the increasing role of Greek shipping which this gave rise to,[43] plus the role of Greek merchants in general in the Aegean and the Mediterranean – led to successive waves of immigration (on the part of the Serbs, Greeks, Vlachs from Epirus and Macedonia).

After their initial, less permanent settlements, smaller or larger groups of people who had departed from their ancestral religious or geographical communities sought permission from the central authorities to form a community (*compagnia/Bruderschaft/Gemeinde*). The groups making these requests were often led by priests or financially powerful merchants,[44] while the privileges they sought related to the right to found a community, build a church (for Orthodox groups) and, in some cases, to set up a school. The privileges usually reflected the general economic and social profile of the given city of reception. Thus, in the case of Trieste, the privileges granted to foreigners can be viewed in the context of the freedoms enjoyed by the city, meaning they were exempted from military service, had the right to purchase land and property and store products, and enjoyed tax breaks, rights of moorage, etc. In this context, the merchant colonies of Trieste had the chance to develop over the long term, thanks to the exceptional opportunities they enjoyed in the transit trade, and to the opportunity available to their members to join and help mould the city's cosmopolitan society.[45] The situation was quite different and varied inland. The Habsburg authorities initially treated the newly arrived merchants on the basis of their religion. The '*Griechen*', '*Greci*' or the '*Greci scismatici*' or the '*Griechen nicht unirte*' (Greeks not united with the Catholic Chruch) were the terms used by the Catholic reception authorities for those who adhered to the *Greci orientali* creed, which is to say members of the Eastern Orthodox Church. In theory, most of the Christian inhabitants of south-eastern Europe – or at least those who moved to central Europe to trade – fell into this category. And, in theory, Serbs (Illirici), Greeks and (Macedonian) Vlachs alike from Macedonia, Thessaly and Epirus enjoyed the privileges applying to this religious category. Having acquired privileges, the merchants proceeded to organize the community that would serve as their institutional representative before the central authorities and among themselves. Apart from Greek and the official language of the particular country of reception (Italian, German), Slavo-Serbian (*Slavjano serbisch*) was often used to draft the communities' privileges and memoranda of statutes. The choice of Greek can be explained by its dominant role in the spheres of trade and education throughout south-eastern Europe at this time. National differentiation would become more intense with the increase in the number of families arriving from the south and the need for the community's women and children to attend the liturgy, and for the latter to be educated. In an atmosphere shaped by the Enlightenment and the ideology of the French Revolution, these were factors that would lead to national awareness, especially between the Greeks and more numerous Serbs (Illirici), who enjoyed the support of the Metropolitan of Karlowitz[46] and the diocese of Szentendre. The signs of national differentiation would become more obvious from the late eighteenth century on as different ethnicities began to acquire different privileges and to establish 'separate' churches. The distinction between Serbs and Greeks would become especially clear in both Trieste and Vienna, as well as in the numerous colonies in Hungary which had a larger Serbian than Greek population as a result of the large influx of Serbs into the area along the Military Frontier from the late eighteenth century on.[47] In contrast, the clashes on a community level between Greeks and Vlachs from Epirus and Macedonia, where Greek-language culture predominated, did not lead to discrete communities.[48] In the world of the mercantile diaspora, people took in the ideology of nationalism with their mother's milk, and it was in the merchant colonies that ideas of creating independent Balkan states, beginning with the establishment of an independent Greece, were nurtured.

For the Austrian authorities, these foreigners formed groups of *acattolici* (not Catholics), of '*Greek*' or *görög* merchants, or *türkischen Untertanen* (Ottoman subjects). Registered on the census *Konskriptionen* as *acattolici*, they would also be subdivided into several subcategories, if the census sought to monitor their progress in educational matters. During the era of *Josephinismus*,[49] Austria concerned itself with monitoring the maintenance of religious education by the inhabitants of the empire. They were usually recorded as '*Greek*' or *görög* merchants, as well as *türkische Untertanen*, on their arrival at the border, along with a precise description of their person, provenance, reason for coming and planned place of settlement.[50] Censuses were also held at regular intervals in the places where they settled, due to the need for constant monitoring, especially in Transylvania and Hungary,[51] where there was a larger influx of arrivals and a more scattered pattern of settlement.

The reactions of the local people and the strengthening of the commercial classes in the empire itself led in the late eighteenth century to a gradual change in policy on the part of the central authorities. Especially in Hungary, the fact that the Greek Orthodox frequently did not adapt to the strict framework of a tariff regime that worked to their advantage after the treaty of Passarowitz involved them in competition with local merchants.[52] After 1774, like most other Ottoman subjects, they had to take the Hungarian oath of fidelity and move their families to their new places of residence if they wanted to continue trading from established shops in Hungarian territory. In Austria, the naturalization of colonists was becoming increasingly common, to the extent that two Greek Orthodox communities were created in Vienna in the 1780s: one around the church of Saint George for the Ottoman subjects, the other around the church of the Holy Trinity for the subjects of the Habsburg emperor.[53] They sought naturalization because of the easier access it brought to local economic *gremia*/institutions and to improve their economic and social standing, but it did not necessarily lead to national and social assimilation. In regions (of Hungary) where the flow of merchants from the south came to a halt in the second decade of the nineteenth century, the road to social Hungarianization was more rapid,[54] though the immigrants' retention of their religion, and the presence of Greek and Serbian schools, preserved the social structure for longer. Starting in the early nineteenth century, the Greek merchants, who had until then settled around the Greek Orthodox churches and communities which had formed the centres of informal but distinct neighbourhoods – known as the *campo dei Greci* in Venice, the *Griechengasse* (Greek street) in Vienna's Fleischmarkt neighbourhood[55] and the *görög utca* (Greek street) in Szentendre – began, in the richer cities of reception at least, to merge into the urban fabric. The organizational commercial conditions, which had required them to live side by side to deal with the practical need of conducting commercial transactions via common small commercial firms and the consequent cohabitation of their members and their auxiliary staff, gradually ceased to hold. It is worth noting that there had never been a need to create neighbourhoods of this sort in cities like Trieste, where almost the entire population of the cosmopolitan *città nuova* were immigrants. It was in this new city that the *acattolici* migrants (Orthodox, Armenians, Jews, Protestants) would 'construct' a city along with Catholics from the surrounding area as well as from south-eastern and the rest of Europe.[56] The Greeks would erect their impressive buildings around the city's financial centre rather than in a separate neighbourhood,[57] and they would participate in the moulding of their city's economy, built environment and society on at least an equal footing, sometimes playing a lead role despite accounting for no more than 3.5 to 4 per cent of its population. In contrast, in Braşov and Sibiu, efforts to found churches within the city walls met with fierce resistance from the powerful local Saxon majority, which was determined to treat the members of the Greek Orthodox *compagnie* as foreigners.[58] The clash of interests between the central Austrian authorities and those of the lower tiers of the local communities is also often clear in the induction of the new arrivals.

According to the above view, the merchant colonies included a second group to be examined, which related precisely to the way in which the sole-trader, family and other commercial enterprises were organized. The aforementioned privileges would allow some of the pioneering itinerant merchants – who arrived by sea from parts of the Venetian Republic (Ionian islands), Ottoman-ruled areas with access to the sea (Epirus, the Peloponnese, Constantinople, the coast of Asia Minor – Smyrna, in particular – and the Aegean islands), but also by caravan from landlocked provinces (the Epirote highlands, Macedonia, Thessaly) – to transform themselves into wealthy merchants who developed commercial practices, contributed to the establishment of family networks linking south-eastern with central and northern Europe[59] – for example linking the areas that produced the raw materials with the regions where they were processed and marketed as industrial or manufactured goods – and played their part in establishing their host societies economically. Thus, it was largely men experienced in marine communication who set off from these regions, men oriented towards the rhythms of trade, usually with an urban background – and who thus chose to settle in foreign ports and, above all, in Trieste, although mountain populations were also on the move, mostly from areas with pastoral economies (Zagorochoria, Metsovo, market towns in western Macedonia) but also from areas with a mixed economy (like Moschopolis, Ioannina the Epirote capital, and Thessaly) which had begun to inject trade activities into their agricultural-pastoral economies in the eighteenth century.[60] Many of these subsequently powerful merchants started their commercial careers as apprentices.[61] They often had to live in small rooms in relatives' houses or in the community, and to pay for their keep in return for learning the secrets and language of the art of commerce. Alternatively, they might work as *garzoni di bottega* (apprentices of sorts)[62] in the merchants' household. We are familiar with the enormous change both in business practices and – still more importantly – in world view and mentality experienced by the great Greek man of letters of the future, Adamantios Korais, who started life as an *apprenti marchand* (merchant apprentice) in Amsterdam (1770–4).[63] Moreover, 'the family form also provided a source of respectable employment for family members.'[64]

Kaiserliche privilegierte Großhändler, Negozianti, commercianti, ditte insinuate nel Tribunale mercantile, ditte in accomandita, shipping insurance firms and shipping associations were the most prominent forms of business associated with the Greek presence in the Habsburg Monarchy. Alongside them, a host of smaller-scale merchants sought financial success or tried at least to secure a living working as commercial agents, secretaries, shop assistants, selling coffee, dyeing red yarn or working as teachers, priests and scholars based in one place or moving among some of them.[65]

Interpersonal relationships in family firms on land, at sea or both, constitute a core axis for readdressing the relationship between south-eastern and central Europe. These firms were of varying duration, short being at about three years, middle at about five to six years or long at six years; after that period they could be dissolved or reformed. They consisted of two–three individuals, who were usually from the same place or family, while companies in which Greeks and Serbs or Jews collaborated began to appear round the turn of the century, without this being the norm. The longest durations are to be found in the late eighteenth century, and are chiefly in the form of the society '*in accomandita*',[66] in which *socii taciti* (silent partners) took part through the provision of capital and *socii attivi* (active partners). In the late eighteenth century, their capital ranged from 10,000 to 300,000 fiorins.[67] These merchants manoeuvred between two or more worlds and countries, and they certainly played their part in blurring the boundaries between the 'semi-peripheral' and the 'peripheral',[68] often playing a leading role – in central Europe at least – in local institutions instrumental in shaping economic conditions (*Borsa, Camera di Commercio, Tribunale mercantile*).[69] In the early part of the period under consideration, businessmen were part of a socio-economic network, along with the environment of the places they started out from and ended up residing. Emotional and moral factors also played a key role in determining economic decisions. 'The early-modern entrepreneur cannot be seen as an independent agent. He was invariably part of a socio-economic network, which exerted a coercive influence on his behaviour.'[70]

The Greek commercial networks around the port of Trieste extended into the Mediterranean, into central Europe and, from the end of the eighteenth century, the Black Sea as well. They were based in commercial firms, shipping investments and backed up by marine insurance companies;[71] they survived in the pluralism of Trieste because they maintained links with the places they had set off from in the Ottoman Levant, and because they retained their local,[72] ethnic and familial cohesion through intermarriage, though a number of their members would, for financial reasons, choose the route of imperial *naturalization* from the late eighteenth century on.[73] Of the forty-five firms approved by the commercial court from 1787 to1815, twenty-five had partners from Smyrna, seventeen from the Peloponnese, ten from Chios, eight from Thessaly and four from Epirus.[74]

The *Griechischer Handelsmann* in central Europe proper formed a category of its own;[75] he did everything he could to acquire the *Niederlassungsrecht* (the right of commercial establishment) required to trade in non-Ottoman goods as well, and succeeded in establishing himself – generally through his terrestrial trading/banking family network which encompassed Vienna, Pest, Constantinople, Ioannina and Trieste (in the case of the Epirote Stavros Ioannou[76]) – for at least fifty years between the late eighteenth and early nineteenth centuries during which time the merchants of Ambelakia and Epirus/Thessaly in general, held onto their monopolistic commercial and production network.[77] Attempted collaborations between capitalist merchants and craftsmen in running the *Türkischrot-Garnfärbereien* (yarns dyed red in the 'Turkish manner') in the form of commercial-artisanal companies proved short-lived due to the Ambelakia monopoly and to the climate. In central Europe, too, and especially in Vienna and Pest, the family forms of company described above were predominant, with agents or subsidiaries based in trading stations throughout south-eastern Europe, especially in places with important commercial fairs (Pazardzik, Philippoupolis/Plovdiv, Monastir/Vitolja, Niš et al.[78]), or in the rest of central Europe as far as Bohemia, Saxony, the international market of Leipzig and Poznan, but also to the Ukraine and Russia. The founding of powerful commercial/banking houses and their relations with local houses (links between the Sinas and Paziazi houses with the Schwarzenberg banking house),[79] the investments in property around the *Fleischmarkt* and *Hoher Markt* (Sinas),[80] imperial naturalization and the search for a means of acquiring grain estates in the Hungarian Banat and, hence, the acquiring of noble titles by some (Hatzimichail, Manoussis, Christoforos Nakos, Johann Georg Paziazi, Simon Georgiou Sinas)[81] are some of the social achievements of the merchants/bankers from the end of the eighteenth century onwards. A number of the large-scale merchants would enter the nobility in both Austria and Hungary.[82]

The *compagnie* operated alongside these family companies, especially in eastern Hungary and Transylvania. These *compagnie* were multi-member, multi-partner incorporations which, transcending the trade guild, allowed for freedom of action and protected their members against their powerful Saxon competitors, in particular.[83]

Since the Greek merchant colonies were chiefly established in urban areas, they, along with the other foreign merchant colonies as a whole, generally contributed to their urban transformation and re-signification as centres of central European industrial production and commerce.

8 COMMUNITY FOR COMMERCE: AN INTRODUCTION TO THE NEZHIN GREEK BROTHERHOOD FOCUSING ON ITS ESTABLISHMENT AS A FORMAL INSTITUTION IN THE YEARS BETWEEN 1692 AND 1710

Iannis Carras

It was in the border town of Nezhin, 'Nizhna' in the Greek sources,[1] in what is today north-eastern Ukraine, that the 'Brotherhood of the Greeks' with its religious and trading privileges and its arbitration court was established in the closing years of the seventeenth century.[2]

The members of this 'Brotherhood of the Greeks' called themselves '*Romioi*', denoting that they were Orthodox Christians of the Ottoman Empire; theirs was thus 'the Brotherhood of the Romioi of Nizhna' or alternatively 'of Kazakia'.[3] In the Russian and Ukrainian texts of the time these *Romioi* are called 'Greeks' or '*Greki*'. It is only in very specific contexts, and towards the end of the century, that the term 'Hellene' is used with respect to this particular group.[4] Though it is true that many members of the 'Brotherhood' spoke Greek only as a second language, it should be noted that the official language of their communal institutions, both secular and religious, was Greek. Following Troian Stoianovich's characterization of these his 'conquering' merchants, this should be considered just as much a Brotherhood of the Balkan Orthodox as a Brotherhood of Greeks, though arguably the distinction would have been lost on most of its members.[5]

Nezhin was far from the precarious coast,[6] and did not lie on any of the significant fluvial arteries linking Ukrainian territories with the Black Sea littoral.[7] The city was, however, ideally suited for the caravan trade connecting the Ottoman Empire through Wallachia, Moldavia and Poland with Muscovy.[8] Further, three fairs annually gave Nezhin pride of place in an expanding network of other fairs serving the town's hinterland,[9] the left bank of the river Dnieper, 'Kazakia' as it was known to the Greeks of the time, and the wider Russian south.[10]

The merchants and others who constituted this Brotherhood traded in a large number of goods: in the seventeenth century slaves (especially, though not exclusively, slaves returning from captivity in the Ottoman Empire),[11] and also, throughout the period under consideration, valuable cloths and clothes, precious stones, holy relics, icons and other select items, wines, spices, delicacies and the like.[12] Perhaps the main reason for their journeying to Moscow and further inland was, however, the quest for fur;[13] governed by strict sartorial laws in Ottoman lands, fur was symbolic of status, being conferred from on high as a demonstration of protection and patronage.[14] It is in the context of this exchange of 'charismatic' goods that members of the Brotherhood prospered.[15]

Following the violent expulsion of most Jews from the region,[16] the Hetman Bogdan Khmel'nitskii ceded trading privileges to Greeks, Armenians and Muslims (in other words to the non-Jewish populations of the Ottoman Empire) in the territories under his control though a Universal (or decree) of 1657.[17] Greeks were first associated with the particular town of Nezhin in a Universal of the Hetman Ivan Samoilovich of 1675.[18] The Brotherhood's founding charter however dates only to 1696, or, perhaps, 1697.[19] It should therefore be clear that Greeks lived and traded in Nezhin before the Brotherhood was established as a formal institution, sanctioned by official – ecclesial and secular – authorities.

As confirmed by a series of Hetmans, and, from 1710 on, by Peter I and his successors, the Nezhin Greeks were granted extensive privileges: not only permission to trade, but also religious liberties, tax concessions, autonomy from local municipal authorities (excluded, for example, from obligations to provide housing for army personnel), and the right to their own arbitration court, the *Kriterion*.[20] Further tax concessions were granted to Greeks trading within Russia proper.[21] Throughout the period under consideration, these privileges or freedoms constituted sources of dispute between the other residents of the region, the Ukrainian and Russian authorities, and the Greeks themselves. Regulations governing the Nezhin Greeks' right to buy houses and property in and around Nezhin, maintaining them tax-free, were a particular source of tension.[22] Though undoubtedly important, it is not the privileges in and of themselves that explain the presence of the Greeks in the region; rather than giving them pride of place, attention should be directed to access to political power enjoyed by merchants; they made use of this power in order to establish, defend, and, at times, extend their privileges.

During the course of the seventeenth and eighteenth centuries, the number of Nezhin Greeks steadily increased. Eighteen Greeks resident in Nezhin are referred to in a list of those who swore allegiance to the Russian Crown in 1682.[23] The final decade of the century was one of rapid growth;[24] a list of the Greeks in Nezhin compiled in view of the commencement of hostilities between Russia and the Ottoman Empire in March 1711 refers to 232 Greeks temporarily or permanently resident in the city,[25] an increase linked to the expulsion of most Greeks from Moscow.[26] Similar numbers are confirmed by other sources later in

the century.[27] Thus 242 Greek males signed a document related to the enthrone-
ment of Catherine II in 1762.[28] More impressively, 164 places of residence in
Nezhin were owned by Greeks at this time.[29] The official 1782 census recorded
408 Greek men and 357 Greek women permanently resident in Nezhin; a further 77 men and 72 women are recorded as Vlachs, Bulgarians or Persians;[30] 17
men and 19 women are referred to as baptized Turks. Thus, at this late date, with
the authorities attempting to distinguish between population groups, more than
800 Orthodox of the Ottoman Empire were permanently resident in Nezhin, a
number that corresponds to some 8 per cent of the town's resident population.[31]
As noted by travellers through Nezhin at the time, theirs was the dominant
influence on the commercial and cultural life of the town.[32]

A note of caution is of course required with all these figures: being mobile
and expert at avoiding the payment of duties in the loosely controlled southern
borderlands, Greeks could and frequently did slip through official attempts to
record them.[33] Further, as was the case in other similar communities, those recognized as official members of the Brotherhood were far fewer than the total
number of Greeks active in any given area.[34] Nonetheless the numbers should
be considered indicative of a considerable Greek presence in Nezhin, and of the
importance of trading routes linking the Ottoman and Russian Empires.

The 1782 census may represent the acme of the Greek community in Nezhin.
Russia's taming of its borderlands and southward expansion, population growth,
and, from the treaty of Belgrade of 1739 onwards, the at first listless but progressively accelerated increase in maritime trade, contributed to Nezhin's demise as a
community at the forefront of international trade.[35] The ease of direct commerce
via the sea led to changes in the product mix and adjustments in the locations
where merchants chose to be based; the privileges of the Nezhin Brotherhood
served, however, as a precedent for the organization of other communities of
the south of the Russian Empire in the second half of the eighteenth century.[36]
It was many of the same merchant families, formerly Nezhinites, that continued
to prosper in this altered world.

Inland Emporion

In 1759 a Greek historian would describe Nezhin as an 'illustrious emporion
... where many Greeks reside for the sake of commerce'.[37] The use of the term
'emporion' is striking; for in many ways, and despite being inland, Nezhin provides a perfect fit for Karl Polanyi's 'port of trade',[38] and the Nezhin Greeks a
parallel to Lois Dubin's and David Sorkin's 'port Jews'.[39] As was the case with
Polanyi's 'port of trade', Nezhin was located in the border regions of empire, in
a no man's land between two worlds, without however being a frontier garrison
like Kiev, which functioned above all as a military and administrative, rather

than trading, centre. With the 'port of trade' at a distance, empire might profit, while simultaneously (as seen with the expulsion of Greeks from Moscow) keeping commerce's corrupting influence at a safer distance.

Clearly, the concept of the 'port Jew' cannot be extended to the Nezhin Greeks without, to put it mildly, 'diluting the historical specificity of the social type'.[40] Unlike Dubin, Sorkin uses the term very much in the context of his analysis of alternative Jewish paths to modernity. Like the 'port Jews', the Nezhin Greeks were associated with migration and commerce; however, though their services were required, they did not reside in an environment that valued commerce as such. If anything, it was the Hetmans and the Russian Court that most treasured their activities, and it was to such Court circles, at least in the initial stages of the community, that the more successful Nezhin merchants aspired.

Members of the Nezhin Brotherhood did show an interest in education, even in education in one of its more secular forms. They planned to establish a school with scholarships for those students who could not afford to pay the fees.[41] Zgouros Katakatzoulos, son of Stylos, a founding member from the region of Ioannina in Epirus,[42] wrote to the scholar Seraphim Mytilinaios.[43] At first Seraphim agreed to Zgouros's proposal. The school was to have been funded, in part, by the Hetman Mazepa.[44] In the end, all three participants in this endeavour fell foul of the Russian state. Zgouros allied himself with Mazepa in the events of 1708–9.[45] Seraphim left Russia disillusioned,[46] eventually entering the service of Charles XII of Sweden.[47] Though members of the clergy educated merchants' sons in informal educational settings,[48] and further attempts to establish a formal school were made during the course of the eighteenth century,[49] an official Greek secondary school was established only in the early nineteenth century.[50] The Nezhin Greeks' interest in education did not therefore deliver tangible results in the medium term.

The most significant differences between the Nezhin Greeks and the social type of the 'port Jew' lie elsewhere however. The Greeks did not face the religious obstacles that had to be surmounted by Jewish traders. Though there were rebaptized Muslims among the Nezhin Greeks, such fluidity of belief should be considered more a characteristic of borderlands, than a parallel to the experience of the *conversos* per se: more 'port of trade' than 'port Jew'. In fact, as will be argued further on, Orthodoxy, and the connections of the religious institutions of the Orthodox east constitute part of the explanation for the Nezhin Greeks' initial accomplishments.

And second, in contrast to expanding trade across the Atlantic seaboard that served as the environment for the western diaspora of the Sephardim, and hence for Sorkin's 'social type', the successes of the Greeks of Nezhin, trading over land with their caravans in tow, were a function of traditional contacts between the Ottoman and Russian Empires.[51] Equating the economic significance of the

Greeks with that of the port Jews would therefore be anachronistic, at least for the seventeenth and part of the eighteenth century; it is not a difference of degree but in kind that is at issue. However, during the course of the eighteenth century, the trading networks of the Nezhin Greeks formed one of the bases for the integration of the northern Black Sea littoral into an incipient world economy, an economy fashioned to a considerable extent by economic developments further west. Thus, far from it being simply 'the capitalist world economy' that expanded 'by virtue of its internal dynamic' à la Wallerstein, it was in part through developments in the Black Sea hinterland that the two systems merged;[52] the role of the Nezhin Greeks in this transition, and the means they employed to manage the changes that accrued, render their community particularly worthy of study.

Even if we reject the utility of the 'social type' as a sufficient explanatory framework, and despite the manifest nature of the differences, contrasting the Nezhin Greeks to the 'port Jew' remains useful. It is such contrasts that mitigate against expanding the term 'port Jew' to cover other social and economic circumstances, as proposed for example by Dubin, circumstances that may better be examined through a variety of theoretical frameworks: those of 'Jews in port cities', of the 'emporion' or 'port of trade', or indeed of diaspora more generally.[53]

Further, contrasting the 'port Jew' with the Nezhin Greek provokes a number of questions, chief among them the legal status of the Nezhin Brotherhood. In particular, to what extent should the Greeks of Nezhin be viewed as a traditional autonomous community, through which, in Sorkin's words, 'the temporal powers, in exchange for the remission of taxes, vouchsafed ... wide-ranging legal authority over its members', or, alternatively, as a merchant corporation or voluntary association. In Sorkin, the question of legal status is closely linked to the fifth and final characteristic for his 'social type', the strengthening of a sense of Jewish identity through the development of communal institutions.[54]

It will be argued here that in the case of Nezhin no unambiguous separation between the Brotherhood's role as a 'traditional community' and its role as a voluntary association can be posited. Rather, in the case of the Nezhin Greeks, the term 'traditional community' requires further examination; though this was a community based on belonging to a shared religion, it should not be whitewashed as 'traditional'. The role of the Nezhin Brotherhood as a voluntary or merchant corporation was instrumental, from the outset, in the reconfiguration of 'community'. This 'community' developed, over the course of the eighteenth century, first into something resembling a merchant corporation, and, later, into a constituent part of the local government of empire. Confusingly, all these elements overlapped, and our perspective on the Brotherhood will necessarily vary depending on the sources we use to examine it.

Community should not therefore be understood as a given; examined from the inside, as it will be here, it was structured to meet the needs of the diverse

Orthodox of the Ottoman Empire who travelled to and through Nezhin from the mid-seventeenth century on. Continually adjusted thereafter to meet alterations in those needs, it impacted upon the identities of the merchants and others involved. Examined from the outside, as it has been elsewhere, it served the requirements of the Hetmans and also of the Russian state as it expanded commercially and militarily southwards.[55]

In analysing 'merchant colonies' or 'trading communities', the term 'community' has all too frequently either been taken for granted, or used as a proxy for the a priori premise of increased trust between members. Neither approach is adequate.[56] In fact, the efforts the Nezhin Greeks made to create and maintain community structures despite their differing backgrounds, should point towards the central importance of community both as a framework for but also as a corollary to commerce. The necessity of creating and re-creating community, both on a local level and over vast expanses, may come to be viewed as a significant parallel between the experiences of the trading Greeks of Nezhin (and elsewhere) and the 'social type' of the 'port Jew'. It is however the formation, parameters and utility of one community, the Nezhin Brotherhood in its early years, that will be analysed here.

Community Created

As based on its first seal dated to 1692,[57] and then on its founding charter, dated to 1696, the Nezhin Greek Brotherhood was established as a 'Stavropegial' community, grouped around the two Greek churches of the town, the Church of the Archangels Michael and Gabriel, and the Church of All the Saints. The term 'Stavropegial' connects the Nezhin Brotherhood to a range of other similar Stavropegial Brotherhoods established on both sides of the Dnieper between the sixteenth and eighteenth centuries, chief among them the Brotherhood of Lviv (Lvov or Lemberg, 'Leoupolis' or 'Leontopolis' to the Greeks of the time).[58] As was the case with the Stavropegial monasteries of the eastern Roman Empire, such communities were not subservient to the local ecclesiastical authorities, but rather directly to the Oecumenical Patriarch himself; in fact, the first *Chrysobule* (an official document or decree), granted to the Nezhin Greeks, though expressly linked to the person of Father Christopher (elsewhere named Father Christodoulos, who had been raising alms for the Greek churches of Nezhin since the 1670s), was issued in 1680 by the Oecumenical Patriarch Jacob.[59]

Prior to the establishment of the Brotherhood as an official institution with its own charter, the Greeks of Nezhin, guided (so they claimed) by their priest Father Christopher,[60] and led by the aforementioned Zgouros, approached the Metropolitan of Kiev Varlaam Iasinskii, the highest religious authority in the region. Responding to their petition, the Metropolitan decreed: ' ... in their Greek Church in Nezhin they are to have a brotherly religious union of a Church Brotherhood ... and they should be subservient to no one else, except to the throne of the Metropolitan of Kiev of the Church of the Holy Wisdom ... '.[61]

These regions having been sundered from the Oecumenical See of Constantinople in 1686, 'Stavropegial' now denoted direct subservience to Kiev. Thus, in the early years of their community, and especially in its first charter, the members of the Brotherhood placed themselves within a framework traditional to the regions in which they had relocated, while simultaneously emphasizing their autonomy vis-à-vis local religious authorities, and their ties to the Orthodox east. Only after receiving permission from the Metropolitan did the Nezhin Greeks approach Ioann Mazepa, 'Hetman of both banks of the Borysthenes', as the Dnieper is termed in Greek, requesting a 'Universal for the Brotherhood Church of God together with privileges and terms'.[62]

The Brotherhood's charter commences by determining a range of issues related to religious observance: the role of priests in the community, their obligations and their earnings;[63] there follow the obligations of those elected to serve in the 'offices' of the Brotherhood, 'offices' that for the most part concerned the Brotherhood churches.[64] According to the charter, any *Romios* could join the Brotherhood should he wish; he had to inform the priest as to his intentions, and the priest summoned the holder of the highest office of the Brotherhood, the 'Protephor' ($\pi\rho\omega\tau\acute{\epsilon}\phi\rho\rho\varsigma$) who, in turn, proposed the new member to the Assembly of the Brotherhood. The prospective member paid his dues and swore an oath to the Mother of God, to the Holy Trinity, to All the Saints and to the Archangels Michael and Gabriel soliciting their mediation on his behalf before Jesus Christ, so that, as the oath taker put it: ' ... I may be considered worthy to become a brother in this church'. Having taken the oath, this latest member of the Brotherhood worshiped the New Testament and prostrated himself before the Brotherhood's twelve office holders.[65] Both men and women could be Brotherhood members,[66] but only the men had the right to vote in the Assembly, to elect and be elected to Brotherhood offices.[67]

It is worth dwelling on the question of the Brotherhood's religious autonomy; such autonomy is perhaps surprising given the fact that the populations of the areas in which the Greeks were trading were also Orthodox. Religious autonomy was important for a number of reasons. First, minor differences in the Orthodox ritual and perceived variations in religious commitment were repeatedly magnified in the eyes of contemporaries. Unfamiliar dress, fasting regulations, or, indeed, Greek incapacity to remain standing during services, were frowned upon.[68] Religious autonomy thus reflected the divide between the Orthodox of the Ottoman Empire on the one hand, and the local populations of the Ukraine and Russia on the other. At the same time, it was an Orthodoxy held in common that served as the basis for the Orthodox of the Ottoman Empire constituting a whole, far from their various homelands, in this their new environment.

The second reason for the importance of religious autonomy for the Greeks of Nezhin should, however, be considered equally important. Many of those Greeks who had travelled through the Ukraine via Nezhin to Muscovy from the sixteenth up until the eighteenth centuries arrived as emissaries of the religious establishments of the Orthodox east, establishments frequently labouring under a proscriptive burden of debt.[69] Kyriak Oikonomou, active collecting sums from Astrakhan on behalf of the Patriarch of Jerusalem, was one such emissary.[70] Diamantis Nikolaou, a lay merchant from Syria, dispatched to Moscow in 1706 by Constantine Metropolitan of Chalkedon, was another.[71] The correspondence between Ioannis Christodoulou from the Morea but based in Moscow, an emissary who was active collecting alms for the Patriarchate of Jerusalem while also trading in years between 1705 and 1707, and 'his friend' Sterios Ioannou, based in Nezhin, survives.[72]

Once past Nezhin and on reaching the borders with Muscovy, these emissaries and their retinue received subsidized transport in the form of carts, food and also shelter from the Russian state.[73] Above all however they received alms, alternatively translated as charity or mercies, *milostynia* in Russian, *zities* or, more formally, *eleimosynes* in Greek. There were both small and also larger donations. In one decree of 1706, Peter I mandated that the total sum in alms that the Russian state was to provide to the monasteries of Mount Athos would vary according to the rank of the visiting clergy and also in proportion to the value of the relics they brought as offerings.[74] A considerable portion of these donations were made in sable rather than cash, both because donations in sable could be made at below market value and also to prevent the outflow of specie from the Muscovite state.[75]

This was not a society exclusively characterized by the exchange of alms, that form of exchange similar if not identical to gift-giving as depicted by Marcel Mauss;[76] it would however seem to have been a society where alms-giving and trade were not fully differentiated, where the exchange of goods had some but not all the characteristics of the seemingly disinterested, highly structured exchange of gifts based on rules of mutual reciprocity. As the poet, deacon and alms collector Kaisarios Dapontes aptly coined it, no archpriest would have been as concerned for the loss of a soul in his charge, as he was at the thought of passing up a *para*, which should perhaps in this context be translated as a 'dime'.[77] The exchange of alms aimed at establishing the obligation of interaction between members of a community; the emerging world of trade based on contracts could not begin to function without the non-contractual underpinnings and social structure that preceded and existed alongside it. Sparing a 'dime' was but one small step from earning it.[78]

Given the lack of differentiation between alms and trade, it is not surprising that the higher clergy served as patrons to Greeks trading in Russian lands: their letters of recommendation were essential for those clergy and laypersons that intended to travel to Russian lands with official passports;[79] they guaranteed trading operations, especially, though not exclusively, through the practice of suretyship;[80] their interventions were useful in legal disputes between Greeks,[81] and also in resolving differences with the authorities.[82] To cite but two examples, the Patriarch of Jerusalem Dositheos intervened in the case of the bankrupted Paulo Christophorou from Constantinople;[83] he also supported a further merchant of Macedonia, Kosmas Kyrilou or Kyrilov, a man sufficiently trusted to convey Ambassador Peter Tolstoi's correspondence between Constantinople and Moscow.[84] The former Archbishop of Thessaloniki Methodios Armenopoulos, who was active in the early years of the eighteenth century in encouraging the emigration of sailors and shipbuilders to meet the needs of Russia's new fleet, intervened repeatedly.[85] Such networks of guarantee based on the letters of confirmation of leading Hierarchs functioned as an essential element in such a mobile society, creating social bonds based on protection.

Greek merchants did not receive such protection for free. Rather they were expected to offer substantial sums to the Holy Sepulchre in Jerusalem, to the Monastery of St Catherine on Mount Sinai, to the various monasteries of Mount Athos, and to a whole range of other monastic communities throughout the eastern Christian world. It is not for nothing that the Patriarch of Jerusalem Chrysanthos repeats such formulae as 'they are contributors to the Holy Sepulchre', or, more simply, uses the term 'our friends', to describe his preferred merchants.[86]

Merchant wills provide testimony of such financial contributions and also reveal the common sense of attachment the Greek merchants of Ukraine and Russia felt for their sacred places. The will of the Nezhin Greek merchant Anania Voinov, originally composed 'in vulgare Greco', which has however survived only in vulgar Latin, is a case in point: 'Primo: Sancto Sepulchro Domini nostri Jesu Christi lego reales septingentos. Monti Sancto de Sina lego reales du centos. In Monti Sancto de Attona, in Sancta Laure, lego reales centu et quinquaginta ...' [First: to the Holy Sepulchre of Our Lord Jesus Christ I submit seventy reals, to the Holy Mountain of Sinai I submit two hundred reals. In the Holy Mountain of Athos, to the Monastery of the Holy Laura I submit one hundred and fifty real ...].[87] The document then proceeds to offer that same sum to all the other monasteries of the Holy Mountain, and also to a number of monasteries in his own homeland, Bosnia. The Nezhin Greek from Kastoria Hadji-kyriazis, son of Ralis, left remittances to the Holy Sepulchre, to the furriers guild in Constantinople, to the Oecumenical Patriarchate, to the churches of Nezhin as well as to the poor of the city, and also to the parishes and poor girls of Kastoria. The Brotherhood of the Nezhin Greeks as a whole was supposed to ensure that the will's provisions were to be carried out.[88] As is evident from their wills, the Balkan merchants of Nezhin felt that they belonged to a particular world: that of the eastern Christian commonwealth.[89] '*Hadji*' repeatedly appended to merchants' names denoted precisely an attachment to the holy places of the east, its owner revealing his status as one who had made the pilgrimage to Jerusalem.[90] It is perhaps not unfair to claim that it was in part through the transfer of financial remittances to the holy places of the east that a common geography – a sense of belonging to a particular set of places – was repeatedly fashioned.[91]

When a merchant did not pay dues promised to the Holy Sepulchre, he ran the risk of excommunication. Should Kyriakis, son of Papa-Oikonomou, a *Romios* from Provat, based in Astrakhan, fail to pay 1,000 kuruş that had been entrusted to him as alms for the Holy Sepulchre, then:

> '... we consider him un-forgiven, excommunicated, and eternally damned by God ... For having caused injustice to the Holy Sepulchre he is no Christian, and deserves nothing less than excommunication. ... for all the Orthodox are children and brothers of the Holy Sepulchre ...'.[92]

This missive, composed by the Patriarch of Jerusalem Dositheos, was read 'in the Church of Saint Nicholas where the Romioi sing their prayers'. Nearly all the Greeks in Moscow on that Sunday in 1702 will have heard its content. Excommunication excluded Kyriakis, and others like him, not merely from the community of living merchants but also from its extension in the hereafter.[93]

It is in the context of such threats by Dositheos and other Hierarchs of the Orthodox east that the religious autonomy of the Brotherhood of the Nezhin Greeks should be understood.[94] For the early years of the community were characterized by an ongoing struggle for control of the community's official institutions: churches, warehouses, school, infirmary and other communal buildings. The Monastery of St Catherine on Mount Sinai owned properties in Nezhin, as did the Patriarchate of Jerusalem, and both used the town as a base for the collection of alms among the populations of the Ukraine and Russia.[95] Dositheos, Patriarch of Jerusalem, petitioned the Tsars Peter I and Ivan V requesting that one of the two Greek churches in the city be transferred to the control of his Patriarchate.[96] Zgouros petitioned the Hetman Mazepa to prevent ecclesiastical control of buildings in Nezhin. The sources record conflicts between those Greeks, for example Hadjikyriakis, who supported the principal position of the Monastery of St Catherine in Nezhin, and those opposed, such as Hadjiparaskevas. Hadjikyriakis and Hadjiparaskevas had been trading partners before they fell out, in part over this issue.[97]

In Nezhin, the struggle was won by those who sought to limit the supremacy of the religious institutions of the Orthodox east.[98] Despite the fact that a priest, Father Christopher, is presented as the principal architect of the Brotherhood, the first charter is clear: lay merchants and not clergy were to serve as the governing organs of the Brotherhood. Such clerics as assisted in the Brotherhood churches were to be at the merchants' beck and call.[99] Crucially, the Brotherhood itself was to supervise the collection and distribution of alms. Every Sunday after the celebration of the liturgy alms were collected in the Brotherhood churches for the monasteries of Mount Athos, the Monastery of St Catherine on Sinai and the Holy Sepulchre.[100] It was through the collection of alms that the Greek churches of Nezhin were completed in their current form.[101] Funds were also distributed to laypersons enslaved in Ottoman lands,[102] and to those in poverty locally.[103] The Brotherhood established its own home for the elderly and a hospital catering to the community's basic medical needs.[104]

The charter specified that as soon as a Greek severed his ties with the Brotherhood, its priests were not permitted to accept him to Communion in the Brotherhood churches.[105] A number of Brotherhood documents confirm that whenever one of its members did not obey 'public opinion', then, 'all ... should regard him as a Judas, and ... he should have no prospects for engaging in any type of activity with the brothers and with the church ... '.[106] The use of the term 'public opinion' was linked to Brotherhood elections: 'thus, again, with opinion held in public, and brotherly love in Christ, we agreed all together, and determined, and decreed ... '.[107] Rather than the decrees of Orthodox hierarchs, it was the decisions of the community as a whole that were supposed to serve as the basis for acquiescence.[108]

The Christian term *'ἀγάπη'* ('love' or 'charity') was repeatedly employed in the Brotherhood's religious but also legal documents, revealing the ideal to which its members were meant to aspire, however much they fell short in practice. One document reads: 'and we came together in love, the first and foremost virtue, which is able to accomplish everything both on earth and in heaven'.[109] Yet, despite the religious overtones, and contra to Dositheos's missive of 1702, it was the Brotherhood itself, through the protection of its patron saints and through the remembrance of the dead, that was to be responsible for this *'ἀγάπη'* and for the salvation or otherwise of its members.[110]

Religious autonomy was not of course the only privilege granted to the Nezhin Greek Brotherhood. For this early stage in the community's existence, however, the connection between the Brotherhood's religious autonomy and other privileges is summed up in the founding documents of the Brotherhood: ' ... in having our churches, we have our Brotherhood, and in having our Brotherhood we have our freedoms, and in having our freedoms we trade, and the benefits accrue, to some greatly, to others less, as God bestows to each ... '.[111]

In contradistinction to Nezhin, very different forms of communal organization were established in Kiev and in Moscow. The Greek church at Kiev was controlled by the Monastery of St Catherine on Mount Sinai;[112] the two Monasteries of Saint Nicholas and of the Epiphany where the Greeks (and, in the second case, both Greeks and Armenians) resided in Moscow were controlled by monasteries on Mount Athos.[113] Given this diversity of communal structures, it would be premature, on the basis of the early years of the Nezhin Brotherhood alone, to suggest a correlation between the needs of traders and secularization. Connections between clergy and merchants were close throughout the eighteenth century: often relatives, they travelled and resided together, both in Nezhin and in the monasteries of Moscow and on route. They owed money to each other,[114] and merchants continued with their substantial contributions to the holy places of the Christian east.[115]

Arguably, reduced access of the Ottoman-based Hierarchy to the Russian Court, part of an ongoing process to regulate admissions from the Ottoman world to Muscovy, played a part in this reconfiguration of community.[116] Changes in the Russian state stance vis-à-vis the giving of alms may have proved significant; eventually these passed to the jurisdiction of the Russian Holy Synod.[117] Such trends had not yet significantly impacted upon the Brotherhood at the time of its first establishment as a formal institution, however. Rather, in creating the Brotherhood, its members sought to establish boundaries protecting themselves and their activities from outside intervention. Or, to make the same point in different terms, at this junction the Greeks of Nezhin sought to reconfigure the religious, political and commercial networks that fostered their trade, reducing their dependence on the higher clergy of the Ottoman east, which had proved so useful during the seventeenth century.

Thus, the members of the Brotherhood relied on the religious dimension to foster communal identity, while at the same time reconfiguring the religious dimension to limit external interventions, thus permitting increased differentiation between alms-giving and trade, and therefore reducing barriers to trade per se. The point being made here is not that trust can exist between strangers, provided the institutional conditions help sustain it, as convincingly argued by Francesca Trivellato,[118] rather, it is that commerce reconfigures community, and that community served, in turn, as the kernel for wider trading networks extending to other groups beyond its confines.

In this context, it is possible to explain how a charter that is framed almost entirely in religious terms, should be viewed as part of an incipient differentiation between secular and religious authority: for the means employed to achieve this differentiation were precisely the religious prototypes common to the time. Thus, the Nezhin Brotherhood in its inception does not constitute a case of secularization; rather, it is the contours of community and the loci of power that can be seen in the process of shifting. Networks are being arranged anew, in some cases destabilized, in others created where previously they may not have existed.

Community Contested

Needless to say, the workings of the Brotherhood did not necessarily correspond to the Brotherhood's first charter. Many of the Brotherhood offices fell out of use, or were entrusted to salaried employees.[119] Though a history of the Brotherhood over the course of the eighteenth century is far beyond the scope of this paper, a number of tensions that characterized the Brotherhood almost from its inception may be considered indicative of the difficulties involved in the creation of a functioning trading community of this type.

Though interventions by the Hierarchs of the Orthodox east may have progressively diminished following the establishment of the Brotherhood, this did not reduce interventions by other authorities. Even early on in the century, the higher clergy were not the only source of patronage: other oft-mentioned protectors of Greek merchants included Alexandros and Nicholas Mavrocordatos, both of them serving for some time in the capacity of Grand Dragoman of the Ottoman Porte,[120] the recurring Hospodars (rulers) of Moldavia and Wallachia,[121] various Hetmans,[122] and, increasingly, any number of Russian state officials.[123]

Following on from the Battle of Poltava in 1709 and with Russian control over Left-Bank Ukraine vastly increased, the Brotherhood required confirmation of its privileges from the tsar himself in order to continue functioning effectively. On 3 February 1710 the Brothers addressed a petition to Peter I, asking him to confirm the freedoms 'of their church' which (they claimed) they had enjoyed up until the time of 'the traitor' Mazepa.[124] It was at this juncture, the Russian-Ottoman war of 1711 looming, that the merchant of Constantinople Savva Raguzinskii, charged with organizing efforts to tempt the Christians of the Ottoman Empire to rebellion, intervened, petitioning Tsar Peter personally. The Brothers achieved what they desired on 11 March 1710.[125] Backdated to that very day, the Brotherhood accorded Raguzinskii its highest honour; he too was included in its ranks.[126]

Whereas this was a case of patronage reinforcing the Brotherhood as a whole, in other cases external influences undermined community. Nezhin Greeks might appeal to Ukrainian and Russian patrons to prevent their being condemned by the organs of the Brotherhood.[127] Furthermore, as part of the bargaining process that characterized the Brotherhood's interactions with the Nezhin Magistracy, with local taxation officers, and with other state organizations, members of the Brotherhood spent much of the eighteenth century in fervent dispute as to whether 'incoming' Greeks from the Ottoman Empire should share the full privileges of those already 'established' in Nezhin.[128]

Contested membership of the Brotherhood contributed to complications with regard to the jurisdiction of the Brotherhood court, the *Kriterion*. For the most part the *Kriterion* functioned as an oral arbitration court, hearing disputes among Greeks that required immediate resolution, predominately, but not exclusively, disputes relating to trade. The *Krites* or judges were chosen by mutual consent. At times 'incomers' and the 'established' insisted on having separate judges, creating added difficulties when disputes arose between members of the two groups.[129] Later, a small number of disputes were also to be settled in court through written proceedings.[130]

The extent of the *Kriterion's* jurisdiction was however unclear. The cloth merchant of Nezhin Alexei Nikolaev journeyed to Moscow in 1721 in order to submit a protest to the Chancery of the Collegium of Foreign Affairs.[131] His trial and subsequent condemnation by the Nezhin Magistracy was, he claimed, unlawful. As he argued, the plaintiffs in his case: 'Alexandrov and Galoktionov are not Little Russians. One is a Greek, the other from Wallachia, and both are merchants. And according to the Tsar's Ukaz ... cases involving Greeks and their servants should be tried in their *Kriterion* in their own tongue'.[132] Quite apart from the question of who was and who was not a Greek, and the impact of this question on the functioning of the *Kriterion*,[133] there was the ongoing dispute concerning whether the court should hear cases between Greeks and non-Greeks – a dispute which spawned considerable and frequently contradictory legislative activity on the part of the Ukrainian and Russian authorities.[134]

The source or authority that the court was charged to dispense was to prove an equally intractable issue. One merchant invoked the legislation of Peter I, of Anna Ioannovna, of Catherine II, in addition to the legal traditions of Little Russia and the *Hexabiblos* of Armenopoulos, in his attempt to avoid referral of his case to the *Kriterion*.[135] Indeed the *Kriterion* could itself take account of the all these legal authorities, as well as the laws of Magdeburg and of the Polish-Lithuanian Commonwealth.[136] This was legal pluralism with a vengeance; in all cases, however, the law was adjudicated by secular, not religious, authorities.[137] The judicial field was thus open to constant reinterpretation, and litigants would repeatedly seek justice in other courts where they felt they were better connected and indeed where differences in the law favoured their claims.[138]

The *Kriterion*, and also other legal entities such as the Nezhin Magistracy, were constantly seeking to define their turf, and thus to maximize the privileges accruing to their constituents. In this context, as the eighteenth century progressed, the autonomy of the *Kriterion* was increasingly viewed as codependent with the autonomy of the Brotherhood as a whole. This development can be viewed through changes in the official stamp of the Brotherhood. As mentioned above, the first stamp of 1692 confirms the Brotherhood's religious character. Later in 1736 the stamp was recast. The new cast of the Greek Brotherhood court included a hand holding a scale with the words, 'Stamp of the Nezhin Greek Arbitration Court 1736, January 1st'.[139] In 1775 a further stamp wrote 'Stamp of Her Imperial Majesty's Court of the Nezhin Greek Brotherhood'.[140] A predominately religious association, the Nezhin Brotherhood transformed over time into a legal and commercial entity.

In sum, even after the establishment of the Brotherhood as a formal institution, its parameters, and also the parameters of the community constantly being recreated around it, remained fluid, and contested. Though many elements of the Brotherhood charter had been discarded long before, the charter itself was officially redrafted in 1773. The new charter balanced the offices of the Brotherhood equally between 'incomers' and the 'established'.[141] In 1785 the Nezhin Brotherhood was replaced by a new formal institution, the Nezhin Greek Magistracy, forming part of a chain of other magistracies directly subservient to the Russian state.[142] Though this new institution continued functioning for almost a century, traders had for the most part been active elsewhere by the time of the Magistracy's abolition in 1873 in the reforms of the Emperor Alexander II.[143]

Community and Commerce

In the changing societal conditions of early eighteenth-century Ukraine, with Greek merchants finding themselves at a distance from the clerical networks that had traditionally furnished them with guidance and support, the potential for a differentiation between different methods of interaction emerged. There was already a tension between alms-giving and trade in 1700, though the two activities may in fact have been mutually supporting; as the eighteenth century progressed trade increasingly disentangled itself from its partner's sticky paws.[144]

The establishment and increasing vibrancy of a community that was less dependent on the patronage and spending power of only a few religious and secular centres of power was part of this process: though the Brotherhood's initial charter is redolent of religious prototypes, a shift away from networks of hierarchical protection and in the direction of networks based on the Russian state, and also on trade as an autonomous sphere of human activity, is evident. The borderlands of the Ukraine with their alacritous population growth and increasing incorporation into the ebbs and flows of international maritime trade should then be judged an appropriate litmus for our comprehension of the transition to a market economy. It is the very early stages in such a transition that have been examined here.

The Nezhin Brotherhood created a common bond between its members irrespective of their place of origin within the Ottoman Empire, differentiating them from other populations of the Ukraine and Russia, while simultaneously conjoining them, by means of patronage and through legally binding institutional arrangements, to the Russian state. Here, halfway to Moscow, the merchants endeavoured 'to be united', as they themselves put it.[145] Indeed, they used the term 'polity' to describe their common undertaking.[146] This was not then a 'traditional community' in the sense implied by Sorkin, though it was a community created, at first, through the sense of belonging to a shared religion. Allegiance to this Brotherhood seems to have permitted a transition from Ottoman prototypes, while recreating, and for a time preserving, a mobile but nonetheless distinct eastern Orthodox diaspora community in Ukrainian and Russian lands.

There is thus a circle at the centre of the network, a basis that permits any given community to create more extensive networks beyond its confines. That circle need not have been religious in any strict sense of the term: the Church may have supplanted kinship, or may be supplanted by ethnic ties, by the Court, or indeed by the courtroom, as occurred with the Nezhin Brotherhood during the course of its eighteenth-century expansion. In the case of the Nezhin Brotherhood in its early years, however, the importance of religious bonds as one explanation for Greeks' commercial development should not be overlooked.

Acknowledgements

The research for this paper constitutes part of my dissertation, I. Carras, 'Trade, Politics and Brotherhood: The Greeks in Russia 1700–1774' (PhD dissertation, Athens University, 2011).

I would like to thank among others G. Arsh, M. Bourbouhakis, E. Chernuhin, N. Chrissidis, G. Harlaftis, O. Katsiardi-Hering, P. Kitromilides and Y. Nikolopoulos for their help and advice.

9 ENTREPRENEURSHIP AT THE RUSSIAN FRONTIER OF INTERNATIONAL TRADE. THE GREEK MERCHANT COMMUNITY/PAROIKIA OF TAGANROG IN THE SEA OF AZOV, 1780s–1830s

Evrydiki Sifneos and Gelina Harlaftis

Taganrog developed as the first city-port in south Russia, part of the strategic plan of the Russian Empire to expand southwards into the Black Sea and the Mediterranean and to create a new economic zone which would later specialize in grain trade.[1] It was the most important port in the Sea of Azov up until the mid-1860s and the second most important of southern Russia after the port of Odessa. It was named after the horn-like shape of the peninsula (*tagan*) which dominates the small inlet of the north-eastern Sea of Azov. In this remote point for international trade, which developed based on the Russian imperial plans for expansion southwards, the Greeks contributed significantly to the integration of the area into the international economy. During the first half of the nineteenth century the large and affluent Greek merchant community or *paroikia* of Taganrog was so dominant in the economic and social life of the town to the extent that the Russian novelist Vassili Sleptsov referred to it as a 'Greek Kingdom'.[2] Greeks brought with them entrepreneurship, in other words capital, technical know-how and their networks in trade and shipping, and promoted the economic development of the area.[3] Despite the fact that the Greek population in Taganrog was smaller than in Odessa it made up a dense ethnic-cultural group which demonstrated dynamism through their economic and social activities.[4] The Greeks of Taganrog changed the look of the town with their endowments, and, as members of the city government and its collective bodies, as grain merchants and shipowners developed the economy of the area and the city's enhancement and embellishment.[5]

This paper explores the first phase of the evolution of the Greek *paroikia*, as is explained in the introduction of this book, from its formation in the last third of the eighteenth century to the first third of the nineteenth century. The theme is studied in the light of new archival material from the rich south Russian and Ukrainian archives. The aim is to examine the establishment of a city-port, and the participation of the Greeks and the mechanisms they developed in opening up paths to the international market. The connection between the southern Russian grain market, the Mediterranean and northern Europe was, in part, an achievement of Greek business.[6]

Greek Merchant *Paroikies*

The issue of the diaspora of the Greeks and the boundaries of their 'homeland' have attracted the attention of many a Greek scholar.[7] I. Hassiotis has defined the Greek diaspora as part of the Greek people that for various reasons have left the traditional lands of the Greek Orthodox east and have settled, even temporarily, in lands and countries far away but continued to keep close cultural ties with their land of origin.[8] The numerous works on the Greek merchant communities of the early modern era have revealed their bonds with their homeland and, more recently, their process of integration into the country of reception. These two trends, between the imagined homeland and the day-to-day reality of the host country constructed the material and spiritual realm of the immigrants towards which they addressed their actions. Recent studies tend to emphasize the interaction among different ethnic groups of the city-ports and the ways they shared the common city space, according to their relation to the institutional framework and to other ethno-cultural groups.[9]

The formation of Greek *paroikies* in eastern and western Europe and the Mediterranean came as a result of the expansion of Greeks in land and sea transport during the eighteenth century.[10] Greeks in the eighteenth century, who were Ottoman or Venetian subjects, linked the eastern Mediterranean and the Black Sea to western Europe through maritime and commercial networks. These expanded, on the one hand through the sea, by the development of a dense web of sea routes that linked the Mediterranean maritime regions, by seafarers based in the Aegean or Ionian islands, and, on the other hand, by land, that is, via mobile groups of organized Greek entrepreneurial families involved in continental trade. They handled international commodities by establishing a chain of Greek merchant *paroikies* that linked their activities during the eighteenth and nineteenth centuries to the large sea-oriented empires, the Venetians, the Spanish, the Dutch, and the British, as well as to the land-oriented empires, the Ottomans, the Austro-Hungarians and the Russians.[11]

With the main interest of western European historians in the Venetian, the French, the English and the Dutch presences in the Mediterranean, there is a limited literature – in other than Greek languages – on one of the most active and mobile diaspora groups in the area, the seafarers of the Levant, Ottoman and Venetian Greeks (see also Chapter 7 by Olga Katsiardi-Hering in the present volume).[12] The economic and social factors that conditioned the emigration of merchants and the growth of their activities lay in the particular circumstances of the eighteenth century.

It was the political and economic conjuncture in both sides, east and west, of the Mediterranean that favoured the expansion of Greek merchant *paroikies* in the whole of the Mediterranean and the Black Sea throughout the eighteenth century. Greeks served and exploited the political and economic policies of the empires: the Ottoman, the Habsburg and Russian in the east, the British, the French and the Dutch in the west. The expansion in each maritime region of the Mediterranean was facilitated by the almost continuous wars and resulting treaties that instigated economic opportunities for 'free traders' and subjects of neutral powers.

Important deep-sea going fleets of large merchant ships were formed in about forty islands and port towns of the Ionian Sea on both the Venetian and Ottoman sides and in the Aegean islands with captains and shipowners experienced in the management and operation of cargo vessels in the long-distance Mediterranean sea trade. By the end of the eighteenth century a 'production system' was thus gradually formed, carrying grain from the eastern Mediterranean with the island fleets of the Greeks consisting of about 1,000 large deep-sea going cargo vessels. The Greek diaspora traders created a 'production system' of closely knit small, medium and large businesses within a loosely organized network. This commercial and maritime web assumed a triple dimension: the local/regional, the national/peripheral and the international. It gave access to ports, agents and financial and human resources, providing the Greek diaspora networks with the strength to internalize many operations and survive international competition. Their cohesion was derived from the business culture they developed, and through shipping they were able to survive economically in the international arena.[13]

Why were the Greeks in Taganrog?

The expansion of Russia along the southern and the eastern coasts of the Black Sea took place during the Age of Empires, a period of intense competition between the colonial western European powers to acquire new lands for exploitation of economic sources. The colonization of the Sea of Azov and the establishment of the city of Taganrog was part of Russia's expansion to the south. The development of grain exports via the Black Sea was a central choice of its strategy to create a new economic zone. To achieve this the Russian Imperial state needed experienced seamen, businessmen and people to populate the new towns and cultivate the land. Thus the Greeks – Venetian/Ionian and Ottoman subjects - with a long tradition in maritime trade were highly significant for the economy of the Sea of Azov region.

Almost all the port towns of southern Russia which were founded at the end of the eighteenth century, from Odessa to Taganrog, became gateways of grain exports during the nineteenth century.[14] The new territories that Russia conquered from the Ottoman Empire attracted a large number of immigrants from central and south-eastern Europe who settled in rural areas, towns and cities and advanced economically.[15] Economic incentives for immigration to new lands were offered to Russians, the populations of central Europe and the inhabitants of the Aegean and Ionian seas. The population of 'New Russia' (Novorossiya) mushroomed from 163,000 in 1782 to 3.4 million in 1856.[16]

The area of New Russia offered different possibilities than those of the north. All the Russian towns on the Black Sea from Odessa to Taganrog were new towns that had been established by immigrants from the end of the eighteenth century to the mid nineteenth. They flourished as gateways of grain export, since the Russian steppes with their precious 'black soil' proved to be ideal grain-producing and supplying areas for the industrializing western Europe.[17] The port towns of southern Russia developed rapidly during approximately the same period that the large American port towns of the Atlantic were also growing. The inhabitants of the urban centres of New Russia, Greeks, Jews, Armenians, Bulgarians, Serbs, Germans, Poles, along with Ukrainians and Russians, set up a thriving and evolving urban society with many self-made businessmen.

Despite the fact that Russian policy for the development of Odessa on the western coast of the Black Sea is better known, the development of Taganrog on the opposite less-accessible eastern edge of the north coast began at least twenty years prior to that of Odessa. The development of Taganrog and the other towns of the Sea of Azov is associated with the overcoming of the major obstacle, that of the access to the Sea of Azov. The geography of this area was special, not only as a result of its shallow waters which did not permit large-capacity vessels to approach the shores, but also due to the weather conditions created in the region.[18] From November to March the ports were forced to cease operations due to the icing over of the sea, and the frequent high winds often caused damage to the ships and brought about shipwrecks. The dangerous weather conditions in the Sea of Azov (storms and gale-force winds) made the depth of the sea fluctuate suddenly from four to twelve feet.[19] A characteristic example of the problems caused is the fact that the construction work for Taganrog port, which took thirty years to be completed, was entirely destroyed three times due to extreme weather conditions.[20]

The development of the town of Taganrog directly correlates to the economic activities and affluence of the Greeks residing in the area. As traders and shipowners the Greeks were almost exclusively involved in the foreign trade of the town which operated as an export port located at the particularly difficult and 'insubordinate' region of the Don Cossacks.[21] The Greeks were co-founders of Taganrog and perhaps this is why they named it 'Taiganio' (Ταϊγάνιο) to be closer in sound to Tanais, the ancient Greek colony. The precious archival material discovered in the state archives of the region of Rostov-on-Don (GARO) presents the history of the foundation of the town on the coast of the country of the Don Cossacks. A town perched on a peninsula on the banks of the Sea of Azov which in some respects is like an island: faced with Lake Mæotis (the ancient name for the Sea of Azov) and backed by steppe land.

The archives reveal the Russian institutional framework within which the Greeks managed to develop an extensive community involved in sea trade. It must not be forgotten that Taganrog was located on the southern border of the Russian Empire in the 1770s and that the chief concern of the government was to populate the town and ensure its economic development. Therefore, the imperial government offered many incentives so as to create permanent settlements in the new port towns and transform them into export gates of the agricultural production of the hinterland. Yet, in terms of port infrastructure and facilities these coastal towns remained backward in comparison to Odessa and the other ports of the Mediterranean.[22] Most ships were obliged to wait at the roadstead in order to be loaded and warehouses were insufficient. Grain had to be loaded and unloaded once more at the Kerch Straits before leaving the Sea of Azov. This situation was unsuitable and risky for the merchandise, it cost time and money and made the eastern businessmen rather reluctant to send their merchandise and to purchase grain in the Sea of Azov ports.

A permanent concern for the Russian government throughout the eighteenth century, aside from access to the Black Sea, was the development of markets in the south and their links to the Mediterranean. Russia's only outlet to the Black Sea in the eighteenth century was via the Sea of Azov.[23] I. Carras's recent study on Greek traders in Russia mentions that the first wave of development in Greek sea trade for the Greeks of the Black Sea is noted during the period 1739–74. The signing of the Treaty of Belgrade (1739) played an important role in opening up the sea trade between the Ottoman and Russian Empires and was particularly significant for the development of the trade of the Black Sea by the Ottoman Greeks, particularly in the Sea of Azov. As the ninth article of the treaty determined, it allowed for 'freedom for trading subjects throughout the Russian Empire to trade in the Ottoman Empire and whatever concerned the Russian trade in the Black Sea. This would be carried out in ships owned by Turkish subjects'.[24] An important route followed by the Greeks in trading between Russia and the Ottoman Empire was via the Sea of Azov, the river Don and the town of Cherkessk.[25] The Greeks developed measurable activity centreing around Temernikov, a port north of the river Don and south of Cherkessk and Taganrog on the banks of the Sea of Azov. Between 1746 and 1760, six to seventeen ships traded in Taganrog.[26] The majority of these ships must have been Ottoman Greeks and many of the merchants were Greek traders of the continental urban centre of Nezhin, which was, together with Moscow, one of the first eighteenth-century mainland towns in which Greek merchants settled. Trade via the Sea of Azov arrived in Moscow having followed a challenging route from Constantinople, via Kerch and Temernikov or via Taganrog, Cherkessk, Voronezh and Toula and operated as an alternative route for the Greek merchants of Nezhin, Constantinople–Nezhin–Moscow.[27]

Finally, foreign trade from southern Russia took a more systematic and extensive form following the victories of the first Russo-Ottoman war and the Treaty of Kuçuk Kainardji (1774) through which Russia not only achieved the much sought-after access into the Black Sea but also successfully gained free sea communications between Russia's southern areas and Europe. The right for ships sailing under the Russian flag to freely pass through the Dardanelles Straits and the lack of a Russian merchant fleet in the southern ports provided a great opportunity for the Greek captains who were sailing in the Aegean and Black Seas under the Ottoman flag to also use the Russian flag. Gradually the right to sail through the Straits was bestowed on others via agreements between the Ottoman Empire and Austria (1784), followed by England (1799) and France (1802).[28] The complete freedom for ships to enter the Black Sea and the Sea of Azov was achieved with the Peace Treaty of Adrianople in 1829.[29]

The Ottoman archives bear witness to a dense sea trade activity particularly in the areas of the Sea of Azov and the Crimea towards the end of the eighteenth century.[30] Many licences were issued to ships owned by Ottoman-Greeks heading towards the Black Sea. Trade between the Ottoman and the Russian Empires comprised grains, preserved meats, animal fats, timber, furs and slaves from the Caucasus.[31] More specifically, during the period 1780–7 a significant number of 212 Greek-Ottoman ships were recorded as trading in the Russian ports of the Black Sea, a figure which reached its peak during the period 1792–1806 with 993 ships.[32] Russia's access to the Black Sea and the Mediterranean trade presented an opportunity for Greeks to expand their trade and shipping activities beyond the Ottoman frontier.

In Greek history the use of the Russian flag by Greeks – Venetian, Ionian or Ottoman subjects – has mistakenly been considered as a panacea for the rise of the Greek shipping in the so-called pre-revolutionary period. New research reveals that Greek shipping in the eighteenth century developed mainly with the use of the Ottoman flag and the support of the Sublime Porte for the greater part of the period 1750–1821. Specifically, during the period of the French and Napoleonic Wars only 6 per cent of Greek-owned ships sailed under the Russian flag.[33] Russian archives reveal that the Russian flag was adopted mainly by members of families who had taken up residence, either temporarily or permanently, along the southern Russian coast.[34] For example, the Ginis family from Spetses and the Koundouri, Couppa, Lykiardopoulo families from Cephallonia (Ionian islands) had members of their kin residing in Taganrog (see Tables 9.1 and 9.6). An excellent example of the Greek-Russian relationship of the time can be seen in the name of Captain Spyros Lykiardopoulos's ship *Prince Alexander and Virgin Mary of Spartia* from Cephallonia in 1786 which sailed under the Russian flag (Table 9.1).[35] Despite the fact that the use of the Russian flag was not so important in the development of Greek shipping, the Russian conquest of the lands on the northern and north-eastern coast of the Black Sea and the spectacular rise in the export of grain from said area were fundamental in the development of Greek shipping.[36]

Table 9.1: A sample of Greek ships sailing under the Russian flag and trading in Russia.

Date of register	Ship	Flag	Captain	Place of origin	Port of arrival	Port of departure	Crew
11/8/1804	*Aghios Nikolaos*	Russian	Ginis Georgis	Spetses (western Aegean Sea)	Malta	Taganrog	43
1/8/1802	*Aghios Nikolaos*	Russian	Ginis Thodoris	Spetses (western Aegean Sea)	Malta	Crimea	22
26/9/1803	*Triton*	Russian	Dakrosis Dimitris	Syros (central Aegean Sea)	Malta	Sebastopol	14
11/9/1806	*Aghios Spyridon*	Russian	Igglesis Spyros	Cephallonia (Ionian Sea)	Malta	Odessa	15
28/1/1786	*Count Alexander Andreovich Besborontiev*	Russian	Koundouris Dionysis	Cephallonia (Ionian Sea)	Malta	Taganrog	16
7/9/1806	*Evangelistria*	Russian	Koundouris Dionysis	Cephallonia (Ionian Sea)	Malta	Taganrog	16
13/10/1785	*Dorothea*	Russian	Koundouris Panagis	Taganrog	Malta	Taganrog	14
11/9/1806	*Great Duchess Maria*	Russian	Coupas Giannis	Cephallonia (Ionian Sea)	Malta	Taganrog	18
22/12/1806	*Aspasia*	Russian	Lazarou Lazaros, son of Andreas	Spetses (western Aegean Sea)	Malta	Taganrog	29
5/11/1786	*Prince Alexander and Virgin Mary of Spartia*	Russian	Lykiardopoulos Spyros	Cephallonia (Ionian Sea)	Malta	Azov	18
5/1/1787	*Karolos Konstantinos*	Russian	Milesis Giannis	Zakynthos (Ionian Sea)	Malta	Black Sea	11
28/9/1806	*Panaghia Agriliotisa*	Russian	Panas Konstantis	Cephallonia (Ionian Sea)	Malta	Taganrog	14
9/10/1805	*Panaghia Plastiriotisa*	Russian	Rosolymos Nikolas	Cephallonia (Ionian Sea)	Malta	Taganrog	15

Source: *Amfitriti* Database, Research Programme of the Ionian University 'Greek Shipping History, 1700–1821', funded by the European Union and the Greek Ministry of Education and included in the 'Pythagoras 1' Operational Programme, 2004–7.

The development of Taganrog, the largest exporting port in the Sea of Azov, began immediately after the signing of the Treaty of Kuçuk Kainardji. Greek settlers were the catalysts for its trade apogee and contributed significantly to the evolution of the town. Greeks from the shipping families of the main shipping centres in the Ionian and Aegean moved after the announcement of Catherine the Great's incentives for the creation of the new port towns in New Russia. In effect it was the businessmen of the sea who opened the Sea of Azov up to international trade at the end of the eighteenth century, loading their ships with Russian grain and transporting it to Malta, Livorno, Genoa, Marseilles and Barcelona. Greeks became competitive in the international market of the Mediterranean. Their success lay in low cost sea transport services and the existing business networks which had been developed throughout the Mediterranean for the transportation of sea trade from the east to the west.[37]

The policy of attracting a population experienced in particular sectors of the economy was widely implemented by the Russian Empire in the lands of 'New Russia' throughout the nineteenth century. Maritime hegemony as a geopolitical and economic strategy for colonial expansion and economic power began from the time of Peter the Great and became a reality during the reign of Catherine II. Furthermore Russia's colonial policy in the south can be seen in the wider context of the Eastern Question and Russia's attempt to provide, as a great European power, 'protection' to a select minority of the Ottoman Empire with the aim of expanding its influence into the neighbouring state. It resulted in a fixed policy of the Russian officials to support the multi-ethnic composition of the southern areas in order to colonize them and exploit the special abilities of each ethnic group in order to ensure economic development.

D. Sherry claims that according to Russian government reports, contained in the Georgian State Archives, the privileges which had been given to the foreigners of the south and particularly to the Greeks for the development of sea trade were aimed at the economic development of the area and the creation of the suitable 'social alchemy' along the coast of the Black Sea in the mid-nineteenth century.[38] Control of the empire's foreign trade via the Black Sea rested entirely in the hands of Greeks, Jews and Armenians. The area from Odessa to the Crimea was mainly dominated by Greeks and Jews and the area from the Azov to Georgia was in the hands of Greeks and Armenians.[39]

The Russian governors attributed economic characteristics to every ethnic minority group. They recognized, for example, the need for the existence of the Cossacks for military purposes, but believed that the Don Cossacks alone could not fulfil the plans for the creation of a new economic zone, and that an urban population was needed which did not exist in the area. The country of the Don Cossacks was considered the most insubordinate in Russia and it was an area with more freedom for its inhabitants in which serfdom was not applied. Due to their location in the frontier zone of the river Don, the Cossacks were granted the right to farm fertile soils and were given fishing rights for the river. However, agriculture spread hesitantly throughout the Don region. Being a military people with the obligation to protect the empire's frontiers, the Cossacks could not successfully contribute to the Russian government's major interest which was to promote the development of a Russian merchant fleet.[40] The Imperial government believed that a heterogeneous ethnic population was necessary to develop the farming, industry and sea trade. In this way the ethnic groups who would be encouraged to immigrate were thought to serve as an example and would encourage the Russians to develop similar activities. It was believed that the Greek presence would enhance the development of sea trade since the Greeks were a ready force who would diffuse their know-how in trade and shipping and would assist with the formation and training of future Russian shipping.[41] As will become evident later, this expectation was indeed confirmed.

The Foundation of the Greek *Paroikia* in Taganrog, 1775–1836

The history of the Greek 'colony' or *paroikia* in Taganrog begins in 1775 and ends at the aftermath of the Russian Revolution, with the victory of the Red Army over the anti-revolutionary forces and their European allies (1919). Although we will deal here only with the first period, the phase of its establishment (1775–1836), we must also refer to the next two phases, which form part of the proposed periodization for the history of the Greek merchant community. Major historical events for the Greek *paroikia* delineate its life cycle. The first phase begins with the foundation of the settlement and ends with the abolition of the Greek Magistrate. The second period, 1837–80, begins with the formation of a single merchant body in the town and the predominance of the grain trade as the principal economic activity of the region and ends with the fraud at the Taganrog customs house in which many Greek merchant houses were implicated. The third, 1881–1919, begins with the trial against the biggest Greek merchant of Taganrog, Mari Vagliano, and ends with the exodus of a significant portion of the Greek population of the city during the Russian Civil War (1919). In this article, we will deal with the initial phase, the settlement of the Greek merchant community.[42]

Catherine the Great's decree of 28 March 1775 inviting Greek seafarers and their families to the newly acquired areas of southern Russia was accepted with relief by the seamen who took part in the Russo-Ottoman war.[43] The houses, the churches and land in the host country would be generously offered by the empress. Tax breaks were given, incentives for trade, free ports were established and the right to self-governance (through the creation of a separate institution for the Greeks, the Greek Magistrate) were among the basic privileges offered.

Amongst the first settlers were the members of the Greek contingent who had initially settled in Kerch-Yenikale and to whom Catherine II had promised 'the transportation of their belongings from the Crimea to the Sea of Azov settlements at her expense'.[44] The two contingents of soldiers settled in Pavlofsk Castle, on the city's hill, while the merchant population settled in Taganrog, in the Greek neighbourhood from which the Greek street begins today (*Gretseskayia Oulitsa*). With Russia's conquest of the Crimea in 1783 the Greek military corps moved to Sebastopol and then on to Balaklava.[45] With the abandonment of the stronghold on the Taganrog hill its radial layout dictated the directions of the first roads in the town. Land was given to the discharged members of the military, while the traders had to make do by themselves.

As the tsarina had promised the higher military officials, soldiers and certain merchants were granted 15,946 desiatines[46] of fertile land[47] which had been initially marked out and calculated by the representatives of the Greek Magistrate (6 August 1811) to be distributed amongst ninety-one lots. Nobles, former military men who had been rewarded with a title for their services to Catherine the Great, active military men (colonels, commanders, corporals), discharged members of the military, citizens, widows and heirs of deceased members of the military and merchants became landowners with plots outside the town. These plots of land could be cultivated and after 1819 they could be inherited by their descendants.[48] Greek landed gentry, who had at their service a good number of peasants, received land in this initial dividing up performed by the representatives of the Greek Magistrate. Some examples of the sharing out of land can be seen with Vice Colonel Georgios Kandiotis who received 479 desiatinas, Major Georgios Kokkinos 523, Georgios Venardakis 261 and Athanasios Houliaras 349.[49] The commander of the Greek battalion, Dimitrios Alfierakis from Mystra in Lakonia, Peloponese, held the land west of Mious River which he named *Lakedaimonovka*, after the ancient Greek name of his homeland. The Greek presence in the area did not allow the Russians to obtain land, which they laid persistent claims to before the emperor.[50] However, despite state support, the majority of Greeks sold their land and shifted to urban occupations and trade activities. Only the nobles, Alfierakis, Venardakis[51] and Houliaras, expanded their landed property. In 1852 their serfs included 393 Orthodox Christian peasants.[52]

After the end of the Russo-Ottoman war in 1775, reforms took place which divided up the empire into provinces of equal-sized population sections called *guberniya*. Each *guberniya* consisted of regional administrations (*uyezds*) which reported to each local governor.[53] The Novorossiya (New Russia) area was divided into two *guberniyas*, Azov and Novorossiya. Taganrog belonged to the *guberniya* of Azov, and was headed by Governor Lt. General Valerii A. Tserchov. Only in the 1890s was it brought within the jurisdiction of the Don Cossack province. The first Greek government body in Taganrog was set up in 1781 in accordance with the decree of the Provincial Chancellor of Azov, under the administration of Tserchov. The decree was in the same spirit as the Imperial Decree of 28 March 1775 which sought to improve the situation and number of Greek immigrants (merchants and petit bourgeois) in Taganrog. This Greek self-government institution, initially called the Board of Trade, was later named the Greek Magistrate when approved by decree of the Governor of Ekaterinoslav, and the proclamation of the commencement of its activities by the Chairman of the Upper Provincial Court.[54]

The creation of the Greek Magistrate was considered necessary not just for administrative reasons to resolve the problems which would arise during the settlement of the Greeks, but also to consult with the Russian authorities (in the name of Greeks) about the provision of services and supplies. A separate body was also set up which would seek to attract and administrate the Russian settlers to the area. Therefore, the Russian Magistrate was founded. Both administrative bodies were under the jurisdiction of the governor. They equally shared rights and duties and their representatives sat on advisory committees which assisted the governor in his work. From the data available, it is clear that the Greek Magistrate had more revenue from the arrival of ships at the port than the Russian one.[55]

The Magistrate, an institution of German origin, was the main administrative body for the cities. It was a critical link between the Governor and the registered inhabitants.[56] In towns and cities where there was a large Greek element, Greek Magistrates were set up which operated in parallel with the Russian ones and reported to the supreme authority, the governor. They had administrative, policing and judicial powers and resolved all civil disputes amongst their members. The control over merchant and petit bourgeois mobility was particularly important, with information on this frequently being reported to the central administration. In 1781, for example, the Greek Board presented to the governor three lists of its members, one for thirty-eight merchants with their capital and possessions, one with twenty-eight individuals who were temporarily missing and one for another thirty-eight Greeks who wanted to register with the Greek Board of Trade.[57] The Greek administrative body was comprised of three elected representatives but important decisions were taken collectively at the meeting of all members of the Greek Board of Trade.[58]

Involvement of Greek merchants in the self-government institutions and the respective committees during the first period of the foundation of the city attracts our attention and confirms B. Mironov's argument of the de facto self-government of the merchants and the petit bourgeois in the pre-reform Russian city administration.[59] Staff shortages and lack of finances made the state delegate part of its power to the local merchants who fulfilled their public service, on many occasions, with great efficiency. They thus became dominant in the administration of city affairs and often defended local interests against government encroachment.

In 1710 under Peter the Great, the Greeks had been granted privileges of administrative autonomy within the Russian Empire. In 1785 the Greek Magistrate in Nezhin was established.[60] In the same year another three Greek Magistrates were founded, the Bosphorus Magistrate which covered the ports of Crimea[61] and the Taganrog and Mariupol Magistrates.

In order to enjoy the privileges granted by the Russians, the Greeks who registered for the Greek Magistrate had to become Russian citizens. The new residents of the territories of the south, stripped as they were of population, no matter what their origin became 'Greek Russians' as E. Karakalos called them[62] and joined the social and professional system of Russian society. In Russia until the end of the nineteenth century the population was divided into four social groups: the nobles, the clergy, the urban population and the rural population. The urban population was divided into four subgroups: the honoured citizens, the merchants, the petit bourgeois and the artisans. Merchants were divided into three guilds and registration in those guilds was open to all who could pay the guild tax.[63]

Guilds were a uniform commercial body which someone had to register with in order to engage in trade. Under Peter the Great, there were two categories, while under Catherine II there were three. In the first category one had to declare a working capital of over 10,000 roubles, in the second between 5,000 and 10,000 roubles and in the third between 1,000 and 5,000 roubles.[64] Holders of a third guild license could only engage in retail trade and were not exempt from military service. Merchants in the first guild could engage in wholesale trade and trade abroad without any limit on their annual transactions. Merchants in the second category had a limit on their annual trading activities for both the empire and abroad. The third guild, which could engage only in retail trade within the empire was abolished in 1865.

The social position of merchants was exceptionally precarious. It depended on how much capital the merchant would declare each year in order to obtain the relevant license. If he went bankrupt or was destroyed due to the impact of frequent military conflicts on trade, the burden of excessive taxation or just bad management of his enterprise, he automatically fell into the petit bourgeois category. His social position and the position of the members of his family was not secure. For that reason a key aim of merchants was for them to acquire titles granted to the nobility. In its attempt to limit the rise of merchants to the nobility, the Russian Government in 1859 devised the title of honoured citizen which was granted to merchants in the first guild after ten years of service.[65]

Members of the Greek community who fell within the jurisdiction of the Taganrog Magistrate were both merchants and petit bourgeois. It was relatively easy to move from one category to the other. In the first years of the Greek *paroikia*, the Magistrate prepared two lists which it submitted to the Russian authorities, one for merchants and one for the petit bourgeois. It had to report the date of their registration, the capital with which each merchant traded, his family members and their precise occupation. The Russian authorities and the Greek administration wanted to know where its members were at any given time.

In the lists for 1795 to 1804, there were 583 registered merchants, 148 petit bourgeois and 70 foreigners. Along with their families, they comprised a total population of 1,569 individuals, an exceptionally high number given the small size of the city (7,000).[66]

Table 9.2: Allocation of merchants from the Greek Magistrate of Taganrog into guilds, 1795–1804.

Guild	No. of merchants	Capital in roubles
First	10	159,100
Second	262	2,126,825
Third	311	642,080
Total	583	2,928,005

Source: Государственный архив Ростовской области [State Archive of the Rostov Region], f. 579 op. 3, d. 2, 'List of Merchants in the Taganrog Greek Magistrate, 1795–1804'.

As is clear from Table 9.2, the ten merchants in the first guild had a registered capital of 16,000 roubles on average. In particular, they were the Cephallonians Pavlos Kountouris, Athanasios Panas and Nikolaos Typaldos, the Santorinian Theodoros Miserlis, the Psariot Nikolaos Koumianos, the Constantinopolitan Michail Zografos, along with Ioannis Popov and Ioannis Fistis.[67] As expected, the majority were merchants in the second and third guilds, in other words all those who had come to Taganrog with small to medium amounts of capital. Both the big merchants and most of those in the second and third categories who were registered with the Greek Magistrate were Greek Ottoman or Venetian citizens. There was also a limited number of Orthodox Balkan merchants who registered with the Greek Magistrate, such as Vassily Goikovich.[68] The same occurred with the petit bourgeois to a larger degree, whose work was related to clerical positions in administrative bodies (the Magistrate, customs office), urban occupations (tailors), services (servants), handicrafts and small industry.

The surnames of the merchants reveal their origins. As one might expect, the majority of the first merchants who settled in Taganrog came from shipping families from the Ionian and the Aegean Seas. Of the 583 merchants, we were able to identify the origin of 199 merchants from the Greek Magistrate of Taganrog. Of that significant sample, it is clear that the Ionians played an important role in populating the city. Of that sample 55 per cent came from the Ionian Sea, while 43 per cent came from the Aegean (see Figure 9.1). Of those merchants from the Ionian Sea, the majority are from the island Cephallonia, followed by Mesolongi, Galaxidi (in mainland western Greece), the islands of Zakynthos, Corfu, Ithaca and Lefkada. In the Aegean Sea, 17 per cent came from the eastern Aegean (the islands of Psara, Chios, Patmos, Lesvos, Kassos and the Asian Minor port Aivali), 13 per cent came from the central Aegean (islands of Santorini, Mykonos and Sifnos) and the remaining 13 per cent from the western Aegean (islands of Hydra, Skopelos and Spetses). The rise of Greek shipping during the eighteenth century is consistent with the opening up of new areas and new sea routes. Moreover, it is well known that the opening up of the Black Sea to global trade and the establishment of Greeks there was of definitive importance not just for creating the Greek state but also for the continued growth of Greek shipping in the nineteenth century.

Table 9.3: Origin of merchants who settled in Taganrog, 1795–1804.

Origin	Number	% of the whole
The Aegean	**90**	**43%**
The eastern Aegean	*30*	*17%*
Psara	14	7%
Aivali (Kydonies)	6	3%
Chios	4	2%
Patmos	3	2%
Lesvos	1	1%
Lemnos	1	1%
Kassos	1	1%
The central Aegean	*25*	*13%*
Santorini	17	9%
Mykonos	6	3%
Sifnos	2	1%
The western Aegean	*25*	*13%*
Hydra	11	6%
Skopelos	6	3%
Spetses	4	2%
Other	4	2%
The Ionian Sea (including the Corinthian Gulf)	**105**	**55%**
Cephallonia	63	32%
Mesolongi	9	5%
Galaxidi	8	4%
Zakynthos	7	4%
Corfu	4	2%
Ithaca	2	1%
Lefkada	1	1%
Other	11	6%
Constantinople	**4**	**2%**
Total	199	100%

Source: Государственный архив Ростовской области [State Archive of the Rostov Region], f. 579, op. 3, d. 2, 'List of Merchants in the Taganrog Greek Magistrate, 1795–1804'.

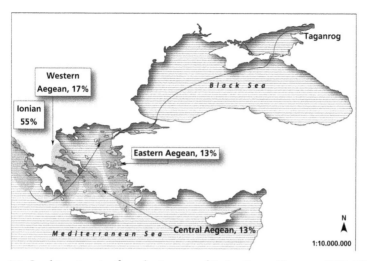

Figure 9.1: Greek immigration from the Aegean and Ionian Seas to Taganrog, 1795–1804.

In parallel with attracting populations, even before the Greek Magistrate was established, the Russian Government ensured that the necessary economic institutions were in place to run and develop foreign trade in the south.[69] Trade at Taganrog without a customs office and quarantine could not exist. In 1776 with imperial consent the customs office was moved from the river Temernik to Taganrog, employees were appointed and the new reduced tariffs took effect for imported and exported products.[70] The detailed customs office list, part of which is presented in Table 9.4, served as an incentive especially for Constantinopolitan merchants who came to trade in the city. The tariff list shown in Table 9.4 is indicative of the trade at Taganrog before grain became important and suggests that Constantinople was the main supplier and recipient of the products of southern Russia.[71]

Table 9.4: Tariff list of products exported from Taganrog, 1776 (in roubles).

Items exported	Purchase price in Taganrog	Export tariff	Fare to Constantinople	Import tariff to Turkey	Unloading charges	Cost	Sale price in Constantinople	profit %
Butter from cows' milk (in *berkovets**)	27.1	2.92	1.65	10.5	0.30	42.47	53	20%
Candles (in *berkovets*)	26.5	2.86	1.65	1.05	0.30	32.36	37.5	14%
Black caviar (in *berkovets*)	23.5	0.85	1.65	1.20	0.30	27.5	38	28%
Iron (long pieces in *berkovets*)	7.80	37.5	1.65	40.5	0.30	87.75	13.40	-65,5%
Iron (sheets in *berkovets*)	15.9	6	1.65	0.60	0.30	24.45	30.90	21%
Sails (in 1000 *arsin*)	160	2.50	1.65	5	0.30	169.45	195	13%
Badger furs (in 100 pieces)	80	7	1.65	3.90	0.30	92.85	135	31%

*   1 *berkovets* is equal to 163.8 kilos; 1 *arsin* is equal to 0.71 metres.

Source: P. Filefksy, П. Филевский, *История города Таганрога* [History of the City of Taganrog] (Taganrog, 1898), pp. 213–15.

The above table reveals that at the end of the eighteenth century exports of certain products to Constantinople, such as furs and caviar, were particularly beneficial generating a profit margin of around 30 per cent. Black caviar was the top export product from Taganrog because its consumption in European markets where it was a luxury item had even greater profits for Constantinople. Caviar was followed by butter from cows' milk, iron sheets and sailcloth. Iron in long rods was to be avoided as its purchase price was high. Imports in the years 1775–7 were primarily in Mediterranean products such as currants, wine, lamb skins and particularly foodstuffs. Most of them came from Constantinople or the wider Ottoman region, such as Turkish syrup sweets, walnuts, dates, olives and fresh fruit as well as green soap.

V. Zakharov reveals that documents from the customs office of the port of Taganrog located in the Vorontsov file in the St Petersburg Archives state that 67 per cent of the ninety merchants engaged in foreign trade in 1793 were Greeks, holding either Russian or Ottoman citizenship.[72] Two thirds of the new colonists came on their own in search of work without their families. When their work was assured, they brought their wives and children. Most families consisted of between three and five members, confirming the average size of families found in other urban communities such as Odessa.[73] The most important colonization data revealed by our sources is that male relatives of the first or second degree often came to settle. This is proved both by the 'List of merchants and petit bourgeois for the period 1785–1804' and by the family registers of Taganrog which indicate the successive migration of brothers.[74]

Table 9.5 highlights the social ranking of the Greek merchant *paroikia* which may be deduced by their specialized activities and assets. Most, eighty-nine per cent, had no property and came to Taganrog with funds or merchandise to set up foreign trade. Of these, fifty-three per cent had no property, yet they possessed considerable capital and were engaged exclusively in foreign trade, while nineteen per cent engaged in foreign and domestic trade. Ten per cent were owners of vessels, engaged in foreign trade and had their own means for transporting their products. Another category of merchants, seven per cent, moved inland dealing in small-scale trade (the second guild) with other cities. From the list of professional occupations of merchants it is clear that the social ranking was based on the acquisition of properties and the type of trade engaged in.

Table 9.5: Social ranking of Greek settlers in Taganrog, 1795–1804.

Assets and business activity	Greek settlers	%
A. Foreign and domestic trade and ships	513	89%
B. Domestic trade	49	8%
C. Ownership of houses and shops	16	3%
Total	578	100%

Source: Государственный архив Ростовской области [State Archive of the Rostov Region], f. 579, op. 1, d. 535, 'List of merchants from Taganrog and Mariupol 1804–1841'.

Real estate properties were a sign of climbing the social ladder and integrating into the host society. Shops, warehouses, homes and landed estates declared the intention of their owners to put down roots and to be assimilated into the Russian society by developing ties with the local population. The capital used to finance foreign trade which was brought in by merchants of non-Russian origin was particularly important because it filtered through to the city's market and was used for certain services and committees. For that reason, merchants were released from military service and personal taxation. As is clear from a letter from the customs authorities to the Greek Magistrate, the Greek merchants who travelled abroad were obliged to leave part of their capital behind as a guarantee which we assume would have financially facilitated the operation of the custom offices and committees.[75] The same happened with merchants, as members of the port committee who financed, together with the municipality and the government, the port infrastructure.

As previously mentioned, engaging in trade meant registering with a guild and becoming a Russian citizen. However, a merchant could retain his nationality for a time period and register as a foreigner or guest merchant. Foreign merchants and petit bourgeois who maintained their nationality were also declared by their place of origin, their occupation and the area of the city where they resided.[76] Foreigners were primarily involved in specialized industrial occupations, services and trade. The police authorities kept a close eye on them to discern any suspicious activities or persons who wanted to subvert the regime or to serve the interests of the foreign powers. Many revolutionaries found refuge in remote cities of the Russian south. For example, Giuseppe Garibaldi, the father of Italian unification, is known to have visited Taganrog in April 1833.[77]

The archives are full of details and interesting facts on foreigners residing in Taganrog. Ambrose Mokkna, of Swiss descent, for example, who claimed to be an officer, and who served for ten years as an architect on the Building Works Committee, was described by the police authorities as 'easily roused, given to secrecy and doubtful forms of behaviour'.[78] Referring to Dimitrios Parvaris, an Ottoman citizen who had arrived with his wife from the Aegean in 1812 and who worked as an employee of the merchant Vagliano, the police stated that his behaviour was 'good, his mind simple and he caused no problems'. Referring to Pavlos Adrianopoulos, an Ottoman citizen who had arrived with his wife in 1811, the police stated that he did not work and stayed with his brother who was a merchant from Odessa.[79]

Although information on the founding of companies is scarce at this period, we know that Greeks were involved in family partnership or partnerships among fellow countrymen. The type of chained emigration among family members who bore the same surname and registered among the merchants of the Greek Magistrate makes us assume that the basic type of enterprise was of family type which allowed merchants to trade with more capital, help their kin and reduce their costs. The advantages of family enterprises in Taganrog are well presented in the monograph on the Sifneo Frères family business that operated in the second half of the nineteenth century but was similar to enterprises of the first half.[80]

Table 9.6: Greek merchant families* in Taganrog,
registered by the Greek Magistrate, 1795–1804.

Surname	Name	Year
Anagnostis	Ioannis	1804
Anagnostis	Dimitrios	1804
Ane(s)tis	Iakovos	1804
Ane(s)tis	Spyridon	1804
Avgerinos	Gerasimos	1798
Avgerinos	Mihail	1800
Bastakis	Stamatis	1795
Bastakis	Ioannis	1804
Bekatoros	Panaiotis	1804
Bekatoros	Vangelis	1804
Bekatoros	Yerasimos	1804
Bertoumis	Manouil	1803
Bertoumis	Panaiotis	1804
Bertoumis	Ioannis	1804
Damianos	Nikolaos	1804
Damianos	Spyridon	1804
Dimakis	Zaharis	1804
Dimakis	Francesco	1804
Divaris	Spyridon	1800
Divaris	Dimitrios	1804
Droutsos	Vassilios	1803
Droutsos	Pantelis	1804
Frangopoulos	Dimitrios	1803
Frangopoulos	Kosmas	1804
Frangopoulos	Marios	1804
Kaleris	Dimitrios	1798
Kaleris	Nikolaos	1804
Kaleris	Georgios	1803
Kaligas	Nikolaos	1803
Kaligas	Zisimos	1804
Kaligas	Georgios	1804
Kaligas	Panagis	1804
Kambanakis	Nikolaos	1800
Kambanakis	Georgios	1804
Kapetanakis	Ioannis	1796
Kapetanakis	Mihail	1800
Kondoglou	Ioannis	1795
Kondoglou	Georgios	1798
Koumianos	Nikolaos	1795
Koumianos	Mihail	1799
Koundouris	Pavlos	1804

Surname	Name	Year
Koundouris	Athanasios	1804
Koundouris	Nikolaos	1804
Linardakis	Grigorios	1797
Linardakis	Antonis	1804
Logothetis	Nikolaos	1797
Logothetis	Georgios	1804
Matako[i]s	Dimitrios	1800
Matako[i]s	Stavros	1804
Mavromatis	Diamantis	1795
Mavromatis	Georgios	1796
Mavromatis	Mattheos	1804
Mavroudis	Ilarion	1795
Mavroudis	Nikolaos	1795
Miserlis	Theodoros	1795
Miserlis	Panaiotis	1800
Mitilinaios	Nikolaos	1804
Mitilinaios	Konstantinos	1804
Moshonisiotis	Ioannis	1795
Moshonisiotis	Dimitrios	1804
Nomikos	Nikolaos	1795
Nomikos	Ioannis	1802
Paleologos	Georgios	1795
Paleologos	Dimitrios	1803
Paleologos	Konstantinos	1804
Panaiotopoulos	Panos	1795
Panaiotopoulos	Pavlos	1795
Panaiotov	Dimitrios	1804
Paniotov	Georgios	1804
Papadopoulos	Panaiotis	1798
Papadopoulos	Athanasios	1803
Papadopoulos	Efstathios	1804
Papapavlos	Dimitrios	1804
Papapavlos	Emmanuel	1804
Politov	Savvas	1795
Politov	Pavlos	1800
Politov	Ioannis	1804
Politov	Georgios	1804
Popov	Ivan	1795
Popov	Anastasis	1800
Popov	Georgios	1803
Poulos	Yerasimos	1798
Poulos	Anastasios	1804
Renieris	Georgios	1804
Renieris	Leontios	1804
Sarris	Apostolos	1802
Sarris	Dimitrios	1802
Spatis	Theodoros	1795
Spatis	Nikolaos	1804
Svoronos	Panagis	1795

Surname	Name	Year
Svoronos	Ioannis	1804
Valsamakis	Nikolaos	1795
Valsamakis	Andreas	1804
Varvarigos	Konstantinos	1803
Varvarigos	Nikolaos	1804
Varvarigos	Ioannis	1804
Velisaropoulos	Komninos	1804
Velisaropoulos	Ioannis	1804
Zaharopoulos	Polihronis	1795
Zaharopoulos	Dimitrios	1902
Zaharov	Leontios	1803
Zaharov	Dimitrios	1804
Zaharov	Georgios	1804
Zaradin	Pavlos	1797
Zaradin	Andreas	1803

* The above Table does not contain all merchants registered in the Greek magistrate. It contains those whose surname is mentioned more than once.

Source: Государственный архив Ростовской области [State Archive of the Rostov Region], f. 579, op. 3, d. 2, 'List of Merchants in the Taganrog Greek Magistrate, 1795–1804'.

Greeks during this first period were also involved in industrial ventures. In 1806, for example, the merchants H. L. Vrakopoulos and I. Manetis opened two macaroni factories but detailed information is scarce. It was during the period of Russian industrialization in the last third of the nineteenth century that Greeks invested also in the industrial sector. Yet manufacturing was never their preferred economic sector. Commercial and seafaring skills prevailed over technological know-how and agricultural capacities.

In 1836 the imperial authorities abolished the Greek Magistrate. The policy of integration and assimilation of foreign citizens attempted by the Russian authorities abolished the privileges which had been granted to useful groups of the population, such as the Greeks. A uniform trade body was set up for all merchants. The number of Greeks in the guilds in relation to the period of the Magistrate appears to have been drastically reduced. Examining the surnames in the list for 1840 it is clear that only 125 were Greek merchants (Table 9.6).[81] Yet the Greeks still remained dominant in the guilds.

Table 9.7: The merchant body of Taganrog, 1840.

Guilds	Russians	Greeks	Greeks as a % of the whole	Total
1st guild	8	18	69%	26
2nd guild	7	8	53%	15
3rd guild	93	99	51%	192

Source: Государственный архив Ростовской области [State Archive of the Rostov Region], f. 579, op. 1, d. 535, 'List of merchants from Taganrog and Mariupol 1804–1841'.

The drop in the number of Greek merchants should come as no surprise as there was a widespread reduction in the overall number of merchants in Russia. In the period from 1809 to 1824 the number of Russian merchants registered in the guilds decreased by two thirds.[82] The frequent price fluctuations, wars, changes in the tariffs, etc. discouraged all those who wished to assume the risk of trading. The increase in the number of honorary citizens, in other words big merchants, reflected the desire of the merchant class to climb the social ladder in order to ensure stability and a better place in society.

We will analyse the Greek members of Table 9.7. In the first guild, there were three Zaharov brothers, Zacharis, Ioannis and Leontios from Constantinople. They were followed by merchants from Cephallonia who were the largest group by number: Michail and Alexandros Avgerinos, Stavros Vagliano, Spyridon Mousouris, Dionysios Koundouris, Michail Metaxas, Haralambos Panas, Dionysios Razis, Pavlos Travlos and Damianos Fokas. The 'golden' list of merchants from the 1840s' first guild included Nikolaos Rallis and Loukas Skaramanga from the island of Chios, Nikolaos Alafouzos from Santorini, as well as Emmanuel Koumanis and Angelis Glykis whose origins could not be identified. It is interesting to note that two thirds of the above families were still engaged in trading activities of the region in 1912.[83] However, new individuals also appear who built a name for themselves in the grain trade over the next forty years, Maris Vagliano and Loukas Skaramanga.

The major boom in trade brought about widespread economic prosperity which was gradually reflected in the planning of the town. According to the constitutive charter of rights and privileges of cities issued by Catherine II in 1785, the planning of provincial cities from above sought to ensure uniformity, standardization, to safeguard public order and also to reflect the strength of public power.[84] The primary concern was to organize trade, to mark out roads, squares and marketplaces which were the areas where citizens could circulate, primarily merchants, artisans and the petit bourgeois. The public administration was also concerned about controlling the movements and accommodation of citizens. Merchants in particular who conducted business abroad and frequently travelled were obliged to publicly disclose their intention to travel abroad in newspapers within a specific deadline before departing.

The city of Taganrog began to develop in a ring shape around the ruined fortress and castle. Residential areas sprang up in three zones (the Peter, Catherine and Alexander zones). Each zone had numbered building blocks and in each block there were numbered properties.[85] The Construction Works Committee of Taganrog (1806) was responsible for the building method and the form of public and private buildings in the city, roadworks, bridges, street lamps and public works. Money came from the municipal fund. The committee, other than the mayor, was comprised of four municipal counsellors from the Greek and

Russian Magistrates. The general street plan had been approved by the tsar and the buildings were constructed in accordance with the general building rules.[86] However, the façades of buildings had to be approved in every single detail by the construction works committee. Any change, even to the colour, meant new plans had to be submitted and approved.

In the period 1806–10, building work was intense. The first priority was to build the commodity exchange (*birzha*) with wooden shops and warehouses, and the customs office building. At the same time, private individuals built wooden houses along the length of the Greek street which were replaced by stone buildings after 1830.[87] In 1806 the Greek wooden church dedicated to Saints Constantine and Helen was constructed, followed by the building that housed the Greek Magistrate, the guards' house (1806–15), the hospital, the post office (1812–16) and the cathedral church dedicated to the Virgin Mary (1823). In 1809 a wooden lighthouse was built at the entrance to Taganrog and floating lighthouses were set to facilitate navigation.[88] The municipal gardens were also laid out in 1806 and the commercial club in 1812.

Major works were built with donations from the Greek residents of the city. The nobleman, Ioannis A. Varvakis, who held the monopoly on sturgeon fishing in the Caspian Sea, wished to move from Astrakhan down to the milder climate of Taganrog in 1809 and marked his arrival in the city with two very important donations: a hospital and a stone church. The Greek community, spurred on by Varvakis's donation, requested that the minister of the interior provide the plans for the stone church of the Holy Wisdom in St Petersburg in order to build the Greek church.[89] The representatives of the Greek community proposed that a twenty-four-bed hospital be built on the same plot. The minister replied that the tsar wished to honour Varvakis with a new noble title after the work was completed, but the architect Mokkna considered that the site was at risk of landslides and the building was particularly large.[90] In the end the Greek church was built with money from the Greek community of the city and Varvakis built the Holy Trinity Monastery (1813) at Jerusalem Square which was dedicated to the Patriarchate of Jerusalem. In line with the legator's wishes, the monastery was built in the Catherine zone of the city in block 17 close to the merchandise market on a plot of land which had been offered by the widow of General Sarandinakis.[91] Today the supplementary building erected by Varvakis as a home for the monks still stands.

Another Greek that marked the city was Gerasimos Typaldos, a merchant from Cephallonia (1788–1825), who donated a sum of money to the city to build a home for seamen and stone steps which would link the Greek street to the seafront.[92] This monument is a symbol of the city because it links the historical centre on the hilltop with the coastal peripheral road, the seafront walk and the yacht club. Typaldos's stone steps set the overall style for the city. This was followed by the municipal park, three outdoor markets, where merchant fairs were held. In 1825 the building intended as a residence for Tsar Alexander I was built. In terms of grandeur it can be compared to the municipal theatre which officially opened in 1827. While staying in Taganrog, Tsar Alexander I died suddenly on 1 December 1825. His body was put on public display in the church of the Greek monastery built by Ioannis Varvakis.

Conclusion

The current study confirms the success of Catherine the Great's 'Greek plan' to invite Greeks to populate the newly founded port cities of New Russia. In the framework of the 'social alchemy' among different ethno-cultural groups in the region the Greeks were needed for their shipping and trading expertise in an effort to activate a new economic zone linked to international trade. Indeed, with regard to the particularities of the Sea of Azov the Greek entrepreneurs possessed both trading and seafaring skills and therefore offered an important advantage over merchants of other nationalities. The lack of a Russian merchant fleet was covered and international links with the European ports were ensured. The Greeks residing in Taganrog managed to successfully compete with all the western European merchants due to their family business organizations and dense networks among relatives and fellow countrymen which provided them with reduced costs. In addition to enjoying local links with the producers of the country of the Don Cossacks they also had international bonds for the transporting and supplying Russian grain. Their coastal and seagoing fleet afforded them a practical monopoly on the transportation of agricultural produce from the shores and rivers of the region towards the moorings of Taganrog and the Mediterranean ports of destination.

Of particular importance was their knowledge of trade organization under primitive conditions with limited infrastructures and state support. The operation of the Greek merchants of the Sea of Azov through family business and their ties with international networks of the Mediterranean ports and England provided them with increased profits and immediate contact between production and consumption without the intervention of middlemen. Another important advantage was the geographical proximity of the Greeks either to the Greek state or the Ottoman Empire with the coastal areas of south Russia. The Greeks had a strong presence in the strategic location of Constantinople prior to the opening of the Black Sea to international trade and throughout the nineteenth to the beginning of the twentieth century. Constantinople was the springboard for expansion to the Sea of Azov as well as being a safe retreat when navigation out of the Black Sea was 'closed' by the Ottoman government. The Greek merchant *paroikia* of Taganrog made a significant contribution to the creation of a new economic zone in the south of Russia and its linkages to international markets via the import/export activities.

NOTES

Zakharov, Harlaftis and Katsiardi-Hering, 'Introduction'

1. F. Mauro, 'Merchant Communities, 1350–1750', in J. D. Tracy (ed.), *The Rise of Merchant Empires. Long-distance Trade in the Early Modern World (1350–1750)* (Cambridge: Cambridge University Press, 1990), pp. 255–86.
2. Ibid.
3. A. Reid, 'Entrepreneurial Minorities, Nationalism and the State', in Daniel Chirot and Anthony Reid, *Essential Outsiders: Chinese and Jews in the Modern Transformation of Southeast Asia and Central Europe* (Seattle: University of Washington Press, 1997), pp. 33–72.
4. P. Curtin, *Cross Cultural Trade in World History* (Cambridge: Cambridge University Press, 1984).
5. A. Cohen, 'Cultural Strategies in the Organization of Trading Diasporas', in C. Mesailloux (ed.), *The Development of Indigenous Trade and Markets* (London: Oxford University Press, 1971), pp. 266–81; S. Vertovec and R. Cohen (eds), *Migration Diasporas and Transnationalism* (Cheltenham: Edward Elgar, The International Library of Studies on Migration, 9, 1999).
6. Curtin, *Cross Cultural Trade*.
7. See I. Baghdiantz McCabe, 'On the Study of Diasporas', in G. Harlaftis, N. Karapidakis, K. Sbonias and V. Vaiopoulos (eds), *The New Ways of History* (London: I. B. Tauris, 2010), pp. 193–210.
8. Two editors of this volume have been involved in writing about Greeks and Jews in a comparative perspective. See G. Harlaftis, 'Mapping the Greek Maritime Diaspora from the Early 18th to the Late 20th Century', in I. Baghdiantz McCabe, G. Harlaftis and I. Minoglou (eds), *Diaspora Entrepreneurial Networks. Five Centuries of History* (Oxford: Berg, 2005), pp. 147–69; G. Harlaftis, 'Mediterranean Entrepreneurial Diaspora Networks during the Long Nineteenth Century', at the international conference in *Competing Networks: Greek and Other Commercial Houses in the Mediterranean during the Long Nineteenth Century*, University of Haifa, 6–7 June 2006, http://tujjar.haifa.ac.il/index.php?option=com_content&task=view&id=26&Itemid=28 [accessed 10 December 2011]; O. Katsiardi-Hering, 'Christian and Jewish Ottoman Subjects: Family, Inheritance and Commercial Networks between East and West (17th–18th Centuries)', in S. Cavaciocchi (ed.), *La famiglia nell'economia europea. Secc. XIII–XVIII / The Economic Role of the Family in the European Economy from the 13th to the 18th Centuries*, Atti della 'Quarantesima Settimana di Studi' 6–10 Aprile 2008 [Forty-fifth Week of Studies 6–10 April 2008] (Florence: Firenze University Press, Fondazione Istituto Internationale di Storia econom-

ica 'F. Datini' Prato, Serie II – Atti delle 'settimane di Studi' e altri Convegni [International Institute of the 'Week of Studies' and other Conferences], 40, 2009), pp. 409–40; Also an outcome of an equivalent conference is the volume M. Rozen (ed.), *Home-Lands and Diasporas. Greeks, Jews and their Migrations* (London and New York: I. B. Tauris, 2008), pp. 169–80; there is a huge bibliography for Jewish diaspora entrepreneurial activities, just to name a few: J. I. Israel, *Diasporas within a Diaspora: Jews, Crypto-Jews, and the World of Maritime Empires (1540–1740)* (Leiden: Brill, 2002); D. Cesarani and G. Romain, *Jews and Port Cities, 1590–1990* (London: Valentine Mitchell, 2006).

9.　Among the huge literature on ancient Greek colonies see A. J. Graham, 'The Colonial Expansion of Greece', in J. Boardman and *N. G. L. Hammond* (eds), *The Cambridge Ancient History*, vol. 3/3: *The Expansion of the Greek World, 8th to 6th Centuries B.C.*, 2nd edn (Oxford, 1982), pp. 83–162. Herodotus frequently uses the word *emporium* to define a trading city. For the term in early modern times see Chapter 9 by Iannis Carras.

10.　The etymology of the word stems from 'παρά/para-' which means 'beside' or 'alongside' and 'οἰκῶ/oiko' which means 'I live/get established'.

11.　For a detailed bibliography see Chapters 8 and 10.

12.　Mauro, 'Merchant Communities', p. 262.

13.　G. Jones, *The Evolution of International Business: An Introduction* (London: Routledge, 1996), p. 149.

14.　Geoffrey Jones for the nineteenth century introduces a typology on British trading companies and suggests three network-based organizational forms. See G. Jones, *Merchants to Multinationals: British Trading Companies in the Nineteenth and Twentieth Centuries* (Oxford and New York: Oxford University Press, 2000), p. 160.

15.　G. Harlaftis, 'Greek Maritime Business in the Nineteenth and Twentieth Centuries: A Paradigm for Comparative Studies on Family Capitalism and Diaspora Networks', in F. de Goey and J. W. Veluwenhamp (eds), *Entrepreneurs and Institutions in Europe and Asia, 1500–2000* (Amsterdam: Aksant, 2002), pp. 71–90. See also G. Harlaftis, 'From Diaspora Traders to Shipping Tycoons: The Vagliano Bros.', *Business History Review*, 81:2 (2007), pp. 237–68.

16.　M. H. Van Den Boogert, *The Capitulations and the Ottoman Legal System: Qadis, Consuls and Beratlis in the 18th Century* (Leiden: Brill, 2005).

17.　J. W. Veluwenkamp, *Archangel. Nederlandse ondernemers in Rusland, 1550–1785* [Arkhangelsk. Dutch Entrepreneurs in Russia, 1550–1785] (Amsterdam: Balans, 2000), pp. 111, 124; O. J. Schmitt, *Levantiner: Lebenswelten und Identitäten einer ethnokonfessionellen Gruppe im osmanischen Reich im 'langen 19. Jahrhundert'* [Levantines: the World and Identities of an Ethnoreligious Group of the Ottoman Empire in the 'Long Nineteenth Century'] (Munich: Oldenbourg, 2005);O. Katsiardi-Hering, 'City-ports in the Eastern and Central Mediterranean from the Mid-Sixteenth to the Nineteenth Century: Urban and Social Aspects', *Mediterranean Historical Review*, 26:2 (2011), pp. 151–70.

1 Veluwenkamp and Veenstra, 'Early Modern English Merchant Colonies: Contexts and Functions'

1.　N. O. Pedersen, 'Scottish Immigration to Bergen in the Sixteenth and Seventeenth Centuries', in A. Grosjean and S. Murdoch (eds), *Scottish Communities Abroad in the Early Modern Period* (Leiden: Brill, 2005), pp. 135–68; K. Zickermann, ' "*Briteannia ist mein Patria*". Scotsmen and the "British" Community in Hambourg' in A. Grosjean and S.

Murdoch (eds), *Scottish Communities Abroad in the Early Modern Period* (Leiden: Brill, 2005), pp. 249–76.
2. See for instance: O. Katsiardi-Hering, 'Christian and Jewish Ottoman Subjects: Family, Inheritance and Commercial Networks between East and West (17th–18th Centuries)', in S. Cavaciocchi (ed.), *The Economic Role of the Family in the European Economy from the 13th to the 18th Centuries* (Florence: Firenze University Press, 2009), pp. 409–40; G. Harlaftis, 'International Business of Southeastern Europe and the Eastern Mediterranean, 18th Century: Sources, Methods and Interpretive Issues', in F. Ammannati (ed.), *Where is Economic History Going? Methods and Prospects from the 13th to the 18th Centuries* (Florence: Firenze University Press, 2011), pp. 389–415.
3. J. W. Veluwenkamp, 'Merchant Colonies in the Dutch Trade System (1550–1750)', in C. A. Davids, W. Fritschy and L. A. van der Valk (eds), *Kapitaal, Ondernemerschap en Beleid. Studies over Economie en Politiek in Nederland, Europa en Azië van 1500 tot Heden. Afscheidsbundel voor Prof. Dr. P. W. Klein* [Capital, Entrepreneurship, and Policy. Studies on Economics and Politics in the Netherlands, Europe and Asia, 1500–Present. Valedictory Collecion of Articles in Honour of Prof. P.W. Klein] (Amsterdam: NEHA, 1996), pp. 141–64.
4. Veluwenkamp, 'Merchant Colonies', pp. 141–64.
5. Ibid., pp. 144, 162, 164.
6. The expression is Jonathan Israel's: J. I. Israel, *Dutch Primacy in World Trade, 1585–1740* (Oxford: Clarendon Press, 1989).
7. M. E. Bratchel, 'Regulation and Group Consciousness in the Later History of London Italian Merchant Colonies', *Journal of European Economic History*, 9:3 (1980), pp. 585–610; A. Grosjean and S. Murdoch (eds), *Scottish Communities Abroad in the Early Modern Period* (Leiden: Brill, 2005).
8. See also Katsiardi-Hering, 'Christian and Jewish Ottoman Subjects', pp. 409–40; Harlaftis, 'International Business', pp. 389–415.
9. J. E. Rauch, 'Business and Social Networks in International Trade', *Journal of Economic Literature*, 39:4 (2001), pp. 1177–1203.
10. W. R. Easterly, *The White Man's Burden: Why the West's Efforts to Aid the Rest Have Done So Much Ill and So Little Good* (New York: Penguin Press, 2006).
11. M. Fafchamps, 'Networks, Communities and Markets in Sub-Saharan Africa: Implications for Firm Growth and Investment', *Journal of African Economies*, 10, AERC supplement 2 (2001), pp. 109–42, on p. 120.
12. A. Greif, 'Contract Enforceability and Economic Institutions in Early Trade: The Maghribi Traders' Coalition', *American Economic Review*, 83:3 (1993), pp. 525–48, on p. 529.
13. Rauch, 'Business and Social Networks', p. 1181; A. Cohen, *Custom and Politics in Urban Africa: A Study of Hausa Migrants in Yoruba Towns* (London: Routledge & Kegan Paul, 1969), pp. 99–100.
14. Veluwenkamp, 'Merchant Colonies'.
15. The word 'network' is a contested term. Here, we apply the definition given by Casson: 'a set of high-trust relationships which either directly or indirectly link together everyone in a social group. A linkage is defined in terms of information flow between people'. See M. Casson, 'Entrepreneurial Networks. A Theoretical Perspective', in M. Moss and A. Slaven (eds), *Entrepreneurial Networks and Business Culture. Proceedings of the Twelfth International Economic History Congress* (Sevilla: Universidad de Sevilla, 1998), pp. 13–28, on p. 15.

16. I. Blanchard, *The International Economy in the 'Age of Discoveries', 1470–1570. Antwerp and the English Merchants' World* (Stuttgart: Franz Steiner Verlag, 2009), pp. 125–7, 139; Bratchel, 'Regulation and Group Consciousness'; B. Murphy, *A History of the British Economy, 1086–1970* (London: Longman, 1973), pp. 200–2, 205; L. A. Clarkson, *The Pre-Industrial Economy in England 1500–1750* (London: Batsford, 1971), p. 142.

17. Murphy, *A History*, pp. 119, 201–2, 208, on p. 202; Clarkson, *The Pre-Industrial Economy*, pp. 140–1.

18. Murphy, *A History*, pp. 119, 201–2, 208; Clarkson, *The Pre-Industrial Economy*, pp. 140–1.

19. R. W. K. Hinton, *The Eastland Trade and the Common Weal in the Seventeenth Century* (Cambridge: Cambridge University Press, 1959), p. 2.

20. J. W. Veluwenkamp, *Archangel. Nederlandse Ondernemers in Rusland, 1550–1785* [Arkhangelsk. Dutch Entrepreneurs in Russia, 1550–1785] (Amsterdam: Balans, 2000), p. 19.

21. Murphy, *A History*, p. 204.

22. Veluwenkamp, *Archangel*, pp. 19, 21, 44–5; Murphy, *A History*, pp. 203–4; T.S. Willan, *The Early History of the Russia Company, 1553–1603* (Manchester: Manchester University Press, 1968; reprint of 1956), p. 275.

23. Murphy, *A History*, p. 204; Willan, *The Early History*, pp. 30, 32, 34, 38–9, 67, 78, 157.

24. D. Ormrod, *The Rise of Commercial Empires. England and the Netherlands in the Age of Mercantilism, 1650–1770* (Cambridge: Cambridge University Press, 2003), p. 61; Murphy, *A History*, p. 205; Clarkson, *The Pre-Industrial Economy*, pp. 140–1; S. E. Åström, *From Cloth to Iron. The Anglo–Baltic Trade in the Late Seventeenth Century. Part 1. The Growth, Structure and Organization of the Trade. Commentationes Humanarum Litterarum*, 33:1–2 (Helsingfors: Societas Scientiarum Fennica, 1963), p. 19; Hinton, *The Eastland Trade*, pp. 1, 5.

25. Ormrod, *The Rise of Commercial Empires*, p. 61; Åström, *From Cloth to Iron*, pp. 25, 35, 133; Hinton, *The Eastland Trade*, pp. vii, 1–3, 34, 36–7, 39–41, 53.

26. Åström, *From Cloth to Iron*, pp. 19–20, 22, 179; Hinton, *The Eastland Trade*, pp. 3, 6, 53–4.

27. Åström, *From Cloth to Iron*, pp. 22–3, 179; Hinton, *The Eastland Trade*, pp. 11, 27, 36, 40–1, 68, 78, 87, 102, 130–1.

28. Hinton, *The Eastland Trade*, pp. vii, 41, 54, 57–8. Quotation, p. 57.

29. Murphy, *A History*, pp. 207–8.

30. R. Davis, *Aleppo and Devonshire Square. English Traders in the Levant in the Eighteenth Century* (London, Melbourne, Toronto: MacMillan, 1967), p. 43.

31. Murphy, *A History*, pp. 207–8.

32. A. C. Wood, *A History of the Levant Company* (London: Frank Cass & Co Ltd, 1964), p. 8.

33. Wood, *A History*, pp. 8–9. Compare Davis, *Aleppo and Devonshire Square*, pp. 44–5.

34. Wood, *A History*, p. 14.

35. Ormrod, *The Rise of Commercial Empires*, p. 62; Murphy, *A History*, pp. 208–9.

36. B. A. Masters, *The Origins of Western Economic Dominance in the Middle East: Mercantilism and the Islamic Economy in Aleppo, 1600–1750* (New York: New York University Press, 1989), p. 25.

37. Ormrod, *The Rise of Commercial Empires*, p. 63; Murphy, *A History*, p. 209.

38. K. Glamann, 'European Trade 1500–1750', in C. M. Cipolla (ed.), *The Fontana Economic History of Europe. The Sixteenth and Seventeenth Centuries* (Glasgow: Fontana, 1974), pp. 427–526, on p. 516.

39. Masters, *The Origins of Western Economic Dominance*, p. 26; H. Inalcik and D. Quataert (eds), *An Economic and Social History of the Ottoman Empire, 1300–1914* (Cambridge: Cambridge University Press, 1994), p. 523; Murphy, *A History*, p. 209.

40. R. Grassby, *The English Gentleman in Trade. The Life and Works of Sir Dudley North, 1641–1691* (Oxford: Clarendon Press, 1994), p. 38; M. Abraham, *The Middle East on the Eve of Modernity: Aleppo in the Eighteenth Century* (New York: Columbia University Press, 1989), p. 45; G. Ambrose, 'English Traders at Aleppo (1658–1756)', *Economic History Review*, 3 (1931–2), pp. 246–67, on p. 246.

41. Inalcik and Quataert, *An Economic and Social History*, p. 523; Abraham, *The Middle East*, p. 45; Masters, *The Origins of Western Economic Dominance*, p. 25.

42. D. Goffman, 'Izmir: from Village to Colonial Port City', in E. Eldem, D. Goffman and B. Masters, *The Ottoman City between East and West: Aleppo, Izmir and Istanbul* (Cambridge: Cambridge University Press, 1999), pp. 79–134, on pp. 90, 94, 105; E. Frangakis-Syrett, *The Commerce of Smyrna in the Eighteenth Century (1700–1820)* (Athens: Centre for Asia Minor Studies, 1992), p.76.

43. E. Frangakis-Syrett, 'Commercial Practices and Competition in the Levant', in A. Hamilton, A. H. de Groot and M. H. van den Boogert (eds), *Friends and Rivals in the East; Studies in Anglo–Dutch Relations in the Levant from the Seventeenth to the Early Nineteenth Century* (Leiden: Brill, 2000), pp. 135–58, on p. 145.

44. Murphy, *A History*, pp. 209–10.

45. H. Koenigsberger, 'English Merchants in Naples and Sicily in the Seventeenth Century', *English Historical Review*, 62 (1947), pp. 304–26, on pp. 307, 312–15, 317–18, 325.

46. Zickermann, 'Briteannia *ist mein Patria*', pp. 250–1; Ormrod, *The Rise of Commercial Empires*, pp. 36–7, 93; Murphy, *A History*, pp. 201–2; Clarkson, *The Pre-Industrial Economy*, p. 141; W. E. Lingelbach, 'The Merchant Adventurers at Hambourg', *American History Review*, 9:2 (1904), pp. 265–87, on pp. 265–9.

47. Clarkson, *The Pre-Industrial Economy*, pp. 142–3; Åström, *From Cloth to Iron*, p. 122; T. S. Ashton, *An Economic History of England. The 18th Century* (1955; London: Methuen, 1959), p. 135.

48. Ormrod, *The Rise of Commercial Empires*, pp. 182, 310, 338; Hinton, *The Eastland Trade*, pp. 89, 93.

49. Ormrod, *The Rise of Commercial Empires*, p. 343; Hinton, *The Eastland Trade*, pp. 90–1.

50. Clarkson, *The Pre-Industrial Economy*, p. 142; Ashton, *An Economic History*, p. 135.

51. Ormrod, *The Rise of Commercial Empires*, p. 343.

52. Murphy, *A History*, pp. 309–10; Clarkson, *The Pre-Industrial Economy*, p. 142; Ashton, *An Economic History*, p. 130.

53. Murphy, *A History*, p. 310; Clarkson, *The Pre-Industrial Economy*, p. 142; Ashton, *An Economic History*, p. 130.

54. Ormrod, *The Rise of Commercial Empires*, pp. 182, 288, 338–43.

55. Ormrod, *The Rise of Commercial Empires*, p. 63; Murphy, *A History*, pp. 292–5, 304–8; Hinton, *The Eastland Trade*, p. 110.

56. Ormrod, *The Rise of Commercial Empires*, p. 63; Murphy, *A History*, pp. 304–8.

57. Åström, *From Cloth to Iron*, pp. 35, 37, 40–1, 48, 69, 133–4, 181.

58. Ormrod, *The Rise of Commercial Empires*, pp. 63, 75–6; Frangakis-Syrett, 'Commercial Practices', pp. 135, 148, 151; Abraham, *The Middle East*, p. 149; Murphy, *A History*, pp. 303–8; Davis, *Aleppo and Devonshire Square*, pp. 27–9; Ambrose, 'English Traders'.
59. Murphy, *A History*, pp. 411–12.
60. Ormrod, *The Rise of Commercial Empires*, p. 329.
61. Ibid., pp. 139, 329.
62. Ibid., p. 342.
63. Aström, *From Cloth to Iron*, pp. 36, 96, 99, 108, 122–3, 139–43, 147–9.
64. Ibid., pp. 149–50.
65. Ibid., pp. 108, 123, 144–6, 148.
66. Ibid., pp. 108, 143.
67. L. Müller, *The Merchant Houses of Stockholm, c. 1640–1800. A Comparative Study of Early-Modern Entrepreneurial Behaviour* (Uppsala: Uppsala University, 1998), pp. 122–4.
68. Åström, *From Cloth to Iron*, pp. 125–8, 150.
69. Ibid., pp. 36, 124, 128, 131–3.
70. V. Zakharov, 'Russian Trade Policy in the 18th Century', in F. de Goey and J. W. Veluwenkamp (eds), *Entrepreneurs and Institutions in Europe and Asia, 1500–2000* (Amsterdam: Aksant, 2002), pp. 55–70.
71. P. W. Klein, '"Little London": British Merchants in Rotterdam during the Seventeenth and Eighteenth Centuries', in D. C. Coleman and P. Mathias (eds), *Enterprise and History. Essays in Honour of Charles Wilson* (Cambridge: Cambridge University Press, 1984), pp. 116–34, on pp. 126–33.
72. Ormrod, *The Rise of Commercial Empires*, pp. 37–8, 93–5, 134, 139, 333.
73. Frangakis-Syrett, 'Commercial Practices', pp. 135, 148, 151; Abraham, *The Middle East*, p. 149; Davis, *Aleppo and Devonshire Square*, pp. 3, 36–7, 66–7; Ambrose, 'English Traders', p. 262.
74. On this shift of western European commercial activities: N. Svoronos, *Le commerce de Salonique au XVIIe siècle* (Paris: Presses Universitaires de France, 1956), pp. 347–8.
75. Frangakis-Syrett, 'Commercial Practices', pp. 135, 148, 151; Abraham, *The Middle East*, p. 149; Davis, *Aleppo and Devonshire Square*, pp. 5, 26, 36–7, 66–7; Ambrose, 'English Traders', p. 256.
76. Frangakis-Syrett, 'Commercial Practices', pp. 135, 148, 151; Abraham, *The Middle East*, p. 149.
77. C. M. Cipolla, 'The Economic Decline of Italy', in B. Pullan (ed.), *Crisis and Change in the Venetian Economy in the 16th and 17th Centuries* (London: Methuen, 1968), pp. 127–45, on p. 127.
78. D. Sella, 'Crisis and Transformation in Venetian Trade', in B. Pullan (ed.), *Crisis and Change in the Venetian Economy in the 16th and 17th Centuries* (London: Methuen, 1968), pp. 88–105, on p. 88.
79. F. C. Lane, 'Venetian Shipping During the Commercial Revolution', *American Historical Review*, 38:2 (1933), pp. 219–39, on p. 224.
80. Cipolla, 'The Economic Decline', p. 135.
81. M. E. Bratchel, 'Italian Merchant Organization and Business Relationships in Early Tudor London', in S. Subrahmanyam (ed.), *Merchant Networks in the Early Modern World* (1996), pp. 1–28, on pp. 4–5, 15, 26.

82. F. Elder, 'The van der Molen, Commission Merchants of Antwerp: Trade with Italy, 1538–1544', in J. L. Cate and E. N. Anderson (eds), *Medieval and Historiograhical Essays in Honor of James Westfall Thompson* (Chicago, IL: 1938), pp. 78–145, on p. 82.
83. Zickermann, 'Briteannia ist mein Patria', p. 261.
84. T. C. Smout, N. C. Landsman and T. M. Devine, 'Scottish Emigration in the Seventeenth and Eighteenth Centuries', in N. Canny (ed.), *Europeans on the Move* (Oxford: Oxford University Press, 1994), pp. 76–112, on p. 86.
85. Zickermann, 'Briteannia ist mein Patria', p. 250.
86. D. Catterall, 'Scots along the Maas, c. 1570–1750', in A. Grosjean and S. Murdoch (eds), *Scottish Communities Abroad in the Early Modern Period* (Leiden: Brill, 2005), pp. 169–90, on p. 175.
87. Catterall, 'Scots along the Mass', p. 184.
88. Bratchel, 'Italian Merchant Organization', p. 23.
89. Ibid., p. 23.
90. Cipolla, 'The Economic Decline', p. 133.
91. Bratchel, 'Italian Merchant Organization', pp. 25–6.
92. Smout, Landsman and Devine, 'Scottish Emigration', p. 82.
93. Pedersen, 'Scottish Immigration to Bergen', p. 149.
94. Ibid., pp. 149, 152, 160.
95. A. Grosjean and S. Murdoch, 'The Scottish Community in Seventeenth-Century Gothenburg', in A. Grosjean and S. Murdoch (eds), *Scottish Communities Abroad in the Early Modern Period* (Leiden: Brill, 2005), pp. 191–222, on p. 216.
96. Grosjean and Murdoch, 'The Scottish Community', p. 205.
97. Smout, Landsman and Devine, 'Scottish Emigration', p. 86.
98. G. Behre, 'Scots in "Little London". Scots Settlers and Cultural Development in Gothenburg in the Eighteenth Century', *Northern Scotland*, 7:2 (1986), pp. 133–50, on p. 133; Grosjean and Murdoch, 'The Scottish Community', p. 216.
99. Grosjean and Murdoch, 'The Scottish Community', p. 216.

2 Dougherty, 'German and Italian Merchant Colonies in Early Modern England'

1. J. L. Bolton, *The Medieval English Economy, 1150–1500* (London: J. M. Dent & Sons Ltd, 1980), pp. 287–319; D. C. Coleman, *The Economy of England 1450–1750* (Oxford: Oxford University Press, 1977), pp. 48–68; M. M. Postan, 'The Fifteenth Century', *Economic History Review*, 9 (1939), pp. 160–7; E. S. Hunt and J. M. Murray, *The History of Business in Medieval Europe, 1200–1500* (Cambridge: Cambridge University Press, 1999), pp. 178–203, 249.
2. S. L. Thrupp, 'Aliens in and Around London in the Fifteenth Century', in R. Grew and N. H. Steneck (eds), *Society and History: Essays by Sylvia L. Thrupp* (Ann Arbor, MI: University of Michigan Press, 1977), pp. 109–12; Bolton, *The Medieval English Economy*, pp. 287–319.
3. A. Luders, Sir T. Edlyn Tomlins, J. France, Sir W. E. Taunton, J. Raithby, W. Elliot and J. Caley (eds), *The Statutes of the Realm*, vol. I (London: G. Eyre and A. Strahan, 1810), pp. 6–41; 28 Edward III c. 13 (1354), required respect and fair treatment of merchant strangers, if a trial was necessary, the jury would consist of half domestic and half foreign merchants; *SR*, 2, 2 Richard II c. 1 (1378), welcomed foreign merchants, their safety was assured, and punishment for those who disturbed them; M. M. Postan, E. E. Rich and E. Miller (eds), *The Cambridge Economic History of Europe*, vol. 3 (Cambridge: Cambridge

University Press, 1965), pp. 42–118. A general overview of the Italian and German merchants in association with England is presented.

4.   F. Mauro, 'Merchant Communities, 1350–1750', in J. D. Tracy (ed.), *The Rise of Merchant Empires* (Cambridge: Cambridge University Press, 1990), pp. 255–66.

5.   E. Power, 'The Wool Trade in the Fifteenth Century', in E. Power and M. M. Postan (eds), *Studies in English Trade in the Fifteenth Century* (New York: George Routledge and Sons, Ltd, 1933), pp. 39–90, esp. pp. 57–8; Hunt and Murray, *The History of Business*, pp. 52–67.

6.   Mauro, 'Merchant Communities', pp. 255–6.

7.   S. Sanjay (ed.), *Merchant Networks in the Early Modern Period* (Aldershot, : Variorum Books, 1996), pp. xiii–xxi.

8.   Some examples of these writings are: T. Mun, *England's Treasure by Forraign Trade 1664* (New York: Macmillan, 1985), pp. 2–6; R. Roberts, *The Character and Qualifications of an Honest Loyal Merchant* (London: Robert Roberts, 1686), pp. 1–14; and G. Malynes, *Consuedtudo vel Lex Mercatoria; or, the Ancient Law Merchant* (1622; Amsterdam: Theatrum Orbis Terrarum, 1979), pp. 6–16; A. Sapori, *The Italian Merchant in the Middle Ages*, trans. P. A. Kennen (New York: Norton, 1970), pp. 65–91. This contemporary book describes the characteristics and development of the Italian merchant and all the knowledge needed to operate successfully in an international situation, especially the last chapter 'The Italians Abroad'.

9.   P. Dollinger, *The German Hansa* (1970; London: Routledge/Thoemmes Press, 1999), pp. 116–29.

10. M. M. Postan, 'The Trade of Medieval Europe: the North', in M. M. Postan, *Medieval Trade and Finance* (Cambridge: Cambridge University Press, 1973), pp. 92–102.

11. Postan, 'The Economic and Political Relations of England and the Hanse from 1400–1475', *Medieval Trade and Finance*, pp. 232–304, esp. p. 299.

12. J. M. Munro, 'English "Backwardness" and Financial Innovations in Commerce with the Low Countries, 14th-16th Centuries', in P. Stabel, B. Blonde and A. Greve (eds), *International Trade in the Low Countries, 14th-16th Centuries* (Leuven and Apeldoorn: Garant Publishers, 1997), pp. 105–67. Although Italian financial services were useful, this author states that with regular trade transactions, England developed the best financial techniques for her particular needs. Thrupp, 'Aliens in and around London', p. 112.

13. A. A. Ruddock, *Italian Merchants and Shipping in Southampton, 1270–1600* (Southampton: University College, 1951), pp. 71–93.

14. J. N. Ball, *Merchants and Merchandise: the Expansion of Trade in Europe 1500–1630* (London: Croom Helm, 1977), p. 36.

15. Power, 'The Wool Trade in the Fifteenth Century', pp. 45–6. Financial gifts were expected by the king and sometimes if they were not given freely, the king was known to use threats or jail to achieve the desired loan.

16. *The Calendar of the Patent Rolls, Edward IV, Edward V, Richard III, 1476–1485* (London: Mackie & Co., 1901), pp. 251, 296. Besides trade advantages, they also provided the following services: the king asked the Italians to bring cloth craftsmen to England to teach their skills; privileges were granted to the Italians for taking care of the king's business in the court of Rome; privileges were granted for taking care of matters in Rome.

17. Dollinger, *The German Hansa*, pp. 244–5.

18. E. B. Fryde, 'Italian Maritime Trade with Medieval England (c. 1270–1530)', in E. B. Fryde, *Studies in Medieval Trade and Finance* (London: Hambledon Press, 1983), pp. 291–337, on pp. 310–11; Mauro, 'Merchant Communities', p. 264; Postan, Rich and Miller (eds), *The Cambridge Economic History of Europe*, pp. 102–3; E. G. Nash, *The Hansa, its History and Romance* (New York: Dodd, Mead and Company, 1929), p. 177.

19. Coleman, *The Economy of England*, pp. 2, 48.

20. A number of statutes will be given as references in the following text. These references are meant to be examples of the point in the text but they do not represent all possible references because there are many repetitions of the same statutes or repetitions with variations throughout the various reigns.

21. J. Hatcher, 'The Great Slump of the Mid-fifteenth Century', in R. Britnell and J. Hatcher (eds), *Progress and Problems in Medieval England, Essays in Honour of Edward Miller* (Cambridge: Cambridge University Press, 1996), pp. 237–72.

22. An example of such a family: A. Hanham, *The Celys and Their World: an English Merchant Family of the Fifteenth Century* (New York: Oxford University Press, 1985).

23. *SR*, 2, 3 Edward IV c. 1 (1463) wool shipped to Calais only, 14 Edward IV c. 3 (1474), 12 Henry VII c. 6 (1496) Regulation of the Merchant Venturers; *SR*, 1, 27 Edward III s. 2 c. 1 (1353) Staple established; E. Power, *The Wool Trade in English Medieval History* (Oxford: Oxford University Press, 1941), p. 102. England became predominant in the wool trade at the staple but did not increase volume of trade; Power, 'The Wool Trade in the Fifteenth Century', pp. 51–8.

24. E. M. Carus-Wilson and Olive Coleman, *England's Export Trade, 1275–1547* (Oxford: Clarendon Press, 1963), pp. 11–17; G. D. Ramsay, *The English Woollen Industry, 1500–1750* (London: Macmillan, 1982), pp. 18–38. Information for this and the following paragraph are drawn from pages 18–38; M. M. Postan, 'The Medieval Wool Trade', *Medieval Trade and Finance*, pp. 342–52; Power, 'The Wool Trade in the Fifteenth Century', pp. 41-62.

25. Sapori, *The Italian Merchant*, pp. 1–91; Thrupp, 'Aliens in and Around London', pp. 102, 112.

26. T. H. Lloyd, *Alien Merchants in England in the High Middle Ages* (New York: St. Martin's Press, 1982), p. 169.

27. R. Brown (ed.), *Calendar of State Papers and Manuscripts, Relating to English Affairs, Existing in the Archives and Collections of Venice and in Other Libraries of Northern Italy*, vol. 1 (London: Longman, Green, Longman, Roberts, & Green, 1864), no. 155, p. 44 and no. 138, pp. 40–1; Power, 'The Wool Trade in the Fifteenth Century', pp. 45–8; R. Bale, 'Robert Bale's Chronicle', in R. Flenley (ed.), *Six Town Chronicles of England* (Oxford: Clarendon Press, 1911), pp. 114–53, on p. 138.

28. W. Childs, '"To oure losse and hindrance": English Credit to Alien Merchants in the Mid-Fifteenth Century', in J. Kermode (ed.) *Enterprise and Individualism in Fifteenth-Century England* (Stroud: Alan Sutton Publishing, 1991), pp. 68–97; Power, 'The Wool Trade in the Fifteenth Century', pp. 62–6. Both English and Italians bought on credit; Postan, 'Credit in Medieval Trade', *Medieval Trade and Finance*, pp. 1–27.

29. Hunt and Murray, *The History of Business*, p. 247. The authors state that the rich and elite fuelled the medieval economy.

30. Fryde, 'Anglo-Italian Commerce in the Fifteenth Century: Some Evidence about Profits and the Balance of Trade', *Studies in Medieval Trade and Finance*, pp. 345–55.

31. D. Keene, 'Sites of Desire: Shops, Selds and Wardrobes in London and other English Cities, 1100–1550', in B. Blonde, P. Stabel, J. Stobart and I. van Damme (eds), *Buyers*

and Sellers, Retail Circuits and Practices in Medieval and Modern Europe (Turnhout, Belgium: Brepols Publishers, 2006), pp. 125–153; R. Britnell, 'Markets, Shops, Inns, Taverns and Private Houses in Medieval English Trade', in Blonde et al. (eds), *Buyers and Sellers*, pp. 109–123.

32. Thrupp, 'Aliens in and Around London', pp. 101–27. Thrupp believes that the English attitude toward foreigners was not necessarily all negative.

33. M. E. Bratchel, 'Italian Merchant Organizations and Business Relationships in Early Tudor England', in Sanjay, *Merchant Networks*, pp. 1–28.

34. Thrupp, 'Aliens in and Around London', pp. 101–27; H. Bradley, 'The Datini Factors in London, 1380–1410', in D. J. Clayton, R. G. Davies and P. McNiven (eds), *Trade, Devotion, and Governance: Papers in Later Medieval English History* (Stroud: Sutton Publishing, 1994), pp. 55–79; G. Holmes, 'Lorenzo de' Medici's London Branch', in Britnell and Hatcher (eds), *Progress and Problems in Medieval England*, pp. 273–85.

35. Fryde, 'Italian Maritime Trade', p. 292.

36. Brown (ed.), *Calendar of State Papers and Manuscripts*, no. 406, p. 118.

37. Fryde, 'Italian Maritime Trade', pp. 292–3, 321.

38. A. A. Ruddock, 'Alien Merchants in Southampton in the Later Middle Ages', *English Historical Review*, 61 (1946), pp. 1–17.

39. Ruddock, 'Alien Merchants in Southampton', p. 9; C. Platt, *Medieval Southampton* (London: Routledge & Kegan Paul, 1973), pp. 152–63.

40. R. Flenley, 'London and Foreign Merchants in the Reign of Henry VI', *English Historical Review*, 25 (1910), pp. 644–55; Brown (ed.), *Calendar of State Papers and Manuscripts*, pp. 1, 118.

41. A. A. Ruddock, 'Alien Hosting in Southampton in the Fifteenth Century', *Economic History Review*, 16 (1946), pp. 30–7.

42. Ruddock, *Italian Merchants and Shipping*, pp. 173–6; Fryde, 'Italian Maritime Trade', pp. 291–333, on pp. 330–1; *SR*, 1, 25 Edward III s. 5 c. 23 (1352), this statute stated that the Lombards were answerable for the debts of other Italians.

43. Postan, Rich and Miller (eds), *The Cambridge Economic History of Europe*, p. 102.

44. T. Wright (ed.), *Political Poems and Songs Relating to English History* (London: Longman, Green, Longman, and Roberts, 1861), vol. 2, pp. 157–205, 282–7; G. A. Holmes, 'The "Libel of English Policy"', *English Historical Review*, 76 (1961), pp. 193–216. The author states that the poem is related to trade and politics and intended to influence government policy.

45. *SR*, 2, 18 Henry VI c. 4 (1439); Fryde, 'Italian Maritime Trade', p. 324. These figures are quoted in a number of other sources.

46. Fryde, 'Italian Maritime Trade' p. 330; G. D. Ramsay, 'The Undoing of the Italian Mercantile Colony in Sixteenth-Century London', in N. B. Harte and K. G. Ponting (eds), *Textile History and Economic History Essays in Honour of Miss Julia de Lacy Mann* (Manchester: Manchester University Press, 1973), pp. 22–49, on p. 22.

47. Bale, 'Bale's Chronicle', pp.143–4; 'Evil May Day 1517', in R. H. Tawney and E. Power (eds), *Tudor Economic Documents* (1924; London: Longmans, Green and Co., 1951), vol. 3, pp. 82–90; *Calendar of Patent Rolls, Edward IV, Henry VI, 1467–1477* (London: Eyre and Spottiswoode, 1900), p. 217.

48. Ruddock, 'Alien Merchants in Southampton', pp. 14–16. The Venetians felt that they were cheated locally and so took their case to the Chancery in London requesting two times the damages and punishment for the wrong doers.

49. Bale, 'Bale's Chronicle', pp. 138, 144; *Calendar of Patent Rolls, 1467–1477*, p. 213.

50. *SR*, 2, 1 Richard III c. 9 (1483–4); I. M. W. Harvey, 'Was There Popular Politics in Fifteenth-Century England?', in R. H. Britnell and A. J. Pollard (eds.), *The McFarlane*

Legacy: Studies in Late Medieval Politics and Society (New York: St. Martin's Press, 1995), pp. 155–74. Ordinary people were expressing their thoughts and concerns and were not afraid to ask their MPs to carry their thoughts to Parliament; *Rotuli Parliamentorum; ut et Petitiones, et Placita in Parliamento; or, Rolls of Parliament*, vol. 6 (London: Parliament, 1767–77), p. 263.

51. *SR*, 2, 1 Henry VII c. 10 (1485); *Rotuli Parliamentorum*, vol. 6, pp. 289–90; S. B. Chrimes, *Henry VII* (Berkeley, CA: Yale University Press, 1972), p. 202.
52. Ramsay, 'The Undoing of the Italian Mercantile Colony', pp. 39, 48.
53. Bratchel, 'Italian Merchant Organizations', p. 2.
54. D. Sella, 'Crisis and Transformation in Venetian Trade', in B. Pullen (ed.), *Crisis and Change in the Venetian Economy in the Sixteenth and Seventeenth Centuries* (London: Methuen, 1968), pp. 88–105; C. M. Cipolla, 'The Economic Decline of Italy', in Pullen (ed.), *Crisis and Change in the Venetian Economy*, pp. 127–45.
55. Ruddock, 'Alien Merchants in Southampton', pp. 1–17.
56. Mauro, 'Merchant Communities', pp. 256–7; Dollinger, 'Consolidation of the Hansa of the Towns', *The German Hansa*, pp. 404–5.
57. Dollinger, 'Charters for the Merchants from Cologne in London (1157)', *The German Hansa*, pp. 380–1.
58. Dollinger, 'Undertaking Given by the English Customs to a Group of Merchants from Dortmund (1340)', *The German Hansa*, pp. 384–5.
59. Dollinger, 'Outrages and Wrongs done to Hanseatic Merchants by the English (1386)' *The German Hansa*, pp. 389–91.
60. Nash, *The Hansa*, p. 183.
61. Dollinger, *The German Hansa*, p. 104.
62. Nash, *The Hansa*, pp. 164–83; Dollinger, *The German Hansa*, pp. 243–6; Postan, 'The Economic and Political Relations of England and the Hanse', in Postan (eds), *Studies in Medieval Trade and Finance*, pp. 232–304, esp. p. 293; On 26 September 2005, the City of London erected a plaque which reads, 'To commemorate six hundred years during which some 400 Hanseatic Merchants inhabited peaceably in the City of London from the XIIIth to XIXth Centuries a German self-governing enclave on this site known as the Steelyard'.
63. Thrupp, 'Aliens in and Around London', p. 111; *Calendar of Patent Rolls, 1476–1485*, for example, pp. 129, 353, 425; Dollinger, *The German Hansa*, pp. 186–91.
64. *Calendar of Patent Rolls, 1476–1485*, pp. 129, 289, 353, 425–6.
65. Dollinger, *The German Hansa*, p. 187; I. D. Colvin, *The Germans in England 1066–1598* (London: Kennikat Press, 1971), p. xvi; Postan, 'Economic and Political Relations of England and the Hanse', pp. 298–300.
66. *Calendar of Patent Rolls, 1476–1485*, pp. 289, 426.
67. Dollinger, *The German Hansa*, pp. 188–91; Chrimes, *Henry VII*, pp. 235–7; Nash, *The Hansa*, pp. 142–51; *SR*, 3, 15 Henry VIII c. 29 (1523), 26 Henry VIII c. 26 (1534), 32 Henry VIII c. 14 (1541).
68. Dollinger, *The German Hansa*, pp. 204–6.
69. Postan, Rich and Miller (eds), *The Cambridge Economic History of Europe*, pp. 105–6; Mauro, 'Merchant Communities', p. 258; Nash, *The Hansa*, p. 174. They had no fear of going to court either.
70. Dollinger, 'Solidarity between English Clothiers and Hanseatics (1468)', *The German Hansa*, pp. 427–8.

71. T. H. Lloyd, *England and the German Hanse 1157–1611. A Study of Their Trade and Commercial Diplomacy* (Cambridge: Cambridge University Press, 1991), pp. 173-201.
72. Lloyd, *England and the German Hanse*, pp. 209–17; C. Ross, *Edward IV* (London: Yale University Press, 1974), pp. 211–12.
73. Lloyd, *England and the German Hanse*, pp. 200–17; *Rotuli Parliamentorum* vol. 6, pp. 65–9.
74. Chrimes, *Henry VII*, pp. 235–6; Lloyd, *England and the German Hanse*, pp. 236–9, 251.
75. Lloyd, *England and the German Hanse*, pp. 213–15. The judgements against the Hanse before 1473 were nullified, German merchants were relieved of any act of war against the English between 1468–74 and parliament reinstated the Hanse.
76. Dollinger, *The German Hansa*, pp. 311, 331; Nash, *The Hansa*, pp. 257–61.
77. Chrimes, *Henry VII*, p. 235.
78. Dollinger, *The German Hansa*, pp. 397–8; M. A. Green (ed.), *Calendar of State Papers, Domestic Series, 1598–1601* (London: Longmans, Green, and Co., 1869), 13 January 1598, no. 14, pp. 5–6.
79. Fryde, 'The English Cloth Industry and the Trade with the Mediterranean c. 1370–c. 1470', *Studies in Medieval Trade and Finance*, pp. 343–4; Ramsay, 'The Undoing of the Italian Mercantile Colony', p. 48.
80. Ramsay, *The English Woollen Industry*, pp. 55–7; Postan, 'Private Financial Instruments in Medieval England', *Medieval Trade and Finance*, pp. 28–64.
81. *SR*, 2, 1 Edward IV s.lc. 9 (1461).
82. *SR*, 2, 3 Edward IV c. 3 (1463); 3 Edward IV c. 4 (1463); 4 Edward IV c. 1 (1464); 4 Edward IV c. 2 (1464).
83. F. J. Fisher, 'The Sixteenth and Seventeenth Centuries: the Dark Ages of English Economic History?', in P. J. Corfield and N. B. Harte (eds), *London and the English Economy, 1500–1700* (London: Hambledon Press, 1990), pp. 131–147. The author states that growth came with new opportunities in existing categories of work.
84. Fisher, 'London as an "Engine of Economic Growth"', in Corfield and Harte (eds), *London and the English Economy*, pp. 185–98; P. Nightingale, 'The Growth of London in the Medieval English Economy', in Britnell and Hatcher (eds), *Progress and Problems in Medieval England*, pp. 89–106.
85. Fisher, 'Commercial Trends and Policy in Sixteenth-Century England', in Corfield and Harte (eds), *London and the English Economy*, pp. 81–103. The author states that the depression in the third quarter of sixteenth century England was the impetus for making economic changes and progress; Coleman, *The Economy of England*, pp. 48–68.
86. Ramsay, 'The Undoing of the Italian Mercantile Colony', pp. 46–9.
87. Coleman, *The Economy of England*, pp. 48–68; Ramsay, *The English Woollen Industry*, pp. 55–7.
88. Fisher, 'Commercial Trends and Policy', pp. 90–3; Ramsay, 'The Undoing of the Italian Mercantile Colony', p. 46; Ramsay, *The English Woollen Industry*, pp. 55–7.
89. Ball, *Merchants and Merchandise*, pp. 30–44, 154; M. Epstein, *The English Levant Company, its Foundation and its History to 1640* (London: G. Routledge and Sons, Ltd, 1908), pp. 20–150; Lloyd, *England and the German Hanse*, pp. 359–62.
90. Ramsay, 'The Undoing of the Italian Mercantile Colony', p. 23; Ramsay, *The English Woollen Industry*, pp. 55–7; Fisher, 'London as an "Engine of Economic Growth"', p. 191; Fisher, 'The Sixteenth and Seventeenth Centuries', p. 136.

3 Pourchasse, 'Dynamism and Integration of the North European Merchant Communities in French Ports in the Eighteenth Century'

1. B. Gautier and P. Voss, 'Les communautés marchandes étrangères dans l'espace urbain bordelais (1620–1715)' ['Foreign Merchant Communities in Urban Bordeaux (1620–1715)'], in J. Bottin and D. Calabi (eds), *Les étrangers dans la ville* [Foreigners in the City] (Paris: Editions de la maison des sciences de l'homme, 1999), pp. 329–43, on p. 328.

2. J. Meyer, 'Négociants allemands en France et négociants français en Allemagne au XVIIIᵉ siècle' ['German Merchants in France and French Merchants in Germany in the Eighteenth Century'], in J. Mondot, J.-M. Valentin and J. Voss (eds), *Allemands en France, Français en Allemagne, 1715–1789* [Germans in France, French in Germany, 1715–1789] (Sigmaringen: Beihefte der Francia, 25, 1992), pp. 103–19, on p. 105.

3. P. Dollinger, *La Hanse* [The Hanse] (Paris: Aubier, 1964), p. 313.

4. Ordonnance de Louis XI du 15 août 1473 [Ordinance of Louis XI, 15 August 1473].

5. J. Mathorez, 'La pénétration des Allemands en France sous l'ancien régime' ['The Entry of the Germans in France Under the Old Regime'], *Revue des Études Historiques* (1916), pp. 34–65, 171–207 and 314–45, on p. 177.

6. P. Pourchasse, *Le commerce du Nord. Les échanges commerciaux entre la France et l'Europe septentrionale au XVIIIᵉ siècle* [Trade with the North. Trade Between France and Northern Europe in the Eighteenth Century] (Rennes: PUR, 2006).

7. J. W. Veluwenkamp, 'International Business Communication Patterns in the Dutch Commercial System, 1500–1800', in H. Cools, M. Keblusek and B. Noldus (eds), *Your Humble Servant. Agents in Early Modern Europe* (Hilversum: Uitgeverij Verloren, 2006), pp. 121–34, on p. 126.

8. J. Cavignac, *Jean Pellet, commerçant de gros (1694–1772). Contribution à l'étude du commerce bordelais au XVIIIᵉ siècle* [Jean Pellet, a Wholesaler (1694–1772). Contribution to the Study of Trade in Eighteenth Century Bordeaux] (Paris: SEVPEN, 1967), p. 87.

9. P. Butel, 'Les négociants allemands de Bordeaux dans la deuxième moitié du XVIIIᵉ siècle', ['The German Merchants in Bordeaux in the Second Half of the Eighteenth Century'], in J. Schneider (ed.), *Wirtschaftskräfte und Wirtschaftswege* [Economic Forces and Economic Ways], vol. 2, *Wirtschaftskräfte in der europäischen Expansion. Festschrift für Hermann Kellenbenz* [Economic Forces in European Expansion. Festschrift for Hermann Kellenbenz] (Stuttgart: Klett-Cotta, Beiträge zur Wirtschaftsgeschichte 5, 1978), pp. 589–611, on p. 601.

10. M. C. Jensen and W. H. Meckling, 'Theory of the Firm: Managerial Behavior, Agency Costs and Ownership Structure', *Journal of Financial Economics*, 3 (1976), pp. 305–60 on, p. 309; An example in A.-M. Carlos, 'Principal-Agent Problems in Early Trading Companies: A Tale of Two Firms', *American Economic Review*, 2 (1992), pp. 140–5.

11. P. Gobain, *Le commerce en son jour ou l'art d'apprendre en peu de tems à tenir les livres de compte à parties doubles et simples par débit et crédit* [Daily Trade or the Art of Learning Rapidly to Keep the Account Books in Single and Double Parts Debit and Credit] (Bordeaux, 1702), p. 31.

12. A. Wegener Sleeswijk, 'La relation problématique entre principal et agent dans la commission: l'exemple de l'exportation des vins vers les Provinces-Unies au XVIIIᵉ siècle' ['The Problematic Relationship Between Principal and Agent in the Commission Trade: the Example of Wine Exports to the Dutch Republic in the Eighteenth Century'], in S. Marzagalli and H. Bonin (eds), *Négoce, Ports et Océans XVIᵉ–XXᵉ siècles, Mélanges offerts*

à *Paul Butel* [Trade, Transportation and Oceans in the Sixteenth-Twentieth Centuries, Mixtures Offered to Paul Butel] (Pessac: PUB, 2000), pp. 29–45, on p. 30.

13. P. Verley, *L'échelle du monde. Essai sur l'industrialisation de l'Occident* [The Size of the World. Essay on the Industrialization of the West] (Paris: Gallimard, 1997), p. 195.

14. D. C. North, *Institutions, Institutional Change and Economic Performance* (Cambridge: Cambridge University Press, 1990), p. 8.

15. G. Rambert, *Histoire du commerce de Marseille*, tome 7, *de 1660 à 1789. L'Europe moins les trois péninsules méditerranéenne, les Etats Unis* [History of Commerce of Marseille, Volume 7, from 1660 to 1789. Europe Excluding the Three Mediterranean Peninsulas, the United States] (Paris: Plon, 1966), p. 831.

16. Verley, *L'échelle du monde*, p. 235.

17. L.-P. Abeille and J.-G. Montaudouin, *Corps d'observation de la Société d'agriculture, de commerce et des arts établis par les États de Bretagne* [Corpus of Observation of the Society of Agriculture, Commerce and Arts Established by the Estate of Brittany], vol. 2, 1759–60 (Paris: n.p., 1772), p. 175.

18. G. Martin, *Nantes et la Compagnie des Indes* [Nantes and the French East India Company] (Paris: Marcel Rivière, 1928), p. 76.

19. J. Israel, *Dutch Primacy in World Trade* (Oxford: Clarendon Press, 1989), p. 367.

20. L. Müller and J. Ojala, 'Consular Services of the Nordic Countries during the Eighteenth and the Nineteenth Centuries: Did they Really Work?', *Research in Maritime History* 22 (2002), pp. 3–4,1 on p. 36.

21. F. Crouzet, 'Le commerce de Bordeaux' ['The Trade of Bordeaux'], in F.-G. Pariset (ed.), *Bordeaux au XVIIIᵉ siècle* [Bordeaux in the Eighteenth Century] (Bordeaux: Fédération historique du Sud-Ouest, 1968), pp. 221–86, on p. 260.

22. F.-K. Huhn, 'Die Handelsbeziehungen zwischen Frankreich und Hamburg, im 18. Jahrhundert' ['Trade Relations Between France and Hamburg in the Eighteenth Century'] (PhD dissertation, University of Hamburg 1952), pp. 34–6.

23. Archives Municipales, Nantes, CC 484.

24. Y.-M. Nouailhat, 'Les étrangers à Nantes au XVIIIᵉ siècle' ['Foreigners in Nantes in the Eighteenth Century'] (Master's thesis, University of Nantes, 1967).

25. G. Treutlein, 'Schifffahrt und Handel zwischen Nantes und dem europäischen Norden von 1714 bis 1744' (PhD dissertation, University of Heidelberg, 1970).

26. Archives Municipales, Nantes, série GG, Église réformée.

27. Butel, 'Les négociants allemands de Bourdeaux', pp. 589–611; M. Espagne, *Bordeaux-Baltique. La présence culturelle allemande à Bordeaux aux XVIIIᵉ et XIXᵉ siècles* [Bordeaux-Baltic Area. German Cultural Presence in Bordeaux in the Eighteenth and Nineteenth Centuries] (Paris: CNRS, 1991); W. Henninger, *Johann Jacob Von Bethmann 1717–1792. Kaufmann, Reeder und kaiserlicher Konsul in Bordeaux* [Johann Jacob Von Bethmann 1717–1792. Merchant, Shipowner and Imperial Consul in Bordeaux], vol. 2 (Bochum: N. Brockmeyer, 1993); Meyer, 'Négociants allemands en France', pp. 103–19; A. Ruiz (ed.), *Présence de l'Allemagne à Bordeaux du siècle de Montaigne à la veille de la Seconde guerre mondiale, Hommage au Goethe Institut de Bordeaux à l'occasion de son 25ème anniversaire* [Presence of Germany in Bordeaux in the Century of Montaigne to the Eve of the Second World War, Homage to the Goethe Institute in Bordeaux on the Occasion of its Twenty-fifth Birthday] (Bordeaux: PUB, 1997); K. Weber, 'Deutsche Kaufmannsfamilien im atlantischen Manufaktur- und Kolonialwarenhandel: Netzwerke zwischen Hamburg, Cádiz und Bordeaux (1715–1830)' ['German Merchant Families

in the Atlantic Manufacturing and Colonial Trade: Networks between Hamburg, Cadiz and Bordeaux (1715–1830)'] (PhD dissertation, University of Hamburg, 2001).

28. Archive départementales de la Gironde, C 4473.
29. Henninger, *Johann Jacob Von Bethmann*, p. 40.
30. C. Huetz de Lemps, *Géographie du commerce de Bordeaux à la fin du règne de Louis XIV* [Geography of the Trade in Bordeaux at the End of the Reign of Louis XIV] (Paris and La Haye: Mouton and EHESS, 1975), p. 489.
31. Butel, 'Les négociants allemands de Bourdeaux', p. 594.
32. Henninger, *Johann Jacob Von Bethmann*, pp. 53–60; Butel, 'Les négociants allemands de Bourdeaux', p. 596.
33. G. Buron, *Le commerce du sel de Guérande* [The Trade of Salt of Guérande] (Morlaix: Skol Vreizh, 1999), p. 103.
34. X. Moutet, 'Négociants et armateurs de Lorient au XVIIIe siècle' ['Merchants and Ship-owners of Lorient in the Eighteenth Century'] (Master's thesis unpublished, University of Nantes, 1974).
35. L. Guillou, 'André Vanderheyde, courtier lorientais et ses opérations (1756–1765)' ['André Vanderheyde, A Broker of Lorient and His Business (1756–1765)'], *Annales de Bretagne et des Pays de l'Ouest*, 33:1 (1918), pp. 13–38, on p. 17.
36. J.-C. Moraud, 'Quelques aspects du commerce morlaisien à la veille de la Révolution, 1781–1789' [Some Aspects of Trade Morlaix on the Eve of the Revolution'], *107ème Congrès national des sociétés savantes, histoire moderne et contemporaine* [107th National Congress of Learned Societies, Modern and Contemporary History] (Brest, 1982), vol. 2, pp. 237–52, on p. 245.
37. A. Lespagnol, *Messieurs de Saint-Malo. Une élite négociante au temps de Louis XIV* [Gentlemen of St. Malo. A Merchant Elite at the Time of Louis XIV] (Rennes: PUR, 1996), p. 94.
38. G. Treutlein, 'Navigation et commerce entre Nantes et les régions du Nord et de la Baltique entre 1714 et 1744' ['Navigation and Trade between Nantes and the Northern and Baltic Regions Between 1714 and 1744'], *Cahiers des Salorges*, 22 (1970).
39. Martin, *Nantes et la Compagnie des Indes*, p. 76.
40. V. Barbour, *Capitalism in Amsterdam in the 17th Century* (Chicago, IL: University of Michigan Press, 1966), p. 130.
41. Archives Affaires Etrangères, Nantes, Amsterdam, 21 February 1724.
42. Ibid., 6 March 1724.
43. P. Jeannin, 'Les pratiques commerciales des colonies marchandes étrangères dans les ports français (XVIe–XVIIIe siècles)' ['The Commercial Practices of Foreign Trading Colonies in French Ports (Sixteenth-Eighteenth Centuries)'], in L. M. Cullen and P. Butel (eds), *Négoce et industrie en France et en Irlande aux XVIIIe et XIXe siècles* [Trade and Industry in France and Ireland in the Eighteenth and Nineteenth Centuries] (Paris: CNRS, 1980), pp. 9–16, on p. 11.
44. P. Bois (ed.), *Histoire de Nantes* [History of Nantes] (Toulouse: Privat, 1977), p. 187.
45. G. Martin, *L'administration de Gérard Mellier* [The Administration of Gerard Mellier] (Toulouse and Nantes: Lion et fils and L. Durance, 1928), p. 207.
46. Or *Edit de révocation de l'Edit de Nantes* [Edict of Revocation of the Edict of Nantes].
47. Henninger, *Johann Jacob Von Bethmann*, p. 41.
48. Archives Municipales Nantes, GG 649.
49. Archives Municipales Nantes, HH 649.

50. J. Mathorez, 'Notes sur la colonie hollandaise de Nantes' ['Notes on the Dutch Colony of Nantes'], *Revue du Nord*, 1 (1913), pp. 1–46, on p. 12.
51. Mathorez, 'Notes sur la colonie hollandaise', p. 42.
52. J. Cambry, *Voyage dans le Finistère. Voyage d'un conseiller du département chargé de constater l'état moral et statistique du Finistère en 1794* [Travel in Finistère. Journey of a Department Adviser Assigned to Look At the Moral and Statistical Conditions in the Finistère in 1794], 1st edn (Paris: Editions du Layeur, 2000, 1836), p. 116.
53. Jeannin, 'Les pratiques commerciales', p. 10.
54. A.-M. Gutierrez-Obadia, 'Mariage dans le négoce français au XVIIIe siècle' ['Marriage in the Eighteenth Century French Trade'], in *Rochefort et la mer*, vol. 3, *Présence maritime française aux XVIIe et XVIIIe siècles* [Rochefort and the Sea, No. 3, French Maritime Presence in the Seventeenth and Eighteenth Centuries] (Jonzac: Publications de l'université francophone d'été, 1987), pp. 103–13, on p. 107.
55. Weber, 'Deutsche Kaufmannsfamilien', pp. 372–9.
56. Butel, 'Les négociants allemands de Bordeaux', p. 598.
57. P. Hintze, *Geschichte des Geschlechts Lüttman in Hamburg* [History of the Lüttman Family in Hamburg] (Hamburg: Selbstverlag, 1928), p. 22.
58. Treutlein, 'Schifffahrt und Handel', p. 137.
59. H. Lüthy, *La banque protestante en France de la révocation de l'édit de Nantes à la revolution* [The Protestant Bank in France From the Revocation of the Edict of Nantes to the French Revolution], vol. 2 (Paris: SEVPEN, 1959), p. 91.
60. Mathorez, 'Notes sur la colonie hollandaise', p. 46.
61. B. Morin, 'Une dynastie de négociants hollandais à Nantes: les Deurbroucq' ['A Dynasty of Dutch Merchants in Nantes: the Deurbroucq Family'], *Bulletin de la Société Archéologique et Historique de Nantes et de Loire-Atlantique*, 134 (1999), pp. 203–12, on p. 205.
62. Archives Départementales de Loire-Atlantique, Nantes, B 5612.
63. Archives Municipales Nantes, GG 649, 6 August 1715.
64. Rigsarkivet, Stockholm, Kommercekolegium, Huvudarkivet a: 347, Skivelser från konsuler Nantes [Skivelser from Consuls Nantes], 12 February 1757.
65. J. Meyer, *L'armement nantais dans la deuxième moitié du XVIIIᵉ siècle* [The Commissioning in Nantes in the Second Half of the Eighteenth Century] (Paris: SEVPEN, 1969), p. 174.

4 Baghdiantz McCabe, 'Opportunity and Legislation: How the Armenians Entered Trade in Three Mediterranean Ports'

1. J. B. Tavernier, *Les six voyages de Jean Baptiste Tavernier, Ecuyer Baron d'Aubonne, en Turquie, en Perse, et aux Indes, pendant l'espace de quarante ans, & par toutes les routes que l'on peut tenir: accompagnez d'observations particulières sur la qualité, la religion, le gouvernement, les coûtumes et le commerce de chaque païs, avec les figures, le poids, & la valeur des monnoyes qui y ont cours,* [The Six Voyages of John Baptista Tavernier, Baron of Aubonne through Turkey, into Persia and the East Indies, for the Space of Forty Years: Giving an Account of the Present State of those Countries, viz. of the Religion, Government, Customs and Commerce of Every Country, and the Figures, Weight and Value of the Money Current All Over Asia] 2 vols (Paris: Chez Gervais Clouzier et Claude Barbin, 1676–7) vol. 1, pp. 39–40. Translation my own.

2. I thank Gelina Harlaftis for inviting me to write with the participants of the panel on 'Merchant Colonies' held in Utrecht in 2009. I was part of the panel on Global Maritime trade, the presentation I gave is published as 'Small Town Merchants, Global Ventures: the Maritime Trade of the New Julfan Armenians in the Seventeenth and Eighteenth Centuries' in M. Fusaro and A. Polónia (eds), *Maritime History as Global History*, *Research in Maritime History*, 43 (St. John's, Newfoundland: International Maritime Economic History Association, 2010). Some of what I could not explore in that article is contained here.

3. G. Rambert and L. Bergasse, *Histoire du commerce de Marseille* [History of the Commerce of Marseilles], publiée par la Chambre de Commerce de Marseille sous la direction de Gaston Rambert [published by the Chamber of Commerce of Marseille under the Direction of Gaston Rambert] (Paris: Plon, 1953–7). This long work is a thorough study of the Archives of the Chamber of Commerce of Marseilles; all the edicts quoted here are found in those archives. The history of Marseille from 1660–1789 is contained in vol. 6, published in 1959.

4. F. Trivellato, *The Familiarity of Strangers: the Sephardic Diaspora, Livorno, and Cross-Cultural Trade in the Early Modern Period* (New Haven, CT: Yale University Press, 2009).

5. J. T. Takeda, *Between Crown and Commerce: Marseille and the Early Modern Mediter-ranean* (Baltimore, MD: Johns Hopkins University Press, 2011).

6. O. Raveux, 'Marseille (1831–1865). Une révolution industrielle entre Europe du Nord et Méditerranée' [Marseille (1831–1865). An Industrial Revolution Between Northern Europe and the Mediterranean], *Annales. Histoire, Sciences sociales*, 1 (2001), pp. 153–76; idem, 'Espace et stratégies industrielles aux XVIIIe et XIXe siècles: exploiter le laboratoire méditerranéen' [Industrial Strategies and Spaces in the Eighteenth and Nineteenth Centuries: Exploiting the Mediterranean Laboratory] *Revue d'histoire moderne et contemporaine*, 2/3 (2001), pp. 11–24; idem, 'Les marchands orientaux et les langues occidentales au XVIIe siècle: l'exemple des "Choffelins" de Marseille' [Oriental Merchants and Occidental Languages in the Seventeenth Century: the Example of the 'Choffelins' of Marseilles], archives: Hyper Article en Ligne-Sciences de l'Homme et de la Société halshs-00429647, Vers. 2 (25 March 2010).

7. Gh. Alishan, *L'Armeno-Veneto: compendio storico e documenti delle relazioni degli Armeni coi Veneziani: primo periodo, secoli XIII–XIV* [Armenian Venice: Historical Compendium of the Documents about the Relationship of the Armenians with the Venetians: First Period, Thirteenth to Fourteenth Centuries] (Venice: Stab. Tip. Armeno, S. Lazzaro, 1893); M. Ughurlean, *Patmut'iwn hayots'gaght'akanut'ean ew shinut'ean ekeghets' woy nots'a i Livoṛnoy k'aghak'i : handerdz haweluatsovk'* [History of the Armenian Colony of Livorno and of the Construction of their Church Accompanied with Appendices] (Venice: Mkhit'arean tparan, 1891).

8. I. Baghdiantz McCabe, 'La diaspora marchande arménienne de la Nouvelle-Djoulfa et sa fonction dans l'État séfévide: un modèle théorique à revisiter' [The Armenian Diaspora of New Julfa and its Function in the Safavid State: a Theoretical Model to Revisit], in C. Mouradian and M. Bruneau (eds), *Grecs et Arméniens en diaspora. Approches comparatives* [Greeks and Armenians in the Diaspora: Comparative Approaches] (Athens: Ecole française d'Athènes, 2007), pp. 77–85.

9. I. Baghdiantz McCabe, *The Shah's Silk for Europe's Silver, The Eurasian Silk Trade of the Julfan Armenians in Safavid Iran and India (1590–1750)* (Atlanta, GA: University of Pennsylvania Texts and Studies, 1999), p. 414, see the Introduction.

10. A. Sanjian, *The Armenian Communities in Syria under Ottoman Domination* (Cambridge, MA: Harvard University Press, 1965), pp. 48–9.
11. The first recorded Julfan presence in Venice dates to 1572 for the trade of bales of Iranian silk. Alishan, *L'Armeno-Veneto*, p. 307.
12. I. Baghdiantz McCabe, 'Princely Suburb, Armenian Quarter or Christian Ghetto? The Urban Setting of New Julfa in the Safavid Capital of Isfahan (1605–1722)', *La Revue des Mondes musulmans et de la Méditerannée*, special issue: *Les non-musulmans dans l'espace urbain en terres d'islam* (September 2005), pp. 414–37.
13. Baghdiantz McCabe, *The Shah's Silk for Europe's Silver*, pp. 85–105.
14. For the converted Caucasian elites and their role see S. Babaie, K. Babayan, I. Baghdiantz McCabe and M. Farhad (eds), *Slaves of the Shah: New Elites of Safavid Iran* (New York: I. B. Tauris, 2004), especially Chapter 3 by I. Baghdiantz McCabe, 'Armenian Merchants and Slaves', pp. 48–80.
15. I. Baghdiantz McCabe, G. Harlaftis and I. Pepelasis Minoglou (eds), *Diaspora Entrepreneurial Networks: Four Centuries of History* (Oxford and New York: Berg, 2005), p. xxii. The literature on trust is very substantial. For a good analysis, see F. Trivellato, 'Sephardic Merchants in the Early Atlantic and Beyond' in R. L. Kagan and P. D. Morgan (eds), *Atlantic Diasporas: Jews, Conversos, and Crypto-Jews in the Age of Mercantilism, 1500– 1800* (Baltimore, MD: Johns Hopkins University Press, 2009), pp. 99–123.
16. See E. Herzig, 'The Commercial Law of the New Julfan Armenians' in S. Chaudhury, G. Gewonean and K. Kévonian (eds.), *Les Arméniens dans de commerce asiatique au début de l'ère moderne* [Armenians in Asian Commerce at the Beginning of the Modern Era] (Paris: Éditions de la Maison des sciences de l'homme, 1997), pp. 63–81; S. Aslanian, 'The Salt in a Merchant's Letter': The Culture of Julfan Correspondence in the Indian Ocean and Mediterranean', *Journal of World History* 19 (2008), pp. 127–88.
17. L. Khachikian, 'Le registre d'un marchand arménien en Perse, en Inde et au Tibet (1682–1693)' [The Account Book of an Armenian Merchant in Persia, India and Tibet (1682–1693)], *Annales-Économies-Sociétés-Civilizations*, 22:2 (1967), pp. 231–78.
18. Baghdiantz McCabe, *The Shah's Silk for Europe's Silver*, Chapter V: 'The New Julfan as Financiers', especially pp. 155–9.
19. Baghdiantz McCabe, *The Shah's Silk for Europe's Silver*.
20. Rambert and Bergasse, *Histoire du commerce de Marseille*, vol. 4.
21. M. Greene, *Catholic Pirates and Greek Merchants: A Maritime History of the Mediterranean* (Princeton, NJ: Princeton University Press, 2010), pp. 23–30.
22. I. Baghdiantz McCabe, *Orientalism in Early Modern France: Eurasian Trade, Exoticism, and the Ancien Régime* (Oxford and New York: Berg, 2008), pp. 37–68.
23. The Vatican archives are the source for this. They have been studied for this earlier period by R. H. Kévorkian et al., *Arménie: 3000 ans d'histoire* [Armenia: 3,000 Years of History] (Marseille: Maison arménienne de la jeunesse et de la culture, 1988).
24. Kévorkian, *Arménie: 3000 ans d'histoire*.
25. Baghdiantz McCabe, *The Shah's Silk for Europe's Silver*, pp. 43–83.
26. H. Berberian, 'Cosmopolitanism and the Sceriman/Sharimanians Family between Isfahan and Venice', talk at CUNY (City University of New York), 17 March 2011. More information should surface on the Sharimanians through Houri Berberian's research. There may be more information contained in the upcoming publication of her husband's 2007 dissertation: S. Aslanian, 'From the Indian Ocean to the Mediterranean: Circulation and Global Trade Network of Armenian merchants from New Julfa, Isfahan, 1605–1747' (Columbia University, May 2007).

27. Baghdiantz McCabe, *The Shah's Silk for Europe's Silver*, pp. 197, 245, 342.
28. Kévorkian, *Arménie: 3000 ans d'histoire*, p. 232.
29. Many scholars had debates about the dates of publication. *Urbat'agirk'* (lit. 'Friday Book', prayers for the sick) (Venice: pr. Yakob Meghapart, 1512).
30. C. Staikos, Χάρτα της ελληνικής τυπογραφίας, η εκδοτική δραστηριότητα των ελλήνων και η συμβολή τους στην Πνευματική Αναγέννηση της Δύσης [The Charta of Greek Printing, the Printing Activity of the Greeks and their Contribution in the Intellectual Renaissance of the West] (Athens: Kotinos, 2002).
31. See I. Baghdiantz McCabe, 'Merchant Capital and Knowledge: the Financing of Early Armenian Printing Presses by the Eurasian Silk Trade', in T. Matthews and R. Wieck (eds), *Treasures in Heaven. Armenian Art Religion and Society* (New York: Pierpont Morgan Library, 1998), pp. 58–73. For early books please see R. H. Kévorkian (ed.), *Catalogue des 'incunables' arméniens, 1511–1695 ou Chronique de l'imprimerie armé-nienne* [Catalogue of Armenian 'Incunables', 1511–1695 or a Chronicle of Armenian Printing] (Geneva: P. Cramer, 1986), especially J.-P. Mahé, 'Préface'.
32. L. Zēk'iean, *Novye dannye ob Armianakh v Italii* [New Findings on Armenians in Italy] (Yerevan: AN Armianskoi SSR, 1978); *Gli Armeni in Italia: Hayerě italioy mēj / coor-dinamento scientifico e redazione del catalogo, Boghos Zēk'iean* [The Armenians in Italy / Scientific Coordination and Writing of the Catalogue by Boghos Zēk'iean] (Rome: De Luca edizioni d'arte, 1990).
33. L. Zēk'iean and A. Ferrari, *Gli armeni e Venezia: dagli Sceriman a Mechitar: il momento culminante di una consuetudine* [The Armenians and Venice: From the Sceriman to Mechitar: the Culminating Moment of a Tradition] (Venice: Istituto Veneto di Scienze, Lettere ed Arti, 2004). On San Lazzaro: T. Yartěmean, *San Lazzaro Island: the monastic headquarters of the Mekhitarian Order (Venice)*, trans. V. Ter-Hevondian (San Lazzaro, Venice: Mekhitarian Pub. House, 1990).
34. Gh. Alishan, *Sisakan teghagrut'iwn Siwneats' ashkharhi* [Sisakan Topography of Siwnik] (Venice: Surb Ghazar, 1893), p. 444.
35. Alishan, *Sisakan*, p. 444.
36. Decreti dei Senato 7 Settembre 1622 cited in G. Berchet, *La repubblica di Venezia e la Persia* [The Republic of Venice and Persia], vol. 1, Torino, 1865, p. 62–4.
37. Decreto dei Cinque Savi decembre 1661, 19 gennaio 1672 and 9 maggio 1676, cited in Berchet, *La repubblica di Venezia*, p. 63.
38. Ibid.
39. Anonymous, *A Chronicle of the Carmelites in Persia and of the Papal Missions of the 17th and 18th Centuries*, H. Chick (ed.), 2 vols (London,1939), vol. 2, p. 1358.
40. H. Yukata, 'Some Characteristics of the Ottoman Capitulations in the Sixteenth Cen-tury: The Cases of Dubrovnik and Venice', *Mediterranean World*, 20 (June 2010), pp. 199-207. For the development of the Ottoman capitulations granted to the European powers, see H. İnalcık, 'Imtiyāzāt, ii' *Encyclopaedia of Islam*, new edn (Leiden: 1971) vol. 3, pp. 1179a–1189b; Chr. Maltezou, Ο θεσμός του εν Κωνσταντινουπόλει Βενετού Βαΐλου (1268–1453) [The Institution of the Venetian Bailo in Constantinople] (Athens: National and Kapodistrian University of Athens, School of Philosophy, 1970).
41. On the exploitation of Venice's problems from the Greek merchants and seamen and the Greek maritime enterprises see more analytically in G. D. Pagratis, 'Greek Com-mercial Shipping (Fifteenth to Seventeenth Centuries). Literature Review and Research Perspectives', *Journal of Mediterranean Studies*, 12:2 (2002), pp. 411–33; idem, 'Venice, the Sea and the Greeks: the Maritime Policy of the Venetian State and the Entrepreune-

rial Activities of the Greek Subjects During the 16th Century', in J.-C. Hocquet and R. Gertwagen (eds), *Venice and the Mediterranean (XIII–XVIII centuries)*, forthcoming.

42. For an overall view of the Venetian dominion in Greek territories see A. Papadia-Lala, *Ο θεσμός των αστικών κοινοτήτων στον ελληνικό χώρο κατά την περίοδο της βενετοκρατίας (13ος–18ος αι.)* [The Institution of the Urban Communities in Greek Territories During the Venetian Dominion (Thirteenth–Eighteenth Centuries)] (Venice: Hellenic Institue of Byzantine and Post-Byzantine Studies in Venice, 2008).

43. Greene, *Catholic Pirates and Greek Merchants*, p. 32.

44. M. Fusaro, 'Un Reseau de Cooperation Commerciale en Mediterrannàe Venitienne: Les Anglais et les Grecs' [A Network of Commercial Cooperation in the Venetian Mediterranean: the English and the Greeks], *Annales. Économie, Sociétés, Civilisations*, 58:3 (2003), pp. 605–25 as cited in Greene, *Catholic Pirates and Greek Merchants*, p. 43.

45. Greene, *Catholic Pirates and Greek Merchants*, p. 41.

46. C. Kafadar, 'A Death in Venice: Anatolian Muslim Merchants Trading in the Serenissima', *Journal of Turkish Studies*, 10 (1987), pp. 191–218, and in S. Subrahmanyam (ed.), *Merchant Networks in the Early Modern World* (Aldershot; Brookfield, VT: Variorum, 1996).

47. Greene, *Catholic Pirates and Greek Merchants*, p. 44. See also literature from Chapter 7 by Olga Katsiardi-Hering in the present volume.

48. Greene, *Catholic Pirates and Greek Merchants*, p. 25.

49. Ibid., p. 29.

50. L. Frattarelli Fischer, 'Gli Armeni a Livorno' [The Armenians in Livorno], in C. Mutafian (ed.), *Roma-Armenia* (Rome: De Luca, 1999); eadem, 'Per la storia dell'insediamento degli Armeni a Livorno nel seicento' [For the History of the Settlement of the Armenians in Livorno in the Seventeenth Century] in Atti del convegno internazionale *Gli Armeni lungo le strade d'Italia* [in the Acts of the International Conferences *The Armenians on the Roads of Italy*], Torino, Genova, Livorno: Giornata di studi a Livorno 8–11 marzo 1997 (Pisa: Istituti editoriali e poligrafici internazionali, 1998).

51. M. Ughlurean, *History of the Armenian Colony of Livorno* (Venice: Mkhitarist Press, 1891), p. 183.

52. Baghdiantz McCabe, *The Shah's Silk for Europe's Silver*, pp. 43–82.

53. Ibid., pp. 79–107.

54. Trivellato, *The Familiarity of Strangers*, p. 78.

55. Ibid., p. 80.

56. Ibid., p. 79.

57. Frattarelli Fischer, 'Per la storia', cited in Trivellato, *The Familiarity of Strangers*, p. 80.

58. Trivellato, *The Familiarity of Strangers*, p. 81.

59. Letter from Colbert to *échevin* et *députés du commerce*, Marseilles 16 February 1670, in *Lettres, instructions, et mémoirs de* Colbert [Letters, Instructions and Memoirs of Colbert], vol. 2, p. 518, cited in T. Takeda, *Between Crown and Commerce: Marseille and the early modern Mediterranean* (Baltimore, MD: Johns Hopkins University Press, 2011), p. 99.

60. M. Cubells, 'Les pratiques politiques à Marseille au milieu de XVIIe siècle' [Political Practices in Marseille in the Middle of the Seventeenth Century], in M. Cubells, *La noblesse provençale du milieu du XVIIe siècle à la Révolution* [Provincial Nobility from the Middle of the Seventeenth Century to the Revolution] (Aix-en-Provence: Université de Provence, 2002), p. 71.

61. Rambert and Bergasse, *Histoire du commerce de Marseille*, vol. 4, pp. 484–5.

62. For more detail on this see Baghdiantz McCabe, *Orientalism in Early Modern France*, Chapter V.
63. Takeda, *Between Crown and Commerce*, p. 23.
64. Rambert and Bergasse, *Histoire du commerce de Marseille*, vol. 5, p. 14. For more on this, see Baghdiantz McCabe, *The Shah's Silk for Europe's Silver*, pp. 294–326.
65. Baghdiantz McCabe, *The Shah's Silk for Europe's Silver*, pp. 295–319.
66. Takeda, *Between Crown and Commerce*, p. 25.
67. Ibid., p. 27.
68. Ibid., p. 53.
69. Colbert to French consuls overseas, 15 March 1669, in *Lettres, instructions et mémoires de Colbert*, 2:453, cited in Takeda, *Between Crown and Commerce*, pp. 97-8.
70. Letter from Colbert to *échevin* et *députés du commerce*, Marseilles 16 February 1670. In *Lettres, instructions, et memories de Colbert*, 2:518, cited in Takeda, *Between Crown and Commerce*, p. 99.
71. Takeda, *Between Crown and Commerce*, p. 99.
72. Colbert to Rouillé in *Lettres, instructions, et mémoirs de Colbert*, 2:679, cited in Takeda, *Between Crown and Commerce*, p. 99.
73. Baghdiantz McCabe, *The Shah's Silk for Europe's Silver*, chapter 10, pp. 194–326.
74. Baghdiantz McCabe, *Orientalism in Early Modern France*, chapters 5–8.
75. Baghdiantz McCabe, *The Shah's Silk for Europe's Silver*, pp. 321–2. See F. Richard, *Raphaël du Mans missionaire en Perse au XVIIe siècle*, [Raphaël du Mans, Missionary in Persia in the Seventeenth Century] vol. 1, *Biographie et Correspondance* (Paris, 1995), p. 280.
76. Baghdiantz McCabe, *The Shah's Silk for Europe's Silver*.
77. Ibid., p. 320.
78. Ibid., pp. 203, 295–307, 383.
79. I have discussed the association of the Armenians and the Huguenots in the gem trade in 'No Diaspora Network is an Island: Competition and Collaboration between Networks', (forthcoming, ed. W. Kokot).
80. Rambert and Bergasse, *Histoire du commerce de Marseille*.
81. Baghdiantz McCabe, *Orientalism in Early Modern France*, chapter 5.
82. Takeda, *Between Crown and Commerce*, p. 100.
83. Baghdiantz McCabe, *Orientalism in Early Modern France*, pp. 86–96.
84. Ibid., p. 127.
85. 'Chambre de Commerce à Monsigneur l'Intendant' (n.d. ACCM, 1585), cited in Takeda, *Between Crown and Commerce*, p. 102.
86. Takeda, *Between Crown and Commerce*, p. 102.
87. Ibid., p. 105.
88. See Kévorkian, *Arménie: 3000 ans d'histoire*, p. 225, who has pointed this out.
89. Archives of the Chambre de Commerce de Marseille, A.C.C.M, B22 dated 1667 in Rambert and Bergasse, *Histoire du commerce de Marseille* vol. 5, p. 11.
90. Raveux, 'Les marchands orientaux et les langues occidentales au XVIIe siècle', Vers. 2 (25 March 2010), p.1, footnote 1.
91. C. D. Tékéian, 'Marseille, la Provence et les Arméniens' [Marseilles, Provence and the Armenians], *Mémoires de l'Institut Historique de Provence*, 6 (1929), pp. 5–65, on p. 32.
92. Raveux, 'Les marchands orientaux et les langues occidentales au XVIIe siècle', Annexes pp. 14–15.

93. O. Raveux, 'Spaces and Technologies in the Cotton Industry in the Seventeenth and Eighteenth Centuries: The Example of Printed Calicoes in Marseilles', *Textile History*, 36:2 (November 2005), pp. 131–45.
94. See their names in the annexes of Raveux, 'Les marchands orientaux et les langues occidentales au XVIIe siècle', p. 15.
95. Raveux, 'Les marchands orientaux et les langues occidentales au XVIIe siècle', p. 6.
96. Tékéian, 'Marseille, la Provence et les Arméniens', p. 32, cited in Raveux, 'Les marchands orientaux et les langues occidentales au XVIIe siècle', p. 7.
97. Raveux, 'Les marchands orientaux et les langues occidentales au XVIIe siècle', pp. 8–9.
98. Ibid., p. 10.
99. Ibid., footnote 37, p. 10.
100. Ibid., p. 11.
101. Raveux 'Les marchands orientaux et les langues occidentales au XVIIe siècle', p. 12; See Kévorkian, *Catalogue des 'incunables' arméniens* and Baghdiantz McCabe, 'Merchant Capital and Knowledge: the Financing of Early Armenian Printing Presses by the Eurasian Silk Trade', in T. F. Mathews and R. S. Wieck (eds), *Treasures in Heaven. Armenian Art Religion and Society* (New York: Pierpont Morgan Library, 1998), pp. 58–73.
102. In Rambert and Bergasse, *Histoire du commerce de Marseille*, p. 19.
103. Kévorkian, *Arménie: 3000 ans d'histoire*, p. 229.
104. 'The merchants who are for the most part Armenians prefer selling their merchandise to the French rather than to the other nations of Europe because they pay in money as opposed to the English or the Dutch who obligate them to taking half of their payment in cloth'. Tavernier, *Les six voyages de Jean Baptiste Tavernier*, vol. 1, p. 79.
105. Baghdiantz McCabe, 'Small Town Merchants, Global Ventures'.
106. Ibid., pp. 137–51.
107. D. Panzac, 'International and Domestic Maritime Trade in the Ottoman Empire during the Eighteenth Century', *International Journal of Middle East Studies*, 24:2 (1997), pp. 189–206.
108. Baghdiantz McCabe, *The Shah's Silk for Europe's Silver*, pp. 281–290.
109. I. Carras, 'Ἐμπόριο, Πολιτική καὶ Ἀδελφότητα: Ῥωμιοὶ στῇ Ῥωσία 1700–1774' [Trade, Politics and Brotherhood: Greeks in Russia 1700–1774], (PhD dissertation, Department of Political Sciences and Administration, University of Athens, 2011).

5 Kotilaine, 'Russian Merchant Colonies in Seventeenth-Century Sweden'

1. For an overview of the literature and Russia's trade patterns, see J. T. Kotilaine, *Russia's Foreign Trade and Economic Expansion in the Seventeenth Century: Windows on the World* (Leiden and Boston, MA: Brill, 2005).
2. A. Soom, 'Ivangorod als selbstständige Stadt 1617–1649' [Ivangorod as an Independent City 1617–1649], *Õpetatud Eesti Seltsi Aastaraamat*, 1935 (1937), pp. 215–316; E. Küng, 'Narva vene kaupmeeskond 17. sajandi teisel poolel. I' [Narva's Russian Merchant Community During the Second Half of the Seventeenth Century I], *Kleio: Ajaloo ajakiri*, 3 (1995), pp. 43–52; idem, 'Narva vene kaupmees- ja kodanikkond 17. sajandi teisel poolel. II' [Narva's Russian Merchant and Burgher Community in the Second Half of the Seventeenth Century II], *Kleio: Ajaloo ajakiri*, 1 (1996), pp. 19–24.
3. A. Attman, *The Russian and Polish Markets in International Trade 1500–1650* (Gothenburg: Ekonomisk-Historiska Institutionen vid Göteborgs Universitet, 1973); idem, *The Struggle for Baltic Markets: Powers in Conflict, 1558–1618* (Gothenburg: Kungl.

Vetenskaps-och Vitterhets-Samhället, 1983); idem, *Swedish Aspirations and the Russian Market during the 17th Century* (Gothenburg: Kungl. Vetenskaps-och Vitterhets-Samhället, 1985).

4. I. P. Shaskol'skii, *Русская морская торговля на Балтике в XVII в. (торговля со Швецией)* [Russian Maritime Trade in the Baltic in the Seventeenth Century (Trade with Sweden)] (St Petersburg: Nauka, 1994); idem, *Экономические отношения России и Шведского государства* [Economic Relations of Russia and the Swedish State] (St Petersburg: Dmitrii Bulanin, 1998).

5. U. Karttunen, *Sortavalan kaupungin historia* [History of the City of Sortavala] (Sortavala: Sortavalan Kirjapaino Osakeyhtiö, 1932), p. 49; E. Kuujo, J. Tiainen and E. Karttunen, *Sortavalan kaupungin historia* [History of the City of Sortavala] (Jyväskylä: K. J. Gummerus Osakeyhtiö, 1970), pp. 30–3; E. Kuujo, E. Puramo and J. Sarkanen, *Käkisalmen historia: Käkisalmen kaupungin ja maalaiskunnan vaiheita* [History of Käkisalmi: Phases of Käkisalmi City and Rural Parish] (Lahti: Lahden Kirjapaino- ja Sanomalehti-Osakeyhtiö, 1958), pp. 42–51; T. Immonen, *Kurkijoen seutu Ruotsin vallan aikana: vv. 1570–1710* [The Kurkijoki District under Swedish Rule: 1570–1710] (Pieksämäki: Sisälähetysseuran Raamattutalon kirjapaino, 1958), pp. 151–4.

6. M. Köhler, *Die Narvafahrt: Mittel- und westeuropäischer Rußlandhandel 1558–1581* [Narva Shipping: Central and West European Trade with Russia 1558–1581] (Hamburg: Verlag Dr. Kovač, 2000).

7. A. Soom, 'De ingermanländska städerna och freden i Stolbova' [The Ingrian Towns and the Stolbovo Peace], *Svio-Estonica*, 3 (1936), pp. 34–45; E. Küng, 'Narva elanikkonna suurusest 17. sajandi keskel' [On the Size of Narva's Population in the Middle of the Seventeenth Century], *Eesti Ajalooarhiivi Toimetised*, 2(IX) (1997), pp. 39–60.

8. A. V. Petrov, *Город Нарва: Его прошлое и достопримечательности в связи с историей упрочения русского госпаодства на балтийском побережье, 1223–1900* [The City of Narva: Its Past and Sights Linked to the History of the Consolidation of Russian Rules in the Baltic Littoral] (St Peterburg: Tipografiia Ministerstva Vnutrennikh Del, 1901), p. 170.

9. Soom, 'De ingermanländska städerna', pp. 36–40, 44; idem, 'Merkantilistlikkude põhimõtete rakendamise esimesi katseid Narvas' [Initial Plans for Establishing Mercantilistic Principles in Narva], *Ajalooline Ajakiri*, 15 (1936) 3–4, pp. 97–115.

10. Soom, 'Ivangorod', pp. 221–9, 266.

11. Soom, 'Ivangorod', p. 304; idem, *Die Politik Schwedens bezüglich des russischen Transithandels über die estnischen Städte in den Jahren 1636–1656* [Swedish Policy Toward Russian Transit Trade through Estonian Cities 1636–1656] (Tartu: Õpetatud Eesti Selts, 1940), pp. 177–8.

12. Soom, 'Ivangorod', pp. 230–41.

13. Soom, 'Ivangorod', pp. 270–5; Kotilaine, *Russia's Foreign Trade*, p. 163.

14. A. Soom, 'Tööstusest Eesti linnades XVII sajandi esimesel poolel' [On Industry in Estonian Towns in the First Half of the Seventeenth Century], *Linnad ja alevid*, 10 (1937) 1, pp. 4–10; idem, 'Ivangorod', pp. 284–5, 302–3; Petrov, *The City of Narva*, p. 166; Küng, 'Narva vene kaupmeeskond', I, p. 44.

15. A. Soom, 'Narvas ryska befolkning och kriget 1656–1658' [Narva's Russian Population and the War of 1656–1658], *Svio-Estonica*, 4 (1937), pp. 165–73; idem, 'Die merkantilistische Wirtschaftspolitik Schwedens und die baltischen Städte im 17. Jahrhundert' [Mercantilist Economic Policy of Sweden and the Baltic Cities in the Seventeenth Century], *Jahrbücher für Geschichte Osteuropas*, N.F., 11 (1963) 2, pp. 183–222.

16. Petrov, *The City of Narva*, pp. 177–8; Küng, 'Narva vene kaupmeeskond', I, pp. 43–6; idem, 'Narva vene kaupmees- ja kodanikkond', II, pp. 19–20; H. Piirimäe, 'Laevandus ja laevaehitus Narvas XVII sajandi lõpul' [Shipping and Shipbuilding in Narva at the End of the Seventeenth Century], *Tartu Riikliku Ülikooli Toimetised*, 785 (1987), pp. 3–25.

17. Soom, 'Die merkantilistische Wirtschaftspolitik', pp. 212–13; M. Ia. Volkov, 'Ремесленное и мелкотоварное производство юфти в России во второй половине XVI – первой половине XVII в'. [Artisan and Small-scale Production of Iuft' Leather in Russia in the Second Half of the Sixteenth–First Half of the Seventeenth Century], *Istoricheskie zapiski*, 92 (1973), pp. 215–52; Kotilaine, *Russia's Foreign Trade*, pp. 194–5, 343, 357.

18. C. von Bonsdorff, *Nyen och Nyenskans: Historisk skildring* [Nyen and Nyenskans: A Historical Description] (Helsingfors: Acta Scietatis Scientarum Fennicæ, 18, 1891), p. 410; E. D. Rukhmanova, 'Русско-шведская торговля на Балтике в середине XVII века', [Russian-Swedish Trade in the Baltic Around the Middle of the Seventeenth Century], *Skandinavskii sbornik*, II (1957), pp. 47–71, on p. 53; A. J. Hipping, [A. I. Gipping,], *Нева и Ниеншанц*, I [Neva and Nyenskans, I] (St Petersburg: Tipografiia Imperatorskoi Akademii Nauk, 1909), p. 157.

19. Bonsdorff, *Nyen*, p. 402; Shaskol'skii, *Russian Maritime Trade*, p. 141; T. G. Aminoff, 'Borgerskapet i Narva och Nyen 1640' [The Bourgeoisie of Narva and Nyen in 1640], *Genealogiska Samfundets i Finland Årsskrift*, 41(1980), pp. 121–38.

20. J. W. Ruuth and A. Halila, *Viipurin kaupungin hjstoria*, II [History of the City of Viipuri, II] (Lappeenranta: Karjalan Kirjapaino Osakeyhtiö-Torkkelin Säätiö, 1974), pp. 99–100; Karttunen, *Sortavalan kaupungin historia*, p. 49; Kuujo, Tiainen and Karttunen, *Sortavalan kaupungin historia*, pp. 30–3; Kuujo, Puramo and Sarkanen, *Käkisalmen historia*, pp. 42–51; Immonen, *Kurkijoen seutu*, pp. 151–4; Kotilaine, *Russia's Foreign Trade*, p. 383.

21. R. B. Miuller, *Очерки по истории Карелии XVI–XVII вв*, [Studies on the History of Karelia in the Sixteenth–Seventeenth Centuries] (Petrozavodsk: Gosudarstvennoe izdatel'stvo Karelo-Finskoi SSR, 1947), p. 166; S. I. Kochkurkina (ed.), *Древний Олонец* [Old Olonets] (Petrozavodsk: Rossiiskaia akademiia nauk, Karel'skii nauchnyi tsentr, Institut iazyka, literatury i istorii, 1994), pp. 58, 64.

22. Kotilaine, *Russia's Foreign Trade*, p. 385; E. Kuujo, *Raja-Karjala Ruotsin vallan aikana* [The Karelian Frontier Under Swedish Rule] (Helsinki: Karjalaisen Kulttuurin Edistämissäätiö, 1963), pp. 77–86.

23. Kotilaine, *Russia's Foreign Trade*, pp. 379–81; J. W. Ruuth, *Viborgs stads historia*, 4 [History of the City of Viborg, 4] (Helsingfors: Helsingfors Centraltryckeri och Bokbinderi Aktiebolag, 1904), pp. 354–5; Ruuth and Halila, *Viipurin kaupungin historia*, II, pp. 150–2.

24. V. Salminen, *Jaakkiman pitäjän historia*, I [History of the Jaakkima Parish, I] (Hämeenlinna: Arvi A. Karisto Oy:n kirjapaino, 1967), pp. 59–61; Immonen, *Kurkijoen seutu*, p. 162; Kuujo, *Raja-Karjala*, p. 122; Kotilaine, *Russia's Foreign Trade*, p. 384.

25. A. Vartiainen, *Kajaanin kaupungin historia*, I [History of the City of Kajaani, I] (Kajaani: Kainuun Sanomain Kirjapaino Osakeyhtiö, 1931), pp. 276–7; Kotilaine, *Russia's Foreign Trade*, pp. 387–95.

26. P. Virrankoski, *Pohjois-Pohjanmaa ja Lappi 1600-luvulla* [Northern Ostrobothnia and Lapland in the Seventeenth Century] (Oulu: Pohjois-Pohjanmaan, Kainuun ja Lapin Maakuntaliittojen yhteinen historiatoimikunta, 1973), pp. 98–105; Vartiainen, *Kajaanin kaupungin historia*, I, p. 107; I. Mäntylä, *Tornion kaupungin historia*, I [History of

the City of Tornio, I] (Tampere: Kustannusosakeyhtiö Sanan Tien kohopaino, 1971), pp. 131, 585–6.

27. K. R. Melander, 'Ruotsin hallituksen ja Tallinnalaisten kauppatuumat Venäjän suhteen ynnä niistä johtuvat riidat Lübeckin kanssa vuosina 1614–1643' [The Trade Plans of the Swedish Government and Tallinn Burghers Regarding Russia and the Disputes with Lübeck Caused by Them in 1614–1643], *Historiallinen Arkisto*, 18:2 (1903), pp. 82–191; idem, 'Die Revaler Zollarende 1623–1629 und die dadurch zwischen Schweden und Lübeck hervorgeruferene Mißhelligkeiten' [The Reval Toll Lease of 1623–1629 and the Disputes Between Sweden and Lübeck Caused by It], *Zeitschrift des Vereins für Lübeckische Geschichte und Altertumskunde*, 14 (1912), pp. 237–72; E. Blumfeldt, 'Statistilisi lisandeid Tallinna kaubaliikluse ja meresõidu ajaloole aa. 1609–1629' [Statistical Data Regarding Tallinn's Trade and Shipping in 1609–1629], *Ajalooline ajakiri*, 14:1 (1935), pp. 1–18, and 14:2, pp. 49–63; Kotilaine, *Russia's Foreign Trade*, pp. 307–10.

28. J. Jenšs, 'Rīgas pilsētas tirdzniecība ar Pliskavu XVII un XVII gs' [Trade of the City of Riga with Pskov in the Sixteenth and Seventeenth Centuries], *Izglītības Ministrijas Mēnešraksts* 1 (1937), pp. 47–53, and 2, pp. 152–64.

29. J. Jenšs, 'Московское торговое подворье в Риге в XVII веке' [Muscovite Guest House in Riga in the Seventeenth Century], *Voprosy istorii*, 11 (1947), pp. 74–9, on pp. 74–6.

30. G. Jensch, *Der Handel Rigas im 17. Jahrhundert: Ein Beitrag zur livländischen Wirtschaftsgeschichte in schwedischer Zeit* [Riga's Trade in the Seventeenth Century: a Contribution to Livonian Economic History during the Swedish Period] (Riga: Nikolai Kymmels Buchhandlung, 1930), p. 237; S. Troebst, 'Stockholm und Riga als "Handelsconcurrentinnen" Archangel'sks? Zum merkantilen Hintergrund schwedischer Großmachtpolitik 1650–1700' [Stockholm and Riga as 'Commercial Rivals' of Arkhangelsk? On the Mercantile Background of Sweden's Great Power Policy 1650–1700], *Forschungen zur osteuropäischen Geschichte*, 48 (1993), pp. 259–94.

31. Kotilaine, *Russia's Foreign Trade*, pp. 339–40; V. V. Doroshenko, 'Протоколы Рижского торгового суда как источник для изучения экономических связей Риги с русскими, белорусскими и литовскими землями в XVII веке' [Records of the Riga Commercial Court as a Source for the Study of Economic Relations between Riga and the Russian, Belorussian, and Lithuanian Lands in the Seventeenth Century], in A. K. Birons (ed.), *Экономические связи Прибалтики с Россией: Сборник статей* [Economic Ties Between the Eastern Baltic and Russia: A Collection of Articles] (Riga: Zinatne, 1968), pp. 117–45, on p. 141; V. Pāvulāne, *Rīgas tirdzniecība ar meža materiāliem XVII–XVIII gs.: No Rīgas ekonomisko sakaru vēstures ar krievu, baltkrievu, ukraiņu un lietuviešu zemēm* [Riga's Trade in Forest Products in the Seventeenth–Eighteenth Centuries: On the History of Riga's Economic Ties with Russian, Belorussian, Ukrainian, and Lithuanian Lands] (Riga: Izdevniecība "Zinātne", 1975), p. 152; K. G. Mitiaev, 'Обороты и торговые связи смоленского рынка в 70-х годах XVII в.' [The Magnitude and Commercial Ties of the Smolensk Market in the Seventeenth Century], *Istoricheskie zapiski*, 13 (1942), pp. 54–83.

32. S. Lang, *Stadsgården och Ryssgården* (Stockholm: Stockholms Stadsmuseum, 1963), pp. 8–9.

33. Kotilaine, *Russia's Foreign Trade*, pp. 334–5.

34. Kotilaine, *Russia's Foreign Trade*, pp. 315–16; E. D. Rukhmanova, *Борьба России за выход в Балтийское море в 1656–1661 годах* [Russia's Struggle for an Outlet to the Baltic Sea in 1656–1661] (candidate's dissertation, Leningrad: Leningradskii gosudarstvennyi Ordena Lenina universitet imeni A. A. Zhdanova, 1954), pp. 57, 59, 77.

35. J. T. Kotilaine, 'In Defense of the Realm: Russian Arms Trade in the Seventeenth and the Early Eighteenth Century', in E. Lohr and M. Poe (eds), *The Military and Society in Russia, 1450–1921* (Leiden and Boston, MA: E. J. Brill, 2002), pp. 67–95.

36. I. P. Shaskol'skii, 'Об основных особенностях русско-шведской торговли XVII в.' [On the Fundamental Characteristics on Russian-Swedish Commerce in the Seventeenth Century], in L. G. Beskrovnyi (ed.), *Международные связи России в XVII–XVIII вв. (экономика, политика, культура):Сборник статей* [Russia's International Relations in the Seventeenth–Eighteenth Centuries (Economics, Politics, Culture): A Collection of Articles] (Moscow: Nauka, 1966), pp. 7–34, on p. 14.

37. S. V. Bakhrushin, 'Торги новгородцев Кошкиных' [Commercial Dealing of the Koshkins of Novgorod], *Uchenye zapiski MGU*, XLI, Istoriia (1940), pp. 35–80, on p. 43; Rukhmanova, 'Russian-Swedish Trade', p. 159.

38. I. P. Shaskol'skii, *Столбовский мир 1617 г. и торговые отношения России со Шведским государством* [The Stolbovo Peace and Commercial Relations Between Russia and the Swedish State] (Moscow: Nauka, 1964); idem, 'Восстановление русской торговли со шведскими владениями в первые годы после Столбовского мира' [The Revival of Russian Trade with the Swedish-controlled Territories in the Years Immediately Following the Stolbovo Peace], *Skandinavskii sbornik*, 11 (1966), pp. 61–80; idem, 'Установление прямых торговых сношений России со Швецией после Столбовского мира' [The Establishment of Direct Commercial Ties Between Russia and Sweden after the Stolbovo Peace], *Srednie veka*, 29 (1966), pp. 139–58.

39. I. P. Shaskol'skii, 'Восстановление русской торговли со шведскими владениями после Валиесарского перемирия 1658 г' [The Revival of Russian Trade with the Swedish Territories After the Valiesaar Truce of 1658], *Skandinavskii sbornik*, 26 (1981), pp. 61–72.

40. Jenšs, 'Muscovite Guesthouse in Riga', pp. 74–6; V. V. Doroshenko, *Торговля и купечество Риги в XVII веке* [The Commerce and Merchants of Riga in the Seventeenth Century] (Riga: Zinatne, 1985), p. 162.

41. Lang, *Stadsgården och Ryssgården*, pp. 8–10; Shaskol'skii, *Russian Maritime Trade*, pp. 90–125.

6 Zakharov, 'Foreign Merchant Communities in Eighteenth-Century Russia'

1. V. E. Syroechkovsky, *Гости-сурожане* [The Surozh Guests] (Moscow and Leningrad: Gosudarstvennoe sotsial'no-ekonomicheskoe izdatel'stvo, 1935), p. 24; V. B. Perkhavko, *История русского купечества* [The History of Russian Tradesmen] (Moscow: Veche, 2008), pp. 122–3.

2. J. W. Veluwenkamp, *Archangel. Nederlandse ondernemers in Rusland, 1550–1785* [Arkhangelsk. Dutch Entrepreneurs in Russia, 1550–1785] (Amsterdam: Balans, 2000), pp. 9, 40.

3. E. A. Rybina, *Новгород и Ганза* [Novgorod and the Hanseatic League] (Moscow: Rukopisnye pamyatniki Drevnei Rusi, 2009), p. 142.

4. I. Lubimenko, *История торговых сношений России с Англией* [The History of Russian–English Trade Relations], vol. 1, *XVI-ый век* [The Sixteenth Century] (Iur'ev: Ministry of Trade and Industry Publishers, 1912), p. 10.

5. Lubimenko, *The History of Russian–English Trade Relations*, pp. 11–12.

6. Veluwenkamp, *Archangel*, pp. 103–4.

7.   Veluwenkamp, *Archangel*, pp. 203–8; V. N. Zakharov, *Западноевропейские купцы в российской торговле XVIII века* [Western European Merchants in Eighteenth-Century Russian Trade] (Moscow: Nauka, 2005), pp. 406–7.

8.   V. N. Zakharov, *Западноевропейские купцы в России. Эпоха Петра I* [Western European Merchants in Russia. Peter the Great's Epoch] (Moscow: ROSSPEN, 1996), p. 25.

9.   J. M. Price, *The Tobacco Adventure to Russia. Enterprise, Politics, and Diplomacy in the Quest for a Northern Market for English Colonial Tobacco, 1676–1722* (Philadelphia, PA: American Philosophical Society, 1961), pp. 38–46.

10. N. G. Hunt, 'The Russia Company and the Government, 1730–1742', *Oxford Slavonic Papers*, 3 (1957), pp. 27–65, on p. 28.

11. Zakharov, *Western European Merchants in 18th-Century Russian Trade*, pp. 46, 51, 56.

12. D. S. Macmillan, 'The Russia Company of London in the Eighteenth Century: the Effective Survival of a "Regulated" Chartered Company', *The Guildhall Miscellany* (April 1973), pp. 222–36, on p. 222.

13. A. V. Diomkin, *Британское купечество в России XVIII века* [British Merchants in Eighteenth-Century Russia] (Moscow: Russian Academy of Sciences, Institute of Russian History, 1998), p. 20.

14. D. K. Reading, *The Anglo-Russian Commercial Treaty of 1734* (New Haven, CT: Yale University Press, 1938), p.156.

15. Reading, *The Anglo-Russian Commercial Treaty of 1734*, p. 156.

16. D. Ormrod, *The Rise of Commercial Empires. England and the Netherlands in the Age of Mercantilism, 1650–1770* (New York: Cambridge University Press, 2003), pp. 74, 355 (Appendix 2).

17. A. Cross, *By the Banks of the Neva. Chapters from the Lives and Careers of the British in Eighteenth-Century Russia* (Cambridge: Cambridge University Press, 1997), pp. 57–63.

18. Российский государственный архив древних актов [Russian State Archive of Old Acts, hereafter RGADA], fond (collection, hereafter f.) 276, opis' (series of documents, hereafter op.) 1, delo (file, hereafter d.) 1668, list (sheet, hereafter l.) 6–7. This list is published in: Zakharov, *Western European Merchants in 18th-Century Russian Trade*, p. 663.

19. E. Amburger, 'Die deutsche Kaufmannschaft St. Petersburgs um 1800' [German Merchants in St Petersburg c.1800], *Herold für Geschlechter-, Wappen- und Siegelkunde* 2 (1941), pp. 135–46, on p.136; V. N. Zakharov, *Western European Merchants in 18th-Century Russian Trade*, p. 102.

20. M. Schulte Beerbühl, 'Staatsangehörigkeit und fremdes Know-how. Die deutschen Kaufleute im britischen Russlandhandel des 18. Jahrhunderts' [Citizenship and Foreign Know-how. German Merchants in Trade with Russia in the Eighteenth Century], *Vierteljahresschrift für Sozial- und Wirtschaftsgeschichte*, 89 (2002), pp. 379–99, on p. 389.

21. Diomkin, *British Merchants in Eighteenth-Century Russia*, p. 126.

22. RGADA, f. 291, op. 1, d. 10070.

23. Cross, *By the Banks of the Neva*, p. 85.

24. RGADA, f. 276, op. 1, d. 257, ll. 4–5.

25. Cross, *By the Banks of the Neva*, pp. 63–4.

26. Ibid., p. 85.

27. Ibid., p. 56.

28. Zakharov, *Western European Merchants in Russia. Peter the Great's Epoch*, pp. 311–15.

29. The list of foreign merchants is published in: Zakharov, *Western European Merchants in 18th-Century Russian Trade*, p. 662.

30. J. W. Veluwenkamp, 'The Purchase and Export of Russian Commodities in 1741 by Dutch Merchants Established at Archangel', in C. Lesger and L. Noordegraaf (eds), *Entrepreneurs and Entrepreneurship in Early Modern Times: Merchants and Industrialists within the Orbit of the Dutch Staple Market* (Den Haag 1995), pp. 85–100, on p. 93.

31. VOC – Verenigde Oost-Indische Compagnie [from Dutch-United East India Company].

32. J. W. Veluwenkamp, *Архангельск. Нидерландские предприниматели в России. 1550–1785* [Archangelsk. Dutch Entrepreneurs in Russia. 1550–1785] (Moscow: ROSSPEN, 2006), p. 233.

33. Amburger Archiv, Osteuropa–Institut, München [The Amburger Archive, East European Institute, Munich], no. 32.020, 32.028, 33.605.

34. Veluwenkamp, *Archangel*, pp. 188–90.

35. V. N. Zakharov, 'Иностранные купцы в Архангельске во второй половине XVIII в.' [Foreign Merchants in Arkhangelsk in the Late Eighteenth Century], in Iu. N. Bespiatykh (ed.), *Русский Север и Западная Европа* [The North of Russia and Western Europe] (St Petersburg: Blits, 1999), pp. 360–87, on pp. 383–4.

36. E. Amburger, *Deutsche in Staat, Wirtschaft und Gesellschaft Russlands. Die Familie Amburger in St. Petersburg, 1770–1920* [German in the Government, Economy and Society of Russia. The Amburger Family in St Petersburg, 1770–1920] (Wiesbaden: Otto Harrassowitz, 1986), pp. 220–1.

37. Amburger, 'Die deutsche Kaufmannschaft St. Petersburgs um 1800', p. 136.

38. RGADA, f. 397, op. 1, d. 465.

39. Northern War (The Great Northern War) was fought between a coalition led by Russia and Sweden in 1700–21.

40. J. Kammerer, *Russland und die Hugenotten im 18. Jahrhundert (1689–1789)* [Russia and the Huguenots in the Eighteenth Century 1689–1789] (Wiesbaden: Otto Harrassowitz, 1978), pp. 86–7.

41. RGADA, f. 276, op. 1, d. 1668, ll. 2–5. This list is published in: Zakharov, *Western European Merchants in 18th-Century Russian Trade*, p. 663.

42. Zakharov, *Western European Merchants in Russia. Peter the Great's Epoch*, p. 42.

43. Familienarchiv Mollwo, Archiv der Hansestadt Lübeck [The Mollwo family archive. The archive of the Hanseatic city of Lübeck], no.. 32.

44. V. Zakharov, A. Krasko and W. Sartor, 'Моллво' [Mollvo], in V. Karev (ed.), *Немцы России. Энциклопедия* [The Germans of Russia. Encyclopedia], 3 vols (Moscow: ERN, 1996–2006), vol. 2, pp. 535–7, on p. 536.

45. A. I. Komissarenko and I. S. Sharkova (eds), *Внешняя торговля России через петербургский порт во второй половине XVIII–начале XIX в. Ведомости о составе купцов и их торговых оборотах* [Russian Foreign Trade via St Petersburg in Late Eighteenth–Early Nineteenth Centuries. Merchant Composition and Trade Turnover Lists] (Moscow: Academy of Sciences of USSR, Institute of History of USSR, 1981), pp. 30–50.

46. Komissarenko and Sharkova (eds), *Russian Foreign Trade via St Petersburg*, pp. 140–54.

47. N. A. Naidenov (ed.), *Материалы для истории московского купечества* [Materials on the History of Moscow Merchants], 9 vols (Moscow: Tipographia Kushnareva, 1886), vol. 4, pp. 449–52, 461.

48. E. Amburger, *Deutsche in Staat, Wirtschaft und Gesellschaft Russlands*, p. 22.

49. V. N. Zacharov, 'Die Herkunft und die familiären Verbindungen deutscher Kaufleute in Russland' [The Descent and Family Ties of German Merchants in Russia], in K. Brügge-

mann, T. Bohn and K. Maier (eds), *Kollektivität und Individualität. Der Mensch im östlichen Europa* [Collectivism and Individuality. People in Eastern Europe] (Hamburg: Verlag Dr. Kovach, 2001), pp. 172–83, on pp. 178–180.

50. V. Zakharov, 'Поппе' [Poppe], in Karev (ed.), *The Germans of Russia*, vol. 3, pp. 122–5, on pp. 122–3.

51. A. Martens, 'Гамбургские купцы в Москве в XVII в.' [Hamburg Merchants in Moscow in the Seventeenth Century], in V. A. Auman, Iu. A. Petrov and V. N. Zakharov (eds), *Немецкие предприниматели в Москве* [German Entrepreneurs in Moscow] (Moscow: Public Academy of Russian Germans, 1999), pp. 44–72, on p. 53.

52. J. H. Schnobel, *Lübeckische Geschlechter* [Lübeck Families], Archiv der Hansestadt Lübeck, ms. S.1449; B. Lammel, 'Der russische Handel der Frankeschen Stiftungen im ersten Viertel des 18. Jahrhunderts' [The Russian Trading of Franke's Foundations in the First Quarter of the Eighteenth Century], in H. H. Bielfeldt (ed.), *Deutsch–Slawische Wechseltigkeiten in sieben Jahrhunderten* [Seven Centuries of German-Slavic Relations] (Berlin: Akademie Verlag, 1956), pp. 157–92, on pp. 159–60; E. Amburger, *Die van Brienen und ihre Sippe in Archangel. Aus dem Leben einer Kolonie* [The van Brienens and their Descendants in Arkhangelsk. From the Life of One Colony] (Berlin: im Selbstverlag des Verfassers, 1936), p. 62.

53. Staatsarchiv Hamburg [Hamburg State Archive], Cl. VII. Lit. Kᵃ. N.1ᵈ. 4a. S.7.

54. I. H. van Eeghen, *Inventarissen van de archieven van de Directie van de Moscovische handel, Directie van de Oostersche handel en reederijen, Commissarissen tot de graanhandel en Comissie voor de graanhandel* [The Inventories of the Archives of the Board of Directors for the Muscovite Trade, Board of Directors for Eastern Trade and Navigation, Grain Trade Commissariat and Grain Trade Committee] (Amsterdam: Gemeentlijke archiefdienst Amsterdam, 1961), pp. 12–13.

55. This kind of company was planned to be set under the guidance of the French consul Henry Lavie in St Petersburg. (S. Baron, 'Henry Lavie and the Failed Campaign to Expand Franco-Russian Commercial Relations (1712–1723)', *Forschungen zur osteuropäischen Geschichte*, 50 (1995), pp. 29–50.

56. Zakharov, *Western European Merchants in 18th-Century Russian Trade*, pp. 196–7.

57. RGADA, f. 291, op. 1, d. 16131, 17613, 18761.

58. O. V. Volosiuk (ed.), *Россия и Испания. Документы и материалы, 1667–1917* [Russia and Spain. Documents and Materials], 2 vols (Moscow: Mezhdunarodnye otnosheniia, 1991), vol. 1, *1667–1779*, no. 42.

59. Volosiuk (ed.), *Russia and Spain*, vol. 1, nos. 94, 109, 166; A. M. Schop-Soler, *Die Spanisch-Russische Beziehungen im 18. Jahrhundert* [Spanish-Russian Ties in the Eighteenth Century] (Wiesbaden: Otto Harrasowitz, 1970), pp. 198, 202–3.

60. W. Tooke, *View of the Russian Empire during the Reign of Catherine the Second and to the Close of the Eighteenth Century*, 3 vols (London: Longman and Rees, 1800), vol. 3, p. 58.

61. Komissarenko and Sharkova (eds), *Russian Foreign Trade via St Petersburg*, pp. 139, 153; I. S. Sharkova, 'Русско–португальские торговые отношения в последней трети XVIII в' [Russian-Portuguese Trade Relations in the Last Third of the Eighteenth Century], in B. N. Komissarov (ed.), *Португалистика в Санкт-Петербурге* [Portugalistika Portuguese studies in St Petersburg] (St Petersburg: Saint-Petersburg University Publishers, 1998), pp. 161–8, on pp. 164, 167.

62. I. I. Ditiatin (ed.), *Столетие С. Петербургского английского собрания, 1770–1870* [The Centennial of St Petersburg's English Assembly, 1770–1870] (St Petersburg: Pechatnia V. I. Golovina, 1870), pp. 43–65.

7 Katsiardi-Hering, 'Greek Merchant Colonies in Central and South-Eastern Europe in the Eighteenth and Early Nineteenth Centuries'

1. On the literature of the Greek diaspora, see O. Katsiardi-Hering, 'Από τις "ελληνικές κοινότητες του εξωτερικού" στην ιστοριογραφία του μεταναστευτικού φαινομένου (15ος–19ος αι.)' [From the 'Greek Communities Abroad' to the Historiography of the Migratory Phenomenon (Fifteenth–Nineteenth Centuries)], in P. Kitromilides and T. Sklavenitis (eds), *Ιστοριογραφία της νεότερης και σύγχρονης Ελλάδας, 1833–2002*, [Historiography of Modern and Contemporary Greece, 1833–2002, IV International Congress, Proceedings] (Athens: Institute for Neohellenic Research, National Hellenic Research Foundation, 2004), vol. II, pp. 223–50.

2. Among the interesting literature on the subject, see G. Harlaftis, 'Το επιχειρηματικό δίκτυο των Ελλήνων της Διασποράς. Η "χιώτικη" φάση (1830–1860)' [The Entrepreneurial Network of Greeks in the Diaspora. 'The Phase of Chios', 1830–1860], *Mnimon*, 15 (1993), pp. 69–127; E. Frangakis-Syrett, 'Networks of Friendship, Networks of Kinship: Eighteenth-Century Levant Merchants', *Eurasian Studies*, 1:2 (2002), pp. 184–205; S. Ramada Curto and A. Molho (eds), *Commercial Networks in the Early Modern World* (San Domenico, FI: European University Florence, 2002); M. Schulte-Beerbühl and J. Vögele (eds), *Spinning the Commercial Web. International Trade, Merchants and Commercial Cities, c. 1640–1939* (Frankfurt am Main: Peter Lang, 2004); M. Stassinopoulou and M. Ch. Chatziioannou (eds), *Διασπορά – Δίκτυα – Διαφωτισμός* [Diaspora – Networks – Enlightenment] (Athens: Institute for Neohellenic Research, National Hellenic Research Foundation, *Tetradia Ergasias*, 28, 2005); I. Baghdiantz McCabe, G. Harlaftis and I. Pepelasis Minoglou (eds), *Diaspora Entrepreneurial Networks. Four Centuries of History* (Oxford and New York: Berg, 2005).

3. I have also included both the German terms, since German was the main administrative language, and the Greek terms, as our subject concerns the Greek merchant colonies.

4. O. Katsiardi-Hering, 'Αδελφότητα, Κομπανία, Κοινότητα. Για μια τυπολογία των ελληνικών κοινοτήτων της Κεντρικής Ευρώπης, με αφορμή το άγνωστο Καταστατικό του Miskolc (1801)' [Confraternity, Company, Community. At a Typology of the Greek Communities in Central Europe, on the Occasion of the Unknown Statute of Miskolc (1801)], *Eoa and Esperia*, 7 (2007), pp. 247–310.

5. The discussion on the 'imperial' aspect of Venice is very rich. See M. O'Connell, *Men of Empire: Power and Negotiation in Venice's Maritime State* (Baltimore, MD: Johns Hopkins University Press, 2009).

6. The old discussion has been revived since 1989. From the rich literature, see P. Katzenstein (ed.), *Mitteleuropa between Europe and Germany* (Providence, RI: Berghahn Publishers, 1997); J. Elvert, *Mitteleuropa: deutsche Pläne zur europäischen Neurordnung (1918–1945)* [Mitteleuropa: German Plans for a New European Reorientation (1918–1945)] (Stuttgart: Historische Mitteilungen, 35, 1999); http://www.idm.at (Institut für den Donauraum und Mitteleuropa); http://en.wikipedia.org/wiki/Mitteleuropa, [both accessed 1 December 2011].

7. V. Bácskai, *Towns and Urban Society in Early Nineteenth-Century Hungary*, trans. M. Uszkay from Hungarian (Akadémiai Kiadó: Budapest, 1989).

8. J. P. Niederkorn, *Die europäischen Mächte und der ‚Lange Türkenkrieg' Kaiser Rudolphs II (1593–1606)* [The European Powers and the 'the Long Turkish War' of the Emperor

Rudolph II (1593–1606)] (Vienna: Verlag der Österreichischen Akademie der Wissenschaften, 1993); B. M. Buchmann, *Österreich und das Osmanische Reich. Eine bilaterale Geschichte* [Austria and the Ottoman Empire. A Bilateral History] (Vienna: WUV–Univ. Verlag, 1999).

9. E. Eickhoff, *Venedig, Wien und die Osmanen (1645–1700). Umbruch in Südosteuropa 1645–1700*, [Vienna and the Ottomans (1645–1700). A Radical Change in Southeastern Europe], 2nd edn (Munich: Georg D. W. Callwey, 1973); I. Pärvev, *Habsburgs and the Ottomans between Vienna and Belgrade, 1683–1739* (New York: Columbia University Press, 1995).

10. H. Heppner and O. Katsiardi-Hering, 'Drei Epochen in einer Stadt. Zum Zeitschichtengefüge im südöstlichen Europa des 18. Jahrhunderts', ['Three Epochs in one City. Texture of Hitorical events in Southeastern Europe in the Eighteenth Century'], in M. Scheutz, W. Schmale and D. Štefanova (eds), *Orte des Wissens* [Places of Knowledge], *Jahrbuch der Österreichischen Gesellschaft zur Erforschung des 18. Jhts*, 18/19 (2004), pp. 357–74, on pp. 369–74.

11. For an extremely detailed depiction of the natural and military landmarks along the Danube, see the *Navigationskarte der Donau* [Navigationmap of Danube], produced by the two engineer/cartographers Ignaz Lauterer and Siegfried Tauferer (Vienna: Kurtzbekischen Buchhandlung, 1789), at http://cartography.web.auth.gr/Kozani/Donau/Navigationskarte.pdf [accessed 1 December 2011]. The map belongs to the Collection of the Municipal Library of Kozani. A first presentation of it was made by E. Livieratos, A. Tsorlini, M. Pazarli, C. Boutoura and M. Myridis, 'On the Digital Revival of Historic Cartography: Treating two Eighteenth-Century Maps of the Danube in Association with Google-Provided Imagery', 24th International Cartographic Conference, Santiago, Chile, 2009, at http://icaci.org/documents/ICC_proceedings/ICC2009/html/nonref/25_6.pdf [accessed 1 December 2011]. I should like to thank the authors for putting the article at my disposal. Of interest in relation to this map, see my forthcoming paper 'Δούναβης: Ποτάμι πολέμων και ειρήνης – γέφυρα ψυχών και ειδών (18ος–μέσα 19ου αι.)' [Danube, a River of Wars and Peace – a Bridge of Souls and Articles], in the volume dedicated to the Metropolitan of Austria, Michael Staikos.

12. J. Alt and L. Ermini, *Donau–Ansichten vom Ursprunge bis zum Ausflusse ins Meer. Nach der Natur und auf Stein gezeichnet von Jacob Alt. Von Belgrad bis zur Mündung ins Schwarze Meer nach der Natur aufgenommen von Ludwig Ermini. Von mehreren Künstlern lythographiert und herausgegeben von Adolph Kunike. Zum Schlusse des Werkes folgt ein erklärender Text von Dr. Franz Sartori* [Danube – Aspects from the Sources to the Outflows to the Sea. Marked on the Stone According to the Nature by Jacob Alt. From Beograd to its Estuary to the Black Sea According to the Nature recorded by Ludwig Ermini. Lithographed by Many Artists] (Vienna: Adolph Kunike, 1824), nos. 175, 183, 211. It is extraordinarily fortunate that we should have, in addition to the *Navigationskarte 1789*, see n. 11 above, this series of 264 lithographs depicting views of cities and locations along the Danube from its source to its estuary made by Jacob Alt and Ludwig Ermini and published in Vienna by Adolph Kunike in 1824. I should like to thank my friends Natasa and Spyros Lalas for making the reprinted lithographs available to me. On the Greek merchant colony of Semlin and Orsova, see I. Papadrianos, *Οι Έλληνες πάροικοι του Σεμλίνου (18ος–19ος αι.). Διαμόρφωση της παροικίας, δημογραφικά στοιχεία, διοικητικό σύστημα, πνευματική και πολιτιστική δραστηριότητα* [The Greek 'Paroikoi'/Colonists in Semlin (Eighteenth–Nineteenth Centuries). The Formation of the Colony, Demographic Elements, Administrative Structure, Cultural Activity] (Thessaloniki: Institute

for Balkan Studies, no. 210, 1988); E. Nikolaidou, 'Συμβολή στην ιστορία τεσσάρων ελληνικών κοινοτήτων Αυστροουγγαρίας (Zemun, Novi Sad, Orsova, Temesvar)' [A Contribution to the History of Four Greek Communities in Austria–Hungary (Zemun, Novi Sad, Orsova, Temesvar)], *Dodoni*, 9 (1980), pp. 323–73.

13. Alt and Ermini, *Donau-Ansichten*, nos. 179 and 210.

14. On the movements and the commercial roads followed by the Greek Orthodox merchants in south-eastern Europe, see V. Seirinidou, *Έλληνες στη Βιέννη (18ος–μέσα 19ου αι.)* [The Greeks in Vienna (Eighteenth to Mid-Nineteenth Centuries)] (Athens: Herodotus, 2011), pp. 31–71; K. Papakonstantinou, Ελληνικές εμπορικές επιχειρήσεις στην Κεντρική Ευρώπη το β' μισό του 18ου αιώνα. Η οικογένεια Πόνδικα [Greek Commercial Entrepreneurships in Central Europe During the Second Half of the Eighteenth Century. The Pondicas Family] (PhD dissertation, University of Athens, Faculty of History and Archaeology, Athens, 2002), pp. 50–90; idem, 'Trading by Land and Sea: the Change of Trading Routes and the Shift of Commercial Centers from Central to Eastern Europe, 18th–19th Centuries', forthcoming in the Proceedings of the Symposium *Greeks in Romania in 19th Cent.*, Historical Archives of the Alpha Bank, Bucharest 3–4 October 2008; I. Mantouvalos, Όψεις του παροικιακού ελληνισμού. Από το Μοναστήρι στην Πέστη. Επιχείρηση και αστική ταυτότητα της οικογένειας Μάνου (τέλη 18ου–19ος αι.) [Aspects of the Greek Diaspora. From Monastir to Pest. Entrepreneurship and Bourgeois Identity of the Manos Family (End of Eighteenth to Beginning of Nineteenth Century] (PhD dissertation, University of Athens, Faculty of History and Archaeology, Athens, 2007), pp. 119–34.

15. Scholars have concerned themselves extensively with this subject. Forthcoming, with a bibliography, see O. Katsiardi-Hering, 'Das Habsburgerreich: Anlaufpunkt für Griechen und andere Balkanvölker im 17–19. Jahrhundert', [The Habsburg Empire: A Point of Destination for Greeks and other Balkan People in the Seventeenth to Nineteenth century] *Österreichische Osthefte*, 38:2 (1996), pp. 170–88; eadem, 'Migrationen von Bevölkerungsgruppen in Südosteuropa vom 15. Jahrhundert bis zum Beginn des 19. Jhts', [Migrations of Populationgroups in Southeastern Europe from the Fifteenth to Early Nineteenth Century], *Südost-Forschungen*, 59/60 (2000), pp. 125–48, which also contains the bibliography.

16. From the rich literature, see H. Feigl and A. Kusternig (eds), *Die Anfänge der Industrialisierung Niederösterreichs* [The Begin of the Industrialisation in Low-Austria] (Vienna: Selbstverlag des Niederösterreichischen Instituts für Landeskunde, 1982), vol. 2; M. Cerman, 'Proto-industrielle Entwicklung in Österreich' ['Proto-industrial Development in Austria'], in M. Cerman and S. D. Ogilvie (eds), *Proto-Industrialisierung in Europa. Industrielle Produktion vor dem Fabrikszeitalter* [Proto-industrialisation in Europe. Industrial Production before the Era of Manufacture] (Vienna: Verein für Geschichte und Sozialkunde, Institut für Wirtschafts- und Sozialgeschichte der Universität Wien, 'Beiträge zur Historischen Sozialkunde, 5, 1994); for additional literature, see O. Katsiardi-Hering, Τεχνίτες και τεχνικές βαφής νημάτων. Από τη Θεσσαλία στην Κεντρική Ευρώπη (18ος–αρχές 19ου αι.). Επίμετρο: Η Αμπελακιώτικη Συντροφιά (1805) [Artisans and Cotton-Yarn Dyeing Methods. From Thessaly to Central Europe (Eighteenth to the Beginning of the Nineteenth Century). Addendum: The 'Company' of Ambelakia (1805)] (Athens: Herodotos, 2003), pp. 53–70 ff.

17. *Maria Teresa, Trieste e il Porto: Mostra storica* [Maria Theresa, Trieste and the Port. A Historical Exhibition] (Udine: Istituto per l'Enciclopedia del Friuli Venezia Giulia, Comune di Trieste, 1981); E. Godoli, *Trieste* (Bari: Edizioni Laterza, Le città nella storia d'Italia, 1984); for more literature on Austrian economic policy in the Adriatic, see O.

Katsiardi-Hering, *Η Ελληνική παροικία της Τεργέστης, 1750–1830* [The Greek 'Paroikia' (Community) in Trieste, 1751–1830] (Athens: Vivliothiki Saripolou, University of Athens, 1986), vol. 1, pp. 1–20; eadem, 'Η αυστριακή πολιτική και η ελληνική ναυσιπλοΐα (1750–1800)' [Austrian Policy and Greek Shipping, 1750–1800)], *Parousia*, 5 (1987), pp. 445–537; on the port's heyday, see the collective volume: R. Finzi, G. Panjek (eds.), *Storia economica e sociale di Trieste* [Economic and Social History of Trieste], *La città dei gruppi* [The City of the Groups] (Trieste: Lint, 2001) vol. 1; R. Finzi, G. Panjek and L. Panariti (eds), *La città dei traffici, 1719–1918* [The City of the Traffics, 1719–1918] (Trieste: Lint, 2003) vol. 2; on a typology of the city-ports see O. Katsiardi-Hering, 'City-ports in the Eastern and Central Mediterranean from the Mid-sixteenth to the Nineteenth Century: Urban and Social Aspects', *Mediterranean Historical Review*, 26:2 (2011), pp. 151–70.

18. The literature on the Greek diaspora is extremely rich: see http://old.arch.uoa.gr/dias-pora/main/index.php [accessed 2 January 2012] and I. K. Hassiotis, O. Katsiardi-Hering and E. A. Abatzi (eds), *Οι Έλληνες στη Διασπορά 15ος–21ός αι.* [The Greeks in the Diaspora, Fifteenth–Twenty-first Centuries] (Athens: Greek Parliament, 2006), pp. 415–39.

19. O. Katsiardi-Hering, 'Central and Peripheral Communities in the Greek Diaspora: Interlocal and Local Economic, Political, and Cultural Networks in the Eighteenth and Nineteenth Centuries', in M. Rozen (ed.), *Homelands and Diaspora. Greeks, Jews and their Migrations* (London and New York: I. B. Tauris, 2008), pp. 169–80, 372–6, on p. 172.

20. See also the map on the Greek-Orthodox communities in Hungary in Ö. Füves, *Οι Έλληνες της Ουγγαρίας* [The Greeks in Hungary] (Thessaloniki: Institute for Balkan Studies, 75, 1965) as well as the map in Hassiotis, Katsiardi-Hering and Abatzi, *The Greeks in the Diaspora*, p. 12; see the crucial recent article, I. Mantouvalos, 'Μεταναστεύσεις διαδρομές από τον χώρο της Μακεδονίας στην ουγγρική ενδοχώρα (17ος αιώνας-αρχές 19ου αιώνα)' [Migration Routes from the Area of Macedonia in the Hungarian Hinterland (Seventeenth Century–Early Nineteenth Century)], in I. Koliopoulos and I. Mihailidis (eds), *Οι Μακεδόνες στη διασπορά, 17ος, 18ος και 19ος αιώνας* [Macedonians in the Diaspora, Seventeenth, Eighteenth and Nineteenth Centuries] (Thessaloniki: Society for Macedonian Studies, 2011], pp. 178–235.

21. Ö. Füves, 'Görög kereskedők a Dunántúlon 1754–1771 közöll' [Greek Merchants in the 'Danube Knee', 1754–1771], *Különlenyomat az tanulmányok 1965, évi XII/1. Számából tanulmányok*, 12:1 (Budapest, 1965), pp. 106–9, on p. 109 and the relevant map; I. Papp, 'Greek Merchants in the Eighteenth Century Jászkunság', *Balkan Studies*, 30:2 (1989), pp. 261–89.

22. The literature on the Greek Orthodox companies of Braşov and Sibiu is extremely rich. See. D. Limona, *Catalogul documentelor greceşti din Arhivele Statului din oraşul Braşov* [A Catalogue of Greek Documents in the State Archives of the Braşov City] (Bucharest, n.p., 1958); O. Cicanci, *Companiile greceşti din Transilvania şi comerţul european în anii 1636–1746* [Greek Companies in Transylvania and the European Commerce in the Years 1636–1746] (Bucharest: Editura Academiei Republicii Socialiste România, 1981); for a bibliographical survey, see O. Cicanci, 'Το στάδιο της έρευνας σχετικά με την ελληνική εμπορική διασπορά στον ρουμανικό χώρο (τον 17ο–18ο αιώνα)' [The State of the Research Relating to the Greek Merchant Diaspora in Romania], *Eoa kai Esperia*, 7 (2007), pp. 409–21. On Braşov and Sibiu in particular, see R. Popa (on Braşov) and C. Suciu and R. Popa (on Sibiu) in E. Gavra (ed.), *Εμπορικοί σταθμοί των Ελλήνων στη Ρουμανία. Ανάδειξη και προβολή του πολιτισμικού μνημειακού αποθέματος του Μείζονος Ελληνισμού* [Greek Commercial Stations in Romania. Shedding Light on the Monumental Hellenic Cultural

Heritage] (Thessaloniki: University Studio Press, 2007), pp. 455–520, 521–605; also see A. Karathanassis, *L'Hellenisme en Transylvanie: l'activité culturelle, nationale et religieuse des compagnies commerciales helleniques de Sibiu et de Brașov aux XVIII–XIX siècles* [The Hellenism in Transylvania; the Cultural, National and Religious Activity of the Hellenic Commercial Companies in Sibiu and Brașov in the Eigthteenth–Nineteenth Centuries] (Thessaloniki: Institute for Balkan Studies, 2003); R. Moașa-Nazare, *Sub Semnul lui Hermes și al lui pallas. Educație și societate la negustorii ortodocși din Brașov și Sibiu la sfârșitul ssecolului al XVIII-lea și începutul secolului al XIX-lea* [Under the Sign of Hermes and Minerva. Education and Society of the Orthodox Merchants in Brașov and Sibiu (End of the Eighteenth Century-Beginning of the Nineteenth Century)] (Bucharest: Editura Academiei Române, 2010); D.-Ei. Tsourka-Papastathi, *Η ελληνική εμπορική κομπανία του Σιμπίου Τρανσυλβανίας 1636–1848. Οργάνωση και δίκαιο* [The Greek Commercial 'Compagnia' in Sibiu, Transylvania, 1636–1848. Organization and Law] (Thessaloniki: Institute for Balkan Studies, 246, 1994); C. Papacostea-Danielopolu, *Οι ελληνικές κοινότητες στη Ρουμανία τον 19ο αιώνα* [The Greek Communities in Romania, in the Nineteenth Century], trans. N. Diamantopoulos from Romanian, with a bibliographical survey by S. Matthaiou (Athens: Institute for Neohellenic Research, National Hellenic Research Foundation, 2010).

23. N. Smilii and V. Kutsenko, *Greki na Ukrainski Terenax. Narissi z Etnitsnoi istorii. Dokumenti, Materiali, Karti* [The Greeks in the Ukranian Lands. Documents, Materials, Maps] (Kiev: Istitut Istorii Ukraini – Natsionalna Akademija Nauka, 2000); *Διαφωτιστές και Ευεργέτες. Έλληνες επιχειρηματίες και κοινωνικοί παράγοντες του 17ου–19ου αι. στην Ουκρανία. Ιστορικο-βιογραφικά δοκίμια* (in Ukranian with a Greek precis) [Enlighteners and Benefactors. Greek Entrepreneurs and Leading Social Figures in the Ukraine, Seventeenth–Nineteenth Century. Historio-biographical Essays] (Kiev: Istitut Istorii Ukraini – Natsionalna Akademija Nauka, 2001); I. Carras, *Εμπόριο, Πολιτική και Αδελφότητα: Ρωμιοί στη Ρωσία 1700–1774* [Trade, Politics and Brotherhood: Greeks in Russia 1700–1774] (PhD dissertation, University of Athens, Department of Political Sciences and Administration, 2011).

24. H. Halm, 'Österreich und Neurußland (1783)' ['Austria and Newrussia (1783)'], *Jahrbücher für Geschichte Osteuropas*, 6 (Breslau, 1941), pp. 275–493; idem, 'Donauhandel und Donauschiffahrt von den österreichischen Erblanden nach Neurußland (1783)' ['The Danube Commerce and the Danube Navigation from the Austrian Hereditary Lands to Newrussia (1783)'], *Jahrbücher für Geschichte Osteuropas*, new series, 2 (1954), pp. 1–52.

25. Alt and Ermini, *Donau-Ansichten*, nos. 233: Kalafat, 248: Ruschtschuck.

26. D. Kontogeorgis, 'Σύσταση και οργάνωση ελληνικών κοινοτήτων της Ρουμανίας. Η περίπτωση του Τζιούρτζιου και της Τούλτσεας (β΄ μισό 19ου αι.)' [The Composition and Organization of Greek Communities in Romania. The case of Giurgiu and Tulcea (2nd Half of the Nineteenth Century)] *Mnimon*, 28 (2006), pp. 209–39.

27. Alt and Ermini, *Donau-Ansichten*, nos. 255, 256.

28. B. McGowan, 'The Middle Danube *"cul-de-sac"*', in Huri İslamoğlu-İnan (ed.), *The Ottoman Empire and the World Economy*, 3rd edn (Cambridge, 2004), p. 175.

29. For more on this, see Katsiardi-Hering, 'Danube, a River of Wars and Peace'.

30. For more details on the Greek merchant colony of Braila, see D. Kontogeorgis's PhD dissertation currently nearing completion at the Faculty of History and Archaeology, University of Athens.

31. Sp. G. Focas, 'The Greeks and the Navigation on the Lower Danube, 1789–1913', in A. Vacalopoulos, C. Svolopoulos and B. Király (eds), *Southeast European Maritime Com-*

merce and Naval Policies from the Mid-Eighteenth Century to 1914, War and Society in East Central Europe, vol. 28, (New Jersey and Thessaloniki, 1988), pp. 117–19.

32. Sp. G. Focas, *Οι Έλληνες εις την ποταμοπλοΐαν του Κάτω Δουνάβεως* [The Greeks on the River Steamers of the Low Danube] trans. Maria Markouplou from Romanian (Thessaloniki: Institute for Balkan Studies, 1975), p. 34, which concerns the Braila–Braşov trade route; Carras, 'Trade, Politics and Brotherhood', p. 80, the maps on pp. 86 and 87 provide a lot of detail on the corresponding commercial initiatives and notes on the role played by Silistra as a Danube crossing point.

33. R. Sandgruber, *Die Anfänge der Konsumgesellschaft. Konsumgüterverbrauch, Lebensstandard und Alltagskultur im 18. und 19. Jahrhundert* [The Beginning of the Consumer Society. Consumer Goods Consumption and Everyday Culture in the Eighteenth and Nineteenth Century] (Vienna: Verlag für Geschichte und Politik, 1982); M. Prinz, 'Konsum und Konsumgesellschaft seit dem 18. Jahrhundert. Neuere deutsche, englische und amerikanische Literatur', ['Consumption and Consumer Society since the Eighteenth Century. New German, English and American Literature'], *Archiv für Sozialgeschichte*, 41 (2001), pp. 450–514; J. De Vries, *The Industrious Revolution: Consumer Behavior and the Household Economy 1650 to the Present* (Cambridge: Cambridge University Press, 2008).

34. M. Çizakça, *Islamic Capitalism and Finance – Origins, Evolution and the Future* (Cheltenham: Edward Elgar, 2011), which includes the relevant rich discussion; on Ottoman industry, see M. Genç, 'Ottoman Industry in the 18th Century; General Framework, Characteristics and Main Trends', in D. Quataert (ed.), *Manufacturing in the Ottoman Empire and Turkey (1500–1950)* (New York: State University of New York Press, 1994), pp. 59–86.

35. Katsiardi-Hering, *Artisans and Cotton-Yarn Dyeing Methods*, pp. 69, 77–95.

36. In recent years, migration policy theories have been applied as far back as the fifteenth century; from the rich literature, see L. Page Moch, *Moving Europeans. Migration in Western Europe since 1650* (Bloomington, IN: Indiana University Press, 1992); J. Lucassen and L. Lucassen (eds), *Migration, Migration History, History: Old Paradigms and New Perspectives* (Bern, Berlin, New York and Vienna: Peter Lang, 1997); K. Bade, *Europa in Bewegung. Migration vom späten 18. Jahrhundert bis zur Gegenwart* [Europe in Movement. Migration from the late Eighteenth Century to the Present] (2000; Munich: C. H. Beck, 2002), pp. 17–83; on south-eastern European migration movements, see Katsiardi-Hering, 'Migrationen von Bevölkerungsgruppen'.

37. F. Mavroidi, *Συμβολή στην ιστορία της Ελληνικής Αδελφότητας Βενετίας στο ΙΣΤ´ αιώνα: έκδοση του Β´ μητρώου εγγράφων (1533–1562)* [A Contribution to the History of the Greek Brotherhood of Venice in the Sixteenth Century: the Publication of the 2nd Register of Documents, 1533–1562] (Athens: Notis Karavias, 1976); from the rich literature on the *stradioti*, see K. Sathas, *Έλληνες στρατιώται εν τη Δύσει και αναγέννησις της ελληνικής τακτικής* [Greek Soldiers in the West and the Rebirth of Greek Tactics] (1885; Athens: Philomythos, 1993), pp. 8–35, the critical introduction by N. Karapidakis; Chr. Maltezou, *'Stradioti': οι προστάτες των συνόρων* ['Stradioti': the Protectors of the Frontiers] (Athens: n.p., 2003).

38. G. Ploumidis, *Το βενετικόν τυπογραφείον του Δημητρίου και του Πάνου Θεοδοσίου: 1755–1824* [The Venetian Printing House of Demetrius and Panos Theodosiou: 1755–1824] (Athens: n.p., 1969); G. Veloudis, *Das griechische Druck- und Verlagshaus Glikis in Venedig (1670–1854): das griechische Buch zur Zeit der Türkenherrschaft* [The Greek Printing

and Editorial House of Glykis in Venice (1670–1854)] (Wiesbaden: Otto Harrassowitz, 1974).

39. From the rich literature on Venice, see M. Manoussakas, 'A History of the Greek Confraternity (1498–1953) and the Activity of the Greek Institute of Venice', *Modern Greek Studies Yearbook*, 5 (1989), pp. 321–94; '*Δημοσία Ιλαρία*. 500 Years Since the Foundation of the Greek Orthodox Community in Venice' (Venice: Hellenic Institue of Byzantine and Post-Byzantine Studies in Venice, 1999); M.-F. Tiepolo, E. Tonetti (eds), *I Greci a Venezia* [Greeks in Venice], Atti del Convegno Internazionale di Studio, Venezia, 5–7 November 1998 [Proceedings of the International Congress, Venice, 5–7 November 1998] (Venice: Istituto Veneto di Scienze, Lettere ed Arti, 2002); B. Imhaus, *Le minoranze orientali a Venezia, 1300–1510* [The Oriental Minorities in Venice, 1300–1510], trans. from French (Rome: Il Veltro, 1997); M. Grenet, La Fabrique Communautaire. Les Grecs à Venise, Livourne et Marseille, v. 1770–v. 1830 [The Communal Fabric. The Greeks in Venice, Livorno and Marseilles, *c.* 1770–*c.*1830] (Florence: European University Institute, Department of History and Civilization, 2010).

40. A. Xanthopoulou-Kyriakou, *Η ελληνική κοινότητα της Βενετίας (1797–1866): διοικητική και οικονομική οργάνωση, εκπαιδευτική και πολιτική δραστηριότητα* [The Greek Community in Venice (1797–1866): Administrative and Economic Organisation, Educational and Political Activity] (Thessaloniki: Aristoteleian University of Thessaloniki, Epistimoniki Epetiris tis Filosofikis Sholis, 1978).

41. S. Koutmanis, 'Όψεις της εγκατάστασης των Ελλήνων στη Βενετία το 17ο αι. [Aspects of the Settlement of Greeks in Venice, Seventeenth Century], *Thesaurismata* 35 (2005), pp. 309–39; idem, 'Το *τρίτο είδος*. Θρησκευτική υβριδικότητα και κοινωνική αλλαγή στην ορθόδοξη κοινότητα της Βενετίας (τέλη 17ου – αρχές 18ου αιώνα)' [The Third Kind. Religious Hybridism and Social Change in Venice's Orthodox Community (Late Seventeenth–Early Eighteenth Centuries)], *Thesaurismata*, 37 (2007), pp. 389–420.

42. M.-D. Peyfuss, *Die Druckerei von Moschopolis, 1731–1769. Buchdruck und Heiligenverehrung im Erzbistum Achrida* [The Printing in Moschopolis, 1731–1769. Typography and the Veneration of Saints in the Archdiocese of Achrid], 2nd edn (1989; Vienna: Wiener Archiv für Geschichte des Slawentums und Osteuropas, 13, 1996), pp. 41–6.

43. Katsiardi-Hering, 'Austrian Policy and Greek Shipping'; G. Harlaftis, *Ιστορία της ελληνόκτητης ναυτιλίας, 19ος–20ός αιώνας* [A History of Greek-Owned Shipping, Nineteenth–Twentieth Centuries] (Athens: Nefeli, 2001). This is the Greek translation of the English original (London: Routledge, 1996) with the addition of the first chapter concerning the Ottoman period, fifteenth–early nineteenth centuries.

44. G. Stefani, *I Greci a Trieste nel settecento* [The Greeks in Trieste in the Eighteenth Century] (Trieste: Monciatti, 1960), pp. 43–88.

45. L. De Antonellis-Martini, *Portofranco e comunità etnico-religiose nella Trieste settecentesca* [Free Port and Ethnic-Religious Communities in Eighteenth Century Trieste] (Milan: A. Giuffre, 1968); E. Apih, *Trieste* (Rome and Bari: Laterza, 1988).

46. I. Draganić, 'Greek and Serbian in the Ottoman Empire and the Habsburg Monarchy in the 18th and at the Beginning of the 19th Centuries', in M. Plamen, I. Parvev, M. Baramova and V. Racheva (eds), *Empires and Peninsulas. Southeastern Europe Between Karlowitz and the Peace of Adrianople, 1699–1829* (Münster: LIT, 2010), pp. 257–63.

47. W. Lukan, '"*Velika seoba Srba*". Der große Serbenzug des Jahres 1690 ins Habsburgerreich' ['"*Velika seoba Srba*". The Big Serbian Migration of the Year 1690 to the Habsburg Empire'], *Österreichische Osthefte*, 33 (1991), pp. 35–54; R. Samardžić, 'Velika seoba

Srba 1690. Godine' [The Big Serbian Migration in 1690], *Sentandrejski zbornik*, 2 (Belgrade 1992), pp. 7–24.

48. G. Hering, 'Der Konflikt zwischen Griechen und Walachen in der Pester orthodoxen Gemeinde' ['The Conflict among Greeks and Vlachs in the Orthox Community of Pest], in idem (ed.), *Dimensionen griechischer Literatur und Geschichte. Festschrift für Pavlos Tzermias zum 65. Geburtstag* [Dimensions of Greek Literature. Publication in Honor of Pavlos Tzermias on his 65. Anniversary] (Frankfurt am Main, New York: Peter Lang, Studien zur Geschichte Südosteuropas, 10, 1993), pp.145–60; V. Seirinidou, 'Βαλκάνιοι έμποροι στην Αψβουργική Μοναρχία (18ος–μέσα 19ου αιώνα). Εθνοτικές ταυτότητες και ερευνητικές αμηχανίες' [Balkan Merchants in the Habsburg Monarchy (Eighteenth–Mid-Nineteenth Centuries). Ethnic Identities and Scholarly Embarrassment], in Stassinopoulou and Chatziioannou (eds), *Diaspora – Networks – Enlightenment* pp. 53–82, and the subsequent literature.

49. From the wide-ranging literature, see W. Schmale, R. Zedinger and J. Mondot (eds), *Josephinismus – eine Bilanz* [Josephinism – a Statement], in *Das Achtzehnte Jahrhundert und Österreich, Jahrbuch der österreichischen Gesellschaft zur Erforschung des achtzehnten Jahrhunderts*, (Vienna, 2007), vol. 22; H. Reinalter (ed.), *Josephinismus als Aufgeklärter Absolutismus* [Josephinism as Enlightened Absolutism] (Vienna: Böhlau, 2008).

50. For details, see O. Katsiardi-Hering, 'Grenz-, Staats- und Gemeindekonskriptionen in der Habsburgermonarchie: Identitätsdiskurs bei den Menschen aus dem Süden', ['Confine-, State- and Community Censuses in the Habsburg Monarchy: Identity Discours among the People from the South'], in M. Stassinopoulou, M. Oikonomou and I. Zelepos (eds), *Griechische Dimensionen südosteuropäischer Kultur seit dem 18. Jahrhundert. Verortung, Bewegung, Grenzüberstreitung* [Greek Dimensions of the Southeastern European Culture since the Eighteenth Century. Resettlement, Movement, Crossing Borders] (Frankfurt am Main: Peter Lang, Studien zur Geschichte Südosteuropas, 17, 2011), pp. 231–52.

51. Ibid.

52. Ö. Füves, 'Görögök Pesten, 1686–1931' [Die Griechen in Pest, 1686–1931] (habilitation thesis, Budapest, 1972), trans. Andrea Seidler into German, pp. 42–60; Z. Ács, 'Marchands grecs en Hongrie aux 17e–18e siècles' ['Greek Merchants in Hungary in the Seventeenth-Eighteenth centuries'], *Études Historiques Hongroises*, publiées à l'occasion du 17e Congrès International des Sciences Historiques (Budapest, 1990), vol. 2, pp. 41–58.

53. S. Eustratiadis, *Ο εν Βιέννη ναός του Αγίου Γεωργίου και η κοινότης των οθωμανών υπηκόων* [The Church of Saint Georges in Vienna and the Community of the Ottoman Subjects] (Alexandria, 1912; reprint with introduction by Charalampos Chotzakoglou, (Athens: n.p., 1997); G. Tsigaras, *Die Kirche zum Heiligen Georg in Wien. Geschichte und Kunst* [The Church of Saint Georges in Vienna. History and Art] (also in Greek) (Thessaloniki: Ministry for Macedonia and Thrace, 2005); Seirinidou, *The Greeks in Vienna*.

54. For more details see Mantouvalos, 'Migration Routes from the Area of Macedonia'.

55. V. Seirinidou, 'Griechen in Wien im 18. Jahrhundert. Soziale Identitäten im Alltag' [Greeks in Vienna in the Eighteenth Century. Social Identites in Everyday Life'], *Das achtzehnte Jahrhundert und Österreich. Jahrbuch der österreichischen Gesellschaft zur Erforschung des achtzehnten Jahrhunderts*, 12 (1997), pp. 7–18.

56. M. Pozzetto, 'Gli uomini che hanno "fatto" Trieste' ['The Men who "constructed" Trieste'], in *La Bora*, 4:5 (Trieste, 1980), pp.16–29, 5:1 (1981), pp. 13–20; A. Millo, *L'elite*

del potere a Trieste. Una biografia collettiva 1891–1938 [The Power Elite in Trieste. A Collective Biography 1891–1938] (Milan: FrancoAngeli, 1989).

57. Katsiardi-Hering, *The Greek 'Paroikia'*, vol. 2, map no. 8.

58. On Saxon settlement in Transylvania since the thirteenth century, see G. Barta et al., *Kurze Geschichte Siebenbürgens* [A Short History of Transylvania] (Budapest: Akadémiai Kiadó, 1990), pp. 175 ff.; on their antagonism towards the Greeks, see Tsourka-Papastathi, *The Greek Commercial 'Compagnia'*, pp. 104–5.

59. On the rich literature, see O. Katsiardi-Hering, 'Christian and Jewish Ottoman Subjects: Family, Inheritance and Commercial Networks between East and West (17th–18th C.)', in S. Cavaciocchi (ed.), *La famiglia nell'economia europea secc. XIII–XVIII* [The Family in the European Economy, Thirteenth to Eighteenth Century] (Florence: Serie II – Atti delle "Settimane di Studi" e altri Convegni 40, Istituto Internazionale di Storia Economica 'F. Datini' Prato, 2009), pp. 409–40.

60. O. Katsiardi-Hering, 'Il mondo europeo degli intellettuali greci della diaspora (sec. XVIII ex.–XIX in.)' ['The European World of the Greek Intellectuals in the Diaspora (End of the Eighteenth to Early Nineteenth Century'], in F. Bruni (ed.), *Niccolò Tommaseo: popolo e nazioni. Italiani, Corsi, Greci, Illirici* [Niccolò Tommaseo: People and Nations. Italians, Corsicans, Greeks, Illyrians] (Rome, Padua: Atti del Convegno internazionale di Studi nel bicentenario della nascita di Niccolò Tommaseo, Venezia, 23–25 gennaio 2003, 2004), pp. 70–85.

61. M. Manoussacas, 'Η αυτοβιογραφία του εμπόρου του Λιβόρνου Αλεξ. Πατρινού και οι εντυπώσεις του από το Παρίσι κατά το μεσουράνημα του Ναπολέοντα (1810)' [The Autobiography of the Merchant Alex in Livorno. Patrinos and his Impressions from Paris During the Apogee of Napoleon (1810)], in *Praktika tis Akadimias Athinon*, 63:1 (1988), Athens, 1989, pp. 235–72.

62. Katsiardi-Hering, *The Greek 'Paroikia'*, p. 401.

63. G. Dertilis, 'Entrepreneurs grecs: trois générations, 1770–1900', in F. Angiolini and D. Roche (eds), *Cultures et formations négociantes dans l'Europe moderne* [Cultures and Traderformations in Modern Europe] (Paris: École des Hautes Études en Sciences Sociales, 1995), pp. 111–19; Frangakis-Syrett, 'Networks of Friendship'.

64. A. Owens, 'Inheritance and the Life-Cycle of Family Firms in the Early Industrial Revolution', *Business History*, 44:1 (2002), pp. 21–46, on p. 21.

65. O. Katsiardi-Hering and M. Stassinopoulou, 'The Long 18th Century of Greek Commerce in the Habsburg Empire. Social Careers', in H. Heppner, P. Urbanitsch and R. Zedinger (eds), *Social Change in the Habsburg Monarchy. Les transformations de la société dans la monarchie des Habsbourg: l'époque des Lumières* (Bochum: Dr Dieter Winkler, 2011), pp. 191–213.

66. Katsiardi-Hering, *The Greek 'Paroikia'*, pp. 422–7.

67. Katsiardi-Hering, *The Greek 'Paroikia'*, Table IV, pp. 579–85; on the Greek firms in Vienna, see Seirinidou, *Greeks in Vienna*, pp. 99–208, 387–406.

68. Theories on the periphery and semi-periphery have been intensely critiqued in recent years. From the rich literature, I shall cite only H. İslamoğlu-İnan (ed.), *The Ottoman Empire and the World-Economy* (1987; Cambridge, New York and Paris: Cambridge University Press/Éditions de la Maison des Sciences de l'Homme, 2004), especially the introduction and Part I; G. Dertilis, *Το κέντρο, η περιφέρεια, η ιστορία. Ενα μεθοδολογικό δοκίμιο* [The Centre, the Periphery and the History. A Methodological Essay], idem, *Ευρώπη. Δύο δοκίμια και τρία σχόλια* [Europe. Two Essays and Three Comments] (Athens: Kastaniotis, 1998), pp. 89–138.

69. For more on this, see Katsiardi-Hering, 'Christian and Jewish Ottoman Subjects', pp. 413–14.

70. A. Wegener-Sleeswijk, 'Social Ties and Commercial Transactions of an Eighteenth-Century French Merchant', in C. Lesger and L. Noordegraaf (eds), *Entrepreneurs and Entrepreneurship in Early-Modern Times. Merchants and Industrialists within the Orbit of the Dutch Staple Market* (Hague: Stichting Hollandse Historische Reeks, 1995), pp. 203–12, on p. 203.

71. The first *Società Greca di Assicurazioni* was established in 1789. It was followed by many other insurance companies with Greeks, Serbs, Italians and Jews as members, Katsiardi-Hering, *The Greek 'Paroikia'*, pp. 449–74.

72. Ibid., pp. 579–92, 729–30.

73. Katsiardi-Hering, *The Greek 'Paroikia'*, pp. 371–92; G. Harlaftis, 'Mapping the Greek Maritime Diaspora from the Early Eighteenth to the Late Twentieth Centuries', in I. Baghdiantz McCabe, G. Harlaftis and I. Pepelasis-Minoglou (eds), *Diaspora Entrepreneurial Networks. Four Centuries of History* (Oxford and New York: Berg 2005), pp. 147–72.

74. Katsiardi-Hering, *The Greek 'Paroikia'*, Table V, pp. 588–91.

75. See, primarily, Seirinidou, *The Greeks in Vienna*.

76. A. Igglessi, *Βορειοελλαδίτες έμποροι στο τέλος της Τουρκοκρατίας. Ο Σταύρος Ιωάννου* [Merchants from Northern Greece at the End of the Tourkokratia. Stavros Ioannou] (Athens: Emporiki Bank, 2004); the son of Ioannou, Georgios Stavrou founded the National Bank of Greece in 1841.

77. O. Katsiardi-Hering, 'The Allure of Red Cotton Yarn, and How it Came to Vienna: Associations of Greek Artisans and Merchants Operating Between the Ottoman and Habsburg Empires', in S. Faroqhi and G. Veinstein (eds), *Merchants in the Ottoman Empire* (Paris, Louvain and Dydley, MA: Peeters, 2008), pp. 97–131.

78. Papakonstantinou, *Greek Commercial Entrepreneurships*, pp. 63–91; Mantouvalos, *Aspects of the Greek Diaspora*, pp. 107–34, 201.

79. A. Lanier, *Die Geschichte des Bank- und Handelshauses Sina* [The History of Sinas' Bank- and Merchant-house] (Frankfurt am Main, Berlin and Vienna: Europäische Hochschulschriften, Reihe III, Geschichte und ihre Hilfswissenschaften, 805, 1998); see also the cases of the commercial firms of Sinas, Paziazi et al. in D. Cerman-Štefanova, *Adelige als Bankiers in der Epoche der Aufklärung, Eine Studie zur Wiener 'K.K. Oktroy-irten Kommerzial-, Leih- und Wechselbank', 1787–1830* [Aristocrats as Bankers in the Enlightenment Era. A Study for the 'K.K. Oktroyirten Kommerzial-, Leih- und Wechselbank' in Vienna 1787–1830] (Vienna: Habilitationsschrift Historisch-kulturwissenschaftliche Fakultät der Univeristät, 2008), pp. 456–61, 530–46.

80. Seirinidou, *The Greeks in Vienna*, pp. 157–61.

81. G. Laios, *Η Σιάτιστα και οι εμπορικοί οίκοι Χατζημιχαήλ και Μανούση (17ος–19ος αι.)* [Siatista and the Hatzimihail and Manoussis Commercial Houses, Seventeenth–Nineteenth Centuries] (Thessaloniki: Makedoniki Vivliothiki, 60, 1982), pp. 126–36, 162–75; idem, *Σίμων Σίνας* [Simon Sinas] (Athens: Academy of Athens, 1972); Cerman-Štefanova, *Adelige als Bankiers*; Seirinidou, *The Greeks in Vienna*, pp. 121, 162–5.

82. Ö. Füves, 'Die bekanntesten geadelten Griechen in Ungarn' ['The Most Famous Ennobled Greeks in Hungary'], *Balkan Studies*, 5 (1964), pp. 303–8.

83. Cicanci, *Companiile grecești*; Tsourka-Papastathi, *The Greek Commercial 'Compagnia'*.

8 Carras, 'Community for Commerce: an Introduction to the Nezhin Greek Brotherhood Focusing on its Establishment as a Formal Institution in the Years between 1692 and 1710'

1. 'Ніжин' [Nizhin] in Ukrainian.
2. For a full bibliography of the Nezhin Greek Brotherhood, see E. K. Chernukhin, *Грецьке ніжинське братство: історіографія та джерела* [The Nezhin Greek Brotherhood: Historiography and Sources] (Kiev: Institute of the History of the Ukraine, 1998).
3. Государственный архив Черниговской области [State Archive of the Chernigov Region, hereafter GAChO] fond (collection, hereafter f.) 101, opis' (series of documents, hereafter op.) 1, delo (file, hereafter d.) 4268, 1773, list (sheet, hereafter l.) 7ob. (verso). '... Οἱ πραγματευτάδες τοῦ ἀδελφάτου τῶν ρομαίων τῆς καζακίας ...'; GAChO, f. 101, op. 1, d. 4272, 1773, l. 17.
4. The term 'Hellene' was first used to describe the Nezhin Greeks by the Enlightenment scholar Evgenios Voulgaris in 1773. É. Legrand, *Bibliographie Hellénique ou description raisonnée des ouvrages publiés par des Grecs au dix-huitième siècle*, (Paris: Louis Petit and Hubert Pernot, 1928), vol. 2, nos. 782, 792, pp. 169, 175–8.
5. T. Stoianovich, 'The Conquering Balkan Orthodox Merchant', *Journal of Economic History*, 20 (1960), pp. 234–313. For a more recent discussion of the question of Balkan merchant identities, see V. Seirinidou, 'Grocers and Wholesalers, Ottomans and Habsburgs, Foreigners and "our Own": The Greek Trade Diasporas in Central Europe, Seventeenth to Nineteenth Centuries', in S. Faroqhi and G. Veinstein (eds), *Merchants in the Ottoman Empire*, Collection Turcica, vol. 15 (Paris, Louvain and Dudley: Peeters Publishers, 2008), pp. 81–95, on pp. 92–3.
6. Precarious, in part, due to the dangers posed by Tatars, Cossacks and a diversity of brigands, not to mention the menace of Russian, Ottoman, Polish and, for a period, Swedish troops.
7. Nezhin is on the river Oster, south-east of Chernigov, a few hours' drive east of Kiev.
8. Ė. G. Istomina, 'Дороги России в XVIII–начале XIX века' [Roads of Russia in the Eighteenth and the Early Part of the Nineteenth Centuries], in Ė. G. Istomina, A. V. Diomkin and Iu. A. Tikhonov (eds), Исследования по истории России XVI–XVIII вв., Сборник статей в честь 70-летия Я.Е.Водарского [Research into the History of Russia from the Sixteenth to the Eighteenth Century, a Collection of Articles to Commemorate the 70th Anniversary of Ia. E. Vodarskii] (Moscow: Russian Academy of Sciences, Institute of Russian History, 2000), pp. 181–209, on p. 203; E. M. Podgradskaia, *Экономические связи Молдавского княжества и Балканских стран с Русским государством в XVII веке* [Economic Relations Between the Principality of Moldavia and Balkan Lands with the Russian State in the Seventeenth Century] (Kisinau: Shiintsa, 1980), pp. 7, 35, 37, 49; K. Kharlampovich, 'До історії національних меншостей на Україні. Грецька колонія в Ніжені (XVII–XVIII ст.). Нарис V. Ніженські греки й торгівля' [On the History of Ethnic Minorities in the Ukraine. The Greek Colony at Nezhin (Seventeenth–Eighteenth Centuries). Essay V. The Nezhin Greeks and Trade], *Записки історико-філологічного товариства Андрія Білецького* [Transactions of the Andrii Bilets'ki Historical and Philological Comradeship], 3 (Kiev, 1999), pp. 87–159, on pp. 92–7.
9. For the fairs, see J. T. Kotilaine, *Russia's Foreign Trade and Economic Expansion in the Seventeenth Century, Windows on the World* (Leiden and Boston, MA: Brill, 2005),

pp. 52–3, 423; M. M. Plokhinskii, *Иноземцы в старой Малороссии. Греки, цыганы, грузины* [Foreigners in Old Little Russia. Greeks, Gypsies and Georgians] (Moscow: Press of G. Lissner and D. Sobko, 1905), p. 67; M. D. Chulkov, *Словарь учрежденных в России ярмарок и торгов* [A Dictionary of Fairs and Markets Established in Russia] (Moscow: Ponamarjov Press, 1788), pp. 135, 215.

10. See the terms for the region, 'περὶ τῆς Οὐκραῖνας, ἤγουν Καζακίας κοινῶς', used in Greek geographies of the time. G. Constantinou, *Παγκόσμιος Ιστορία τῆς Οἰκουμένης ..., Τόμος Πρῶτος, Περιέχων τὸ Βασίλειον τῆς Μεγάλης Ρουσσίας ἤτοι Μοσχοβίας* [Complete History of the World ..., vol. 1, Containing the Kingdom of Great Russia, that is Muscovy] (Antonios Zapas, 1759), pp. 135–6, 141. Though 'Kazakia' covered a wider area, the left bank of the Dnieper is often, anachronistically, termed the 'Hetmanate'.

11. D. N. Ramazanova, 'Греческие купцы в России во второй половине XVII в' [Greek Merchants in Russia in the Second Half of the Seventeenth Century], in A. P. Pavlov (ed.), *Торговля, купечество и таможенное дело в России в XVI–XVIII вв. Сб. Материалов международной научной конференции* [Trade, Merchantry and Custom Duties in Russia from the Sixteenth to Eighteenth Centuries. Collection of Articles of an International Scientific Conference] (St Petersburg: Institute of Russian History, St Petersburg State University, 2001), pp. 106–9. Sailors destined for service in the Russian fleet might be considered commodities of a similar nature.

12. For the range of products traded, see V. Savva, 'Материалы из архива нежинских греческих братства и магистрата' [Materials from the Archive of the Nezhin Greek Brotherhood and Magistracy], *Сборник Историко-Филологического Общества при Институте кн. Безбородко* [Collection of the Historical Philological Society at the Institute of Prince Bezborodko], 6:1 (Nezhin, 1909), pp. 7–11. Only trade in luxury items was profitable, due to the high additional costs of caravan transport. See B. McGowan, 'Part III. The Age of the Ayans, 1699–1812', in H. Inalcik and D. Quataert (eds), *An Economic and Social History of the Ottoman Empire 1300–1914* (Cambridge: Cambridge University Press, 1994), pp. 637–758, on p. 738.

13. Kotilaine, *Russia's Foreign Trade*, p. 194; R. H. Fisher, *The Russian Fur Trade 1550–1700* (Berkeley and Los Angeles, CA: University of California Publications in History, 1943), pp. 67–9, 123–9, 181, 187, 211, 217.

14. M. Berindei, 'Contribution à l'étude du commerce Ottoman des fourrures Moscovites. La route Moldavo-Polonaise, 1453–1700' [Contribution to the Study of the Ottoman Trade of Muscovite Furs. The Moldav-Polish Route, 1453–1700], *Cahiers du monde russe et soviétique* [Notebooks of the Russian and Soviet World], 12 (1971), pp. 393–409, on p. 395. On the significance of fur and Ottoman sartorial regulations, see S. Faroqhi, 'Introduction, or Why and How one Might Want to Study Ottoman Clothes', in S. Faroqhi and C. K. Neumann (eds), *Ottoman Costumes: From Textile to Identity* (Istanbul: EREN, 2004), pp. 15–49; M. C. Zilfi, 'Goods in the Mahalle: Distribution Encounters in Eighteenth-Century Istanbul', in D. Quataert (ed.), *Consumption Studies and the History of the Ottoman Empire 1550–1922. An Introduction* (New York: State University of New York Press, 2000), pp. 289–312, on pp. 306–7.

15. The activities of the Nezhin Greeks should therefore be viewed in relation to the furriers guilds of the Ottoman Empire, and, in particular, that of its capital. For the furriers guild in Constantinople, see M. D. Chulkov, *Историческое описание российской коммерции при всех портах и границах от древних времян до ныне настоящего ...* [A Historical Description of Russian Commerce from all Ports and Borders from Ancient Times to the Present ...] (St Petersburg: Imperial Academy of Sciences, 1786), vol. 2, book 1, p.

198. For 'charismatic' goods, see C. A. Bayly, '"Archaic" and "Modern" Globalisation in the Eurasian and African Arena, c.1750–1850', in A. G. Hopkins (ed.), *Globalisation in World History* (London: Pimlico, 2002), pp. 47–74, on pp. 52, 66.

16. V. Eingorn, *К истории иноземцев в Старой Малороссии, Отзыв об исследовании М.М. Плохинскаго, издание Императорскаго Общества Истории и Древностей Российских при Московском Университете* [On the Story of Foreigners in Old Little Russia, a Review of the Study by M. M. Plokhinskii Published at the Imperial Society for the Study of Russian History and Antiquities at Moscow University] (Moscow: Imperial Society for the Study of Russian History and Antiquities, 1908), p. 6. For the Jews in the Russian Empire during the eighteenth century, see B. Nathans, 'The Jews', in D. Lieven (ed.), *The Cambridge History of Russia*, vol. 2, *Imperial Russia, 1689–1917* (Cambridge: Cambridge University Press, 2006), pp. 184–201, on pp. 186–8.

17. A. A. Fedotov-Chekhovskii, *Акты Греческаго Нежинскаго Братства* [Documents of the Nezhin Greek Brotherhood] (Kiev, 1884), pp. 43–4. The privileges were corroborated by the Hetmans that followed Khmel'nitskii, see Fedotov-Chekhovskii, *Documents of the Nezhin Greek Brotherhood*, pp. 53–8; C. P. Lascarides (ed.), *Το Καταστατικό της Ελληνικής Εμπορικής Κοινότητας στη Νίζνα Ουκρανίας* [The Charter of the Greek Commercial Community in Nezhin, Ukraine] (Ioannina: Panagiotes Pournaras, 1997), pp. 7, 13. For the Armenians in the region, see Y. Dashkevych, 'Armenians in the Ukraine at the Time of Hetman Bohdan Xmel'nyc'kyj (1648–1657)', *Harvard Ukrainian Studies*, 3–4:1 (1979–80), pp. 166–88; I. Baghdiantz McCabe, *The Shah's Silk for Europe's Silver, The Eurasian Silk Trade of the Julfan Armenians in Safavid Iran and India (1590–1750)* (Atlanta, GA: University of Pennsylvania Texts and Studies, 1999), pp. 280–90.

18. Fedotov-Chekhovskii, *Documents of the Nezhin Greek Brotherhood*, p. 53; K. Kharlampovich, *Нариси з історії грецької колонії в Ніжині (XVII–XVIII ст.)* [Essays on the History of the Nezhin Greek Colony (Seventeenth and Eighteenth Centuries], *Записки історико-філологічого відділу, ВУАН* [Transactions of the Historical and Philological Department, Pan-Ukrainian Academy of Sciences], 24 (Kiev, 1929), on pp. 11–13.

19. Fedotov-Chekhovskii, *Documents of the Nezhin Greek Brotherhood*, pp. 12, 15, 53, 55–7; Lascarides, *The Charter*, pp. 5, 10, 17, 123.

20. *Полное Собрание Законов Российской империи* [Complete Collection of Laws of the Russian Empire, hereafter PSZ], vol. 4, no. 2260, pp. 481–2, 11 March 1710; *PSZ*, vol. 11, no. 8656, pp. 709–11, 3 November 1742. Fedotov-Chekhovskii, *Documents of the Nezhin Greek Brotherhood*, pp. 64–8, 79–84; Kharlampovich, 'Essays on the History of the Nezhin Greek Colony', pp. 24, 29–31, 48.

21. Podgradskaia, *Economic relations*, pp. 91–2, 95–6; E. M. Podgradskaia, 'Таможенная политика Русского государства по отношению к купечеству стран Юго–Восточной Европы, входивших в состав Оттоманской империи (XVII в.)' [Customs Policies of the Russian State Toward the Merchants of South-Eastern Europe, Belonging to the Ottoman Empire (Seventeenth Century)], in Ia. S. Grosul (ed.), *Карпато–дунайские земли в средние века* [Carpatho-Danubian Lands in the Middle Ages] (Kisinau: Shiintsa, 1975), pp. 229–47; S. A. Pokrovskii, *Внешняя торговля и внешняя торговая политика России* [Foreign Trade and Foreign Trade Policy of Russia] (Moscow: Mezhdunarodnaia kniga, 1947), pp. 84, 96–7, 116.

22. Kharlampovich, 'Essays on the History of the Nezhin Greek Colony', pp. 32, 48, 56–62, 74.

23. E. K. Chernukhin, 'Книга пожертв грецького ніжинского братсва 1696–1786 рр'. [The Offerings Book of the Nezhin Greek Brotherhood, 1696–1786], *Записки*

Історико-Філологічного товариства Андрія Білецького [Transactions of the Andrii Bilets'ki Historical and Philological Comradeship], 1 (Kiev, 1997), pp. 91–102, 144–79, on p. 91; Eingorn, *On the story of foreigners in Old Little Russia*, p. 17.

24. Kharlampovich, 'Essays on the History of the Nezhin Greek Colony', p. 18.
25. Российский государственный архив древних актов [Russian State Archive of Old Documents, hereafter RGADA], f. 124, Малороссийские Дела [Little Russian Affairs], d. 12, 1711, ll. 1–26; Podgradskaia, *Economic relations*, p. 80. See also Kharlampovich, 'Essays on the History of the Nezhin Greek Colony', p. 25. Kharlampovich, 'On the History of Ethnic Minorities in the Ukraine', pp. 88–9; Chernukhin, 'The Offerings Book', p. 92.
26. For a decree of 1700, one of several from the end of the seventeenth and the early eighteenth centuries, ordering Greeks to leave Moscow for Nezhin, see Ia. S. Grosul (ed.), *Исторические связи народов СССР и Румынии в XV-начале XVIII в. Документы и материалы* [Historical Relations of the Peoples of the USSR and Romania from the Fifteenth until the Beginning of the Eighteenth Centuries. Documents and Data] (Moscow: Nauka, 1970), vol. 3, p. 141.
27. GAChO, f. 101, op. 1, d. 4285a, 1779, ll. 1–4; Chernukhin, 'The Offerings Book', p. 92; Lascarides, *The Charter*, p. 49.
28. GAChO, f. 101, op. 1, d. 11, 1762–4, ll. 1, 6, 10–12.
29. Kharlampovich, 'On the History of Ethnic Minorities in the Ukraine', p. 89.
30. Persians, in other words, Armenians. I intend to write a further article on the important question of collaboration between Greeks and Armenians in the wider region.
31. A. Shafonskii, *Черниговского наместничества топографическое описание с кратким географическим и историческим описанием Малыя России ...* [Topographical Description of the Chernigov Region with a Brief Geographical and Historical Description of Little Russia ...] (Kiev: Kiev University Press 1851), pp. 467–78; N. K. Storozhevskii, *Нежинские Греки* [Nezhin Greeks] (Kiev: Kiev University Press, 1863), p. 14; M. Berezhkov, *Город Нежин в начале XIX века, по описанию московских путешественников (заметки к истории города)* [The City of Nezhin in the Early Nineteenth Century, According to the Writings of Travellers from Moscow (Notes on the History of the City)] (Nezhin: E. F. Venger, 1895), p. 12.
32. I. M. Dolgorukii, 'Славны бубны за горами, или путешествие мое кое куда 1810 года' [Tambourines Sound Glorious on the Other Side of the Mountains, or My Travel Somewhere in 1810], in *Чтения в Императорском Обществе Истории и Древностей Российских при Московском Университете* [Readings of the Imperial Society for the Study of Russian History and Antiquities at Moscow University], book 2, April–June, book 3, June–September (Moscow, 1869), pp. 1–170, 171–356, on p. 308.
33. Carras, 'Trade, Politics and Brotherhood', pp. 134–49.
34. Similar observations have been made for the trading community at Sibiu, to cite but one example. D.-E. Tsourka-Papastathi, *Η ελληνική εμπορική κομπανία του Σιμπίου Τρανσυλβανίας 1636–1848, οργάνωση και δίκαιο* [The Greek Company of Sibiu in Transylvania 1636–1848, Organization and Law] (Thessaloniki: Institute for Balkan Studies, 246, 1994), p. 38.
35. R. E. Jones, 'Opening a Window on the South: Russia and the Black Sea 1695–1792', in M. Di Salvo and L. Hughes (eds), *A Window on Russia, Papers from the V International Conference of the Study Group on Eighteenth-Century Russia* (Rome: La Fenice, 1996), pp. 123–8.
36. First Elisavetgrad (Elizavetgrad) and later others, such as Taganrog, Cherson and Odessa. V. Iastrebov, 'Греки в Елисаветграде, отрывок из истории колонизации

1754–1777 гг'. [The Greeks of Elisavetgrad, Excerpt from the History of a Colonization, 1754–1777], *Kievskaia Starina*, 8:4 (1884), pp. 673–84, on p. 678; G. L. Arsh,
'Переселение греков в Россию в конце XVIII–начале XIX века' [Migration of Greeks
to Russia at the End of the Eighteenth and the Beginning of the Nineteenth Century],
in Iu.V. Ivanova (ed.), *Греки России и Украины* [The Greeks of Russia and the Ukraine]
(St Petersburg: Aletheia, 2004), pp. 36–49, on p. 38. In these later cases however Russian
authorities were keen to ensure that Greek privileges were more clearly prescribed than
was the case in Nezhin.

37. '... ἐμπόριον περίφημον ... εἰς τὴν ὁποίαν κατοικοῦσιν πολλοὶ Ρωμαῖοι δ' αἰτίαν τῆς
πραγματείας', Constantinou, *Complete History of the World*, p. 141.

38. R. B. Revere, '"No Man's Coast": Ports of Trade in the Eastern Mediterranean', in K.
Polanyi (ed.), *Trade and Markets in the Early Empires* (New York and London: Free Press,
1957), pp. 38–63, on pp. 51–2; S. C. Humphreys, 'History, Economics and Anthropol-
ogy: The Work of Karl Polanyi', *History and Theory*, 8 (1969), pp. 165–212, on p. 191.

39. D. Sorkin, 'The Port Jew: Notes Toward a Social Type', *Journal of Jewish Studies*, 50:1
(1999), pp. 87–97; L. C. Dubin, *The Port Jews of Habsburg Trieste: Absolutist Politics
and Enlightenment Culture* (Stanford and California: Stanford University Press, 1999),
pp. 198–225.

40. D. Sorkin, 'Port Jews and the Three Regions of Emancipation', in D. Cesarani (ed.), *Port
Jews: Jewish Communities in Cosmopolitan Maritime Trading Centres, 1550–1950* (London: Frank Cass, 2002), p. 31.

41. Lascarides, *The Charter*, pp. 89, 177, 191–3.

42. Chernukhin, 'The Offerings Book', pp. 145–7; Lascarides, *The Charter*, pp. 18–20;
S. Pavlenko (ed.), *Військові кампанії доби гетьмана Івана Мазепи в документах*
[Military Campaigns of the Epoch of Hetman Ivan Mazepa in Documents] (Kiev: Kiev-
Mohyla Academy Publishers, 2009), no. 85, p. 391.

43. A scholar of mixed repute who had spent some time in the College of the Greeks in
Oxford prior to journeying to the Russian Empire. A. Helladius, *Status Praesens Ecclesiae
Graecae* (Nuremburg: n.p., 1714), pp. 249–87.

44. RGADA, f. 52, Сношения России с Грецией [Russian Relations with Greece], op. 1, d.
15, 1704, l. 22; f. 52, op. 1, d. 15, 1705, l. 6ob. For Mazepa's involvement in the funding
of the Nezhin school, see also D. Papastratou (ed.), *Ο Σιναΐτης Χατζηκυριακής εκ Χώρας
Βουρλά, Γράμματα – Ξυλογραφίες 1688–1709* [The Sinaite Hatzekyriakes from Vourla,
Letters – Woodcuts 1688–1709] (Athens: Hermes–Istos 1981), p. 101.

45. Peter I, *Письма и бумаги императора Петра Великого* [Letters and Papers by the
Emperor Peter the Great] (vol. 1–13, vol. 6, July–December 1707), ed. I. A. Bychkov (St
Petersburg: State publishers, 1912), pp. 443–4; Peter I, *Letters and Papers* (vol. 7, January–June 1708), ed. I. A. Bychkov (Petrograd: First state publishers, 1918), pp. 772–3,
824; Peter I, *Letters and papers* (vol. 8, July–December 1708), ed. A. A. Preobrazhenskii
(Moscow: Academy of Sciences of the USSR, 1948), p. 946; Grosul, *Relations of the
Peoples of the USSR and Romania*, pp. 300, 358; Papastratou, *The Sinaite Hatzekyriakes*,
pp. 101–2; Chernukhin, 'The Offerings Book', p. 145. Zgouros died in Mazepa's camp
in Gadiach a few months prior to the battle of Poltava. S. Pavlenko (ed.), *Доба гетьмана
Івана Мазепи в документах* [Epoch of the Hetman Ivan Mazepa in Documents] (Kiev:
Kiev-Mohyla Academy Publishers, 2008), no. 578, pp. 724–35; Pavlenko, *Military campaigns*, no. 85, p. 391.

46. RGADA, f. 52, op. 1, d. 15, 1705, ll. 1–2, 8ob–9.

47. G. Esipov (Г. Геσίποβ), 'Ὁ Ἑλλην κληρικὸς Σεραφείμ' [The Greek Cleric Seraphim], trans. K. Palaiologos, *Parnassos*, 4:1 (1880), pp. 28–51, on pp. 28, 37. Following his return to Russia in 1731 Seraphim was dispatched to Siberia. V. N. Makrides, 'Στοιχεία για τις σχέσεις του Αλέξανδρου Ελλάδιου με τη Ρωσία' [Facets of Alexander Helladius's Relations with Russia], *Mnemon*, 19 (1997), pp. 9–39, on pp. 33–4.

48. GAChO, f. 101, op. 1, d. 4251, 1771, l. 2ob. See also Архив внешней политики Российской империи [Archive of Foreign Affairs of the Russian Empire, hereafter AVPRI], f. 7, Московская Контора КИД [Moscow Office KID], op. 4, d. 122, 1770, ll. 1–2.

49. The historian Bantysh-Kamenskii (Николай Николаевич Бантыш Каменский, 1737–1814) studied in a Greek school in Nezhin; G. M. Piatigorskii, 'Александровское греческое училище в Нежине (1817–1919 гг.)' [The Alexander Greek School in Nezhin (1817–1919)], in G. L. Arsh (ed.), *Греческая культура в России XVII–XX вв.* [Greek Culture in Russia Seventeenth–Twentieth Centuries] (Moscow: Institute of Slavic Studies, 1999), pp. 51–71, on p. 52. For a Greek school in Nezhin in 1749, see Fedotov-Chekhovskii, *Documents of the Nezhin Greek Brotherhood*, p. 79.

50. K. Kharlampovich, 'Нарис VI: Просвітницька й благодійна діяльність Ніжинської грецької громади' [Essay VI: Educational and Philanthropic Activities of the Community of the Greeks of Nezhin], in *Записки історико-філологічного товариства Андрія Білецького* [Transactions of the Andrii Bilets'ki Historical and Philological Comradeship], 4 (Kiev, 2003), pp. 131–64, on pp. 133–42.

51. Berindei, 'Contribution à l'étude du commerce Ottoman', pp. 393–409.

52. I. Wallerstein, H. Decdeli and R. Kasaba, 'The Incorporation of the Ottoman Empire in the World-Economy', in H. Islamoğlu-İnan (ed.), *The Ottoman Empire and the World Economy* (Cambridge: Cambridge University Press, 1987), pp. 88–97, on p. 88. See the argumentation in Bayly, '"Archaic" and "Modern" Globalisation', p. 50.

53. L. C. Dubin, '"Wings on their feet ... and wings on their head": Reflections on the Study of Port Jews', in D. Cesarani and G. Romain (eds), *Jews and Port Cities 1590–1990: Commerce, Community and Cosmopolitanism* (London, Portland, OR: Vallentine Mitchell, 2006), pp. 14–30, on p. 17. For a critique of David Sorkin's concept of the 'social type', see C. S. Monaco, 'Port Jews or a People of the Diaspora? A Critique of the Port Jew Concept', *Jewish Social Studies: History, Culture, Society*, 15:2 (2009), pp. 137–66, on p. 159.

54. Sorkin, 'The Port Jew: Notes Toward a Social Type', pp. 90–1.

55. Carras, 'Trade, Politics and Brotherhood', pp. 572–83.

56. For a discussion of this issue, see I. Baghdiantz McCabe, G. Harlaftis and I. Pepelasis–Minoglou (eds), *Diaspora Entrepreneurial Networks: Four Centuries of History* (Oxford and New York: Berg, 2005), p. xxii; Dubin, 'Wings on their feet', pp. 22–3.

57. The Brotherhood's first official seal depicted Jesus Christ and all the saints with the inscription: 'The Year 1692'; Storozhevskii, *Nezhin Greeks*, p. 10.

58. For such 'Stavropegial Brotherhoods', see I. Isaievych, *Voluntary Brotherhood: Confraternities of Laymen in Early Modern Ukraine* (Edmonton and Toronto: Peter Jacyk Centre for Ukrainian Historical Research Monograph Series, vol. 2, Canadian Institute for Ukrainian Studies, 2006), pp. 40–68. For the Lviv Brotherhood, see Iu. E. Shustova, *Документы Львовского Успенского Ставропигийского Братства (1586–1788), Источниковедческое Исследование* [Documents of the Lvov Stavropegial Brotherhood of the Dormition of the Mother of God (1586–1788). A Study of the Sources] (Moscow: Russian Academy of Science, Institute of Universal History, 2009), pp. 77–95.

For the terms 'brotherhood', 'parish', 'diaspora', 'colony' and alternatives used to describe merchant communities in Greek history, see O. Katsiardi-Hering, Ἀπὸ τις "Ἑλληνικές κοινότητες του Ἐξωτερικοῦ" στην ιστοριογραφία του μεταναστευτικού φαινομένου (15ος-19ος αι.)' [From 'Greek Communities Abroad' to the Historiography of the Phenomenon of Migration (Fifteenth–Nineteenth Centuries)], in P. M. Kitromilides and T. E. Sklavenites (eds), Ιστοριογραφία της νεότερης και σύγχρονης Ελλάδας 1833–2002 [The Historiography of Modern and Contemporary Greece 1833–2002], Proceedings of the fourth International History Congress, vol. 2 (Athens: Institute for Neohellenic Research, National Hellenic Research Foundation, 2004), pp. 223–49, on pp. 229, 241.

59. Thus limited religious freedoms were first granted to the 'church of Nezhin' by the Oecumenical Patriarch in 1680. GAChO, f. 101, op. 1, d. 4225, 1680, l. 1ob. Fedotov-Chekhovskii, *Documents of the Nezhin Greek Brotherhood*, pp. 2–3.

60. Fedotov-Chekhovskii, *Documents of the Nezhin Greek Brotherhood*, pp. 6–7; Pavlenko, *Epoch of the Hetman Ivan Mazepa*, no. 463, pp. 488–9; Lascarides, *The Charter*, pp. 4–5, 10, 17, 27–30, 112, 123–4.

61. '... при церкви их Греческой Нежинской, имети союз духовный братолюбный церковного братства ...'; Fedotov-Chekhovskii, *Documents of the Nezhin Greek Brotherhood*, pp. 12–15. For Zgouros, see Lascarides, *The Charter*, pp. 6, 111, 123.

62. '… γράμμα ονηβερσσάλι τη εκκλησία του θεού τη Αδελφότιτη …'. Lascarides's transcription of the text is monotonic. Lascarides, *The Charter*, pp. 6–7, 12, 111, 123–4; Also Fedotov-Chekhovskii, *Documents of the Nezhin Greek Brotherhood*, pp. 12–15; Kharlampovich, 'Essays on the History of the Nezhin Greek Colony', pp. 20–1.

63. Lascarides, *The Charter*, p. 142.

64. Ibid., pp. 70, 156.

65. Ibid., pp. 83–5, 181–2.

66. For references to women members of the Brotherhood, see Chernukhin, 'The Offerings Book', pp. 156, 158, 161.

67. In the elections, beads were used for ballots. Gogol had witnessed the Brotherhood elections, satirizing them in a now-lost early work. G. B. Samoilenko, *Нежин – город юности Гоголя* [Nezhin – Town of Gogol's Youth] (Nezhin: Nezhin State Pedagogical University, 2002), pp. 110–12.

68. For one discussion of such differences, see I. Luk'ianov, *Путешествие в Святую Землю старообрядца московского священника 1710–1711, в царствование Петра Великого* [The Journey to the Holy Land of the Old Believing Moscow Priest 1710–1711, During the Reign of Peter the Great] (Moscow: n.p., 1864), pp. 38–44.

69. The donation of alms by Muscovy to the ecclesiastical institutions of the Orthodox east dates at least from the time of the granting of an autonomous See to Moscow by the Oecumenical Patriarch Jeremiah II in 1589. N. F. Kapterev, *Характер отношений России к православному Востоку в XVI и XVII столетиях* [The Nature of Relations of Russia with the Orthodox East in the Sixteenth and Seventeenth Centuries] (Sergiev Posad: M.S. Elova bookshop, 1914), pp. 60, 105, 153 and passim.

70. RGADA, f. 52, op. 1, d. 17, 1702, l. 1.

71. RGADA, f. 52, op. 1, d. 10, 1706, l. 1; f. 52, op. 1, d. 7, 1705, ll. 1–2, 7. For other examples, see RGADA, f. 52, op. 1, d. 26, 1703, l. 5; f. 52, op. 3, d. 102, 1718, l. 3.

72. RGADA, f. 52, op. 1, d. 11, 1705, l. 1, 3–3ob, 17–18, 21. Similarly, prominent Greeks are reported travelling to London not for trade, but for charity. J. Harris, 'Silent Minority: The Greek Community of Eighteenth-Century London', in D. Tziovas (ed.), *Greek*

73. RGADA, f. 52, op. 1, d. 29, 1712, l. 1; f. 52, op. 1, d. 7, 1704, l. 2; f. 52, op. 1, d. 29, 1712, l. 1.; f. 52, op. 1, d. 4, 1708, l. 1ob–2.
74. Peter I, *Letters and Papers* (vol. 4, 1706), ed. A. F. Bychkov (St Petersburg: State publishers, 1900), p. 433.
75. R. Hellie, *The Economy and Material Culture of Russia 1600–1725* (Chicago, IL and London: University of Chicago Press, 1999), p. 530.
76. M. Mauss, *The Gift: The Form and Reason for Exchange in Archaic Societies*, trans. W. D. Halls (New York and London: W.W. Norton, 1990), pp. 18, 33.
77. Ἀρχιερεὺς δὲν ἀγρυπνεῖ, καὶ τόσο δὲν τρομάζει, / Μὴ τοῦ χαθῆ καμμιὰ ψυχή, καὶ κόπον δὲν κοιτάζει, / Οσον ἐγὼ ὁ μάταιος πάντοτε ἀγρυπνοῦσα, / μὴ χάσω ἄσπρο ἢ παρᾶ, κ᾽ ἔτρεμα κ᾽ ἐπονοῦσα᾽, K. Dapontes [Καισάριος Δαπόντες], *Κῆπος Χαρίτων* [Garden of the Graces], ed. G. Sophocles (Athens: Hermes, 1880), p. 143.
78. For more on the bearers of Russian alms to the east, note K. Chrysohoides, ʽΙερὰ Ἀποδημία. Τὸ προσκυνηματικὸ ταξίδι στοὺς Ἁγίους Τόπους στα μεταβυζαντιμᾶ χρόνιαʼ [Holy Migration. The Pilgrim's Journey to the Holy Lands in Post-Byzantine times], in I. Viggopoulou (ed.), *Τὸ ταξίδι ἀπὸ τους αρχαίους ἕως τους νεότερους χρόνους* [Travel from Ancient to Modern Times] (Athens: Institute for Neohellenic Research, National Hellenic Research Foundation, 2003), pp. 99–110; C. Stamatopoulos, 'Bref aperçu de l'histoire des quêtes athonites en Russie', *Russie mille ans de vie chrétienne, Les études théologiques de Chambésy*, 10 (Chambésy, Genève, 1993), pp. 245–57; C. Roggel, 'The Wandering Monk and the Balkan National Awakening', *Études Balkaniques*, 1 (1976), pp. 114–127; Kapterev, *The Nature of Relations of Russia with the Orthodox East*; idem, *Сношения иерусалимских патриархов с русским правительством с половины XVI до конца XVII столетия* [Relations of the Patriarchs of Jerusalem with the Russian Authorities from the Mid-Sixteenth until the End of the Seventeenth Centuries], Православный Палестинский Сборник [Orthodox Palestine Review] (St Petersburg: Orthodox Palestine Society, 1895).
79. Kapterev, *The Nature of Relations of Russia with the Orthodox East*, p. 256.
80. Suretyship was one of the basic means for insuring contracts, ensuring the payments of debts, the return of travellers, appearance in court and other similar activities. D. L. Ransel, 'Character and Style of Patron–Client Relations in Russia', in A. Mączak (ed.), *Klientelsysteme im Europa der Frühen Neuzeit* [Client-systems in Europe in Early Modern Times] (Munich: Oldenbourg Verlag, 1988), pp. 211–31, on p. 212. Examples in Kharlampovich, 'On the History of Ethnic Minorities in the Ukraine', p. 145; RGADA, f. 52, op. 1, d. 11, 1700, ll. 6, 14.
81. The newly enthroned Oecumenical Patriarch Gavriil intervened in 1703 in a question of the inheritance due to the merchant Christophoros Manuilov. RGADA, f. 52, op. 1, d. 15, 1703, l. 2ob-3. For other examples, see RGADA, f. 52, op. 1, d. 20, 1709, l. 1ob; f. 52, op. 1, d. 34, 1705, 3ob.
82. RGADA, f. 52, op. 1, d. 26, 1703, ll. 5–7.
83. Dositheos's letters are addressed either to Peter I or to Fedor Alexeevich Golovin, RGADA, f. 52, op. 1, d. 1, 1705, l. 54; f. 52, o. 1, d. 4, 1705, l. 1–1ob, 6ob; f. 52, op. 1, d. 1, 1706, l. 6ob.
84. RGADA, f. 52, op. 1, d. 1, 1706, l. 64. See also RGADA, f. 52, op. 1, d. 13, 1707, l. 16ob–17ob.
85. RGADA, f. 52, op. 1, d. 2, 1706, l. 1–1ob.

86. Chrysanthos became Patriarch of Jerusalem in 1707 and remained Patriarch until 1731. RGADA, f. 52, op. 1, d. 1, 1707, l. 30ob–3ob. See also RGADA, f. 52, op. 1, d. 1, 1707, l. 17.
87. Voinov was a factor for Savva Raguzinskii, RGADA, f. 52, op. 1, d. 6, 1712, l. 3.
88. The will is dated to 5 November 1725, E. Pelagides, *Ο Κώδικας της Μητροπόλεως Καστοριάς, 1665–1769* [The Codex of the Metropolis of Kastoria, 1665–1769] (Thessaloniki: Macedonian Library, 1990), no. 121, pp. 38–9.
89. Like all such terms, 'Orthodox commonwealth' should be used with caution. In this context, it is not intended as an alternative to the complex and diverging identities of the Orthodox of the Ottoman Empire in the seventeenth and eighteenth centuries. Anania Voinov might be described as a Bosnian, or perhaps a Serb, and equally as a Greek of the Nezhin Brotherhood. His will, however, speaks louder than any anachronistic description; it is the sense of identity conveyed in this document, and others similar to it, that the term 'Orthodox commonwealth' seeks to portray. For use of the term 'Orthodox commonwealth', see P. M. Kitromilides, 'Από την ορθόδοξη κοινοπολιτεία στις εθνικές κοινότητες: το πολιτικό περιεχόμενο των ελληνορωσικών πνευματικών σχέσεων κατά την τουρκοκρατία' [From the Orthodox Commonwealth to Ethnic Communities: the Political Content of Greek-Russian Cultural Ties During the Period of Ottoman Domination], in *Χίλια Χρόνια Ελληνισμού–Ρωσίας* [One Thousand Years of Greeks in Russia] (Athens: International Chamber of Commerce, 1994), pp. 139–65.
90. If we are to accept the testimony of their names, then these were merchants who identified themselves above all with the practice of pilgrimage. See, for example, Hadji Thoma Ivanov, RGADA, f. 158, Приказные дела новых лет [Chancery Affairs from Recent Years] op. 2, kn. (kniga, book) 12, 1715, l. 5.
91. An interesting parallel to Jewish and Armenian experiences.
92. '… διατὶ ὃλοι οἱ Ὀρθόδοξοι εἶναι τοῦ Ἁγίου Τάφου τέκνα καὶ ἀδελφοὶ …', see n. 93 for details.
93. The above passages from the epistle of the Patriarch are to be found in RGADA, f. 52, op. 1, d. 1, 1701, l. 15. For the continuation of this affair, see RGADA, f. 52, op. 1, d. 17, 1702, l. 1. For trans-Saharan caravan networks organised along similar lines, see A. K. Bennison, 'Muslim Universalism and Western Globalisation', in A. G. Hopkins (ed.), *Globalisation in World History* (London: Pimlico, 2002), pp. 74–98, on p. 86.
94. The Oecumenical Patriarch was nominally Primus inter Pares, but in fact the Patriarchal throne in Constantinople was seriously weakened for most of the eighteenth century.
95. In 1711 Greeks gathered in various houses in order to be counted. These included buildings of the Monastery of St Catherine and also of the Patriarchate of Jerusalem, RGADA, f. 124, d. 12, 1711, l. 19–19ob.
96. Pavlenko, *Epoch of the Hetman Ivan Mazepa*, no. 463, pp. 488–9.
97. The conflict is mentioned in a letter of Ioannikios, Archbishop of Sinai, dated to 1698. Papastratou, *The Sinaite Hatzekyriakes*, pp. 62, 100–2.
98. As emphasized in the aforementioned decree of the Metropolitan of Kiev Varlaam Iasinskii. Fedotov-Chekhovskii, *Documents of the Nezhin Greek Brotherhood*, pp. 12–15.
99. Lascarides, *The Charter*, p. 55.
100. Ibid., pp. 77, 171.
101. A. A. Dmitrievskii, 'Греческие нежинские храмы и их капитальный вклад в церковно-археологический музей при Киевской Духовной Академии' [The Greek Churches of Nezhin and their Principle Endowments in the Church-Archaeological Museum at the Kiev Theological Academy], *Pravoslavnoe obozrenie*, 1 (1885), pp. 370–400, on p. 375;

Kharlampovich, 'Essays on the History of the Nezhin Greek Colony', pp. 15–16; Chernukhin, 'The Offerings Book', p. 144.
102. GAChO, f. 101, op. 1, d. 4226, 1734, l. 22.
103. GAChO, f. 101, op. 1, d. 4276, 1730 on, l. 60; f. 101, op. 1, d. 4226, 1734, l. 17, 35. Fedotov-Chekhovskii, *Documents of the Nezhin Greek Brotherhood*, p. 79; Lascarides, *The Charter*, pp. 63, 77.
104. Thus Zgouros made a donation to the Brotherhood hospital. Chernukhin, 'The Offerings Book', p. 145. For the home for the elderly, see Kharlampovich, 'Essays on the history of the Nezhin Greek colony', p. 20; Lascarides, *The Charter*, pp. 87–8, 136.
105. Lascarides, *The Charter*, pp. 14–15.
106. The particular document dates to 21 March 1731, GAChO, f. 101, op. 1, d. 4285a, 1779, l. 2ob; 'public opinion', in other words 'γνώμιν κοινὴν', GAChO, f. 101, op. 1, d. 4273, 1773, l. 1; GAChO, f. 101, op. 1, d. 4285a, 1779, l. 2–2ob; f. 101, op. 1, d. 4272, 1773, l. 2ob.
107. GAChO, f. 101, op. 1, d. 4273, 1773, l. 1.
108. For the importance of such expressions in the organization of communal power structures, see A. Black, *Guilds and Civil Society in European Thought from the Twelfth Century to the Present* (London: Methuen, 1984), pp. 22, 134, 137.
109. GAChO, f. 101, op. 1, d. 4272, 1773, l. 2. See also Chernuhin, 'The Offerings Book', p. 144.
110. '... for their spiritual salvation, and eternal remembrance ...', notes the Brotherhood book of donations, Chernuhin, 'The Offerings Book', p. 144.
111. '... ἔχωντες τας εκκλησίας μας, ἔχωμεν και το Αδελφάτον μας, ἔχωντες το Αδελφάτον ἔχωμεν τας ελευθερίας, ἔχωντας τας ελευθερίας πραγματευόμεθα και ωφελούμεθα ποίος πολύ, ποίος ολιγώτερον καθώς καθενός ο Θεός δώση ...'. Lascarides, *The Charter*, p. 126.
112. N. Petrov, 'Греческий Екатерининский Монастырь в Киеве' [The Greek Monastery of St Catherine in Kiev], in *Trudy Kievskoi dukhovnoi akademii*, 37:1 (Kiev, 1896), pp. 55–112, on p. 99.
113. 'Epiphany', in other words 'Богоявление'. O. Alexandropoulou, 'Η ελληνική μονή Αγίου Νικολάου στη Μόσχα. Στοιχεία από την ιστορία των ελληνορωσικών σχέσεων στο δεύτερο μισό του 17ου αιώνα' [The Greek Monastery of St Nicholas in Moscow. Facets of the History of Greek-Russian Relations in the Second Half of the Seventeenth Century], *Mesaionika and Nea Ellinika*, 6 (2000), pp. 111–54, on p. 138.
114. For such debt relations, see the case of the merchant Nikolaos Hadji Aggelis who provided a loan to Ioannikios the Archimandrite of the Monastery of St Nicholas, AVPRI, f. 2, Внутренние Коллежские Дела [Internal Collegiate Affairs], op. 6, d. 3643, 1763–9, ll. 150–3, 156, 166, 173; AVPRI, f. 13, Письма разных лиц на русском языке [Letters of Various Individuals in Russian], op. 2, d. 967, 1765, l. 2.
115. For an example from Nezhin from 1733, see Kapterev, *Relations of the Patriarchs of Jerusalem*, p. 428.
116. *PSZ*, collection 1, vol. 2, no. 659, p. 75, 22 August 1676; *PSZ*, collection 1, vol. 2, no. 693, p. 104, 28 May 1677; *PSZ*, collection 1, vol. 2, no. 818, p. 264, 17 April 1680. For changes in church state relations during the seventeenth century, see R. O. Crummey, 'The Orthodox Church and the Schism', in M. Perrie (ed.), *The Cambridge History of Russia*, vol. 1, *From Early Rus' to 1689* (Cambridge: Cambridge University Press, 2006), pp. 618–39. See also N. A. Chrissidis, 'Creating the New Educated Elite: Learning and Faith in Moscow's Slavo-Greco-Latin Academy, 1685–1694' (PhD dissertation, Yale University, 2000), pp. 47–50.

117. Kapterev, *Relations of the Patriarchs of Jerusalem*, pp. 472–3; idem, *The Nature of Relations of Russia with the Orthodox East*, pp. 271–75; P. Stathi, Χρύσανθος Νοταράς Πατριάρχης Ιεροσολύμων [Chrysanthos Notaras Patriarch of Jerusalem], Ανάλεκτα της καθ᾽ ημάς Ανατολής [Proceedings of the Greek East] (Athens: Society for the Study of the Greek East, 1999), pp. 162–3.

118. F. Trivellato, *The Familiarity of Strangers: the Sephardic Diaspora, Livorno and Cross-Cultural Trade in the Early Modern Period* (New Haven, CT and London: Yale University Press, 2009), pp. 177–223.

119. Chernukhin, 'The Offerings Book', p. 158; Lascarides, *The Charter*, pp. 173–80.

120. Alexandros Mavrocordatos provided capital for trade to the merchant Hadjiparaskevas among others. Grosul, *Historical Relations of the Peoples of the USSR and Romania*, p. 233. Nicholas Mavrocordatos intervened on behalf of the merchant Dmitri Michailov Merjan, RGADA, f. 52, op. 1, d. 3, 1714, l. 8ob.

121. Among them Constantin Brancoveanu of Wallachia (Voievod, 1688–1714), RGADA, f. 52, op. 1, d. 4, 1703, l. 8ob. See also Storozhevskii, *Nezhin Greeks*, pp. 7–8.

122. Among them Daniil Apostol (Hetman, 1727–34), Kharlampovich, 'On the History of Ethnic Minorities in the Ukraine', p. 144.

123. For example, Ambassador Peter Tolstoi. RGADA, f. 52, op. 1, d. 16, 1704, p. 1.

124. In Russian: 'изменника', Kharlampovich, 'Essays on the History of the Nezhin Greek Colony', p. 24.

125. RGADA, f. 52, op. 3, d. 99, 1710, l. 3; *PSZ*, collection 1, vol. 4, no. 2260, pp. 481–2, 11 March 1710; Chulkov, *A Historical Description of Russian Commerce*, pp. 66–7.

126. Chernukhin, 'The Offerings Book', p. 158. For more on Raguzinskii, see N. I. Pavlenko, *Птенцы гнезда Петрова* [Fledgelings from Peter's Nest] (Moscow: Mysl', 1994), pp. 331–66.

127. See the case of the Greek Stouka, who had considerable debts. Kharlampovich, 'Essays on the History of the Nezhin Greek Colony', p. 33.

128. The distinction between 'incomers' ('εἰσερχόμενοι') and the 'established' ('ἐγκάτικοι') is evident already in Russian and Greek documents from the early years of the Brotherhood. Chernukhin, 'The Offerings Book', p. 150; Kharlampovich, 'On the History of Ethnic minorities in the Ukraine', p. 131; Fedotov-Chekhovskii, *Documents of the Nezhin Greek Brotherhood*, p. 14. Tensions between the two groups became more acute from the 1730s on however. GAChO, f. 101, op. 1, d. 4285a, 1779, l. 2–2ob, 4; GAChO, f. 101, op. 1, d. 4272, 1773, l. 17.

129. Kharlampovich, 'Essays on the History of the Nezhin Greek Colony', pp. 18, 21, 40–1.

130. Ibid., p. 42.

131. This institution replaced the Posolskii Prikaz.

132. AVPRI, f. 124, Малороссийские дела [Little Russian Affairs], f. 124, op. 1, d. 14, 1721, l. 9, 20.

133. The question of the differentiation of the Greeks from the other populations of the Ukraine and Russia belongs to a different paper. Nonetheless, it is worth noting that as the century progressed the burghers of Nezhin increasingly complained that non-Greeks shared the Brotherhood's privileges. GAChO, f. 101, op. 1, d. 87, 1786–90, l. 65–65ob. See also Kharlampovich, 'Essays on the History of the Nezhin Greek Colony', pp. 57–8, 70–1.

134. Kharlampovich, 'Essays on the History of the Nezhin Greek Colony', pp. 67–8.

135. His appeal was to the Little Russian College. Savva, 'Materials from the Archive of the Nezhin Greek Brotherhood', pp. 27–8, 33.

136. Storozhevskii, *Nezhin Greeks*, p. 10; Lascarides, *The Charter*, p. 13; Kharlampovich, 'Essays on the History of the Nezhin Greek Colony', p. 92.
137. For a discussion of legal pluralism, see S. E. Merry, 'Legal Pluralism', *Law and Society Review*, 22:5 (1988), pp. 869–96.
138. Thus even Greeks might prefer: 'that the issue be presented at the Nezhin Magistracy': GAChO, f. 101, op. 1, d. 4267, 1773, l. 2; f. 101, op. 1, d. 4248, 1771, l. 1. See also GAChO, f. 101, op. 1, d. 4259, 1771, ll. 2–3. On other occasions disputants might bypass the *Kriterion* and appeal directly to the Little Russian College, GAChO, f. 101, op. 1, d. 4255, 1771, l. 1–1ob.
139. 'Печать нежинскаго греческаго компромиссиальнаго суда 1736 года, генваря 1 дня', Storozhevskii, *Nezhin Greeks*, p. 10; Kharlampovich, 'Essays on the History of the Nezhin Greek Colony', p. 38.
140. 'Печать Ея Императорскаго Величества Суда Нежинскаго Греческаго Братства', Storozhevskii, *Nezhin Greeks*, p. 10; Kharlampovich, 'Essays on the History of the Nezhin Greek Colony', pp. 20, 38, 68.
141. Lascarides, *The Charter*, pp. 39, 46.
142. *PSZ*, collection 1, vol. 22, no. 16250, p. 441, 1 September 1785.
143. Kharlampovich, 'Essays on the History of the Nezhin Greek Colony', p. 1.
144. I note the use of the term 'structural differentiation of functions' to describe this process. 'Structural differentiation' encompasses the division of labour but is not confined to the economic field. It also refers to the specialization of institutions. D. Rueschemeyer, *Power and the Division of Labour* (Cambridge and Stanford, CA: Stanford University Press, 1986), pp. 2–3, 51, 141–2.
145. GAChO, f. 101, op. 1, d. 4272, 1773, l. 2ob.
146. 'πολιτεία', see GAChO, f. 101, op. 1, d. 4285a, 1779, l. 4.

9 Sifneos and Harlaftis, 'Entrepreneurship at the Russian Frontier of International Trade. The Greek Merchant Community/*Paroikia* of Taganrog in the Sea of Azov, 1780s–1830s'

1. On Russia's southward expansion, see R. E. Jones, 'Opening a Window on the South: Russia and the Black Sea, 1695–1792', in L. Hughes and M. di Salvo (eds), *A Window on Russia: Papers from the V International Conference of the Study Group on Eighteenth-Century Russia* (Rome: La Fenice, 1996), pp. 123–30.
2. Letter to his wife L. F. Lomofskaya-Nelidova, 6 October 1877, quoted from A. Tsymbal, 'Οι Έλληνες ως επικεφαλής της Δημοτικής Δούμας του Ταγκανρόκ [Greeks at the Head of the Duma of Taganrog]', in E. Sifneos and G. Harlaftis (eds), *Οι Έλληνες της Αζοφικής, 19ος αι.* [Greeks in the Sea of Azov, Nineteenth Century] (forthcoming). See also G. Harlaftis, 'Ο "πολυεκατομμυριούχος κύριος Μαράκης" Βαλλιάνος, το σκάνδαλο του Τελωνείου Ταγκανρόκ και οι 144 καταστροφές του Αντόν Τσέχωφ [The 'Multimillionaire Mr. Marakis' Vagliano, the Scandal of the Taganrog Customs Office and 144 Disasters of Anton Chekhov], *Τα Ιστορικά*, 54 (2011), pp. 79–122.
3. E. Sifneos, 'Merchant Enterprises and Strategies in the Sea of Azov Ports', *International Journal of Maritime History*, 22:1 (June 2010), pp. 259–68.
4. According to the 1897 All-Russian Census the Greek-speaking population of Odessa was 5,086 inhabitants and of Taganrog 1,006. See *Первая всеобщая перепись населения Российской империи 1897 года* [The first All-Russian Population Census of 1897], vol.

XLVII, Chersonskaya Gubernia, Odessa (Moscow, 1904), pp. 2–3 and *Первая всеобщая перепись населения Российской империи 1897 года* [The First All-Russian Population Census of 1897], Oblast' voiska Donskogo (Moscow, 1905), pp. 2–3. For an analysis of the 1897 census and the Greeks, see E. Sifneos and S. Paradisopoulos, 'Οι Ελληνες της Οδησσού το 1897: διαβάζοντας την πρώτη επίσημη ρωσική απογραφή [The Greeks in Odessa in 1897: Revisiting the First Official Russian Census], *Ta Istorika*, 44 (June 2006), pp. 81–122.

5. On the architectural choices of the Greeks of Taganrog, V. Colonas, 'Architectural Expression of the Greeks in the Nineteenth-Century Cities of the Sea of Azov Region: The Case of Taganrog', *International Journal of Maritime History*, 22: 1 (June 2010), pp. 269–78. On the cultural features of the Greek merchant diaspora in south Russia, E. Sifneos, 'Business Ethics and Lifestyle of the Greek Diaspora in New Russia: from Economic Activities to National Benefaction', in A. Kuijlaars, K. Prudon and J. Visser (eds), *Business and Society. Entrepreneurs, Politics and Networks in a Historical Perspective*, Proceedings of the Third European Business History Association (EBHA) Conference 'Business and Society', September 24–26, 1999, (Rotterdam, The Netherlands: Centre of Business History, 2000)

6. See for example the case of the trading firm Sifneos Bros. (1850–1919) in E. Sifneos, *Ελληνες έμποροι στην Αζοφική. Η δύναμη και τα όρια της οικογενειακής επιχείρησης* [Greek Merchants in the Sea of Azov. The Power and Limits of a Family Business] (Athens: Institute for Neohellenic Research, 2009).

7. For Greek merchant communities/*paroikies* in central Europe see Chapter 7 by O. Katsiardi-Hering. Indicative bibliography on other merchant *paroikies* in the Mediterranean see Chr. Hadziiossif, 'La colonie Grecque en Egypte 1833–1856' (PhD dissertation, Université Paris-Sorbonne Paris IV, Ecole Pratique des Hautes Etudes, IV Section, Paris, 1980); O. Katsiardi-Hering, *Η Ελληνική παροικία της Τεργέστης, 1750–1830* [The Greek 'Paroikia' [Community] in Trieste, 1751–1830] (Athens: Vivliothiki Saripolou, University of Athens, 1986); D. Vlami, *Το Φιορίνι, το Σιτάρι και η Οδός του Κήπου. Ελληνες Εμποροι στο Λιβόρνο, 1750–1868* [The Florin, Wheat and the Street of the Garden. Greek Merchants in Livorno, 1750–1868] (Athens: Themelio, 2000); A. Mandilara, 'The Greek Business Community in Marseille, 1816–1900. Individual and network strategies' (PhD dissertation, European University Institute, Florence, 1998). A selected list of the literature on the Greek communities in Russia includes P. Herlihy, 'Greek Merchants in Odessa in the Nineteenth Century', in I. Sevcenko and F. E. Sysyn (eds), *Eucharisterion: Essays Presented to Omeljan Pritsak on His Sixtieth Birthday by His Colleagues and Students*, 2 vols (Cambridge, MA: 1979), vol. 1, pp. 399–420; eadem, 'The Greek Community in Odessa, 1861–1917', *Journal of Modern Greek Studies*, 7:2 (1989), pp. 235-51; G. Harlaftis, 'The Role of the Greeks in the Black Sea Trade, 1830–1900' in L. R. Fischer and H. W. Nordvik (eds), *Shipping and Trade, 1750–1950: Essays in International Maritime Economic History* (Pontefract: Lofthouse Publications, 1990), pp. 63–95; eadem, *A History of Greek-Owned Shipping: The Making of an International Tramp Fleet, 1830 to the Present Day* (London: Routledge, 1996); V. Kardasis, *Diaspora Merchants in the Black Sea: The Greeks in Southern Russia, 1775–1861* (Lanham, MD: Lexington Books, 2001); I. Pepelasis Minoglou, 'The Greek Merchant House of the Russian Black Sea: A Nineteenth-Century Example of a Trader's Coalition', *International Journal of Maritime History*, 10:1 (1998), pp. 61-104; J. A. Mazis, *The Greeks of Odessa: Diaspora Leadership in Late Imperial Russia* (New York: Boulder, distributed by Columbia University Press, 2004); E. Sifneos, 'The Dark Side of the Moon: Rivalry and Riots for Shelter and Occupation between the Greek and Jewish Populations in Multi-

Ethnic Nineteenth-Century Odessa', *Historical Review/La Revue Historique*, 3 (2006), pp. 189–204; eadem, 'Business Ethics and Lifestyle of the Greek Diaspora in New Russia: From Economic Activities to National Benefaction', in A.-M Kuijlaars (ed.), *Business and Society: Entrepreneurs, Politics and Networks in a Historical Perspective* (Rotterdam: Center of Business History, 2000), pp. 455–68; eadem, Ἐθνικός αυτοπροσδιορισμός σε ένα οικονομικά μεταβαλλόμενο περιβάλλον. Η μαρτυρία ενός έλληνα εμποροϋπαλλήλου από το ρώσικο εμπόριο σιτηρών' [National Self-Determination in an Economically Changing Environment. The Testimony of a Greek Trading Employee from the Russian Grain Trade], in M. A. Stassinopoulou and M.-C. Chatziioannou, 'Diaspora – Networks – Enlightenment', *Tetradia Ergasias 28*, (Athens: Institute for Neohellenic Research , The National Hellenic Research Foundation 2005), pp. 116–25; O. Selekou, *Η καθημερινή ζωή των Ελλήνων της διασποράς δημόσιος και ιδιωτικός βίος (19ος–αρχές του 20ού αιώνα)* [Everyday Life of the Greek Diaspora, Nineteenth to the Beginning of the Twentieth Century] (Athens: EKKE, 2004); E. Sifneos, 'Οι αλλαγές στο ρωσικό σιτεμπόριο και η προσαρμοστικότητα των ελληνικών εμπορικών οίκων [The Changes in the Russian Grain Trade and the Adaptability of the Greek Merchant Houses]', *Ta Historica*, 40 (2004), pp. 53–96; Sifneos and Paradeisopoulos, 'Οι Έλληνες της Οδησσού το 1987 [The Greeks in Odessa in 1897], pp. 81–122; I. K. Hassiotis, *Οι Έλληνες της Ρωσίας και της Σοβιετικής Ενωσης* [The Greeks of Russia and the Soviet Union] (Salonica: University Studio Press, 1997); G. L. Arsh, *Этеристское движение в России* [The Filiki Etaireia in Russia] (Moscow: n.p., 1970); I. V. Sapozhnikov and L. G. Belousova, *Греки под Одессой: Очерки истории п. Александровка с древней-ших времен до начала XX века* [Greeks in the Region of Odessa. Historical Studies about Alexandrovka from the Ancient Times to the Present Day] (Odessa: n.p., 1999); Y. V. Ivanov (ed.), *Греки России и Украины* [The Greeks of Russia and Ukraine] (St Petersburg: Aleteia, 2004); O. B. Shliakhov, 'Судновласники Азово-Чорноморського басейну наприкінці XIX – на початку XX ст.' [The Shipowners of the Azov and the Black Sea, Late Nineteenth beginning–Twentieth Century], *Ukrain'skii istorichnii zhurnal*, 1 (2006), pp. 61–72; S. Novikova, 'Внесок греків в економічний розвиток північного Приазов'я (друга половина XIX- початок XX ст.)' [The Contribution of the Greeks to the Economic Development of the Northern Azov (Second Half of the Nineteenth Century–Early Twentieth Century)] (PhD dissertation, Ukraine Institute of History, Ukraine National Academy of Science, 2005).

8. I. K. Hasiotis, 'Continuity and Change in the Modern Greek Diaspora', *Journal of Modern History*, 6 (1989), p. 9–24; idem, *Επισκόπηση της Νεοελληνικής Διασποράς* [A Survey of the History of Modern Greek Diaspora] (Thessaloniki: Vanias, 1993), pp. 19–20.

9. Sifneos and Paradeisopoulos, 'The Greeks in Odessa in 1897'; Sifneos, 'The Dark Side of the Moon'; M. Vassilikou, 'Greeks and Jews in Salonika and Odessa: Inter-ethnic Relations in Cosmopolitan Port Cities', *Jewish Culture and History*, 4:2 (2001), pp. 155–72; Harlaftis, 'The "Multimillionaire, Mr. Marakis"'.

10. For analysis of the meaning of *paroikia* see the Introduction of the present volume.

11. M.-C. Chatziioannou, 'Greek Merchant Networks in the Age of Empires (1770–1870)', in I. Baghdiantz-McCabe, G. Harlaftis and I. Pepelasis-Minoglou (eds), *Diaspora Entrepreneurial Networks. Four Centuries of History* (Oxford and New York: Berg, 2005), pp. 371–81; G. Harlaftis, 'The "Multimillionaire, Mr. Marakis"'.

12. G. Harlaftis, 'The "Eastern Invasion". Greeks In The Mediterranean Trade And Shipping in the Eighteenth and Early Nineteenth Centuries', in M. Fusaro, C. Heywood and M.-S. Omri (eds), *Trade and Cultural Exchange in the Early Modern Mediterranean: Braudel's Maritime Legacy* (London: I. B. Tauris, 2009), pp. 223–52. See also G. Harlaftis,

'International Business of Southeastern Europe and the Eastern Mediterranean, Eighteenth Century: Sources, Methods and Interpretive Issues', in F. Ammannati (ed.), *Dove va la storia economica? Metodi e prospettive. Secc. XIII–XVIII* [Where is Economic History Going? Methods and Prospects from the Thirteenth to the Eighteenth Centuries], Atti della 'Quarantaduesima Settimana di Studi', 18–22 April 2010 [Proceedings of the 'Forty-fifth Week of Studies', 18–22 April 2010] (Florence: Florence University Press, 2011), pp. 389–415.

13. See G. Harlaftis, 'From Diaspora Traders to Shipping Tycoons: The Vagliano Bros.', *Business History Review*, 81:2 (2007), pp. 237–68 and G. Harlaftis and K. Papakonstantinou (eds), *H ναυτιλία των Ελλήνων, 1700–1821* [Greek Shipping, 1700–1821] (Athens: Kedros, forthcoming), chapters 1, 8 and 9.

14. N. V. Riasanovsky, *A History of Russia*, 5th edn (1963; New York; Oxford: Oxford University Press 1993), pp. 254-75; V. N. Zakharov, 'Внешнеторговая деятельность иностранных купцов в портах Азовского и Черного морей в середине и второй половине XVIII в' ['The Development of Foreign Trade by Foreign Merchants in the Azov and the Black Sea Ports in the Second Half of the Eighteenth Century'], *Vestnik Moskovskogo universiteta*, ser. 8, *Istoria*, 4 (2004), pp. 85–102; P. Herlihy, *Odessa. A History (1797–1914)* (Cambridge, MA: Cambridge University Press, 1986).

15. Kardasis, *Diaspora Merchants in the Black Sea*; Harlaftis, *A History of Greek-Owned Shipping*, pp. 3–38.

16. P. Herlihy, 'Russian Grain and the Port of Livorno, 1794–1865', *Journal of European Economic History*, 5 (1976), pp. 79–80.

17. M. Harvey, 'The Development of Russian Commerce in the Black Sea and its Significance' (PhD dissertation, University of California, 1938); S. Fairlie, 'The Anglo-Russian Grain Trade, 1815–1861' (PhD dissertation, University of London, 1959); Herlihy, *Odessa. A History*.

18. Sifneos, 'Merchant Enterprises and Strategies'.

19. S. Osborn, 'On the Geography of the Sea of Azov, the Putrid Sea, and Adjacent Coasts', *Journal of the Royal Geographical Society of London*, 27 (1857), pp. 133–48.

20. P. Filefsky, *История города Таганрога* [History of the City of Taganrog] (Taganrog, 1898).

21. On the Don Cossacks see S. O'Rourke, *Warriors and Peasants: the Don Cossacks in Late Imperial Russia* (Basingstoke: Palgrave Macmillan, in association with St Antony's College, Oxford, 2000).

22. E. Sifneos, 'Can Commercial Techniques Substitute Port Institutions? Evidence from the Greek Presence in the Black and Azov Sea Ports (1780–1850)', in Consiglio Nazionale delle Ricerche (CNR), Istituto di Studi sulle Societá del Mediterraneo (ISSM) [National Research Council (CNR), Institute of Studies on the Mediterranean societies (ISSM)], *Istituzioni e traffici tra età antica e crescita moderna* [Institutions and exchanges from the ancient to modern times] (Napoli, 2009), pp. 77–90.

23. On the importance of Greeks in the Kazakh area (modern-day Ukraine), with a focus on Nezhin, who had extended their activities as far as the Sea of Azov, see I. C. Carras, 'Εμπόριο, Πολιτική και Αδελφότητα: Ρωμιοί στη Ρωσία 1700–1774' [Trade, Politics and the Brotherhood of the Greeks in Russia 1700–1774] (PhD dissertation, Department of Political Science and Adminsitration, National and Capodistrian University of Athens, 2011), pp. 97, 103.

24. Carras, 'Trade, Politics and the Brotherhood', p. 97.

25. Ibid., pp. 93–100.

26. Ibid., p. 98.
27. Ibid., pp. 68–87.
28. Harvey, 'The Development of Russian Commerce', pp. 19–21.
29. Ibid., pp. 36–8.
30. H. Inalcik and D. Quataert (eds), *An Economic History of the Ottoman Empire, 1300–1914* (Cambridge: Cambridge University Press, 1994), pp. 209–16.
31. C. King, *The Ghost of Freedom. A History of the Caucasus* (Oxford: Oxford University Press, 2008), pp. 53–63.
32. H. V. Aydin, 'Greek Merchants and Seamen in the Black Sea 1780–1820', in Harlaftis and Papakonstantinou (eds), *Greek Shipping*, chapter 18.
33. Harlaftis and Papakonstantinou (eds), *Greek Shipping*, chapter 6.
34. *Amfitriti* Database, Research Programme of the Ionian University 'Greek Shipping History, 1700–1821', funded by the European Union and the Greek Ministry of Education and included in the 'Pythagoras 1' Operational Programme, 2004–2007.
35. The ship is named after the church of the village of Spartia in Cephallonia. Spartia belongs to the province of Levatho, a region in Cephallonia renowned for its seafarers.
36. Harlaftis and Papakonstantinou (eds), *Greek Shipping*; G. Harlaftis, *A History of Greek-Owned Shipping* (London: Routledge, 1996).
37. About the productivity and competitiveness of the fleet of the Greeks in the eighteenth century, Harlaftis and Papaconstantinou (eds), *Greek Shipping*, chapter 9.
38. D. Sherry, 'Social Alchemy on the Black Sea Coast, 1860–1865', *Kritika: Explorations in Russian and Eurasian History*, 10:1 (2009), pp. 7–30.
39. A. J. Rieber, *Merchants and Entrepreneurs in Imperial Russia* (Chapel Hill, NC: University of North Carolina Press, 1982), pp. 68–70.
40. Sherry, 'Social Alchemy'.
41. Ibid.
42. For the growth of the Taganrog *paroikia* from the 1840s to the First World War see E. Sifneos and G. Harlaftis (eds), *Οι Έλληνες της Αζοφικής, 19ος αιώνας* [The Greeks of the Azov, Nineteenth Century] (forthcoming), chapter 2.
43. Catherine II's decree towards Count Orlov, 28 March 1775.
44. Catherine II's decree, 21 May 1779, Exhibited Document, Museum of the City of Mariupol.
45. O. C. Safonov, *греческих легионов в России, или нынешнее население Балаклавы* [The Remains of Greek Legions in Russia or Balaklava's Current Population]], *Zapiski Odeskovo Obshestva Istorii*, vol. 1, (Odessa, 1849), 1, pp. 250–73.
46. 1 dessiatine = 1.09 hectares = 2.7 acres.
47. Catherine II's decree, 21 April 1808.
48. Filefsky, *History of the City of Taganrog*, p. 107.
49. Ibid., p. 103.
50. Ibid., p.106.
51. Dimitrios Venardakis was born in Taganrog in 1800. At the age of 30 he left his military career and became secretary of the holder of the alcohol monopoly in the Charkov district. He was managing the Taganrog office of the state monopoly on alcohol. He donated his property to the Russian and the Greek state by sponsoring the publication of Ad. Korais's 'Greek Library' collection. See "Δημήτριος Βεναρδάκης» [Dimitrios Venardakis] in *Βοβολίνη Μέγα Ελληνικόν Βιογραφικόν Λεξικόν* [Vovolini Big Greek Dictionnary of Biographies],vol. 1 (Athens: Kerkyra, Economia publishing, 1958), pp. 158–62.

52. Государственный архив Rostov области [State Archive of the Rostov Region, hereafter GARO] fond (collection, hereafter f.) 226, opis' (series of documents, hereafter op.) 21, delo (file, hereafter d.) 633, 'Greek Church of Saints Constantine and Helen, Taganrog, List of Church Attendees According to their Estate Status, 1852'.

53. I. de Matariaga, *Russia in the Age of Catherine the Great* (London: Phoenix, 1981), pp. 287–91.

54. GARO, f. 579, op. 1, d. 409, report of the Greek Magistrate to the military governor of Taganrog, governor of the city and holder of many titles, Apollon Andreevich Dashkov, 2 June 1803.

55. GARO, f. 579, op. 1, d. 82, office of the governor, record of revenues of the Greek and Russian Magistrates from ships calling at the port 1804–5.

56. de Madariaga, *Russia in the Age*, pp. 91–2.

57. GARO, f. 579, op. 1, d. 409, 11 July 1781.

58. GARO, f. 579, op. 1, d. 409.

59. B. Mironov, 'Bureaucratic- or Self-Government: the Early Nineteenth Century Russian City', *Slavic Review*, 52:2 (June 1993), pp. 233–55.

60. Carras, 'Trade, Politics and the Brotherhood', pp. 241–52.

61. M. A. Arantzioni, *Греки Криму: історія і сучасне становище (етнокультурна ситуація та проблеми етнополітичного розвитку* [The Greeks of the Crimea: History and Current Situation (Ethno-cultural Status and Problems of Ethno-political Development] (Simferopol: Regional Annexe of the National Institute of Strategic Research in Simferopol, 2005), pp. 20–1.

62. E. Karakalos, a Greek judge who travelled in Russia in 1894 in order to promote the export of raisins from the Peloponnese into the Russian market, made a clear distinction among Greeks and Greek Russians or assimilated Greeks in Taganrog; E. Karakalos, *Ημερολόγιον περιοδείας προς Διάδοσιν της Κορινθιακής Σταφίδος (1894–1895)* [Diary of a Tour for the Promotion of the Raisins of Corinth (1894–1895)], ed. K. Papoulides (Athens: Kyriakidi Bros., 2009), p. 76.

63. Rieber, *Merchants and Entrepreneurs*, p. xxiii.

64. de Madariaga, *Russia in the Age*, p. 300 and Rieber, *Merchants and Entrepreneurs*, p. xxiii.

65. Rieber, *Merchants and Entrepreneurs*, pp. 33, 36.

66. GARO, f. 579, op. 3, d. 2, 'Lists of Merchants, Petit Bourgeois and Foreigners, 1795–1802 and 1803–1804 of the Greek Magistrate'.

67. Their names have been transliterated according to the Greek language.

68. GARO, f. 579, op. 3, d. 2, 'List of Merchants of the Taganrog Greek Magistrate, 1795–1804'.

69. On these first attempts which did not succeed, see Zakharov, 'The development of foreign trade'.

70. Customs office at the delta of the river Temernik which joined with the river Don, which was created in 1749 so that the Don Cossacks could develop trade relations with Greek, Turkish and Armenian merchants.

71. Filefsky, *History of the City of Taganrog*, pp. 213-15.

72. See Zakharov, 'The Development of Foreign Trade'.

73. See Sifneos and Paradisopoulos, 'The Greeks in Odessa in 1897'.

74. GARO, f. 579 op. 3 d. 2, 'List of Merchants in the Taganrog Greek Magistrate, 1795–1804'.

75. GARO, f. 579, op. 3, d. 2, 'Letter from the Office of the Mayor of Taganrog to the Greek Magistrate', 7 April 1804.

76. GARO, f. 579, op. 3, d. 3, 'List of Foreigners Resident in Taganrog, 1812'.
77. V. I. Ratnik, 'Даты в истории города Таганрога' [Historical Dates of the City of Taganrog], *Enciklopedia Taganroga* (Taganrog: Anton, 1998), pp. 452–80.
78. GARO, f. 579, op. 3, d. 3, 'List of Foreigners Resident in Taganrog (Catherine Zone), 1812', from which the relevant comments come.
79. Ibid.
80. Sifneos, *Greek Merchants in the Sea of Azov*.
81. GARO, f. 579, op. 1, d. 535, 'List of Merchants of Taganrog, 1840'.
82. Rieber, *Merchants and Entrepreneurs*, pp. 34-5, Table. 1.1.
83. GARO, f. 577, op. 1, d. 92, 'List of Merchants of Taganrog, 1912'.
84. D. Brower, *The Russian City Between Tradition and Modernity, 1850–1900* (Berkeley, CA: University of California Press, 1990), pp. 16–22.
85. Colonas, 'Architectural Expression'.
86. *Полное собрание законов Российской Империи* [Collection of the Laws of the Russian Empire] (St Petersburg, 1857), vol. 12, pp. 26–68.
87. GARO, f. 577 inventory 1; E. B. Gorobets, 'Введение каталога архитектурных чертежей' [Introduction to the List of Architectural Designs].
88. GARO, f. 581, op. 1, d. 27, 'Taganrog Building Committee'.
89. GARO, f. 579, op. 1, d. 251, 'Letter from the Greek Magistrate to the Ministry of the Interior', 23 September 1808.
90. GARO, f. 579, op. 1, d. 251, 'Office of the Taganrog Town Governor. The Construction of the Greek Church and Hospital in Taganrog by the Landowner Varvatsi', 12 January 1808–30 December 1809.
91. Ibid.
92. On the asylum for aged and disabled seamen, see *Taganrog Vestnik*, 14 January 1894.

INDEX

Page numbers in italics refer to figures and tables and those including 'n' refer to notes.

For Product Safety Concerns and Information please contact our EU
representative GPSR@taylorandfrancis.com
Taylor & Francis Verlag GmbH, Kaufingerstraße 24, 80331 München, Germany

www.ingramcontent.com/pod-product-compliance
Ingram Content Group UK Ltd.
Pitfield, Milton Keynes, MK11 3LW, UK
UKHW021616240425
457818UK00018B/589